BAMBOOZLED!

Ivan P. Hall, born on an American missionary college campus in Sofia, Bulgaria in 1932, received his B.A. in European History from Princeton, an M.A. in International Relations from the Fletcher School, and his PhD in Japanese History from Harvard in 1969. He is the author of *Mori Arinori* (1973) and *Cartels of the Mind: Japan's Intellectual Closed Shop* (1997). The latter was chosen by *Business Week* as one of the "Ten Best Business Books of 1997." Since 1999 he has been a visiting professor in Japanese history (pre-modern, modern, and intellectual) at Temple University of Japan in Tokyo.

BAMBOOZLED!

How America
Loses the Intellectual
Game with Japan
and Its Implications
for Our Future
in Asia

IVAN P. HALL

AN EAST GATE BOOK

M.E.Sharpe
Armonk, New York
London, England

An East Gate Book

Library of Congress Cataloging-in-Publication Data

Hall, Ivan P., 1932–
  Bamboozled! : how America loses the intellectual game with Japan and its implications
for our future in Asia / Ivan P. Hall.
    p. cm.
  "An East Gate book."
  Includes bibliographical references and index.
  ISBN 0-7656-1005-1 (alk. paper)—ISBN 0-7656-1006-X (pbk.: alk. paper)
    I. United States—Relations—Japan. 2. Japan—Relations—United States. 3.
Japan—Foreign public opinion, American. 4. Public opinion—United States. 5. United
States—Foreign relations—Psychological aspects. I. Title.

E183.8J3 H24 2002
303.48′273052—dc21   2002019095

Printed in the United States of America

The paper used in this publication meets the minimum requirements of
American National Standard for Information Sciences
Permanence of Paper for Printed Library Materials,
ANSI Z 39.48-1984.

∞

BM (c)   10   9   8   7   6   5   4   3   2   1
BM (p)   10   9   8   7   6   5   4   3   2   1

In Loving Memory of

HELENA GUIBNER

1876–1968

Contents

III: Self-Delusion
"And Elliptical Billiard Balls"
American Roots of Wishful Thinking

Acknowledgments

Coming to the end of an extended interpretative essay, my acknowledgments run briefer yet deeper here than the customary many-nods-to-many-people from authors who have had help in working through large amounts of new material.

For sustaining my faith in the merit and feasibility of this book my immediate and heartfelt thanks go to Steven C. Clemons, James Fallows, and Doug Merwin in the United States and to Eamonn Fingleton, Brian McVeigh, and Cynthia Worthington in Japan. Without their unflagging moral support, intellectual companionship, and practical assistance, my manuscript never would have made it all the way to the printed page.

In the middle ground stand three formative scholarly guides who gave me the tools and inclination to take a critical, practically minded, intellectual-historical look at the Japan-United States tie. I have been indebted over the years, respectively, to Albert M. Craig for kindling my enduring curiosity about ideas in Japan; to Donald Fleming for laying out with unforgettable panache the locus classicus of intellectual history at the confluence of great events with great ideas; and to Chalmers Johnson for setting a high standard for intellectual honesty and courage in thinking and writing about things Japanese.

Further back still, in a lifelong career that has swung (like this book) between the two worlds of scholarship and public affairs, I am grateful to those in decades past including Allan B. Cole, Wilson P. Dizard, and the late Edwin O. Reischauer, who with generosity of spirit and much practical support gave me a helping hand in crossing the barriers between their own profession, as the case might be, into the other.

I should like to acknowledge generous permission from former editor-in-chief Owen Harries to rework, mainly into Chapters 5 and 6 of this book, several paragraphs from two articles that I published in *The Na-*

tional Interest: "Samurai Legacies, American Illusions" (No. 28, 1992), and "Japan's Asia Card" (No. 38, 1994–1995).

For keeping the ball rolling in the home stretch, my thanks go to my agent, Henning Gutmann, for placing the manuscript, to Sue Warga for her deft and sympathetic editing of this book, and to Patricia Loo and Angela Piliouras at M.E. Sharpe. And finally, a very special word of gratitude to Mikio Kato and the unfailingly courteous and helpful staff of the International House of Japan for making my recent stints of research and teaching in Japan a real pleasure.

Prologue
In the Shadow of 11 September

One month before this book went to the publishers, the terrorist attack on the World Trade Center and the Pentagon altered forever the way Americans and the West at large would be able to view the world around them.

Seen from the immediate geostrategic perspective, there was little that seemed more gratifying than the Japan-America tie—or less relevant than a critical account of the intellectual relationship between the two peoples. Indeed, as the Japanese government rushed to cut a check for $10 million in aid to a grieving New York, and as the aircraft carrier *Kitty Hawk* with its support vessels steamed out of hospitable Japanese ports for battle duty in the Arabian Sea, the trade imbalances the United States had endured for the past three decades as the price of its defense links with Tokyo must have seemed to many Americans like the bargain of a century. So why nitpick *now?*

If we look at the impact of 11 September on the national psyche and worldview, however, there are lessons for the road ahead that Americans can glean from their long and often bumpy intellectual relationship with Japan. These patterns of ignorance, misperception, gullibility, and self-deluding nonchalance should provide some useful guideposts as our country scrambles to bring the entire Islamic world into some sort of intellectual focus, and as we seek (as an imperative of our very survival) to forge a broader antiterrorist comity and step up ties with Russia, India, and China—nations that are nuclear-armed, beset with severe internal problems, and bereft of any long-shared intellectual and cultural heritage or political alliance with the United States.

It was not only the Cold War that died its final death on 11 September 2001 but also the peculiar interim ideology known as globalism—the demise, to be sure, not of its unimpeachable ideal of a free-trading and democratic international order, but of triumphalist America's assumption that we could get there on addle-brained automatic, leaving it to the manifest destiny of our invincible economic system and without thinking too much about foreign affairs. Paul Kennedy (writing in *Time*, 1 October 2001) called for the "retooling" of a new "Grand Strategy," one that would have to be pursued in peacetime as well. Most American pundits traced the tragedy first and foremost to a failure of intelligence— and I would only add that we would do best to take that in both senses of the term.

There is none more eager than I to see Osama bin Laden brought to terrible, swift justice, but having been posted to Afghanistan and Pakistan with the foreign service for three years (1958–61), I found it bizarre to hear some Americans talk of carpet-bombing into the stone age a prostrate people that diplomatic wags in far happier days would joke was proudly advancing from the thirteenth century into the fourteenth. If our sheer ignorance of the Islamic world was the first parallel to the earlier instance of Japan, another was our wild swing in images. Transmogrifying the Taliban at the drop of a hat from heroes into villains and switching Pakistan back and forth from doughty ally to bad boy, our understanding in each case was driven by our own raw strategic need of the moment, with little stabilizing grasp of the political, social, or ideological constants of those two countries.

Eerily reminiscent of our Japan tie, too, was our Cold War reflex for overstating the moderate nature of politically backward Arab regimes as long as they were pro-American. The same can be said of our assumption of broad regional homogeneities as we fail to see how much separates the Japanese from their East Asian neighbors, or to perceive the West Asian emotional rift dividing the Arab world from the broader Iranian cultures, including Afghanistan. What has been lacking above all in both cases is a broadly informed public discussion in the United States similar to the one we can sustain about Europe—dragging our Asian or Middle Eastern experts out of obscurity to give us the media fix for a crucial moment or two, then switching those areas off our crisis-of-the-week radar.

At the same time, our track record with the Japanese suggests some useful caveats against too much mea culpa about "cultural misunderstanding." The conflation of civilizational differences with political agendas presents an all-too-tempting area for special pleading. As British prime minister Tony Blair told the Labor Party at Brighton on 2 October 2001, no failure of foreign policy could morally justify the murder of seven thousand innocent civilians (Blair's figure at the time). Some Americans, too, were quick to recall American intervention or concern on behalf of the beleaguered Muslim populations in Bosnia, Kosovo, and Chechnya—rebutting the canard of an anti-Islamic Christian crusade. As Fareed Zakaria pointed out (in *Newsweek,* 1 October 2001), the rise of radical Islam owes much to the way in which certain Arab states such as Egypt and Saudi Arabia have "resisted economic and political modernization with disastrous results." In other words, it's not all America's fault, and, at some point in the rhetorical exchange between peoples, nations have to take at least some of the responsibility for their own problems.

In short, we need to set our thinking straight, on both the pros and cons of our global partners and adversaries. What these times call for in American understanding of international crises is a kind of street smarts— not the substitution of sentimental exoticizing for exotic demonizing.

I judge it best to confine discussion of these tragic new circumstances to this prologue, with no further attempt to shoehorn their possible implications into the chapters that follow on Japan, except for the occasional obvious reference—not only because most of this volume pertains to an incontrovertible record of the past but, more to the point, because it is simply impossible to know as of late 2001 where we Americans, our Japanese friends, or the great globe itself will be come the prospective time of publication in spring 2002.

Ivan P. Hall
Tokyo
11 December 2001

Introduction
The Old Deal: Why Our
Muddled Thinking Matters

This book is about the way the United States repeatedly has allowed
itself to be misled intellectually and psychologically by Japan. As such,
it is more about the American mind than about the Japanese. It is about
the illusion, the collusion, and the self-delusion we have permitted to
degrade and bedevil the intellectual relationship with our premier political partner in Asia and our greatest economic rival in the world:

1. The *illusion* of preferred images that Japan would like us to
   hold of it. Bamboozled!
2. The *collusion* of Americans and Japanese in sustaining Tokyo's
   intellectual and psychological gamesmanship toward the United
   States. Co-bamboozled!
3. The *self-delusion*, anchoring the other two, that all too often
   takes command of the American mind when we turn our unsteady gaze toward Japan. Auto-bamboozled!

"But wait a minute!" today's American reader may well interject.
"What's all this Japan bashing and paranoia about? Didn't that go out of
fashion after the 1980s? Isn't Japan flat on its back, out of the running,
desperate to remodel itself American-style?"

Alas, no. And hence, in part, the motivation for this book. Indeed,
there has been something bizarre and deeply disturbing for a U.S. citizen living in Japan at the turn of the millennium in having to watch his

fellow Americans get another country—a nation so important for our own future—so dreadfully wrong.

Yet it is not the particulars of our misreading of Japan (once again) that have been so unnerving. It is, rather, the sheer breathtaking scale of the national nonchalance and naïveté in which it has been taking place— that broader intellectual context of the U.S.-Japan relationship, which is the main focus of this volume. If we can't "get Japan right" despite our far greater ties and leverage with that country, what does that portend for our understanding of the other emerging non-Western great powers such as China, India, or Russia? This is especially problematical in a shrinking and suddenly dangerous new world where we will have to lean less on armed might than on diplomacy, intelligence, and psychological sophistication to bring and keep peoples and states that are culturally and politically very different from us on our side in a protracted war on international terrorism and in laying the foundations for a peaceful world order beyond that.

* * *

From 1999 to 2001 it was clear to anyone with their feet on the ground in Tokyo that Japan was swinging to the right, digging in its heels against American economic prescriptions, and developing its own visions for post–Cold War Asia—that is to say, moving further and further away from, not toward, the United States in all but the narrow area of military cooperation. Yet all these trends remained counterintuitive to America's financial, governmental, and media elites back home, who continued to view Japan from the stratosphere of our reigning economic triumphalism. Wall Street, the Washington Beltway, and our national punditocracy showed no letup in their orthodox doctrine that Japan is slowly but surely falling into line as a U.S.-style free trader and liberal democracy eager to play the American proconsul in Asia.

Americans who care about foreign affairs seem to have entered the twenty-first century thoroughly convinced that Japan is washed up and no longer worthy of our serious economic and political concern or at- tention. What a relief it would be if that were true—if Japan could in- deed be safely relegated to its ancient niche in the American mind as a wisp of quaint exotica! Indeed, an alarming number of Americans have become too tired, squeamish, or otherwise reluctant to think of Japan as either powerful or problematical, let alone both. The first would be bad news, the second too much of a mental effort.

The past decade, we reassure ourselves, was an unmitigated disaster for the Japanese—and so we see it continuing today. As of early 2002 Japan's economy remains stuck in a seemingly intractable recession, with social and governmental reforms hopelessly mired in the sloughs of Tokyo's old-style politics. As Japanese banks collapse ignominiously, foreign securities and insurance traders push through the grudgingly opened doors, their eyes agleam with the promise of fat New Economy profits. And just look at the rest of Asia! It no longer flies in formation behind the Japanese lead goose but jumps to the crack of the American reformist whip as it recovers from the financial debacle of the late 1990s.

Surely, we congratulate ourselves, Japan's fall from grace—more than any other event since the disappearance of the Soviet Union—proves once and for all the superiority of the American economic, political, cultural, and educational model. This model is not only superior but also applicable the world over, as Washington's gobbler replaces Tokyo's goose as top bird in a new age of globalization.

Surely, we tell ourselves, the revisionists who critiqued Japan a decade ago were wrong, if not bordering on racist. And finally, soothing ourselves with a choice of two comfortable scenarios, we decide we can safely relax our intellectual grip on things Japanese. Either Japan eventually will prove too weak to be of any great consequence—a pleasant, complaisant "middling power" for the continued delectation of American aesthetes—or, should it indeed regain its position as a geopolitical heavyweight, it will come back in our own image, reemerging as a powerful partner to push free markets, democratic institutions, and American policy goals in Asia while lining up its regional neighbors to dance the turkey trot.

But wait a minute. What if we have been getting it all wrong, or most of it?

What if Japan is in fact *both* stronger than we like to think *and* less inclined than we fancy to reinvent itself along American lines? Worse yet, what if Japan has deliberately insinuated such false hopes and rosy misperceptions into the American mind to its own advantage? And, most embarrassing of all, what if Uncle Sam has been bamboozled even more by his own intellectual gullibility and patented philosophical nostrums than by any intellectual manipulation by the Japanese?

Those are the three basic messages of this book: not only, in Part I, *that* we have been getting Japan wrong but, more importantly, in Parts II and III, *why*.

This volume is intended less as yet another book *about* Japan than as a critique of the American mind *on* Japan, and its practical consequences—a much rarer literary animal. American and other Western readers have too long viewed reporting on Japan as something "out there." "Hey, tell us all about it," we demand of our journalists and scholars in our on-and-off spurts of attention, not realizing how much our own hopes, images, and mental habits work to shape any new information.

Indeed, America's insouciant, inattentive hubris about Japan today resembles nothing quite so much in its subliminal tenacity as those unexamined preconceptions about American women in the 1950s that Betty Friedan called "the problem that has no name." Labeling it "the feminine mystique," Friedan went on to dredge up the stagnant pool of received truths about the role and capabilities of women and expose them to the harsh light of public awareness and rational scrutiny.[1] With Japan today we simply have it the other way around: a household name, but with no problem attached to it.

The Old Deal

Whether we have been hoodwinked by Tokyo or self-anesthetized by Washington, our notion of "no problem" is of critical importance for the American national interest right now because it will go a long way toward determining the fundamental choice on Japan policy facing the U.S. government. Ten years out of the Cold War and with a radically altered world situation, we can at this time either unimaginatively continue or creatively revise the strategic Old Deal we struck with Japan during the Cold War decades. In that bargain, Tokyo traded base facilities and foreign policy subordination to Washington in return for unlimited access to America's market and its scientific, media, and academic institutions while keeping its own society and economy closed to the outside world.

As a matter of fact, our present state of bamboozlement is largely (although not entirely) the product (and prerequisite) of that Old Deal. Simply stated, as Japan's economy from the 1970s gradually caught up with that of the United States it became essential for the Japanese (and for the American keepers of U.S.-Japan harmony) to deflect rising American impatience with the economic and intellectual price being paid for Japan's political and military cooperation. Apart from the external threat from the Communist bloc, in recent decades four axioms were added to our common wisdom on Japan: first, that too much market-opening pressure would provoke an anti-American nationalism among the Japanese that would threaten our forward-based strategy in the Western Pacific; second, that we had to opt for the Japanese right against the Japanese left whatever the consequences for Japan's own democracy; third, that our own cultural ignorance and insensitivity were at the root of our "misunderstandings," and we needed to learn to be humble and never, ever, offend the Japanese; and fourth, that Tokyo was honestly groping its way toward an American-style open-market economy, given enough time and patience from our side.

These intellectual bromides have left the United States inordinately sanguine about Japan's economic intentions today, too shy about our own actual leverage, and too easily blackmailed by any whiff of anti-Americanism. They have rendered our Japan experts excessively dependent on Japanese money, our public leaders overly deferential to American propagandists for Tokyo's interests, and our policy makers too willing to encourage Japan's rising illiberal elements against the declining democratic camp. They have turned our minds away from the exclusive nature of Japan's growing ties to Asia and seduced us into waiting pathetically on a "third great opening" of Japan and on the imminent emergence of a new Japanese individualism.

During the 1990s, of course, our idea of an economically weakened Japan—oddly combined with the increasing dependence of the U.S. economy on Tokyo's huge holdings of U.S. Treasury bills—only served to strengthen America's acceptance of the Old Deal and the intellectual cosmos it had spawned. And if the initial postinauguration moves of the Bush administration in early 2001 seemed bent on locking the United States more firmly than ever into the old Cold War compact, the new war on global terrorism may well tempt us to extend that status quo indefinitely.

The October 2000 study by the Institute for National Strategic Studies (the so-called Armitage Report) glowingly envisioned Japan "in the midst of its greatest social and economic transformation since the end of World War II" and was a compendium of Old Deal nostrums. Named after its panel chair, former Defense Department official Richard Armitage (who was soon to be appointed George W. Bush's deputy secretary of state), the report praised the new retrogressively statist drift in Japan as evidence of "a new respect for the sovereignty and integrity of the nation-state." Condescendingly offering Japan the junior partnership enjoyed by Britain after World War II, it warned Americans about pressing too much "short-term pain" on Japan's "risk-averse" political system.

In a speech to the American Enterprise Institute on 1 December 2000, Bush's new economic adviser went even further to urge the suspension of *gaiatsu,* or external market-opening pressures, altogether. Lawrence Lindsey also recommended giving Japan a wide-open door to the American market as it endured the pain of long-postponed fundamental reforms. This was a gratuitous, patronizing gesture, tantamount to giving away the farm after three decades of hard-fought trade negotiations.

There are powerful, if motley, forces on the American side that would welcome a reaffirmation of the Old Deal. Business, financial, and academic ideologues convinced of the inevitable advance of American-led free trade will weigh in against any pressures to force Japan to open its markets further. Members of the new plutocratic upper class emerging on the cusp of the New Economy—those among them who are willing to play junior partner to other nations' industries as long as their own pockets are generously lined—may resist arguments from the broader American national and social interest. The U.S. military, moving beyond the artificial pumping up of a new Chinese bogey to confront real enemies in the Middle East, may well chafe at Japan's present constitutional restraints on further rearmament and, willy-nilly, help the Japanese right wing tighten the noose on Japan's languishing democracy. American lobbyists and cultural interlocutors for Japan in any case will not want to see their turf diminished, and if an anxious public climate turns hostile to exploring the downsides of our Japan relationship, it is virtually guaranteed that they will have little serious intellectual competition.

On the other hand, there remains the ever-so-outside chance that an administration of now certified foreign policy realists and pragmatists eventually might head in the opposite direction. Bush's trade officials may simply tire of Tokyo's resistance to playing things our way. The manufacturing sector of the Republicans' big-business backing may insist on genuine reciprocity from the Japanese, particularly if the U.S. economy continues to slide. The Pentagon and our geopolitical pundits may well find themselves driven toward a long-term accommodation with China, fitting Japan into a more balanced mosaic of East Asian ties. And, at a humbler level, the day may yet come when American universities once again esteem teaching and scholarship as the true hallmark of a Japanologist, rather than the number of bilateral policy conferences attended in resort settings at Maui or Hakone.

The Japanese, too, might find themselves liberated—in their case, from their own gullibility and intellectual manipulation by the United States. They might be liberated, for example, from that narrow beam of American attention that sees Japan only in terms of the grand U.S. strategic interest—never, be it for better or worse, as Japan in its own right. And they might be freed from the foolish fancy that America's Japan-touting crowd actually has Japan's objectives at heart or that they are in any way representative of the broader American public.

But those are Japan's problems to solve. This book is for the American side. And, should our creative revision of the Old Deal ever come, it will have been driven in the first instance by new, or as yet untried, ideas.

Why Our Muddled Thinking Matters

In short, this book is intended as a contrarian essay not only questioning many of our comfortable assumptions about Japan but also showing how we have allowed both Japanese PR and our own habits of mind to sustain them. As the relative power of the United States starts to decline throughout Asia, Americans will have to mobilize the one underutilized weapon left in our strategic armory—our intellectual resources. And there is no better guide or handbook of errors to that end than our repeated failures in the intellectual game with Japan.

In the single decade of the 1990s Americans went from fearing to flouting to practically forgetting the Japanese. When Tokyo in 1995 virtually won the two all-important debates over market opening and the interpretation of World War II, the United States hardly noticed the fact of its defeat. We remain ignorant or unconcerned to this day about the ways in which Japan has manipulated our minds and emotions on trade and security matters over the past three decades. We seem almost too lazy to grapple intellectually with the deeper forces of Japanese politics, society, and thought whenever we wonder where that nation is headed next. We prefer to settle for the shallow new determinism of bank failures and economic indicators—or the cotton candy of Tokyo's incessantly heralded but undelivered regulatory reforms.

Toward the close of the decade we Americans often asked ourselves what the Japanese were planning for us and for the rest of the world in the coming century. A renewed push in due course toward economic dominance? An anti-Western alignment over time with the rest of Asia?

A compliant junior partnership, as in the past, with the United States?

With hope or anxiety, as the case may be, we still continue to speculate on the relative likelihood of these and other scenarios without realizing three important things: first, that what Tokyo in fact will do still depends to a great extent on what Washington does; second, that the directions in which the Japanese economic, political, and cultural elites, given the opportunity, would actually like to take their country may be very different from the courses on which most Americans hope and assume Japan already is set; and third, that simply *seeing* those differences is the first—and most neglected—step we need to take toward ensuring more favorable outcomes for the United States, to say nothing of Japan's Asian neighbors.

To be more specific:

1. Are there points we may be getting wrong about the directions in which Japan actually has been tugging?
2. If so, how has our misunderstanding been fed by the binational delivery system now massively in place for purveying what Americans want to hear, rather than what they should be told?
3. And what makes us so vulnerable intellectually and psychologically to such persuasion?

The game being played here is intellectual in the very broadest sense of the term. It has run the whole gamut from philosophical ideas, historical perceptions, emotional hang-ups, and psychological stratagems to the financial, organizational, and rhetorical structures that have been established for our bilateral dialogue—such as it is.

Those Americans who would play this game with Japan successfully must be ready for hidden persuasion and topsy-turvy logic more in keeping with Madison Avenue and Alice's Queen of Hearts than with our erstwhile ideological adversary, the Kremlin. They will find themselves dealing with the most extraordinary attempt in history by one nation—in aggressive pursuit of its national interest—to influence the entire intellectual system of a peacetime ally. As part of that drive, they will be confronted with the emotional manipulation of American self-esteem and guilt, and they will find themselves grappling less with reasoned arguments than with personalistic appeals, evasive answers, and circumlocutory thinking.

Above all they will face three daunting tasks. They will have to parry politically inspired pronunciamentos about events and intentions in Japan, with respect to which most of their countrymen will be too poorly informed to make a sound judgment for themselves. They will have to keep a sharp eye on the counterforce sent out against them not only by Tokyo but also by those American political and intellectual leaders who prefer to assist Japan in its psychological stroking. And they will have to clear their own minds of the accumulated cobwebs of traditional American thinking on Japan.

* * *

The three parts and nineteen chapters of this book challenge a variety of accepted wisdom about Japan and Japan-U.S. relations, drawing both on hitherto neglected evidence and on alternative interpretations of matters already well known.

Part I deals with certain crucial misreadings of Japan. America's stated foreign policy goals of freer markets and more democratic societies in a peaceful Asia require the cooperation of Tokyo on all three counts. Such collaboration in turn requires a strong and growing intellectual commitment among the Japanese themselves to the ideals of free trade, political liberalism, and an enlightened leadership in Asia. Open markets, democracy, and a cosmopolitan worldview are mutually supportive forces that we assume already are working to line up the Japanese as our continuing junior partner in Asia.

But can we really place our bets on an open market in Japan when so much expressed opinion there points to the continuation of mercantilism by one means or another? Is it wise to assume the steady maturing of Japanese political democracy when it is the voices of right-wing nationalism that grow stronger day by day? What signs do we have, at all, of a more generous mind-set toward the rest of Asia? And what indication, really, do we see of the alleged shift to a more individual-centered sense of self and civic responsibility that would help to underpin all of these worthy aims at the personal (or existential) level? Has postwar Japan had any great (or even lesser) national leaders combining political and physical courage with moral conscience on the order of Korea's Kim Dae Jung, the Aquinos in the Philippines, Willy Brandt of Germany, or our own Martin Luther King Jr.?

Indeed—to wrap up all of our hopes in one open-sesame—dare we believe in the recently heralded coming of a "third revolution" or "third opening" of Japan as dramatic as those following the Meiji Restoration of 1868 or the Allied occupation after 1945? The six chapters of Part I suggest that we cannot, at least not without a great deal of caution about the intellectual spin influential Japanese may be putting on the answers to these questions in order to sustain our own wishful illusions.

Part II suggests why we have not been able to get an open, nonmanipulative transpacific discussion of these issues similar to the dialogue that spans the Atlantic. The main reason for this is the interposition of a binational intellectual cartel for sweetness and light in Japan-U.S. relations that exempts Japan from the sort of critical scrutiny we have always applied without any hesitation, embarrassment, or guilt to our public discussions of Russia, China, Germany, or India. The six chapters of Part II challenge the growing acceptance among Americans that there is nothing problematical about Japan's cultural lobbying in the United States—indeed, that it serves our own national interest. We will look at the impact of money, organization, and personal motivation on this game. But we will do so less from our recent anxiety about economic takeovers across America or about political lobbying in Washington than from a concern about the transpacific intellectual channels for discussion that are being dammed up, diverted, or dug more and more to Japan's own liking.

The seven brief chapters of Part III, finally, argue that American self-delusion (for well over a century now) deserves much of the blame for our continuing misperceptions of Japan and for our intellectual vulnerability to the blandishments of the Mutual Understanding Industry.

* **

What a pity it would be if it took another ten years for Americans to realize the full cost of our colossal inattention and euphoria toward Japan during the 1990s. For the longer we persist in our mental leave of absence from Japan, the less practical leverage the United States will have to back up its intellectual suasion—and, conversely, the less chance our thus eroded suasion will have of promoting America's practical interests with Japan. Not only will Japan be traveling even further down roads contrary to our misplaced expectations, but also it will be doing so as America's relative position in East Asia starts to wane on all fronts. Slowly but surely this will come politically from the phasing out of old bilateral Cold War ties. Economically it will be pushed by the constantly advancing regional integration and a fresh Asian distrust of Western nostrums in the wake of the late-1990s financial crisis. Strategically it will be driven by the ineluctable rise of China, and eventually Japan itself, as independent and formidable military powers.

To brake the slippage the United States might, for a change, try putting brain over brawn and mobilizing the one great asset it has allowed to go rusty: its wits.

Unfortunately, the intellectual game already has been lost for the closing decades of the twentieth century. But that does not mean we have to go on losing in the twenty-first—not if we are willing to undertake a critical review of our defeats in this arena and summon the political will and clear thinking needed to get it right next time.

Too much of the long-term national interest is at stake here not to give it a try. And far too much nonsense has recently passed for profundity in this department to let the march of time bury it without any comment, or at least a well-deserved laugh or two at our own muddled mind on Japan as a source of not-so-innocent merriment. For, with apologies to Gilbert and Sullivan, our intellectual bamboozling by Japan has been all too much like the Mikado's punishment of having to play pool "on a cloth untrue, with a twisted cue, and elliptical billiard balls!"

* * *

Indeed, the tale here reaches into American soils as disparate as strategic obsession, academic funding, and a nation's philosophical proclivities. The story cries out for the impish wit of an H. L. Mencken debunking the national verities of his day. It begs for the cosmic belly laugh of a Mark Twain skewering his fellow countrymen's naiveté about other peoples. It waits for a Tom Wolfe deflating the socially chic intellectual fads of self-fancied American elites. And it languishes for an elegant gift like Gore Vidal's in rendering fatuities from other times and places familiar—and thereby vulnerable to our laughter—by stripping away their protective coatings of historical distance and cultural exoticity.

My much humbler aim in these pages is simply to provide a vade mecum for my fellow Americans as well as others who have sensed something askew in their intellectual relationships with Japan and want to do something about it. Most of the writing on this subject to date has been tied to a narrow focus on economic disputes as viewed from the political cockpit of Washington, D.C., with its hardball lobbying over trade issues. It is time now to place these and other American frustrations with Japan in a broader context of ideas and emotions in both countries, including a much closer scrutiny of noneconomic thinking in Japan.

I make no pretense to scholarly depth or journalistic detail in this extended polemical essay on a number of topics, any one of which might well make a book in its own right. What I do try to bring to the broader subject are three decades of Japan-based professional and personal involvement in many of the situations here encountered, together with a skeptical and mildly irreverent mind. At the very least, I would hope to convey to others some sense of what it is like to be caught up in this oddish intellectual milieu.

I was trained in the 1960s at Harvard University as a Ph.D. in Japanese history with a particular focus on the intellectual development of modern Japan from the mid-nineteenth century to the present. This followed three years with the Foreign Service (specifically, the United States Information Service) as assistant cultural attaché at the American embassy in Kabul, Afghanistan, and at the consulate in Dhaka, East Pakistan (now Bangladesh). My discussion in Part I of Japan's approved self-images and tactics of persuasion owes much to my eight years of graduate-school immersion in Japanese history and language and to the writing of a biography of Meiji Japan's first minister of education and ambassador to the United States, Mori Arinori.[2]

That academic background exposed me to the long historical sweep of Japanese institutions, ideas, and sentiments against which we have to judge the actual prospects for any major changes in national direction today, particularly those changes hoped for by so many Americans grasping after the straw of the moment—and touted by Japanese spokesmen only too eager to sustain those expectations.

Beginning in 1970 I plunged into the practical side of Japanese intellectual life in Tokyo, getting an insider's view of the financial, organizational, and motivational aspects of the goodwill industry we shall look at in Part II. For six years I served as a foreign correspondent for the old *Philadelphia Bulletin,* as Harvard's Japan representative for its successful $8 million fund-raising drive for a new Japan institute, and as the Harvard-Yenching Institute's liaison for university ties throughout East and Southeast Asia. Eight years then followed as a cultural diplomat under our Tokyo embassy, representing the federal government's Japan-

U.S. Friendship Commission for bilateral exchanges in education, scholarship, journalism, and the arts.

It was all immensely good fun and an educational extension I never could have gotten from books. In all these roles I functioned as a card-carrying member of the mutual-understanding crowd, with missionary zeal at first, but progressively disenchanted as I came to see the debilitating interplay of Japanese manipulation and American gullibility. Moreover, I watched and played the goodwill game not only in Japan but also on regular short assignments to Washington, D.C., and during trips throughout the United States on behalf of the Friendship Commission.

From 1984 to 1993 I returned to academe as a professor for three years apiece at Tsukuba, Keio, and Gakushuin Universities—respectively, Japan's newest national university, its oldest private campus, and the college that traditionally schools the imperial family. I was blessed with an unusually high cut of Japanese students in my lecture courses, in both English and Japanese, on the history of American thought and on Japan-U.S. cultural relations. These young captives provided me with an opportunity to explore the historical roots of the Japan-U.S. intellectual nexus today. And that exploration increasingly opened my eyes to the frequently self-hobbling impact of America's own heritage of ideas on our practical dealings with Japan throughout the twentieth century. Japanese intellectual historians have written tomes on the impact of American ideas on their own country, and there is a small but growing literature on the reverse flow of Japanese thought (mainly aesthetic, religious, and psychological) into the United States. To the best of my knowledge, however, no one has ever written—not even amateurishly, as I admittedly do in Part III—on the function of the American mind as a self-inflicted stumbling block in our relationship with Japan.

Finally, in the late 1990s, I published my second book, *Cartels of the Mind*.[3] This exposed the barriers Japan still maintains against foreign participation in its legal, media, academic, and scientific institutions—despite a century of intellectual borrowing from the West and decades of prospering from an open global economy. Whereas *Bamboozled!* deals with the intellectual interplay on the mutual surface of U.S.-Japan relations, *Cartels* explored Japan's own institutional impediments to a healthy dialogue with the world at large.

When a friend once ribbed me saying, "Ivan, you're a Japan jack-of-all-trades and master of none," I liked the "all trades" bit better than the "none." But I do think I have had enough experience from enough angles on Japan to qualify the following chapters as "notes from the underground"—a counterintuitive challenge to our conventional wisdom that the intellectual game Japan plays with America (and others) hardly matters any more.

Let us start, then, by looking at some of our current illusions.

I
ILLUSION

"On a Cloth Untrue"
Japanese Mentalities,
American Misreadings

CHAPTER ONE

Economic Mirage
The Asian Crisis
and "Change"

Every now and then the Japanese do tell Americans something very honest and important straight to our face—and we still fail to hear it.

One evening in the spring of 1998 I paid out 5,000 yen, over $40, to attend an intimate dinner in Tokyo that was billed as a private exchange of ideas between the recently arrived American ambassador, former House Speaker Thomas S. Foley, and a blue-ribbon group of Japanese ex-ambassadors and a former cabinet minister to discuss the Asian economic crisis.

I shall honor the off-the-record nature of the occasion by not disclosing the date, venue, sponsor, or names of the other participants. But it was such an obviously prearranged setup to pepper the American envoy with a sequence of well-orchestrated Japanese special pleadings that I, at least, felt used. In lieu of a refund, then, I choose to allow others a wee peek through the curtains at the quintessential Japan-U.S. intellectual charade that was played out that evening before the small captive audience of paying guests like myself—a charade that encapsulates all that is wrong with our bilateral dialogue.

What transpired had about as much spontaneity as one of those Japanese consultative councils, known as *shingikai*, that are regularly convened by Tokyo's government ministries to air new policies before members of the Japanese private sector, incorporate cosmetic mention of alternative views, and induce the ratification of a "consensus" as close as possible to predetermined bureaucratic goals.

3

To avail myself of one of the evasive gimmicks of Japan's own newspaper journalism, let me say that it was A, over his sherbet and coffee, who led off for three of the top-drawer Japanese invitees. Turning to Mr. Foley, A regretted that there were so many things—nonperforming assets, a worsening public debt position, and an aging population—that made it difficult, alas, for Japan to reflate its economy and stimulate consumer demand. Chiming in, B admonished that Japan's ruling conservative party was getting rather annoyed by American criticism and Washington's pressures for action. C then—in the presence of three current Southeast Asian ambassadors to Tokyo, and with an insouciance suggesting he felt sure the American envoy would swallow it—trotted out the shopworn line that there was nothing more Japan wanted to buy from that region, that it already had all it really needed from Asia. In other words, no more imports from the struggling neighborhood, thank you—and, it went without saying, none from the booming United States, either.

There it was—a classic replay, in defense of Japan's closed market, of poor-mouthing, veiled threats, and sheer intransigence.

By way of lonely dissent, one of the American guests referred wryly to another off-the-record powwow that had just been held in Southeast Asia on the same subject. There, before a much larger group of leaders from around the Pacific Rim, the U.S. delegation had asked whether the Japanese really expected Washington to agree to a division of labor in the Asian rescue operation whereby America would provide all the markets while Japan merely shelled out the cash. That, another foreign guest chortled, would have blown the top off American public sentiment if the American journalists, sworn to silence at that earlier conference, had chosen to report it.

What a pity they didn't, since it would have exposed as utterly quixotic Uncle Sam's main article of faith—that a more open Japanese market would drive recovery in the smaller Asian economies, and eventually lead Japan itself to buy into our free trade ideology.

The American ambassador did speak out in defense of his country's interests, but he seemed compelled to sweeten his gentle ripostes with friendly advice to the effect that the Japanese were not sufficiently adept at packaging their foreign policy messages or at advertising their own contributions. To someone who had been following the Japan-U.S. economic dialogue for over a quarter century, it was all too depressingly familiar. Here was the grand, overarching canard of that badly skewed dialogue, assiduously advanced by Japan's spokesmen and patronizingly echoed by too many high-level Americans—namely, that it is the lack of sufficient bilateral communication and mutual understanding rather than Tokyo's deliberate mercantilist policy that keeps churning the U.S.-Japan trade tensions.

Why did the Japanese, then, with a message they really wanted Uncle Sam to hear, insist on muzzling the American reporters attending both of these conferences? And why did the U.S. envoy, given a protected forum in which to deliver hard truths, opt to sugarcoat them with patronizing irrelevancies? Answer those two questions, and you have got the nub of this book.

For the Japanese it was just another exercise in their by now analyzed-to-death game of dual realities: that of covering the *honne* of their true intention with the *tatemae* of a more pleasing facade. It seems reasonable to deduce that they wanted to get the *honne* of their own tough message (and counterpressure) through to the administration in Washington without risking uproar in the U.S. Congress, public, and press. Those were the elements in the American body politic to be mollified with the *tatemae* of vaguely promised changes in all of the areas we will look at in Part I.

Ambassador Foley, for his part, was operating in the standard framework for Japan-U.S. dialogue, the antiquated constraints of which are explored in the final two parts of this book. From the venue itself to much of the guest list, we found ourselves in the friendly ambience of a transpacific continuum of individuals and institutions dedicated to Japan-U.S. friendship, the cardinal rule of which—now chiseled in stone—has been "Never offend the Japanese" (Part II). And that peculiar orientation of the American mind is, in turn, a fossilized carryover from the 1960s with its Cold War campaign to sensitize Americans to things Japanese—an attitude still deeply ingrained among the diplomatic and academic experts who set the tone of our policy on Japan (Part III).

Uncle Sam's Unsteady Focus

Japan's response to the so-called Asian financial crisis—and America's reaction to that response—should have laid bare the widening gap between American expectations of Japanese economic behavior and the actual direction the Japanese leadership seems most inclined to go in. The Asian crisis, starting in 1997 and coming on top of the economic slump Japan had been experiencing since 1993, could have been our wake-up call. Unfortunately, we have been unwilling to look more closely at what Japan actually has been doing (or *not* doing) or to listen more closely to what Japanese have been telling each other as opposed to what they say for our consumption. Instead, we have chosen to run with our triumphalist fancies that Tokyo is at last turning to our own neoclassical models for free trade and a free economy, with sweeping deregulation and political reform to those ends being only a matter of time now.[1]

The implications of our economic mirage of twenty-first-century Japan go well beyond the specifically economic focus of this chapter. First and foremost, this particular illusion has been the archetype of our entire mucked-up intellectual relationship with Japan. It exemplifies the way Japanese spin abets America's false hopes—all to the benefit of Japan. The spin works, alas, because it is convenient for both countries. It allows Tokyo more time to pursue its *honne,* to rummage up new bottles for old wine unburdened by foreign pressures for real change. And it is easier for Americans to accept the Japanese *tatemae* and ride the wave of our simplistic expectations than it is to get an intellectual handle on some of the murkier—but more determinative—aspects of Japan.

Second, our economic mirage typifies and connects with all of the other convenient misperceptions of Japan laid out in the following chapters of Part I of this book. It also represents the final reckoning of our cumulative failures over three decades to meet Japan's rhetorical onslaught over trade issues head-on (Part II, Chapter 7). Indeed, the wider the gap between America's economic wishful thinking and Japan's true economic thrust, the sharper the snap will be on our side when we do wake up, and the nastier the outburst in Japan of an anti-Americanism the emotional chemistry of which we still fail to understand (Chapter 2). To be sure, the future course of Japan's economic, trade, and security policies will be set mainly by trends in Japanese politics, social values, and mind-sets toward Asia and the West—internal factors relatively independent of the American tie. But here, too, we harbor too many comfortable illusions. These include (in Chapters 3 through 6) our complacency about Japan's steady shift toward the political and intellectual right, our failure to discern among Japan's much-weakened left some of the last holdouts of early postwar American-style democratic values, our wishful thinking about Japan's recrudescent historical attitudes toward Asia, and our misplaced hopes for the outbreak of a new, Western-style individualism in Japan.

Third, the bewildering shifts in our economic images during the 1990s are no more than the most recent twist in America's unstable intellectual focus on Japan for over a century and a half—the broader pattern of which we will return to in Part III.

Indeed, the past decade has seen four sharply contrasting American attitudes of paranoia, indifference, triumphalism, and self-recrimination follow each other roughly in that order, to the point now where they are all loosely intertwined in the American psyche. Each strand lies there, waiting to be plucked out from the others and woven all by itself to fit the future scenario most congenial to any given propagandistic purpose or literary ambition. This includes, of course, Japan's intellectual apologists, both Japanese and American, whom we shall look at in Part II. The trouble with all these images, however, is that they derive too narrowly from our perceived shifts in Japan's economic performance, which provides too limited a guide to that country's future direction.

The 1990s opened with the emotional carryover of our late 1980s paranoia about an unstoppable Japan. The United States had been experiencing profound problems with its great Asian partner, problems that threatened to erode American economic competitiveness, living standards, and perhaps ultimately our way of life. And they were being created by a Japan that was not at all nor ever would be, in James Fallows' phrase, "more like us."[2] As the Japanese at the height of their "bubble economy" went about snapping up American corporations, real estate, cultural trophies, and indigent colleges, our deepest fears seemed all too real.

Then, by the middle of the decade, an uncanny lull in American concern with Japan seemed to be settling in, a sudden drop from the intense interest and anxiety at the start of the 1990s. The lull, initially deriving from a sense of exhaustion and defeat, was sustained through the latter half of the decade by a surge of disdainful overconfidence. And this was somewhat oddly accompanied in a minor, self-incriminating key by a few lonely voices blaming Japan's postwar faults on the United States itself.

Was it possible, by the middle of the decade, that Americans no longer even cared? Was Japan bashing giving way to Japan passing? During 1995 the Japanese press, always alert to pick up (or manufacture) new catchphrases, noted with an odd combination of pique and relief that the mood of the American public toward Japan seemed to be shifting. Having been blocked in his efforts to penetrate the Japanese market, Uncle

Sam was now turning his trade attentions to China and the other East Asian nations, with a corresponding loss of interest in Japan.

Thomas L. Friedman, the foreign affairs columnist for the *New York Times,* aptly dubbed it "Japan fatigue."[3] Indeed, save for the occasional protectionist bleat from Pat Buchanan during the primary phase, the United States went through the entire 1996 presidential election campaign without any public attention to Japan-related issues. The almost palpable sense of frustration and futility of the early 1990s was by the middle of the decade translating into intellectual ennui—a portentous willingness, it sometimes seemed, to write off the losses and simply stop trying, thereby handing the Japanese the final victory by default. Americans in 1996 looked back on the repeated failures of the administration's market-opening diplomacy and on their president's slackening of his earlier leadership toward the emerging region of APEC (the Asia-Pacific Economic Cooperation forum) just as the post–Cold War order was entering an era of uncertainty in East Asia. Following the rape of a twelve-year-old Okinawan girl by three American servicemen in 1995, Americans had watched the eruption in Japan of strong public sentiment against the continued presence of U.S. bases in that country just as our government was pledging to keep the American military commitment at present strength levels throughout the region until the year 2015. Clearly, the nation was poorly prepared to deal with a Japan that showed signs of becoming increasingly nationalistic, Asia-oriented, and touchy about its ties to the United States.

By 1997, however, a tired American mind had turned into a triumphalist one as the full extent of Japan's economic woes became apparent. Americans were equally inattentive now, but for a very different reason. What with its bank failures, political scandals, languishing stock market, and souped-up press reports of a painfully restructuring workforce, postbubble Japan to many Americans had simply disappeared "down the toilet" (as one well-known New York editor put it to me). The awesome Asian colossus of the 1980s was no longer viewed as a threat to the United States, which was enjoying historical highs on Wall Street and a resurgent dollar. Out of fright, out of mind—to recast the old adage.

This dumbing down of the American consciousness occurred despite Japan's continuing status as the world's second economic power (with a GDP nearly five times the size of China's), its weight as the major source of the U.S. trade deficit, and its hold on roughly 40 percent of foreign-owned U.S. Treasury bonds. After the broader financial crisis broke out in Southeast Asia in the summer of 1997, too many American commentators were making the fatuous claim that the "Asian," meaning Japanese, economic model was now discredited. The family cronyism, consumer orientation, unbridled speculation, and dependence on foreign capital that drove the debacle in Thailand and Indonesia could not have been further from the tightly run financial self-reliance, alert government guidance, market protectionism, and postponed consumer gratification of the old Northeast Asian model that had propelled Japan, Korea, and Taiwan toward economic stardom. Indeed, Japan's own woes largely stemmed from the betrayal by its bankers and fiscal overseers of its own patented model. Hardly any Americans, however, saw that distinction, and it was only the flickering awareness that Tokyo might still somehow pull the United States down the economic tubes with it that kept a few sober American minds focused on Japan.

In the mid-1990s yet another rationale for Japan passing was being formulated in terms of a penitent withdrawal into noninterference. As frustration overseas so often leads to the search for scapegoats at home, some American writers were now casting their country as a Frankenstein that had created its own Japanese monster. Uncle Sam had no one but himself to blame for the economically protectionist, politically stagnant, and socially misshapen country created by the involvement of the CIA and Washington's resuscitation of Japan's political reactionaries as part of our anti-Communist strategy during and after the occupation.[4] This perspective tends to underplay the threat from the then expansionist Stalinist bloc and the choices and opportunities that were practically available to Americans or Japanese at the time. But it does provide a fresh moral impetus for going easy on Japan.

In a word, at century's close, various forces have been converging in the American mind to incline it to hand over to the Japanese, gratis, the entire postwar tussle of ideas.

Taken together, these contradictory and jerky reactions encapsulate the current dual-mindedness of the United States toward Japan. It is fun being able to play God once again to the Japanese economy, saving it from an allegedly impending downfall. On the other hand, the shattering impact on the United States of such an imagined collapse simply underlines how powerful Japan actually has become—sufficiently so to hold the well-being of all Americans in the balance. And should the U.S. economy once again falter, our current nonchalance about Japan will prove to have been no more than a passing blip on the American psyche.

The Logic of American Expectations

Passing blip or profound insight? Who has got it right, anyway, about Tokyo's true intentions with regard to market opening, or about Japan's gradual integration into a world economy run along Anglo-American principles of free economies and free trade? Short of the verdict of history five to ten years hence, the best we can do now is to lay out the logic of America's stated hopes (and Tokyo's spin) on one side against Japan's ostensible direction as deduced by more skeptical Japanese and Western observers. These two competing intellectual paradigms—each the reverse image of the other—are built on sharply opposed economic philosophies, on contrasting perceptions of Japanese weakness and strength, on dissimilar evaluations of the pace of change and the meaningfulness of recent reforms, and on divergent views of Japan's coming economic role in Asia.

"Gotcha!" has been the American stance toward East Asia since 1997, when the tiger cub economies of the region followed the Japanese mother cat into a financial tailspin. Not only was there palpable gloating over the downturn for Asians, who throughout the 1980s had twitted Uncle Sam mercilessly over his flawed economic thinking and performance, but the debacle also was taken to have discredited once and for all the alleged model for the Asian economic "miracle," as "model" nations went flat while the U.S. economy simply kept growing. As Mortimer B. Zuckerman editorialized early on in *U.S. News & World Report* after Japan's stock market crash and collapse in real estate prices in 1997: "Let us celebrate an American triumph. . . . The mantra is privatize, deregulate and do not interfere with the market."[5]

Top American officials from President Bill Clinton and Treasury Secretary Robert Rubin on down—with the good-doing sternness of Calvinist predestinarians—lectured the hapless Asians on the need to restructure themselves for more effective participation in the world economy, now inevitably to be run along American lines. Japan in particular was pressed, with much impatience, to assist its neighbors and pay its dues to the world trading system by reflating its economy and opening its markets further to Asia—as the United States did in its recent rescue of Mexico.

It was assumed that because Japan *should* do so, it *would* do so—as if the unexpected regional crisis could of itself persuade Tokyo to cave in at long last to decades of American entreaty. Far from it. Indeed, Japan was talking back like never before, as when Ambassador Kunihiko Saito in a public forum in Washington scolded U.S. officials for making their "frank comments" (read: criticism and advice) publicly rather than through private channels with regard to Japan's 16-trillion-yen stimulus package of April 1998.[6] Saito apparently had forgotten the very open way in which Japanese bureaucrats had taunted the Americans for their economic problems a decade earlier. But the point was that he himself was saying no—very publicly and very clearly.

Economic Determinism Redux

Lurking behind—indeed, driving—America's economic mirages of Japan over the past decade has been our triumphant new economic determinism, with its facile assumption that it is economic difficulty that will force Japan into policy directions more to our liking. This rests in turn on the insufficiently examined premise that the cause-and-effect sequence here will run from economics to politics and society and eventually to values and ideas—a leaf that the gnomes of lower Manhattan seem to have stolen, oblivious of the irony, right out of Karl Marx.

The assumptions, more specifically, seem to be that a crisis of nonperformance in a particular economic sector—namely, the banking mess from 1997, with the consequent foreign inroads into that field—will finally catalyze genuine enactment of the drastic regulatory, administrative, and political reforms promised but stalled ever since 1993. These, together with the combined pressures of a rapidly aging population and the need to outsource Japanese manufacturing abroad, will combine to erode established patterns of seniority-based lifetime employment, intercorporate *keiretsu* (affiliated group) solidarity, employee loyalty and deference, pursuit of market share over profitability, and the bureaucracy's leverage over the Japanese economy and parliamentary system. This onslaught, in turn, will expunge Japan's deeper psychological heritage of group-oriented personal behavior, submissiveness toward higher authority, and ethnocentric nationalism. (Triumphalist analysts all have their particular prime movers and sequence of causes, but for the most extensive recent compendium of many of these upbeat prognoses one could do worse than browse the pages of Milton Ezrati's *Kawari: How Japan's Economic and Cultural Transformation Will Alter the Balance of Power Among Nations*.)[7]

Finally, it is assumed that all of the foregoing will propel Japan—

albeit with many a twist and turn—toward the convergence with U.S.-style political individualism, private sector supremacy, civil society, and open markets that will be required to realize America's liberal-capitalist and democratic vision for Asia. The end product will be a switch of Japan's grand national purpose and worldview from self-protective insularism and mercantilism to a genuinely open economy and society taking an intellectually cosmopolitan lead on the Asian and world stages.

Actually, one could argue that this sequence was stood on its head during Japan's two great 180-degree turns in its modern history. It was a fresh mandate of ideas and the reconceptualization of national goals that catalyzed changes under both the new Meiji regime after 1870 and the Allied occupation after 1945. These brought in their wake new political dispensations that, in the end, crafted the economic mechanisms that would best serve the new national goals of military and economic catch-up with the West after 1870 and of continued catch-up by pacifistic and strictly economic means since 1945.

It is this too narrow focus on the Japanese economy—in ignorance, neglect, or bowdlerization of more determinative power-political and attitudinal factors—that has moved the giddy seesaw of our shifting takes on Japan over the last ten years and spawned today's cottage industry of writing speculative scenarios on Japan in the twenty-first century based almost exclusively (if selectively) on economic projections. For prophets content with mathematical equations, economic determinism is the easy way out.

Yet history, if only we listened, would tell us how relatively little the ups and downs of the Japanese economy during the Meiji or prewar eras, for example, affected Japan's overall course, which was being set by deeper forces of political purpose and cultural values. Historians, of course, will continue to dispute the hierarchy of causes. And it is true, for instance, that sectoral hardships in agriculture did help to fan anti-foreign nationalism in the 1880s and 1930s, just as the new spurts of foreign trade in the 1870s and 1920s helped to raise the Western cultural presence along with a certain mood of cosmopolitanism. But neither the maturation of the new industrial economy after 1900 nor the quick recovery from the Great Depression ahead of Europe and America in the early 1930s deflected Japan from the internal authoritarianism and external expansionism that drove its so-called Meiji state, the ethos and structure of which collapsed only with the total military debacle in World War II.

The popularity of neoclassical economics in American (and British) political dogma, policy thinking, and media punditry throughout the 1990s derives, of course, from the successful taming of stagflation during the Reagan and Thatcher years, from the end of the Cold War with its primacy of political anxieties, and from the conceit of the sole remaining superpower—so well expressed in Francis Fukuyama's *The End of History and the Last Man*—that the world will now flock to our own economic and political models without our having to think too hard about social, cultural, or intellectual differences.[8] In short, we are being treated here to the most recent twist on the theory of societal convergence—toward our own American model.[9]

Our current triumphalism toward Japan rests, further, on the superior performance of our own economy over the past decade and on some other factors we will leave to our final chapter. These include the fad of economically modeled and politically denatured rational-choice theory in U.S. academe that has turned our budding Asia specialists away from the earlier emphasis on language-competent historical and anthropological area studies—precisely, the more taxing and subjective exploration of the noneconomic dimensions of Japan. By the same token (as we shall revisit in Chapters 17 and 18), the broader roots of our economic obsession were planted with our initial admiration of Japan's stunning success during the 1970s, followed by our growing fear of it by the 1980s.

Weaker Nation + Stronger Individuals = Change

The dogmatic certainty of America's economic philosophy for East Asia feeds on the dramatization of Japan's current troubles. This fuels the conviction that weakness and vulnerability are about to force dramatic changes, to be shouldered by a new breed of individualistic Japanese waiting in the wings. Tales of personal hardship and retrenchment make the headlines, from a spate of suicides among owners of small companies to university honors graduates no longer able to pick and choose among Japan's blue-chip firms and the brand-name luxury stores on Waikiki that have gone out of business with the drastically reduced flow of Japanese tourists to Hawaii.

One of the starkest prognoses came from the pen of the *New York Times* Tokyo bureau chief Nicholas D. Kristof in his Parthian-shot dispatch upon leaving Japan in July 1999. Like other declinists, Kristof stresses the impact of a shrinking working-age population, together with a productivity growth rate under 0.5 percent—much less than half that of the United States—and government welfare policies perversely wed to "picking losers" among declining companies, towns, and industries and "subsidizing them on a grand scale." From his sources he suggests that Japan's influence is on the wane, destined to become (in the words of Columbia University economist Hugh T. Patrick) a "middling power" with little prospect of leading Asia and with living standards frozen at the present level—but with the silver lining that "ordinary Japanese may live more enjoyable lives in a less crowded country."[10]

The main problem with writing off the economic challenge from Japan—absolutely, as the declinists in effect have done—is that it ignores the future projection of latent material and social strengths under altered circumstances, as the Axis powers (or Japan a half century later) were to learn to their chagrin about the economically "ailing giant" of America during the 1930s or 1980s.

So, willy or nilly, the market openings the Japanese have so long resisted are simply bound to come. On the eve of Prime Minister Keizo Obuchi's visit to the United States in May 1999, the *New York Times* pronounced that—no laughing anymore—"Japan is really opening up its economy this time."

"After visiting Tokyo a few weeks ago," the *Times'* Thomas L. Friedman insisted, "I left convinced that Japan has indeed begun its third great modernization." After those triggered by the arrivals of Commodore Perry in 1853 and Douglas MacArthur in 1945, "the third is being driven now by the invisible hands of globalization: the Internet and global capital flows are breaking the shell around Japan like a nutcracker."[11] Indeed, the friend he had just visited at the Japanese Foreign Ministry had told him that his son wanted to be a fund manager rather than a banker—the premier private sector choice of his father's generation— since Japan's major banks were crumbling. More recently, in a parallel family tale from the high bureaucracy, an old friend of mine at the Ministry of International Trade and Industry told me how *his* daughter had turned down a corporate promotion to remain in a bureau where the work was more meaningful to her personally. Here at last, by implication, was a new generation of more self-directed young Japanese.

Not to be left behind, Japan's most authoritative ex officio spokesman on the subject has been quick to chime in. Briefing about twenty foreign correspondents on his government's newly unveiled policy paper for "economic rebirth" in August 1999, Economic Planning Agency chief Taichi Sakaiya likened Japan to a volcano about to blow its top off (*funka chokuzen*) with a new gospel of "freedom," receding government, and no more administrative guidance—a revolution without a change of rulers.[12] What the world had been witnessing to date was just a series of "small magma eruptions."[13]

Significant portions of the arguments made to foreign publics that Japan is indeed changing hang on anecdotal straws in the wind relating to the alleged growth of individualistic attitudes and behavior among business leaders, salaried workers, bureaucrats, and young Japanese returning from Western educations abroad. And here, indeed, is the level of new social values on which any genuine and lasting change would have to rest.

"Japan Inc. Tries to Put Individualism to Work," proclaimed the lead article of the *New York Times* business section for 9 October 1997. The Japanese were experimenting with "an executive breed indigenous to the U.S.," with a new style of "corporate individualism." The article, by Sheryl WuDunn, featured a twenty-eight-year-old technology-development manager in a small Internet access provider who dyes his hair brown, keeps his own hours, occasionally takes a day off for windsurfing, and typifies the creative whiz kid whose time has at last come. "Nonconformity," concluded the *Times,* "is suddenly in." Japan's big corporations also had studied America's economic resurgence and were looking for ways to inject individual creativity into their cumbersome management processes. The giant NEC (Nippon Electric), for example, was showcasing an entrepreneurially minded midlevel manager it had cut loose to launch his own highly profitable multimedia systems firm—admittedly ensuring his success, however, by buying 60 percent of the spin-off company's product.

Newsweek had already jumped on the change-is-coming bandwagon. "Nowadays . . . the Japanese are putting more value on individual happiness," enthused the 25 August 1997 issue, its opening paragraph in bold blue oversized type quoting Masayuki Suo, author and director of *Shall We Dance?* This film had captured the hearts of moviegoers in the United States and Japan with its depiction of a salaryman (*sarariman*, a white-collar worker) in his late thirties who, in defiance of Japan's corporate norms and robotic stereotypes, and after much dithering, had steeled himself to have a little fun on weekday evenings by attending a social dancing school and romancing his instructress, rather than going drinking with the office crowd. Some American viewers came away from this poignant box-office hit by one of Japan's new crop of young directors claiming to have heard the starting gun of a paradigm shift in the Japanese values governing the individual's role in society.

Japan's public intellectuals, too, have been taking a fresh look at playwright Masakazu Yamazaki's contention a few years back that his countrymen were pioneering a new social ethic of "soft individualism"—a superior mutant that would discard the offensive rugged edges of its Western counterpart.[14] Yamazaki, who has drawn on medieval themes for some of his plays, looks to the reemergence of the more insouciant and freewheeling temperament that characterized his countrymen during their warring-states period from the 1460s to the 1560s, before the national unification process under the Tokugawa shoguns set in with its freezing of social status and its international seclusion policy after 1600. It had been an era of swashbuckling regional strongmen, of fast-paced social mobility both up and down, of constantly negotiated and betrayed political loyalties, and of plucky Japanese merchants (sometimes doubling as pirates) who roamed the "Southern Seas" establishing Japanese trading settlements—minicolonies—throughout Southeast Asia.

One is hard put to find any slackening of the tight-lipped hauteur among Japan's national bureaucrats in Tokyo, but one British journalist remarked after a news-gathering trip to the provinces that he had found some of the younger prefectural officials "practically American" in their frank and open manner: "Japan is changing. Yes, Ivan, it *is* changing."

Another refrain, heard every time Japan seems particularly unresponsive to foreign entreaties, is that the younger generation is changing and will eventually take care of it—just you wait! Tim Larimer, *Time*'s Tokyo correspondent, wrote a cover story for the 3–10 May 1999 double issue arguing, in essence, that rude behavior—in a land venerating harmony—points the way to great changes. With a cover featuring a teenage Japanese girl with a nose ring and eyebrow rings, Larimer noted the "decline in politeness, squatting in public, dyeing hair blonde, tanning, teenage prostitution, [and] chaotic schools where students assault teachers." "Suddenly," he concluded, "the rules are changing before the kids have a chance to rewrite them. It may be that a revolution isn't a choice, but a necessity."

More often, the catalyzing potential of youth has been attributed to those youngsters who have returned to Japan after a secondary education abroad in the countries where their parents were professionally stationed. Their independent spirit, honed at Western or Western-oriented schools in the United States, United Kingdom, Singapore, Switzerland, or São Paulo, will rub off—so the hope goes—on their nontraveled classmates at Japanese universities. Japan's growing international commitments will then put these *kikokushijo*, or "repatriated children," at a premium for employment by Japan's corporate and mass media establishments, from which they will work their leaven of internationalization on the broader populace.[15]

Lastly, American observers in particular tend to assume that people everywhere are at heart individualists—or would-be individualists—as laid down by John Locke and in the Declaration of Independence. Their natural-state egos, we think, are as sharply individuated as ours. And if they are experiencing difficulty in rising to self-awareness and self-expression, it is because of some outwardly imposed, oppressive carapace that merely needs to be lifted. Allow a handful of Japanese banks to collapse; let the big American brokerage firms in; follow the precepts of the Securities and Exchange Commission (SEC), the International Monetary Fund (IMF), and Milton Friedman; tame Tokyo's mandarin bureaucrats; lift, perhaps, Japan's constitutional restraints on a "normal" military establishment—and, lo and behold!—the Japanese will emerge as liberated individualists.

At the level of institutional change, the immediate Western hope is that banking reforms in the wake of an unprecedented financial mess, together with tax cuts and public expenditures to stimulate the economy, may combine to give the individual investor, consumer, and entrepreneur an invigorating new role in Japan's society and economy. To provide a legal and political framework for the gradual retreat of bureaucratic power, much faith has been placed in successive prime ministers' support of administrative retrenchment and in the recent electoral reform to eliminate multiparty deadlock and permit the emergence of a two-party system based on genuine considerations of policy as opposed to the old factional politics. Indeed, the enthusiasts argue, the game has already opened in Japan's financial sector, which now offers an ever-widening cornucopia of lucrative entries for go-getting American banking, securities, and management-consulting firms.

A Japanese economy and political system successfully revamped and reenergized along democratic and free-enterprise lines will then attract regional neighbors toward its drastically Americanized model, making Japan our natural partner for the further realization of U.S. objectives in Asia. So go our illusions.

The Counterpoint of Japanese Realities

Now, how does this logic of American economic hopes and expectations stack up against the counterparadigm of Japanese views and intentions? Here, with many interrelated issues to consider, we need to keep the bottom line in mind: whether or not Japan is prepared to become a genuine free trader, opening its markets to foreign goods and its society to the human interaction with foreign peoples that goes with an increasingly interdependent global community. If that intention were at all in the cards, the Asian economic crisis would have been a good place to start. Instead, faced with the necessity to work its way out of an economic pinch, Japan chose once again to aggravate global trade tensions by increasing exports to others, particularly the United States.

The causes underlying Tokyo's "great refusal" on trade are critical for the debate now unfolding both there and abroad about Japan's role in the post-Cold War world order—or, indeed, about the very nature of that new order itself. For Japan is the only country in today's world capable of mounting a real challenge to America's universalistic gospel of liberal capitalist democracy. Communist fossils and orphans such as China and Russia may choose not to follow us, but they are unlikely to create a successful and appealing particularistic alternative.

Here I am thinking less of Japan's classic growth model (which may retain some regional appeal) than of its future projection onto the entire global trading system of the essentially parasitic economic relationship it has enjoyed with the United States over the past half century—this time with parts of East Asia safely in its own corner.[16] What I have in mind is less a formal currency bloc or Co-Prosperity Sphere than a national or regional entity that manages to grow rich while remaining exclusive and beggar-thy-neighbor in its economic behavior. Driven by mercantilist and cultural nationalist ideas, this global player would continue to benefit from the post–General Agreement on Tariffs and Trade international order by playing along with the World Trade Organization and other rule-setting regimes just enough not to be thrown out. And others would tolerate it because they were unwilling to risk trade wars or endanger political ties.

Mercantilism for Aye

To start once again with ideas, the philosophical underpinning of Japan's train of causes goes dramatically against the grain of America's own ideological assumptions. Where economic freedom was anchored for Americans in the nation's very founding for the "pursuit of happiness," Japan's core national principle from the Meiji Restoration to this day has been the defense of the nation by catching up with the West, subordinating individual Japanese rights and comforts to that purpose. Liberal, business-oriented Meiji intellectuals such as Yukichi Fukuzawa and Eiichi Shibusawa who read J. S. Mill or Herbert Spencer did so mainly to evoke an entrepreneurial spirit as against the antibusiness prejudices of old Confucian Japan, but within the overall purpose of government-led modernization for national security. The Meiji oligarchs went even further and took their economic cues from the mercantilism of Friedrich List.

While America played away with the unfettered economy of the Coolidge era, Tokyo's bureaucrats in the 1920s were already crafting a licensing system to contain the inroads of early foreign multinationals such as Ford or Royal Dutch/Shell into a Japanese market more open then than it is today. "Industry-rationalizing" cartels under state guidance were introduced from 1929, and as the world lurched toward war in the 1930s "reform bureaucrats" and some of Prince Fumimaro Konoe's brain trusters in the Showa Research Society (Showa Kenkyukai) drank deeply of corporatist ideas from fascist Italy and Hitler's Germany.

What gives these dry economic ideas their peculiar ideological grip in Japan is the way they have been ethically internalized as a self-abne-gating social contract based on a familistic concern for all other elements of Japanese society—racially defined. These precepts may not represent true feelings, but as official norms in a group-oriented context, they make an open intellectual questioning of them very awkward. For the sake of a dwindling farm population, urban consumers put up with the high price of rice. To be nice to Mom and Pop, large retail chains are a no-no. And, for everybody's sake, foreign competitors must be kept at bay, both as a moral duty and as a patriotic imperative. Australian writer and long-term Japan resident Murray Sayle captured it best with his sobriquet: "ethno-economics, Japanese style."[17]

And what of the custodians of the mercantilist flame? Despite frothy antibureaucratic protests over the past decade, just how far have the old underlying expectations of the Japanese people toward their government officials actually changed?

In 1881 Japan crossed one of those tragic historical watersheds—one thinks, for example, of the Kennedy assassination in 1963, or that cosmic snap heard against the evening sky at the end of Chekhov's *Cherry Orchard.* In an internal palace coup among the ruling oligarchs of the early Meiji period, effective power passed from Shigenobu Okuma and his coterie of liberal-minded intellectuals, who had been advocating the introduction of an English-model constitution with parliamentary sovereignty, to an autocratic clique leaning ideologically toward Berlin.

That cabal of power-protective Restoration ex-samurai under the baton of Hirobumi Ito went on to craft in strict secrecy—without any constitutional convention or other input from the Japanese people—a constitutional system patterned after that of Bismarck's Germany, embellished by Japan's own emperor mythology. Under that Meiji constitution of 1890, the bureaucrats—already the spiritual legatees of the Tokugawa samurai civil leadership—were placed (along with the military) in the direct personal service of the emperor, in a central administration not answerable to the new Diet. Like the ministries and "transcendental" cabinets they took their orders from, they were considered to be loftily above and superior to—not, as with modern democratic civil servants, simply detached from—the nation-threatening factionalism and personal egotism, as they saw it, of the grubby party-political world.

The harder edges here were somewhat softened, of course, after World War II. But prophets of imminent change too glibly pass over the question as to just what it would now take—in a group- and nation-oriented society such as Japan's—to genuinely undermine the strength of this historically and organically continuous elite.

Peter Drucker reminds us of the remarkable staying power of bureaucratic elites, including those of the modern European democracies. Even when discredited by scandals and incompetence, they manage to hang on wherever they have been based neither on wealth nor on birth but on meritocratic function, especially when no "universally accepted replacement" is in sight—criteria all applicable to Japan today. This is because they provide a bulwark, even in democracies, against social or political breakdown. As in Europe today (and the United States during the New Deal), the national social weal takes primacy over economics not only among Japan's political, bureaucratic, and business leaders but among the Japanese people at large. "In most developed countries other than the United States," Drucker notes, "the economy is considered a restraint on policies rather than their major, let alone sole, determinant. Ideology and, above all, the impact on society come first."[18] Drucker declines to see Tokyo's delays in tackling the banking crisis as "mere political cowardice," since "to Tokyo's ruling coterie, procrastination and delay appear the only rational policies" in ongoing defense of Japan's social objectives.[19]

While writing off Japan's business, professorial, or professional elites as unacceptable replacements, Drucker (as a management guru, perhaps) oddly overlooks Japan's parliamentary arm—that is to say, the elected representatives of the people, whose peculiar weakness and subordination to bureaucracy have been agitating Japan's reformist politicians and sympathetic foreign political observers. Even if the Diet was to move closer to party supremacy, however, there has been little evidence after seven years of stalled reforms to suggest the emergence of any fundamental difference between the political parties, between the parties and the bureaucracy, or between the government and the electorate on keeping Japan's markets closed. Japanese people still think of themselves more as job holders, producers, and loyal company workers than as individual consumers—and they are grateful for protection, whatever leadership can supply it.

Over the grand sweep of postwar history Japan's bureaucrats have on the whole delivered, and there is still too much fear that, in a genuinely free economy, the players would fail to keep either the national interest or broader public interests sufficiently in mind. The burden of proof still lies, I think, with those who would argue otherwise. Similarly, too much has been made of the turf battles among Japan's bureaucrats—what else is new in the bureaucratic cosmos?—as a cause of policy immobility.[20] The same goes for their recent financial fumblings and expense-account scandals, as though those were a sure opening for the greater assertion of parliamentary control.

The celebration by Western commentators of an economically driven tectonic shift in Japanese social psychology seemed particularly bizarre at the time of the Upper House elections in July 1998. With a sense of national crisis and public disgust with their bureaucratically dominated political system at an all-time post-1960 high, this would have been the occasion, if ever, for a modest political earthquake. The protest vote for independents at the expense of the ruling Liberal Democrats was indeed enough to compel Prime Minister Hashimoto to resign. But with the Liberal Democratic Party (LDP) still in control of the Lower House of the Diet, and an opposition still short on convincing leaders and ideas, the nation was content to stand by as the conservatives muddled ahead with the old politics of factional balance rather than policy orientation in choosing the lackluster old consensus maker Keizo Obuchi as the new premier. As Obuchi went on to craft an even stronger LDP with possible openings to other conservative elements such as the Liberal Party and the current legatees of the old Buddhist-oriented Komeito (Clean Government Party), the Japanese electorate still seemed to prefer the collective security of sticking with their old and flawed but familiar patron, the LDP. When in doubt or danger or confronted by the more powerful, "roll up in a long thing," as the traditional aphorism has it: *nagai mono ni wa makarero*.

Change: Things Are Seldom What They Seem

Japan's longstanding philosophical acceptance of protectionism and bureaucratic leadership is not likely to be budged by current developments that have fired the expectations of an impatient West. Our triumphalists seem to have forgotten how strong Japan actually is.

Glen S. Fukushima, a former trade negotiator and recent president of the American Chamber of Commerce in Japan (1998 and 1999), has deplored the tendency of foreign observers to conflate Japan's nonperforming loans in the banking sector and a record-breaking postwar recession with the financial crisis in Southeast Asia, attributed to the evils of "crony capitalism" and "government intervention." Fukushima reminds us, "This misses the fact that Japan constitutes seventy percent of the East Asian economy and its economy is seven times the size of China's, 10 times Korea's, 20 times Indonesia's and 53 times Thailand's. Japan is endowed with world-class technology, a highly skilled work force, a $130 billion current account surplus and $240 billion in foreign currency reserves." The decline in living standards has been marginal, and the suicides among small firm owners sensationally reported out of all proportion to Japanese business as a whole. The problem, in short, is that Americans have been focusing too much on Japan's financial problems while overlooking its manufacturing prowess, where cost reduction measures will boost competitiveness once demand picks up.[21]

More concretely to that point, Tokyo-based Irish financial author Eamonn Fingleton has long stressed the three great weapons of economic strength still held by Japan: copious savings, an unparalleled stock of capital equipment, and well-honed organizational skills.[22] This ensures Japan continued clout in world markets by virtue of its well-tended "hard industries" with their superior capacity for creating jobs, exports, and high wages. Having retained its upstream production facilities for materials, components, and the machines that make them, Japan, according to Fingleton, is destined to show up America's current faith in the supremacy of postindustrial services such as computer software, entertainment, and finance as well as our tendency to confuse downstream snap-together assembly lines in the United States or developing countries with advanced manufacturing.[23]

After all, Japan's cumulative total current-account surplus—the widest and most meaningful measure of trade—in the decade of the "depressed" 1990s came to $987 billion, or 2.37 times the comparable figure of $416 billion for the "booming" decade of the 1980s. Similarly, in little-noticed IMF financial statistics, Japan's net external assets jumped from $294 billion to $1,153 billion in the first nine years of the 1990s, while America's net external liabilities rocketed from $49 billion to $1,537 billion during the same period. These ballooning trade surpluses during the so-called lost decade of the 1990s were driven by the huge strides Japan was making in capital-intensive areas of advanced manufacturing, building a number of crucial monopolies in goods vital to the continued functioning of the world economy.[24]

Fingleton was one of the very few Tokyo-based economic commentators who in the late 1980s predicted both the Japanese stock market and real estate crashes of the early 1990s as well as the consequent banking problems. He believes that the portrayal of the Japanese economy as a basket case by Western bankers and journalists—echoing what they get from the Japanese government and press—has disastrously misled the United States in shaping an effective trade policy toward Japan. For his reminders in two books of continuing Japanese strength and ambitions, Fingleton in early 1999 was singled out for attack over the Internet by two Tokyo-based foreign securities executives with a more pessimistic view of Japan's chances. Challenged by Fingleton to a public debate in Washington before American experts, his opponents first counteroffered to air the matter in the Japanese language before a group of heavyweight Japanese economists and financial experts in Tokyo, but subsequently declined to debate him in any public venue.[25]

The problem with the announcement of a "third revolution" is that it has to start with ideas. Indeed, I recall former ambassador to Japan Edwin O. Reischauer in the early 1970s calling in the course of a university speech in Osaka for a change in attitude as profound as the one that had marked the Meiji Restoration. Unfortunately, the critical difference from

the first and second revolutions is that the two earlier ones were catalyzed by overwhelming foreign threats—the threat of military attack in
the first case, and the actual Allied occupation and direct dictation of
Japanese reform in the second. Scholars, for example, largely agree that
the fall of the Tokugawa and the reforms of Meiji never would have
occurred when they did without that foreign connection.

As for all those harbingers of individualism being served up by the
American press, the question they all beg is: How powerful are they
relative to competing forces in Japan, and are they anywhere near the
cumulative threshold required for a meaningful catalytic effect?

To anyone who has worked for any length of time within the actual
human web of Japanese organizations—as opposed to merely studying
them from the outside—these prognoses of incipient individualism will
seem premature, if not downright fanciful. For years Japanese corporations have given leeway to certain creative individuals within the scope
of corporate purposes, like the maverick company official feted by the
New York Times. This is little more than a subplot of the broader game
by which the Japanese government from the Meiji era onward has consistently encouraged the energies of the private sector and harnessed
them to its own broadly guided goals. Even Sony and Matsushita, the
two great postwar sagas of Horatio Alger–like self-invention, got in step
quickly with Japan's business and political establishments once they
"made it" and were let in. The business sector in Japan has never had,
nor aspired to, the sort of independent power that enabled its American
counterpart to practically run the U.S. government during the 1880s and
1890s or to tell Washington's bureaucracy to get the hell out of the way
a hundred years later. Looking at Japan through the lenses of our own
historical experience, we Americans place far too much faith in the power
of gentle creep.

By the same token, the search by Masayuki Suo's dancing-school
hero for greater self-fulfillment during his private time does not imply
any greater willingness to challenge group mores on the job—what would
be a truer measure of any individualism with pathbreaking implications.
Modern Japanese literature and thought are littered with examples of
writers and thinkers who, despairing of the possibilities for effective
political or social activism, retreated into the quiet of their studies or
into intellectual positions and pursuits no longer challenging the political and social order.[26] Much the same trait, incidentally, was noted of
nineteenth-century German intellectuals—the same tragic disjunction

of inner thoughts and outward political reality,[27] still captured today by the melancholy German campfire song "Die Gedanken sind Frei" (Thoughts [at least] are free). But if thoughts are not permitted to lead you any further, what good is that?

Many ordinary Japanese, too, have cultivated artistically or intellectually rich lives, but in strict apolitical privacy. Foreign observers often have confused stylistically individualistic statements in dress or hobbies—like the dancing school—with a more significant personal independence. How many junketing journalists in Tokyo fifteen to twenty years ago read a newly liberated Japanese youth into the so-called Bamboo-Shoot Tribe, known as the *takenoko zoku?* These were the teenagers who on Sunday afternoons dyed their hair orange and slipped into outrageously psychedelic costumes to gyrate manically to souped-up rock music on the boulevard near the Meiji Shrine in the Harajuku district. Insufficiently noted was the fact that they did so in large, immaculately synchronized groups, rather than in a solo act before crowds of onlookers, like the American break-dance show-offs on Fifth Avenue. Or that, once the sun went down, they changed in a twinkle into their black school uniforms to melt into the subway crowds headed home, their noses poked into Monday's junior high school assignments.

Yamazaki's "soft individualism," too, seems more like a toning down of the hard old Japanese groupism than a milder form of the strict self-direction and personal accountability we normally associate with the concept of individualism in the West. And a less autocratic and standoffish manner with foreigners, while certainly welcome among lesser provincial officials, will not signify real change until it infects the attitudes of Japan's central bureaucrats—not only toward prying foreign journalists but, far more importantly, toward ordinary Japanese citizens. And that is something of which I have yet to hear, read, or see a single instance.

Tim Larimer's regiment of rude young rebels doesn't seem to get beyond an unstructured, sullen anger lacking in the individual discipline and civic sense that will be needed to crack Japan's conformist front—and not just another version of the philosophical anomie and personal rootlessness that tends to afflict individual Japanese whenever their group structures break down. It is hard to see outbreaks of student violence and the (now very easy to do) flouting of older conventions as a harbinger of individualism based on personal choice and responsibility.

As for the college youths returning from a high school education abroad, my own observation after teaching a hundred of them at three of

Japan's leading universities is that they eventually have to conform to their stay-at-home peers and company colleagues, who tend to be less open, more content with affluence, and much more prickly about foreign criticism.[28] Indeed, what awaits the openly principled challenger of conformity is the complete professional ostracism that befell the maverick American-trained physician, the late Dr. Masao Miyamoto, who joined Japan's Ministry of Health after twelve years' successful practice in the United States. Questioning unproductive procedures and refusing to waste his off hours on trivial but customary office socializing, Miyamoto found himself successively demoted from the central ministry to the quarantine office at Yokohama and finally to the quarantine shed at Kobe—the very bottom of the career line. Fortunately for his finances and our understanding of Japan, Miyamoto resigned to write a best-selling exposé of his own "quarantining" from Japanese society that made him a popular luncheon speaker on both sides of the Pacific.[29]

The greatest drag on change comes, of course, from the solid and mutually supportive structures of established interests, the broad lineaments of which have been sketched from the inside by Japanese observers such as Akio Mikuni, head of Japan's leading bond-rating agency.[30] What holds genuine financial reform and economic liberalization back, according to Mikuni, is the politically engineered suppression of consumption in order to mobilize savings for Japan's export-driven developmental capitalism. The tax code and the low interest rates mandated for bank and postal savings have discouraged consumption at the household level and permitted the socialization of financial risk through implicit credit guarantees passed downward from the governmental to the banking to the corporate sectors. These guarantees have sustained Japan's massive capital outlays for production facilities and permitted Japanese firms to neglect corporate and investor profitability in their pursuit of global leadership in technology and market share. This reliance of the political economy on external rather than internal demand also leads to an overcapacity in capital plant that drives Japan's export surges and creates incessant political tension with Tokyo's trading partners.

There is much else that has buttressed this structure, including a labor market stabilized through lifetime employment, the symbiotic logrolling among vested business, parliamentary, and bureaucratic interests, and the lack of transparency and accountability in loss allocation. The bottom line for Mikuni, however, is political and intellectual. "Japan," he warns, "is still mired in feudalistic thinking and social structures. No social revolution has occurred to create full-fledged Japanese citizens, a democratic political system, or a market economy. The policy elite will thwart any serious challenge as long as it can maintain its instruments of control over the economy, suppress consumption, maximize savings, and rely upon external rather than internally generated demand to keep the Japanese industrial machine going."[31] What it will take to turn the corner, Mikuni warns, is no less than a fully independent judiciary as final arbiter in economic disputes, an investigative press more interested in finding the truth than in protecting the social order, a genuine opposition imposing political control on the bureaucracy, and shareholders who can discipline management.[32] A far cry, I might add, from what we have in Japan today.

Mikuni characterizes the hand wringing by Japanese elites over weak yen-dollar rates whenever they occur as "little more than crocodile tears."[33] Financial author R. Taggart Murphy, a former international banker long resident in Japan, similarly challenged Western misperceptions that the "Big Bang" of financial reforms announced in 1997 could lead to the dawn of "Anglo-Saxon"-type capitalism (as the modish term had it), rather than just a ten-year window of opportunity during which foreign financiers would be free to make serious money in Japan in everything from retail banking to mutual fund markets.[34] It would be no more than a grace period, however, while Japanese financial institutions absorbed the cutting-edge expertise required to make them internationally competitive, at which point—as in the past, Murphy reminds us—they would find ways to send the foreigners packing.[35]

Reform: Skim Milk Masquerades as Cream

What convincing evidence have we had that this massive structure of vested interests may at last be yielding to an onslaught of reform?

Unfortunately, the whole process and purpose of Japanese reform—regulatory, administrative, and political—has been not only overestimated but basically misunderstood by many Western observers as an honest if glacially slow trajectory toward Anglo-American-style liberal, free-trading capitalism. We keep missing time after time the deliberate emasculation of key deregulation proposals, the continuation of old administrative governance in new guises, the distracting sideshow nature of the recently touted electoral innovations, and, above all, the unchanging mercantilist objectives behind what is—and is not—being done.

In July 1999 the cabinet of Prime Minister Keizo Obuchi unveiled a
sweeping plan for "economic rebirth"—long on vision, short on details,
and aiming for the year 2010—to loosen restraints on competition, reduce government influence, make markets more efficient, expand consumer options, and give better returns to investors. In a nutshell, the aim
was to alter the way Japan does business. "The future Japan should not
be led by government initiative but by competition of free individuals,"
intoned Economic Planning Agency chief Taichi Sakaiya.[36]

But wait a moment—haven't we been there before?

In the opening sentence of their 1998 group study of the regulatory
and administrative reform movement in Japan since the early 1980s,
political scientists Mark Tilton and Lonny Carlile posed what had been
the guiding question for their Japanese and American fellow researchers: "Can Japan dismantle its developmentalist regulations so as to open
its markets meaningfully to imports and provide the market opportunities desperately needed by its Asian neighbors?"[37] Finding no indication
of "a groundswell of business support for strong antibureaucratic,
promarket reforms,"[38] the two coeditors of *Is Japan Really Changing Its
Ways? Regulatory Reform and the Japanese Economy* noted that their
contributors "concur strongly on the point that the regulatory reform
measures implemented so far have had a relatively small, marginal impact with respect to increasing competition and the role of the 'market'
in the Japanese economy."[39] Indeed, what strikes the reader most of all
is how little the reform movement, even at its most zealous, was concerned with opening Japanese markets to imports by gradually conform-
ing Tokyo's trade practices to international standards—one of the most
striking Western misreadings of Japan in recent years.

Most often reform measures were disabled before they got off the
ground or were pegged at a cosmetic level, as with the abortive attempts
to devolve some of the budgetary, monetary, and bank regulation functions of the Ministry of Finance (MOF) and to reform the opaque and
discretionary nature of its powers.[40] The Securities Exchange Surveillance Committee (SESC), set up in 1992, lacked the teeth to fulfill the
independent regulatory function of its American model (the SEC). It
remained an in-house operation of MOF and failed abysmally to moni-
tor, predict, or expose the racketeer extortion scandal that shook Japan's
top brokerage houses and disgraced the MOF in 1997. Similarly, the
Financial Supervision Agency (FSA) established in 1998 as the new
watchdog for banks has been given much of its staff from MOF and can

only liaise with other government agencies through the Financial Reconstruction Commission (FRC), which is under direct cabinet control.[41]

With regard to administrative reform, there is nothing yet on the horizon like the total abolition of the Civil Aeronautics Board under President Jimmy Carter to open up genuine U.S. airline competition. Massive resistance from pork-barreling politicians has stymied the reform—let alone privatization—of the huge postal savings system that still vacuums up the bulk of Japanese household savings at rock-bottom rates to help underpin the government's promotion of industries deemed most essential to national development. Tokyo's mixed government-private sector advisory commissions set up to streamline the administrative structure have been staffed by the very bureaucrats whose own jobs were on the line. Japan's numerous quasi-governmental bodies (the *tokushu hojin,* "special legal entities"), one of the alleged targets of reform, serve as one of the major retirement havens for former officials, who help to bind these nominally autonomous bodies to their sponsoring ministries. The attempt to reduce their numbers in 1983 ended, not surprisingly, in token cuts, with functions simply transferred or rescrambled in a new table of organization.

Only time will tell whether the same smoke-and-mirrors game has not been played with the plan developed from 1997 by Prime Minister Ryutaro Hashimoto's Administrative Reform Council and enacted into legislation on 6 January 2001, when the number of government ministries and agencies was almost halved, from 22 to 13. This superficially impressive streamlining of the table of organization, too, threatens to result in relatively minor reductions in official personnel and little meaningful dent in state powers. Indeed, the shuffle may leave some of the most problematical players, such as Construction or Posts and Telecommunications, with even more relative power than before as they take over the commanding role in their respective groupings of newly amalgamated ministries.

Finally, with foreign pressures directed (or directable) mainly toward governmental change, we are prone to forget that the restraints on competition imposed by private trade associations and informal cartels (as in steel) remain largely intact.

The real—and largely unperceived—reason for all this foot-dragging is that the goals and conceptualization of Japanese deregulation have been fundamentally different from those in Britain and the United States. The very term for it, *kisei kanwa,* means only the "relaxation" of regulations, not their removal. Unlike the American movement that in the late 1970s sprang out of a broad national political consensus to attack stagflation by reducing the functions of the state in the U.S. economy, deregulation in Japan emerged from a much lower and ad hoc level of ideas and decision making. It started as a gimmick by Tokyo's financial bureaucrats to get out of a budgetary pinch in the general account that had ballooned sevenfold during the latter half of the 1970s as a result of vote-getting social welfare and pork barrel policies. With tax hikes no longer politically acceptable, the emphasis shifted to slimming down bureaucratic agencies in the interests of greater efficiency and effectiveness for the national interest.

Similarly, where U.S. deregulation sought to expand consumer benefit, Japan's has been aimed at strengthening international competitiveness—including, to be sure, some nominal proposals designed to stave off foreign complaints and pressures. "The regulatory reform movement," in Tilton's words, "must be understood as a corrective and complement to Japan's system of developmentalist capitalism rather than an attempt to overthrow it."[42] In sum, little of this was performed as a concession to the Western trade negotiators huffing and puffing at the porte cochere.

The single solid reform promised and actually delivered by the new coalition governments since 1993 has been the political one—namely, the new electoral system eliminating the postwar multiple-seat constituency system. As we shall see in Chapter 3, however, the road this opens up leads less toward economic liberalization than to a massive new conservative dominance, shifting the balance of power toward the neonationalist element, many of whom remain opposed to genuine deregulation but are eager to push the country further to the right on military, educational, and constitutional issues. The effort by wishful-thinking Westerners and PR-conscious Japanese to present the new electoral setup as an earnest of, or substitute for, economic reforms has been either muddleheaded or disingenuous.

The Asian Equation

Finally, what likelihood is there that the rest of Asia after its financial crisis will end up more on Washington's side of the economic argument —perhaps even dragging Tokyo with it—rather than the other way around?

To paraphrase what a top executive of one of America's giant multinationals doing business throughout Asia told me, requesting anonymity: "Japanese corporations have been networking like mad, and successfully, all over the region, and they don't want American businesses in. The Americans are acting very cavalier and not doing anything about it. So the result is the same, whether it's being orchestrated by high Japanese government policy or not. A Bamboo Curtain *is* emerging."

The Asian crisis, ironically, has provided Japan with the opportunity to strengthen both economic ties and ideological rapport with its neighbors even as regional statesmen berate Tokyo for its refusal to assist them by opening its own markets—and for having the gall to knock them even lower by competing with their own recovery strategy of exporting to the American market.

According to Hong Kong-based economic writer and consultant Edith Terry, assiduous networking from 1985 to 1995 succeeded in creating a "vast, largely closed production loop across Asia" featuring Japanese intracompany trade whereby Japan-affiliated corporations in East Asia supply 80 percent of their production to each other and buy 80 percent of their materials from Japan. Replicating Japan's domestic *keiretsu* ties and joined to Asia's national economies through production linkages, this Japanese regional system is virtually impervious to outside suppliers. From 1997 Japanese government emergency assistance by way of export credits, insurance, and the ongoing technical training of local employees placed priority on the region's Japanese affiliates ahead of indigenous companies. This enabled initially stricken manufacturers of automobiles, electronics, and car parts to weather the crisis and turn themselves into even more powerful launching platforms for the United States and other world markets. A strong dollar in dollar-denominated regional trade raised their profits from exports to America while lowering the cost of parts imported from Japan, and enabled them to buy out or increase stakes in joint ventures with local Asian firms hard hit by the sudden devaluation of their own currencies.[43]

In a precrisis study in 1996, economic historian Kozo Yamamura and political scientist Walter Hatch already had characterized as "embraced development" the process by which Japan's business and government elites collaborate to move their production facilities offshore in pursuit of an expanded and exclusion-prone regional production zone in Asia, tightly held through Japan's strategic control of technology.[44] These two Japan scholars likened the rapidly growing Asian economies to the famed diving cormorants of Nagoya, which wear rings around their neck, preventing them from consuming their catch and instead forcing them to turn it over to the fisherman (Japanese business). Terry further likens the Japanese government to the source of financing for the fishermen's boats. For Japan it has been a marvelous formula, one that allows the regional affiliates to repatriate or keep most of their profit in Japanese hands while at the same time taking credit for catalyzing their Asian host country's industrialization.

Terry traces American nonchalance in the face of Japan's economic reconquest of its own backyard essentially to American ignorance and inattention. This includes our prevailing stereotype of a hopelessly weakened Japan, the political uses of that stereotype by U.S. and IMF officials to unlock congressional bailout funding for the region and to browbeat Tokyo into undertaking structural and market-opening reforms, and our sheer obliviousness to the scale of the Japanese presence in Asia and its massive buildup in the mid-1990s. For example, Japanese firms had invested $111 billion in Asia, most of it over the single decade leading up to 1998.

In stark contrast, Japan's economic activities in East Asia have always been backed by ideas and by a well-thought-out sense of purpose. The crisis aid in 1998 to Japanese affiliates derived from a political response at the highest level, just as the regional integration of Asia with Japan serving as its "brain" was laid out in a 1988 policy study by the Economic Planning Agency.[45] In an interview with Terry in 1998, Takato Ojimi, the Ministry of International Trade and Industry (MITI) official in charge of cooperation with developing countries, openly admitted to the active pursuit of a division of labor between the rest of Asia and Japan. Nothing new there—I had heard it more than two decades ago from another MITI man, a longtime personal friend of mine recently at the vice ministerial level, who was grousing to me at the time about the perverse insistence of the Canadians on developing their own manufacturing base, unlike the more sensible Australians, who were complying with a natural Japan-led division of labor in the Pacific.

Not surprisingly, Japan's articulated economic strategies pointedly omit the notion of import promotion. As Ojimi noted in an aside reminiscent of those special pleadings to Ambassador Foley: "There are no strictly effective means to convince consumers to import Asian products. And we can't mobilize additional means to support the industries that might expand imports, because we'd run into both World Trade Organization restrictions [one is tempted to ask which ones] and our own political problems. Many of the items that we might expand, such as agricultural products, would run against Japanese interests and politics."[46]

This reminds me of another dinner party, two decades ago, where the wife of a very high Japanese official (detained on business) responded to her American hostess' lament over the price of the glazed quail dinner she had just set before us by reminding us how all Japanese stood behind their farming communities, high price tags or no. One never ceases to be amazed at the way Japanese elites seem instinctively primed to proclaim the national policy on trade—rather like the American gun enthusiast's reflexive invocation of the Second Amendment.

I saw the network in action—indeed, fell into its web—one weekend during the tense U.S.-Japan trade negotiations in early 1995 when I was invited to address a group of three dozen upper-level corporate and government executives at a luxurious mountainside lodge near Hakone. They had been gathered there by the Economic Planning Agency with the express purpose, I was told, of weaving closer ties between the two sectors—a set piece of consensus building, the meticulous formality of which was exceeded only by its two-day boredom. Doing my best as a private citizen to argue the U.S. position, I ran into a steel wall of rebuttals and velvet-gloved put-downs in the group sections, which left me wondering where on earth my own embassy had gone and hidden itself.

As with so much else in America's economic mirage of Japan, we hurt ourselves most when we push the extreme position of our globalized free trade argument and assume that financial crisis alone will force Japan and others to restructure their economies à l'américaine. Chalmers Johnson, widely recognized as the prime mover of 1980s revisionism on Japan, has argued that the crisis in Asia, far from vindicating the universal applicability of neoclassical economics, shows the price that Asians, including Japanese, have had to pay for neglecting some of the central tenets of the revisionist model of Northeast Asian development capitalism. With their excessive importing of consumer goods and lack of effective piloting agencies like Japan's MITI (and, in the case of Indonesia, a nepotistic political economy), the Southeast Asians never were true followers of the Japanese model, which Tokyo itself strayed from with its lax oversight of financial institutions and the postbubble structural corruption in its corporate sector.[47]

As one of the first journalists to catch the point, Joseph Stieglitz of the *New York Times* noted of the original Thai crisis that the cause was "inadequate oversight, not overregulation" and that "our emphasis should not be on deregulation, but on finding the right regulatory regime to reestablish stability and confidence."[48]

Japan may well be the gainer, too, from Asia's intellectual and emotional responses to the crisis. There are various reasons (as we shall see in Chapter 5) why many Asians still lean politically and culturally more toward the West and would much prefer not to come under any broader Japanese hegemony. But money talks, and it is Japan that now has the money and is willing to put out. America, to be sure, has the markets. But we find ourselves in a catch-22 in which about the only effective tool left for prying open regional Asian markets is the threat of closing ours—thereby undercutting our chief source of appeal now that we have lost our old Cold War security leverage.

George Soros has argued the case against unbridled international movement of capital, while many others in the West have voiced concern about the political destabilization and destruction of social safety nets inflicted on developing societies by unfettered global laissez-faire. Southeast Asians have been particularly resentful of America's moral hectoring on their economic plight, along with the draconian financial cleanup measures dictated to them by the IMF at the very time Washington was bailing out its own "crony capitalist" hedge-fund fat cats at U.S. taxpayers' expense.[49]

The press played up the vitriolic confrontation at the 1998 APEC summit in Kuala Lumpur between Soros, the world's leading currency speculator, and Malaysian prime minister Mahathir Mohamad, Asia's sourest anti-Western voice. But if these two can chime in together on some of the perils of globalization (if not on Soros' share of responsibility for it), then we know that the latter-day epigoni of Adam Smith are in deep trouble, at least in Asia.

Tokyo was quick to stretch the public-relations value of its initiative in organizing the initial $16 billion international bailout for Thailand as well as its own total contribution of $19 billion (as against America's $8 billion) in untied balance-of-payments support programs for Asia through the IMF. It made a public show of its displeasure at America's nixing of a Japan-led Asian Development Fund that would have excluded the West, and it challenged the primacy of the U.S.-dominated IMF. Accused at Kuala Lumpur by the U.S. trade representative, Charlene Barshefsky, of trying to use the Asian Development Fund to buy Asian votes against further U.S. market-opening measures, the Japanese foreign ministry shot back that the U.S. government was possessed by an "evil spirit"—a phrase, as Chalmers Johnson notes, uncomfortably reminiscent of Ronald Reagan's "evil empire" epithet.[50] Speaking of the entire region's rush to help Thailand ahead of a hesitating United States, Japan's vice minister of finance, Eisuke Sakakibara, suggested the long-term fallout: "What is important is that it shows that the Asia-Pacific region is approaching these issues with solidarity."[51]

A tougher trade policy in straightforward defense of American interests would not be inconsistent with a more realistic calculation of the economic needs and nostrums of others. Both would strike a blow for intellectual honesty against the chimera of an Americanizing global economy running on addle-brained automatic. The greatest danger will come if we fail to work out a more cosmopolitan philosophy for the world economy that is credible to others, while at the same time allowing our own "city on a hill" to dim further under the shadows of racial tension, economic inequality, violence, and public incivility. In that case, we, of all people, may well close the great emotional and intellectual gulf between Japan and Asia that we explore in Chapter 5 as Japanese and other Asians alike gradually shed their long postwar legacy of trust, respect, and affection for the United States—in that order.

Bottom-Line Caveats

The evidence to date should make it clear that Tokyo has not yet committed itself to those goals of open markets and effective deregulation for which many Americans hoped the Asian crisis would provide the opportunity—or final push. Americans and others who still hold out hope for a more gradual and voluntary change in course must first explain why Japan so adamantly refuses to take the first and most essential step of all—namely, dropping its attitudinal resistance toward imports. Until that time comes, the vested interests and intellectual struts of mercantilism may bend a bit under foreign or domestic pressures, like tall stalks of bamboo swaying in the wind, but without ever snapping to permit genuine free trade.

Indeed, as Japan and Asia begin to experience even modest starts toward recovery, Americans need to reckon with two rather unpleasant possibilities. One is that Japan's window of time-under-pressure may prove to have been too narrow to force a real change of national purpose —if there ever was one in the cards. Second, and worst of all, there is no guarantee that great changes, if and when they do come, will be hewn to our own prescription or liking. A more self-assertive Japan—grown peevish over American trade pressures and inevitably breaking loose from its military and geopolitical dependence on the United States—should prove more, not less, likely to strike out on its own economic way, perhaps in tandem with the rest of Asia.

Whatever Japan's future direction in the world economy, it will be set by the internal compass of Japanese politics, social values, and attitudes toward America and Asia. Unfortunately, the same combination of American hopes and Japanese spin that deflect our gaze from economic realities will see to it that our illusions in these areas, too, remain as favorable as possible to Japan. Indeed, America's intellectual naiveté toward Japan during the Asian financial crisis is just the latest of Tokyo's rhetorical routings of Washington over three decades of trade disputes. Therefore, before turning to our noneconomic hopes for Japan with respect to political reform, democracy, Asian leadership, and individualistic values, we need to review our clumsiness in parrying Tokyo's ultimate and most dangerous emotional ploy: the implicit threat of anti-Americanism leading to a final, wrenching break.

CHAPTER
TWO

Anti-Americanism
Sayonara
as the Ultimate Blackmail

When terrorists crashed their hijacked airliners into New York's World Trade Center at 9:45 P.M. Tokyo time, Junichiro Koizumi was eating dinner with his secretary at a hotel near his official residence. Heading back to the office to meet his hastily assembled crisis management task force, the Japanese prime minister arranged for a government spokesman to pronounce his country's "anger at terrorism" at 1:00 A.M., then went home to bed, leaving behind as one of his first publicly recorded personal comments a tepid "It's scary because it's unpredictable." Then, at 10:50 A.M. the following morning, 12 September 2001, Koizumi finally appeared on national TV—in contrast to the leaders of Britain, France, and even Russia, all of whom had condemned the acts and expressed support for the United States in news conferences called immediately after the attack.

Manhattan's Tragedy in the Shadow of the *Ehime Maru*

To be sure, there were widespread expressions of horror and sympathy from the Japanese public, with 66 percent as of early October supporting the U.S. military strikes as Tokyo hastened to respond with humanitarian aid for the Afghans, diplomatic and intelligence cooperation, and logistical backup of U.S. forces within the constraints of Japan's pacifist constitution. There was nowhere in Japan's government, however, anything remotely like the impassioned reminder of Germany's defense minister, Rudolf Scharping, to his fellow countrymen that "we owe our freedom, unity, and economic reconstruction" to the Americans, "and we are *not* going to be fair-weather friends."[1]

As Japan's media (like the press everywhere) pounced on the theme of the Islamic world's longstanding grievances with the United States, Japanese intellectuals were suddenly discovering cultural bonds and empathetic resonances with a major world civilization regarding which they had shown very little interest, knowledge, or respect up to the day before Ground Zero. Indeed it was the Muslim "guest workers" from South Asian countries that the nation was quickest to disinvite once the bloom was off the economy. The Islamic and Japanese religious and philosophical traditions stand at opposite ends of the spectrum running from strict monotheism to pluralist eclecticism, so it was odd to hear no less a figure than former LDP prime ministerial candidate Koichi Kato declare that Japan would be especially welcome in the Afghan crisis region since it was a non-Christian nation. Perhaps, one could argue, because it had never been a colonial power in the Middle East—but hardly on the basis of religious rapport. And it was a bit of a stretch—if fully predictable—to read in Tokyo's leftish dailies of Pakistanis and Japanese now being united by the common bond of having suffered at the hand of America.

Indeed, the most striking difference between the Japanese and European responses lay less in actions promised or effected than in the former's evident lack of emotional bonding. One proximate cause of psychological distancing almost surely lay in the way the Japanese people for over six months had been nursing their national grievance over the inexcusably careless sinking of the fisheries training ship *Ehime Maru* a few miles off Oahu by the U.S. submarine *Greenville* on 9 February 2001.

Having myself arrived in Honolulu the day after the *Ehime Maru* tragedy and only two days after closing down my seaside cottage at Misaki—a small fishing port near Tokyo from which many of these student vessels commence their transoceanic runs—I was gripped by the poignancy as well as the utter stupidity of the disaster in which nine lives were lost. The four teenage victims were not members of Japan's examination-obsessed elite youth, just simple coastal folk from remote Ehime prefecture aspiring to no more than an honest fisherman's living. I had chatted with their trainers in Misaki's public baths and had often viewed their floating classrooms tied up at the Misaki docks—hand-

some, immaculately white ships riding high in the water, more like min-
iature passenger liners than the low-slung, net-entangled boats connoted
by the media's use of the term "fishing trawler." It was eerie and heart-
breaking to see one of them photographed at the bottom of the Oahu deep.

Weeks rolled by, however, as apologies from the American president,
ambassador, and military commanders on down the line all failed to
slake Japan's seemingly unquenchable thirst for American penitence and
prostration. Indeed, it was if no matter who apologized or how, the Japanese would find some cultural or other reason to deem it inadequate.
This, too, was in contrast to the shorter-lived Italian outrage when a
plane flown by a daredevil U.S. Marine Corps fighter pilot cut the wires
of a ski-lift cable car in 1998, plunging twenty gondola riders to their
deaths hundreds of feet below.

After a while I began to wonder if some elements in Japan—not, to
be sure, the honest anger of the nine grieving families or the public at
large, but Tokyo's media and government establishments—were not
abusing the tragedy by turning it into a protracted game of emotional
blackmail, overplaying the card of righteous indignation to win maximum future political leverage over the United States in trade and other
bilateral issues.

The American press quickly fell to chanting Tokyo's mantra that the
Japan-U.S. tie itself was now at stake. No one bothered to report the
routine courtesies by which, within three weeks after the sinking, a Coast
Guard helicopter had flown miles out into the Pacific to lift a seriously
ill Japanese fisheries trainee to the safety of a Honolulu hospital. Or
how a sister ship of the *Ehime Maru* out of Akita prefecture had changed
course to rescue four Americans from a dismasted sailboat three hundred miles south of Hawaii's big island.

When Richard Cohen in his *Washington Post* column of 27 February
2001 argued that certain Japanese, "from editorial writers to opportu-
nistic politicians[,] are demanding more than they are entitled to" and
noted the "epic hypocrisy" of those who had yet to apologize for an
entire war now harping on an accident without intent to harm anyone,
our monitors of cultural sensitivity read him the riot act. America's Asia
hands also had a field day illuminating the divergent Japanese and American concepts of remorse, apology, and the afterlife—all of which was
true enough at the level of individual grief but not really relevant to the
high-stakes political game being played out at the nation-to-nation level
as one apology after another was pronounced defective. Hurt most per-

haps by Japan's stony unwillingness to forgive were members of Hawaii's Japanese-American Christian congregations, who, caught between the two cultures, had tried so hard to mediate the emotional tension.

Providing the clue to all this hype—so disproportionate to the event itself or to the practical value to Japan of its American alliance—was a lecture entitled "Nationalism Emerging in Japan," delivered at the University of Hawaii on 16 February by one of Japan's leading unofficial spokesmen, Yukio Matsuyama. Warning in reference to the *Ehime Maru* disaster that Americans and Japanese would have to work together now to contain the rise of anti-American nationalism in Japan, the former *Asahi* editor added that this would require the toning down of Washington's pressure on Tokyo to open its markets.

Striking as the *Ehime Maru* incident was, Japan's emotional temperature toward the United States had started to drop in 1997 with the onset of Asia's financial crisis. On 23 June 1997 the Dow Jones industrial average fell 192.25 points, or 2.47 percent, its biggest loss of the year to date. Traders surmised that the main impetus had come from a speech by Japanese prime minister Ryutaro Hashimoto at Columbia University in which he warned that unless the U.S. government moved to stabilize the dollar-yen exchange rate, Japan would sell its American Treasury bonds and switch into gold.

Aides to Hashimoto—the first postwar premier who actually seemed to enjoy berating and putting down the United States in public—were quick to issue the standard explanation that he had been misinterpreted. There were increasing expressions of anti-American pique throughout the nation, however, as Japan's economic doldrums of the mid-1990s became entwined with the broader Asian financial crisis of 1997–98 and as Americans enjoyed a new curve of prosperity, joined the IMF in hectoring the region on how to clean house, and rode triumphant through the recent breaches into the Japanese banking, securities, and insurance sectors. The new anti-Americanism was in the nature of a broadly based, gradual swell—and, like all tidal waves at their inconspicuous point of origin, all the more ominous for it.

On the right, the Dietman novelist Shintaro Ishihara, who had stunned the United States in 1989 with his provocative *The Japan That Can Say No,* suggested Japan ought to start a fund to buy defunct Japanese banks and businesses to keep them out of the hands of foreigners (meaning mainly the Americans, bent on world economic domination), and urged his government to stop buying U.S. T-bills. From the center, ruling LDP secretary general Koichi Kato roundly stated that Japan would not carry out the large-scale tax cuts desired by the United States and that Japan would be its own judge of how best to deal with its economic slump.

Three intellectuals further to the left—in an April 1998 article (in Japanese) entitled "Arrogant America, Submissive Japan"—fretted over the possibility of a real plunge into anti-Americanism, beyond which lay the specter of a xenophobic, ultranationalist rejuvenation of the old emperor-centered mentality that still "lurks in every nook and cranny of the Japanese landscape," as one of them put it. Japan was being "raped" by the newly upgraded bilateral defense guidelines, lamented former socialist Dietman Masao Kunihiro, and the entire international community was turning anti-American as it encountered the contumely of unrestricted U.S. economic and military power. Nonfiction writer Yoshimi Ishikawa was irked by the way American financial wizards and their Asian acolytes were now carrying the dogmas of the Harvard Business School worldwide, just as their forebears had once spread Christianity. And television news commentator Tetsuya Chikushi spoke of the "second defeat" of Japan in the financial war just lost, and of cultural Americanization masquerading as "globalization." In its posture toward the United States Japan was "obedient on the surface, but defiant at heart."[2]

What is extraordinary about these well-known voices reflecting the entire political spectrum and popular mood in Japan is that not one of them chooses to speak from the standpoint of their country's enormous wealth and relative good fortune, or from a sense of noblesse oblige and responsibility to others less well off, or from the calmer self-confidence one would otherwise expect from what is still the world's second-largest economy. The Japanese appear to be trapped in their obsession with America—the one and only nation toward which they still feel in some respects inferior, as if the great globe itself hardly counted.

The Emotional Chemistry of Japan's Anti-Americanism

Tokyo's ultimate and most dangerous form of psychological blackmail, of course, has been to hint at a collapse of the Japanese public consensus favoring close political and security ties with the United States. It is a blade, however, that can cut both ways. It is more slippery and less retractable than, say, the straightforward economic intimidation of being in a position to trigger a U.S. stock market crash by ordering Japan's financial institutions to dump their American Treasury bonds.[3]

This is because the threat of a rupture in the security tie, to be credible as a foreign policy weapon, rests on a four-part dynamic. It requires, first of all, convincing evidence of anti-American sentiment in Japan. Second, such feelings are best galvanized from a Japanese sense of victimization by the United States. Third, the virulence of that obsession largely depends on the willingness of the national leadership to stoke it. And fourth, the whole thing hinges on the continuing reluctance of American officials and intellectuals to challenge the premises of this victim mentality and call Japan's bluff.

Whether the gamble Tokyo takes with this game may at some point overstep its original intent and induce a break—or whether the Japanese actually would prefer and are now discreetly laying the ground for such a break—is a mystery that the near future may very well clear up. The task for Americans is to see that a game is being played. We rely too exclusively on the bland percentage benchmarks of polls tracking Japanese attitudes toward the United States without searching for their underlying chemistry. Joseph C. Grew, our envoy to Tokyo from 1932 to 1942, had a shrewd sense of the way certain powerful Japanese elements were turning anti-American sentiment on and off like a faucet—and a sharp nose for the manipulation thereby of American emotions that would put to shame his successors at the U.S. embassy today. Yet in reading his diary, *Ten Years in Japan,* one is struck by the extent to which even he managed to fret over public opinion as though it were a genuinely autonomous political force in 1930s Japan.

Tokyo in the past has been skillful in using Washington's defense objectives to muzzle U.S. economic complaints. This works most effectively when applied to American military bases in Japan—the most sensitive Yankee nerve of all—since these installations are the core of the U.S. forward strategy in Asia and the whole point of its security treaty with Japan. Nothing scares Uncle Sam more than the threat of "*Sayonara*—Yankee go home!" and it is to this end that Tokyo from time to time plays its victimhood card.

As of 1998 70 percent of Japanese polled still supported their U.S. alliance, while wanting to see troop levels reduced. But when the Diet in 2000 approved a mild upgrading of Japan's rear-area support for American military operations in the surrounding region there was widespread left-of-center protest, and by the end of the decade there were powerful voices throughout Tokyo's political establishment calling for an elimination of Japan's annual $4 billion subsidy toward the stationing of U.S.

forces on its soil. Worse yet—and from the normally pro-American hawk-ish right—Ishihara, the popular new governor of Tokyo, was no sooner in office than he began peppering the U.S. embassy with his loud public demands to get our bases out of the country altogether.

Japanese reaction to the abduction and rape of a twelve-year-old Okinawan schoolgirl by three American military personnel in October 1995 gave a foretaste of how the binational tie might someday unravel. This single incident provoked an outburst of national indignation so adamant and sustained as to make some observers wonder whether the Japanese—apparently unable or unwilling to separate the crime, how-ever heinous, from the broader issue of American bases—really wanted the bases at all. Public apologies by President Clinton, the U.S. ambas-sador to Japan, Walter F. Mondale, and the secretary of defense, Will-iam J. Perry, did little to quiet the furor.

The explosion of pent-up anger among the Okinawans themselves was all too predictable and understandable, given their long-simmering sense of maltreatment and neglect by both the Japanese and Americans, and their entrapment in an environment of military installations so dense that no citizenry in the United States or Europe in the peaceful 1990s would for one minute tolerate it. What was shocking was the apparent strength of mainlander sentiment for the consolidation, reduction, or even withdrawal of American bases. It had the Tokyo government—and even much of Japan's otherwise indignant press—scrambling to remind the public of the value of their U.S. security umbrella.

Two years later, it was clear that the mainland Japanese cared very little about the patent plight of the Okinawans, as they assented to a set of cosmetic base consolidations on that island worked out by the Clinton and Hashimoto governments that allowed the Japanese to enjoy the con-tinued benefits of American protection without having to accept any transfer of U.S. military into their own prefectures. The great main-lander outburst of 1995 turned out to have been little more than a peri-odic anti-American emotional binge.

Nevertheless, there has been a palpable cooling in Japanese senti-ment toward the United States ever since the soft touch on trade during the Reagan years and the Mike Mansfield ambassadorship gave way to sharper economic talk from Presidents Bush and Clinton and their re-spective envoys, Michael Armacost and Walter Mondale. This gradual distancing from America—with an occasional emotional bound, but usually on cat's feet—has expressed itself mainly in undertones of contempt when Japan senses itself the stronger (as around 1990) or in bouts of peevishness when it thinks itself the underdog (as of 2000). Unlike the earlier anti-Americanisms of Japan's political left (which did not rule out an admiration for American ideals or a personal liking for Americans) or of the politico-cultural right (whose paeans to U.S. Cold War policy veiled its guts antipathy), this new virus reflects a pervasively perceived erosion of both American virtue and power.

This is partly the result—as some American observers tried to warn— of talking tough to Japan about trade without meaning it, or of actually getting tough without being prepared to handle the emotional backlash. The Japanese, who are quicker than most to bow to force majeure and cooperate with perceived moral superiors, are also the quickest to resent abuse from a morally eroded, retreating hegemon. As the economist Kurt Singer, a German Jew who spent the years 1931 to 1939 in Japan, wrote in a paragraph that should be required reading for the entire U.S. foreign policy establishment:

> They are peculiarly sensitive to the smell of decay, however well screened; and they will strike at an enemy whose core appears to betray a lack of firmness. . . . Japan swings with astonishing promptness from enmity and self-assertion to friendship, conciliation, submissiveness, whenever she bites on granite.[4]

I recall the political scientist and ubiquitous rightish TV panelist Susumu Nishibe, the featured autumn festival speaker in 1992 at Gakushuin University, where I was teaching, commencing his two-hour lecture on democracy before several hundred unblinking undergraduates with this disclaimer: "Let me say at the start that I detest America to the marrow of my bones" (*hone no zui made kirai desu*). Imagine the uproar at any U.S. campus if an American pundit were to announce publicly that he "detested" Japan!

Americans may find it difficult to envision a form of anti-Americanism without helmeted students snake-dancing in the streets under Marxist banners, or without the overtly needling French-style cultural put-downs of Mickey Mouse and Colonel Sanders. In a land still saturated and in love with American popular culture, the turning of the Japanese screw proceeds at the deeper and more malignant level of hidden hurts, self-contempt, and a simple alertness to join the crowd in what has been proclaimed to be the new *muudo,* or mood of the times.

Around 1991 the abstract, politically connoted term *han-bei* (anti-America) was displaced by the more personal *ken-bei* (dislike of America) and *bu-bei* (contempt for America)—the Sino-Japanese character *bu* combining visual nastiness with the scorn the Japanese ear associates with the lip-voiced sonant *b* (like the Bronx-cheer overtones of *boob* or *blubber* in English). Although this relabeling broadly reflected the shift in popular sentiment, one suspects that some of it originally may have been intentionally manufactured and then took on a life of its own. Indeed, Yoshimi Ishikawa claimed to have been the author of *ken-bei* as his own personal reading of the emergent public mood. In any case I first heard it from my freshman class on political ideology, where my students in solemn unison one morning asked me if I was aware of this portentous buzzword now catching on throughout Japan.

If the term was indeed fabricated at the time, we might infer yet another attempt to frighten Uncle Sam with the hobgoblin of anti-Americanism, or perhaps even the preliminary steps to prepare the Japanese public emotionally for the foreign policy option of a major break with the United States. That break could come if and when Tokyo decides—whether by grand design, or through the inertia of vested interests, or through some unfortunate outcome of the ongoing Asian financial crisis or "war on terrorism"—that the effort to join the world by genuinely opening up Japan's economy and society is more troublesome than establishing a defensive primacy over its own region. At that time the anesthesia of accumulated anti-American grievances might be required to neutralize the considerable residue of familiarity, trust, and affection, even, for the United States at the grassroots level, and to numb any anxiety over an untested rush into the arms of Japan's technologically inferior Asian neighbors.

Should that day come, there will have been a quarter century's warm-up of literary anger and alarmism to draw upon for it. Vulnerability is victimhood in its potential mode, and a flourishing subgenre of paranoiac potboilers has for years harped on Japan's precariousness in a hostile world—many of them from the pen of respected establishment figures. Taichi Sakaiya, a former MITI trade official turned author and popular TV guru, had two thousand Japanese demonstrators storming the American embassy at the end of his 1978 political novel, *Hibiwareta Niji* (The rainbow cracked), which featured a Carteresque president seeking reelection on an anti-Japanese protectionist platform, including an embargo on U.S. soybean exports. "American pigs over Japanese people," screamed the Tokyo press—the choice before Japan being either "surrender" to the United States or the "honorable death" of a firm stand. It never occurred to Sakaiya's characters that a little trade reciprocity might have provided a less Wagnerian ending to his fancy-bred crisis.[5]

And who was it in mid-1998 that the new prime minister, Keizo Obuchi, appointed as head of the Economic Planning Agency to deal specifically with Japan's stagnant economy and banking crisis? None other than Taichi Sakaiya.

Two nonfiction books in a similar vein came from the pen of Harvard- and MIT-trained freelance critic Naoki Komuro in 1980 and 1981. In *Amerika no Gyakushu* (America's counterattack) he warned that the United States and Japan eventually would revert to their natural enmity, while in *Amerika no Hyoteki* (America's target) he speculated that as the United States and Soviet Union both declined economically they would gang up on Japan in a "second Yalta Conference." Unidentified submarines would start sinking Japanese tankers in the Indian Ocean, bringing Japan to its knees.[6]

More disturbing to the American embassy and the Japanese-American Citizens' League (JACL)—both of whose protests fell on deaf ears— was the decision by the quasi-governmental NHK (the Nihon Hoso Kyokai or Japan Broadcasting Corporation) to run as its Sunday evening prime-time drama special for 1984 the TV serial *Sanga Moyu* (Mountains and rivers aflame), adapted from the best-selling novel about divided loyalties during World War II, *Futatsu no Sokoku* (Two fatherlands), by Toyoko Yamazaki. Here was the closest thing to an official endorsement of middlebrow anti-Americanism.

Every week of that year millions of Japanese families were treated to a succession of anti-American images as the series sought to extract from the wartime experience of Japanese-Americans the last possible drop of self-pity for the Japanese "proper": The FBI, only days after Pearl Harbor, barking questions (how crude of them!) at a gentleman in Los Angeles who still kept his portrait of the emperor (how loyal!) prominently displayed. The second of three sons born to the immigrant family sailing "home" just in time to join the imperial army, stirred to his last bioaesthetic gene by the sight of Mt. Fuji over the steamer rail. The eldest son (played by Kabuki star Koshiro Matsumoto, no less) committing suicide after his schizophrenic efforts to straddle American democracy and Japanese sensitivities. And the third son, the only one to opt for an unadulterated American identity, as the brash, shifty-eyed, deracinated villain of the piece—an "informer" for the U.S. authorities and a pastiche of unflattering stereotypes.

The climax of victimhood stoking came, of course, with the media buildup to the fiftieth anniversary of the atomic bomb in the summer of 1995, when the Japanese showed signs of using the immolation of Hiroshima and Nagasaki to move toward a one-sided admission of wartime aggression vis-à-vis Asia, reposition themselves among the victims of the West, and shift the opprobrium to America. As the United States proceeded with its low-key ceremonies at Pearl Harbor to commemorate the end of the Pacific War, right-wingers in Japan shot down a resolution in the Diet to admit Japan's responsibility for the conflict. With its well-intentioned modesty at the climactic anniversary of V-J Day, the United States may well have squandered the last historical occasion to make its own case abundantly clear to the Japanese people and to its own posterity.

The Persistent Residues of World War II

More basically, Americans persistently fail to challenge Japan's overdrawn sense of victimization going all the way back to Commodore Perry's black ships, or to face the fact that there is little guilt or remorse toward the United States with respect to World War II. Speaking for the government in August 1991, deputy chief cabinet secretary Nobuo Ishihara averred, "It will take tens or hundreds of years before the correct judgment is delivered on who is responsible for the [Japan-U.S.] war," while former prime minister Noboru Takeshita raised Western eyebrows with his publicly expressed "private view" that historians have yet to pin the blame on Hitler for the tragedy in Europe.[7] Japan's leading Freudian theorist, Takeo Doi, writing of the cultivation of *higaisha ishiki* (victimhood consciousness) among his countrymen, once surmised that, "the Japanese tend to feel wronged and to dwell on their being imposed upon to the extent that such a state of mind becomes often an important ingredient of their identity." According to Doi, Japan may have taken on the United States, a formidable opponent, in 1941 "not because she calculated she could win a war, but only because she wanted her opponent to be involved into [*sic*] war, so that her opponent would feel guilty afterward."[8]

Indeed, a typical Japanese docudrama on the 1937–45 conflict might open with Mitsubishi bombers over China (politely, from a hazy height), proceed to sensational shots of the Pearl Harbor attack (well done!), continue with the metal Niagara of U.S. Navy offshore shelling (such brute force!), and conclude with the Hiroshima cloud and prostrate crowds sobbing outside the imperial palace. I myself once watched a Tokyo University historian conclude his NHK educational TV series by remarking that the war had indeed been dreadful—but listing only the Japanese casualties.

Unfortunately, the controversy over the Smithsonian's exhibit of the *Enola Gay* in 1995 showed how close America's own amnesiac postwar generation has come to losing its historical perspective on the Pacific War. The original text for the exhibition argued that "for most Japanese, it was a war to defend their unique culture against Western imperialism." This was a screed to warm the heart of the most unreconstructed Japanese chauvinist, one that ignored the millions of Asians who lost their lives to Japan's aggression, and a view that many Japanese today would still reject. Congress and the veterans, however, should have insisted less on playing down the sufferings of the Japanese than on playing up the pain inflicted by them, along with Tokyo's expansionist policies leading to the war and the suicidal fanaticism of military leaders willing to prolong it to the last sixth-grader.

History has few if any examples of a nation that started and lost a war against so many opponents and yet, after so many years, still nurses so much pity for itself as does postwar Japan. The Hiroshima and Nagasaki Atomic Bomb Exhibitions that toured American universities and municipal galleries every year from 1995 through 2001 (with the exception of 1999) were welcome and appropriate, but would Japan conceivably allow a similar display, put together by its erstwhile victims, to travel to universities and museums in Japan? The mere suggestion seems doomed to failure—judging by the experience of the small western Japanese city of Hirakata in 1996, when it caved in to right-wing threats and canceled an exhibit planned by its local museum of paintings depicting the Nanking Massacre by Chinese artists residing in New York.

By 1998 Japan's assertion of victimhood, denial of guilt, and national amnesia about its erstwhile rampage throughout neighboring Asia was hitting full throttle. The leitmotif of the theater-packing movie exonerating Hideki Tojo, *Puraido: Unmei no Toki* (Pride: The moment of destiny), is that young Japanese went to their battle deaths out of a self-sacrificial idealism to liberate India from the white man. This is a gargantuan distortion of the historical truth, with the screenplay making no reference at all to the agonies Japan meted out to the Chinese, Korean, and Southeast Asian peoples—or to their possible opinion on the subject today.[9] No wonder, then, with some raised eyebrows even in New Delhi, that Beijing and Seoul lodged official protests against this film, which enjoyed the highest box-office gross for a Japanese movie in 1998. The story breathed not a word of remorse about the 1930s or the role General Tojo and the military he headed had played in the snatching of Manchuria, the decimation of civilian rule at home, or their disastrous wager on a confrontation with the United States. It was as though history had begun in 1945 with the gentle, bumbling old granddaddy tending his tomato plants as the American MPs came by to arrest him.

The bulk of this film's action takes place at the Tokyo war crimes trial, with hyped-up performances by foreign actors playing the vindictive American prosecutor (Joseph B. Keenan), a consistently inebriated Australian chief judge (William F. Webb), and the sad-eyed, dissenting Indian justice from Bengal (Radhabinod Pal). Ah, that India again! The unfairness of victors' justice at the International Military Tribunal for the Far East is, to be sure, the arguable point here, although hardly a new one considering the wide assent it has long enjoyed throughout the world.

More shocking than the sponsorship of *Pride* by right-wing intellectual activists has been the willingness of Tokyo's politically centrist establishment to bestow its imprimatur on the film. Dramatically suggesting how far Japan's center has traveled to the right on World War II was an op-ed piece in the conservative *Sankei Shinbun* of 6 July 1998 (translated in the next day's *Japan Times*) by Hisahiko Okazaki, former ambassador to Saudi Arabia and one of Japan's most intellectually articulate retired diplomats. This was a favorable review of *Pride,* dwelling only on the trial segments of the movie and recommending it to foreign audiences. "Americans have only to show again their recent magnanimous practice of accepting all revisionist views of history," purred Okazaki, "then the Japanese would hold them in better respect."

Granted that Tojo as an individual was no clone of Adolf Hitler, it is still impossible to imagine a similar rehabilitation—say, of Hermann Göring, a closer functional equivalent—being filmed by a coterie of revanchist Germans in the late 1990s without the whole world coming down on the Federal Republic's neck, not even if the screenplay had been pegged to an accusation of victors' justice at the Nuremberg trials and to a cooked-up retrospective war aim of liberating the Ukrainians from Communism.

Japan gets away not only with this retrogressive fancy but also with a broad political and ideological slide to the right that has no counterpart in today's Germany, save at the academic level of Friedrich Nolte's resolutely challenged historical revisionism. This is because neighboring Asia's lack of leverage on Tokyo is compounded by the ignorance, inattention, wishful thinking, disbelief, and sheer mental impatience of the distant West in dealing with any bad news out of Japan that is not somehow tied to economics. Also responsible for this indulgence are the American intellectual inhibitions we shall explore in Part III (including but not limited to our A-bomb guilt, our patronizing do-goodism, and the non sequiturs of our aesthetic, multiculturalist, and cultural-relativist takes on Japan).

Of greater impact than the Tojo film on the serious intellectual climate in Japan since the middle of the decade has been the boldness of established university professors of the younger cultural right, such as Nobukatsu Fujioka, Akira Nakamura, and Kanji Nishio, in calling for a "correct" historical view of the war that would reject the "masochism" foisted on Japan after 1945 by the Americans and Japan's own Marxist left. To that end they have sought to shove the recently renewed international interest in the Nanking Massacre and the wartime army's "comfort women" under the rug of casuistry or denial. They also campaigned (if, in the end, unsuccessfully) against the brief references to these two issues that were added to the "unpatriotic" officially approved school history textbooks in 1997—textbooks that the rest of the world has long viewed as being far too soft on the war. All this is part of a broader nationalistic trend, to which we shall return in the next chapter, but to these minds it seems as if the only way for Japan's younger generation to move on to a decent pride of country is to walk around the blemish of 1931–45—rather than through it, as the Germans as a nation did.

I had been in Nanking as a tourist only a month before attending a press seminar organized in Tokyo on 12 June 1998 by several members of this group to refute Iris Chang's best-seller, *The Rape of Nanking: The Forgotten Holocaust of World War II*. At the massacre memorial museum at Nanking I had been struck by the quiet shabbiness of the place, so unlike the high-tech sophistication of Japan's recently refurbished atomic bomb museum at Hiroshima. As the small midweek line of plainly dressed Chinese visitors shuffled through, the faded photographs spoke eloquently enough of their awesome burden. Apparently the only one there who could read German, I was transfixed by the pages of photostatted typescript pinned to one wall, wherein the card-carrying Nazi businessman John Rabe described the horrors he had witnessed in a letter saluting *"Mein Führer!"* and begging Hitler, of all people, to intercede with Tokyo to stop the slaughter.

It was uncanny, then, at the Foreign Correspondents Club of Japan, to watch a panel of unsmiling, flint-eyed academics shuffling through statistics; passing around Japanese war correspondents' photos showing Chinese children and Japanese soldiers smiling at each other on 25 December 1937—at which time the carnage was still in full cry; asking how and where so many could have been buried when the ground was mostly frozen; and waving their blackboard pointers over maps of the same terrain I had just walked across in China on my own. For them it was all a numbers game, as if getting the dead down from three hundred thousand to thirty thousand really mattered much when the greater moral horror lay in the nature of those wanton, face-to-face killings of unarmed individuals that went on for weeks without any Japanese in authority seeking to stop it. As the Australian historian Gavan McCormack has pointed out, history for these activists of the intellectual right lacks intrinsic standards of truth or evidence and "is subject to the ultimate moral imperative of whether or not it serves to inculcate a sense of pride in being Japanese."[10]

This reluctance to face historical facts, despite a half century's passing, underscores the urgency of persuading the Japanese to back off their victimhood game. There will be no real maturity in our transpacific dialogue until they do so, and no country can come to terms with itself and others, much less aspire to international leadership, without facing up to its own darker past, as others have at least tried to do—the Germans with respect to the Nazi era, the Russians with the legacies of Stalinism, and the United States with its historical burden of racial discrimination and the wartime "relocation" of Japanese-Americans to internment camps.

Perhaps the time has come for an eloquent American countertestimony. One could envision, for example, a richly visual documentary film on the recorded behavior of Japan's militarists, quasi-fascists, and ultranationalists at home and abroad from 1931 to 1945 to illustrate what the United States was fighting against and the sort of resistance we would have encountered in any invasion of the Japanese mainland. Let the film be a bit partisan and pro-American for a change—sponsored, if no others come forward, by the veterans' organizations themselves, funded exclusively from American coffers, and unencumbered by any binational committee fudging up a "balanced" view. The Japanese, after all, have never asked Americans to contribute any balance to their own heavily slanted documentaries and dramas about the war—preferring to keep them rather like an exclusive, family-only wake.

But let us turn now to the domestic roots of Japan's renascent rightism.

CHAPTER THREE

New Old Right
Reactionaries in Neoconservative Garb

As of mid-2001 Japanese politics seemed set on an irreversible slide toward the right, with liberal and left-wing alternatives in increasing disarray and the whole gamut of nationalist causes pushing toward broad public acceptance.

While the hoary mutterings of former prime minister Yoshiro Mori about Japan as the "land of the gods, centering on the emperor" could be written off as the obiter dicta of a political buffoon with the lowest popularity of any postwar premier, the wild acclaim of the Japanese electorate and Western press for his successor—the bouffant-haired, "maverick," heavy-metal rock fan Junichiro Koizumi—was truly disturbing. Winning a handsome ratification in the Upper House election of July 2001, Koizumi's celebrity glamour tended to obscure the contradictions in his mix of expansionary and belt-tightening proposals for economic recovery, as well as his general endorsement of the old right-wing conservative agenda for constitutional revision leading to unrestricted rearmament.

Beijing and Seoul, at least, were on to the game as the Ministry of Education refused to withdraw its approval of a new high school textbook prettifying Japan's conduct in World War II, and as Prime Minister Koizumi himself paid a controversial official visit to the Yasukuni war heroes' shrine in mid-August, thereby at one stroke demolishing three years' worth of South Korean–led efforts to reach a new "future-oriented" emotional rapprochement with Japan.

Our discussion, therefore, shifts now from the external arena of Japan's emotive manipulation of the bilateral debate with the United States on trade and security issues to the internal arena of ideas within Japan itself.

A sober reexamination of the Japanese domestic intellectual scene is in order for Americans and others who believe that we are about to see the emergence in Japan of a clearer dedication to political democracy, together with an enlightened rethinking of Asia and a commanding new ethical individualism—in a word, the flowering of a liberal-minded, outward-looking civil society.

These internal questions are the subject of the following four chapters, and our correct judgment on them is essential to our estimates of where Japan may actually be headed on the external front. For it is precisely such changes in the domestic arena of political choices, cultural identity, and social values that will determine whether the Japanese do or do not make a serious (as opposed to merely tactical) commitment to the expectations we hold for them in foreign affairs—including free trade with us, the promotion of democracy and human rights in Asia, and a cosmopolitan leadership role regionally and in the world.

Unfortunately on all these points we have allowed our illusory hopes to run ahead of a more critical reading of Japanese political and social mentalities. Indeed, the images we now hold are all too congruent with the answers Tokyo's political and cultural spokesmen regularly give to the questions a concerned world keeps asking about the future of democracy, attitudes toward Asia, and individualism in Japan:

1. After a half century, what are the actual condition of Japanese democracy and the prospect for long-heralded political reforms that would lead to a more open economy and society?
2. Will Japan continue to follow America's vision for post–Cold War Asia, acting in the manner of a compliant junior partner, as it has in the past, or does it have its own stock of ideas to draw on for the region?
3. Finally—and critical to the first two questions—what are the values that actually drive the Japanese, and is a Western-style individualism really on the verge of breaking out?

To these three inquiries, Tokyo's typical replies seek to assure us:

1. That an antistatist liberalization of economic and political institutions akin to American neoconservatism is in the offing,

one that will make Japan more like us in its trade behavior and pursuit of democratic goals, and that what's left of the left in contemporary Japan is largely irrelevant to U.S. interests,

2. that the Japanese, as cultural bridgers between East and West, are with us in the reconception of post–Cold War Asia,

3. that even where Japanese social values differ the most from ours, they still hold out valuable lessons for us in communal harmony and getting along together.

These intellectual bromides give Americans the response they most want to hear or, at the very least, raise expectations that change is proceeding in the hoped-for direction. To be sure, these PR images are frequently buttressed by mirages that have been self-induced by foreign observers themselves. Moreover, it is only fair to point out that each of the political and cultural statements encoded in Tokyo's preferred images usually gives only one side of a debate on which the Japanese people themselves actually hold numerous and conflicting opinions.

Indeed, a little more truth in advertising would suggest three rather different realities:

1. As to the political image of neoconservatism: Some of the Japanese "reformers" who have appropriated that American-style mantle actually draw ideologically on some of Japan's more regressive old-right traditions. This calls for caution (particularly on the part of U.S. conservatives) in empathetically equating the American and Japanese conservative or right wings. By the same token, Americans need to know more about the critical historical role played by the left in nurturing and maintaining Japan's political liberalism. (See Chapters 3 and 4.)

2. As to our image of Tokyo's role in Asia: Japan's recrudescent pan-Asianism, if left unchallenged as to its conceptual premises, threatens not only to further complicate Japan's touchy emotional relationship with the West but also to undermine its intellectual and psychological resources for a constructive cultural and political engagement with neighboring Asia and the Pacific region. (See Chapter 5.)

3. And finally, as to the social image of group harmony: While Japan's legacy of Asian philosophies and its celebration of group cooperation have useful ethical insights for all Westerners, we

have—as the era of rampant Japanese militarism fades into the past of our grandfathers—forgotten an important root of Japanese values in the old samurai ethic. Although now largely transmuted into economic aggressiveness, this ethic still anchors Japanese solidarity (and insularity) in forms and degrees of individual self-denial and group militancy that set Japan apart from both the West and the rest of Asia. (See Chapter 6.)

Japan's New Political Map

To start with our American perceptions of Japanese conservatism (the subject of this chapter), we tend to make four rather casual assumptions: first, that Japan is on an irreversible trajectory toward a more perfected modern democracy on the British parliamentary model; second, that Japanese and American conservatisms are essentially similar, especially in their more recent neoconservative manifestations; third, that Japan's backward-looking and chauvinistic right wing is without serious influence today; and fourth, that the pro-American stance on the Japanese right may be taken at face value.

For obvious reasons it would be convenient for Tokyo if the rest of the world continued to view political Japan through the old lens of centrist, pro-Western stability—both more reassuring and easier to comprehend. However, to properly understand the strength of Japan's new right-tilting nationalism—as well as the roots of anti-Americanism on both the right and the left—foreign observers need to move beyond the ideological paradigm that held true for postwar Japan up to the early 1990s.

That paradigm (in terms of both parties and political ideas) featured an enormous, philosophically bland, and seemingly unbudgeable center—one that was conservatively inclined, pro-American, and anchored in the Liberal Democratic Party. That great centrist umbrella was able to co-opt or work with the more traditionalist and nationalistic factions of the LDP right wing, the ideologically laconic Buddhist-related Komeito (KMT, or Clean Government Party), and the Democratic Socialist Party (DSP) on the moderate left.

Balancing and checking that great center, yet never strong enough to displace it, was the Marxist and anti-American left. Ideologically concentrated in the universities, the labor unions, and the "progressive" press (typified by the newspaper *Asahi* and *Sekai* magazine), this left wing was led in parliament by the old doctrinaire Japan Socialist Party (JSP)—for decades the major opposition party—with the frequent cooperation of a small but rock-solid Japan Communist Party (JCP).

Far off in right field, discredited by the lost war and judged to be of no consequence any longer, were the raucous superpatriotic kooks of the miniscule ultrarightist splinter groups outside the party system, who blared forth from their loudspeaker trucks the slogans and marching music of Japan's militaristic and emperor-worshiping prewar past.

Today, that paradigm has shifted strikingly to the right. To cram a pachyderm into a peapod: The old party-political left has virtually self-destructed, at the very time that the ideological boundary between right and center continues to bend steadily in favor of the right.

Driven from office after thirty-eight years of one-party rule by the double whammy of political scandals and a busted bubble economy, the LDP in 1993 found itself in the opposition for the first time since its establishment in 1955, deserted by a large number of self-styled reformists bolting from both the traditionalist right and liberalist left wings of the party. For about one year these two types of ex-LDP reformist rebels managed to govern together under Prime Ministers Morihiro Hosakawa (August 1993–April 1994) and Tsutomu Hata (April–June 1994) by forging anti-LDP coalitions with the smaller centrist DSP and KMT and (in the case of Hosokawa) the JSP.

This partial breakup of the LDP in 1993 spelled the collapse of the old moderate-conservative center of Japan's political gravity. Since 1994 what we have been witnessing on the party-political scene is an extended game of musical chairs to determine whether the future center of Diet power will settle more to the right or more to the left of the old 1955–93 system.

Three basic factors are in play here. First, and especially in terms of ideas, this will continue to be primarily a struggle between the more traditionalist and liberal types of the ex-LDP reformist rebels with their alternative visions for twenty-first-century Japan. The former (typified by the powerful backstage mover Ichiro Ozawa) are more nationalistic and statist in thrust and have been seeking a powerful new dominance of the right in Japan's political balance. Calling for stronger military and international postures together with a neoconservative limbering up of the LDP's old regulated welfarist economy, they nevertheless tend to lean on a top-down, bureaucrat-friendly political style. The latter (typified by the Democratic Party of Japan's founder, Naoto Kan) are more cosmopolitan and civic-oriented and have been groping their way toward a widely based liberal counterforce in cooperation with a variety of citizens' groups and reformist elements from the moderate-socialist left. Emphasizing a genuine, bottom-up democratization of Japanese politics, they are nevertheless far more cautious about dismantling the old LDP's long-standing centrist commitments to the war-renouncing Article Nine of the constitution and to social welfare as a major concern of government.

Second, the one thing to emerge clearly from the events of 1994 to 2001 is that the shrunken LDP will remain a major political force. The Japanese electorate has shown itself reluctant thus far to shed its trust in the pragmatic experience of the LDP, repeatedly returning coalition cabinets where the LDP was essential to the mix while not permitting it to govern again on its own—precisely the lesson, once again, of the Lower and Upper House elections of June 2000 and July 2001, respectively.

Third, we can rule out as major influences on the new party-political balance both the ultrarightist sectarians (who are not in the Diet) and the now severely marginalized old Marxists, including the JCP and the tattered remnants of the socialist left wing. These extremes will of course continue to feed ideas and emotions into the political discourse, but with the voting public more inclined now to listen with its right rather than left ear.

To summarize eight years of party fissions and fusions, both the more liberal and more traditional forces have attempted to organize a stronger parliamentary presence around their contrasting visions for Japan. Neither of these two forces, however, has succeeded in creating a stable new electoral base, and their ideals and programs have been blurred by the imperatives of coalition strategy on which all of the political parties now depend. What too many Western observers persisted for most of the 1990s in viewing as an era of change and reform, simply because the old LDP no longer called the tune, has in fact been little more than an interval of indeterminate flux—indeed, of political confusion and stasis, as expressed in Tokyo's slow and inept responses to the banking crisis and economic recession,

Although the jury is still out as to the winner in this murky to-and-fro of political parties, it is important for American interests that we sort out the ideas and ideals at stake here—and that we capture the contrasts between liberal versus authoritarian values revealed not only by *what* is said (at the level of formal program) but also by *how* it is said (the spirit, or mind-set, behind it).[1]

It was during the anti-LDP coalition cabinets of Hosokawa and Hata that the LDP rebels of both stripes had their brief day in power. Generally speaking, those of the more liberal tendency were to be found in Hosokawa's Nihon Shinto (Japan New Party) and the small Sakigake (Harbinger) party, into which ex-LDP liberal Masayoshi Takemura had drawn Naoto Kan and other members of the moderate-left Shakai Minshu Rengo (Social Democratic League). The more nationalistic rebels were to be found in the Nihon Shinseito (Japan Renewal Party) of Ichiro Ozawa, which also included as its nominal leader the more liberally inclined Tsutomu Hata. These two cabinets failed to produce any of the hoped-for initiatives on bureaucratic downsizing, deregulation, campaign finance, or market opening, bringing into law only the electoral reform bill of 1994. This abolished the old multiple-seat constituency system in both houses of the Diet that had made it possible for the opposition JSP to maintain its strength as Japan's second largest political party. The new electoral system of single-seat districts combined with proportional representation was a victory chiefly for Ichiro Ozawa and his goal of squeezing out the old left in favor of a two-party system based on two alternating conservative parties.

With Hosokawa done in by a money scandal and Hata ousted on a vote of no confidence, the second stage of the post-1993 interregnum followed with the allegedly odd cohabitation of the Japan Socialist Party with the rump LDP and liberal Sakigake parties under the cabinet of Tomiichi Murayama (June 1994–January 1996), Japan's first socialist prime minister since 1947. The cohabitation continued when the LDP took over the prime ministerial reins under Ryutaro Hashimoto (January 1996–July 1998), the JSP and Sakigake remaining in the cabinet until the Lower House elections of October 1996 and cooperating in a noncabinet alliance with Hashimoto after that. In fact, this ideological crazy quilt of a coalition was less a marriage of cynical convenience and socialist sellout—as the popular image had it—than one of calculated self-preservation, both the LDP and JSP being anxious to check a further swing toward the Ozawa-centered forces on the right.

Murayama's JSP socialists—fearing virtual extinction if they stuck with their rigid old dogma, and prodded rightward by the new centrist-oriented labor union grouping known as Rengo—came out in basic if lukewarm recognition of Japan's Self-Defense Forces and the Japan-U.S. security treaty, and changed their name to the Social Democratic Party of Japan (SDPJ). Their punishment came from the left, with a major erosion of Diet seats and old constituencies, but those looking for a pragmatic liberal left welcomed the move. Meanwhile, other socialist politicians were forming small groups that similarly moved toward the center. The rump LDP, for its part—despite the nationalistic rhetoric of the economically hapless Hashimoto—was still too attached to its old centrist mainstream moderation, including the present peace constitution, to relish a reunion with the more hawkish of its erstwhile defectors.

Two major new parties emerged in opposition to the Murayama-Hashimoto axis, each basically representing one of the two contrasting rebel visions. It was Ozawa's Shinshinto (New Frontier Party), a more powerful right-leaning umbrella fusing the conservative forces within the old Shinseito and the Democratic Socialist Party, that posed the threat gluing the LDP-JSP alliance together and functioned as the dominant opposition force from 1994 to its collapse in late 1997. Serving as the largest opposition party since then has been the Democratic Party of Japan, or DPJ (in Japanese, Nihon Minshuto), founded in 1996 and led by the popular and "populist" Naoto Kan, the former LDP liberal-wingers Yukio and Kunio Hatoyama, and former Shinseito prime minister Tsutomu Hata. This group (which we will revisit in the next chapter) has been the most hopeful forerunner to date of what might yet become a viable liberal alternative someday.

What transpired in 1999–2001, however, was a lurch to the right. Having struck out on its own as a one-party minority government under the first cabinet of Keizo Obuchi (July 1998–January 1999), the LDP with Obuchi's second cabinet entered into a conservative-conservative coalition with Ozawa's new Liberal Party (LP, in Japanese, Jiyuto), the rightmost element of the now defunct Shinshinto. Ozawa—the repeated disrupter of Japan's parliamentary right in his quest to pull it together more firmly on his own terms—had reestablished his retinue as the LP following the nasty breakup of the Shinshinto in December 1997 that pitched some of its more moderate members into Kan's new DPJ. In March 2000 Ozawa withdrew his LP from what had become a tripartite coalition with the LDP and New Komeito (basically the old Komeito renamed), being replaced as third partner by the tiny new Conservative Party (Hoshuto). In April the old LDP workhorse Yoshiro Mori took over as prime minister upon the death of Obuchi and saw his LDP-led coalition retain a reduced but workable majority in the Lower House after the June elections.

By then, however, the LDP-LP coalition had railroaded through the Diet—with the extracabinet cooperation of the New Komeito, and without the customary interparty consultation and deliberation on the Diet floor—a succession of new laws that the DPJ, SDPJ, and JCP opposition bitterly protested as being regressive in substance and/or procedure. Indeed, Japan's preeminent Western-oriented cultural critic, Shuichi Kato, and many other intellectuals on the liberal left denounced these measures as the first snap in the unraveling of Japan's postwar democratic heritage toward a more statist and chauvinistic order.[2]

The new legislation of 1999 included the symbolically touchy reofficialization of the flag (the red-disk rising sun) and national anthem (originally an ode to the Meiji emperor). Long in general use, but henceforth mandatory in the schools, they remain to all on the left (and to most Asians) deeply seared into the collective memories of Japan's wartime ultranationalism. Although their emotional temperature does not match that of the Nazi symbols, the step backward is a bit as if today's reunified Germany were to abandon the historical red-black-and-gold flag of German republicanism for the more authoritarian red-black-and-white standard of the Second and Third Reich, and require schoolchildren to sing once again the banished first verse of Haydn's noble anthem—the explicitly chauvinist call to national unity of "Deutschland Über Alles."

In early 2000 the Obuchi-Ozawa team forced through a majority-friendly reduction of the Lower House seats set aside in 1994 for proportional representation, giving the opposition virtually no opportunity for debate as they did so. The coalition's cavalier posture on a move with constitutional implications prompted Sir Hugh Cortazzi—Britain's former ambassador to Tokyo and a Japan scholar in his own right—to write in the *Japan Times* of 10 February 2000, "I began to think the government's behavior did pose a potential threat to democratic institutions in Japan." Also passed in the legislative rush of 1999, and indicative of new emphasis on social control, were a series of bills to fight organized crime together with a new law designed to allocate ten-digit numbers to all Japanese residents and store personal information in a computer network that linked local authorities.

Legislation was also approved to implement the updated Japan-U.S. defense cooperation guidelines negotiated in 1997 to permit rear-area support by Japan's Self-Defense Forces given an emergency in the "areas surrounding Japan." While Washington wondered why it had taken Tokyo so long to approve relatively tame measures such as search-and-rescue operations or the inspection of ships during economic sanctions,

Japan's pacifist camp focused on the apparently open-ended new definition of the approved reach of future Japanese military operations, worrying that it eventually might encompass the entire East Asian littoral—the old Co-Prosperity Sphere. And, indeed—as if to confirm those very fears—Japan in October 2000 sent naval vessels for the first time to participate in a multination submarine rescue exercise held in waters near Singapore, a move that provoked shrill warnings from the Chinese about the stirring ghost of Japanese militarism.

These were changes all right, ones that threw the opposition into an unprecedented panic about the powerful "Ji-Ji-Ko" (LDP-LP-Komeito) steamroller with its absolute majority in the Lower House, able to push forward willy-nilly with other measures and perhaps, before too long, with constitutional revision itself. This sense of siege betrayed itself in the idealistically intended but poorly executed opposition boycott of Diet budget hearings, led by the DPJ in early 2000, to protest the unilateral manner in which the Ji-Ji-Ko alliance had forced through the bill reducing the number of seats elected by proportional representation.

Americans, too, should ask themselves whether Japan's "changes" in a nonliberal direction (or manner) are what we—in the long run—really want.

Return of the Nativist

Essential to this new rightward thrust has been the intellectual underpinning building up toward it over the past quarter century. Here, under the American-sounding sobriquet of neoconservatism, a group of older politicians and younger public intellectuals that I have dubbed the New Old Right has been busily refurbishing in modern and increasingly acceptable guise some of the key intellectual assumptions and psychological appeal of Japan's prewar nationalism and statism.

This infiltration of right-wing ideas into establishmentarian respectability is a trend I first warned of in the *National Interest* in 1992. The Australian ambassador in Washington at that time, Rawdon Dalrymple, who had recently served as envoy to Tokyo, countered in the next issue that I had overstated my case, particularly by featuring LDP right-winger Shintaro Ishihara, the author of *The Japan that Can Say No*, whom many Western observers were still writing off as a marginal maverick.[3] Eight years later, with Hideki Tojo and the Nanking Massacre being treated to a concerted public whitewash and Ishihara now running Tokyo, one of the world's largest cities, my point may have become clearer. Those who in the year 2000 persist in discounting Ishihara now stress the simple populist appeal of his dramatic new tax on Japan's Tokyo-based banking giants and his twitting of the central government's slowness in making decisions. But we are now clearly at a political watershed when Japan's largest metropolis—well to the left of the nation in the 1960s and 1970s with its socialist governor, Ryokichi Minobe—now opts for a leader whose rightist political visions we shall return to in a moment.

The tragedy of Japan in the 1930s was not that the far right took over the machinery of government directly, as in Hitler's Germany or Mussolini's Italy, but that the militarist and chauvinist extremists— propelled by a powerful nativist ideology—managed to drive a politically supine and intellectually timid civilian establishment ever further toward internal authoritarianism and external aggression. Similarly, the danger from Japan's reviving rightists today is not that they will replace the center, but that they will simply push the established order more and more in their own direction by commanding once again the high ground of national sentiment and ideas. By the same token, just as anti-Americanism can fester without the overt symptoms of collegians snake-dancing in the streets, so does the creep of Japan's rightish nationalism today take place more at dinner tables, on TV talk shows, in popular fiction, and in the mainstream press than through the occasional pistol shot or sword slash at its liberal or leftist opponents.

These liberals and leftists, too, need to be better understood by the West as a whole. For among the ideological wreckage of Japan's old left lie a surprising number of intellectual shards that we would immediately recognize as being liberal in spirit, even from the old Marxist camp. As we shall see in the next chapter, it is only out of the more liberal-minded Japanese hailing variously from the old center and the old left— political groups still divided by long-standing party, factional, and ideological loyalties—that a new counterbalance to the reinvigorated right might hopefully be fashioned. A tall order, quixotic perhaps, but one that deserves the informed encouragement of democratically minded peoples everywhere.

* * *

Pragmatically oriented Americans often grow restless with seemingly arcane Japanese political ideas, forgetting that they can have serious consequences for the United States. After all, it was the collapse of the liberal intellectual climate in 1920s Japan that helped paved the way for Pearl Harbor. To those who pronounce the age of ideology dead, I say: Just look under the surface of all those talking heads on Japanese TV, if you know the language, or those English-speaking Japanese panelists at international conferences, and you'll find the old guts premises—be they from the left or from the right—still there as an overriding psychological bent, even if not spelled out in as much dogmatic detail as before.

Unfortunately, our policy experts and media pundits too often have lacked the intellectual patience and application to fathom political discourse in other countries and cultures. The Iranian revolution, the spread of religious fundamentalism in the Muslim world, and the escalation of radical Islamic terrorism represent recent and increasingly tragic examples. Earlier, in meeting the Soviet threat to Western Europe in the late 1940s, it took America's intellectual cold warriors some time to get over the simplistic notion that "Red is Red," thereby lumping together all socialists (even Britain's Labour Party) with the Communists as our common enemy. That delayed the eventual enlisting of Western Europe's democratic-socialist left as an effective ideological ally—once the wiser perception sank in that they, like we, had made political freedom their primary commitment, ahead of the economic system.

Looking at Japan today, Americans similarly have to overcome their visceral antipathy to nonauthoritarian foreign left wings and seemingly feckless opposition forces to see our way through to common liberal values against a more serious threat. In the case of Europe that meant swallowing our distaste for socialist economics in the interest of a common front against Stalinist political tyranny. In Japan our distaste has been for the pacifist, neutralist, and often anti-American stance of the left in the area of foreign policy; whereas the greater threat over the long run should be seen in the erosion of liberal values from the right, inside Japan itself.

Historically speaking, Japan's eras of relative cosmopolitanism toward the outside world have corresponded to periods of ascendant political liberalism and individualistic values at home, as in the 1920s or the early postwar decades. Japanese liberalism has always been a delicate flower of Western rationalism transplanted onto inhospitable ethnocentric soil. Its philosophical constructs and institutional models have been drawn at one time or another from Protestant Christianity and Christian Socialism; from Lockean and Rousseauean doctrines of human rights and popular sovereignty; from British, French, and American nostrums for parliamentary democracy and constitutional government; from classical nineteenth-century English liberalism, Anglo-German idealism, and Fabianism; and from twentieth-century West European Marxist socialism of the revisionist (i.e., parliamentary-democratic) school. Despite these diverse intellectual roots, it is a pity that Japanese liberals, preoccupied with their contending capitalist and socialist economic visions, have failed to make more—until the 1990s—of their common and overarching value of individual and political freedom.

During the postwar period this liberal intellectual heritage was vastly strengthened institutionally by the new U.S.-sponsored constitution and the initial occupation reforms, but it was still split in half between the two great conservative and leftist camps of the so-called 1955 System, which finally collapsed in 1993. During those four decades, two major forces tended liberal ideas. One was the liberal capitalist center—the moderate conservatives of the then ruling Liberal Democratic Party, and the more progressive elements in Japan's business community. The other was the moderate right and center of the socialist camp and its affiliated labor unions—leaving out, as politically authoritarian, the Japan Communist Party and the extreme-left Marxist-Leninist ideologues of the old Japan Socialist Party.

Those currents of liberalism-cum-cosmopolitanism have always run afoul of sundry types of emperor-, family-, race-, or nation-fixated nativisms—openly celebrated for their blood-and-soil nonrationality. Up to the end of World War II, this ethnocentric Japanism was buttressed by Western statist nostrums taken in the Meiji Period from the Second German Empire and, during the 1930s, from Nazi Germany and fascist Italy. The whole bag of ideas has been hostile not only to internal democratic freedoms but to an openness toward the outside world as well. The Meiji constitution (1890–1945)—with its extended ideological scaffolding in the prewar educational and legal systems—combined a Bismarckian-style bureaucratic and imperial statism with a moral absolutism centered on the emperor system and family state, as politically concocted from Shinto mythology and Confucian ethical precepts of loyalty and obedience. Strands of European corporatism and a virulent antimodernist strain of racial-cultural nationalism entered the mix during the 1930s. What collapsed after 1945 were more the institutional struts of this authoritarian heritage than its attitudinal lineaments. These have survived right up until today in a powerful and arrogant bureaucracy, in close government-to-business and intercorporate cooperation as to the economy, and in the renewed harping of prominent Japanese intellectuals on racial purity and cultural uniqueness.

Deepest of all in the psyche of Japan's postwar right has lurked the stain of military defeat on the national and imperial honor. In practical terms this has translated into a detestation of the new democratic dispensation that blocks their way toward an emotionally satisfactory expiation through the reestablishment of the older ideology at home and the reassertion of Japanese power abroad. Until recently these inward-looking ideas have been the historical stock in trade of the ultranationalist fringe with its ties to the criminal underworld of the *yakuza*—and also, more respectably expressed, of the political and cultural conservative right. For years our own anti-Communist imperatives in East Asia drew nearly all of these right-wing forces to our side while aligning much of Japan's moderate left against us. For decades Americans in Japan have watched with embarrassment from the sidewalks as the black or olive-green sound trucks of the ultraright thundered by, trumpeting their anti-Soviet slogans at earsplitting volume and flying the Stars and Stripes insouciantly from their rooftops.

Today, with the Cold War over, it should be easier for us to distinguish our truer ideological cousins. But not all that easy, alas, because of the peculiar way in which Japan's liberals themselves have been scattered along the political spectrum, often at odds with one another and politically allied through their parties to distinctly illiberal elements on the LDP right-wing or JSP left-wing extremes.

This anomaly goes deeper than, say, our nuanced disagreements on political versus economic democracy in the United States. The American political mind seeking liberal intellectual resonances in postwar Japan runs up against an exasperating bifurcation between objective and institutional political values, on one hand, as against more subjective humane and individualistic values, on the other—two sets of values that in our own political experience would come bundled in a single package. To be specific, America's economic, political, and foreign policy perspectives have been most closely shared by Japan's moderate conservatives—who nevertheless have been allied in the Liberal Democratic Party with the residue of Japan's old right. Meanwhile, our emphases on the dignity of the individual, on human rights, and on the importance of civil courage have on the whole been more faithfully tended by the moderate left—even though they, in turn, have been tied in parliament to the far left of hard-core Marxism-Leninism.

I am, of course, using the concepts of liberalism and democracy here in broad-brush, layman's parlance—in the sense that this is what we are seeing more of today in Argentina, Poland, South Korea, and Taiwan than was present in those countries ten or twenty years ago. And I do so throughout this volume without raising the more technical and semantic argument raised by some American Japanologists as to whether the terms *liberalism* and *democracy* are applicable to the Japan of the 1920s, or even whether *fascism* is applicable to that of the 1930s.[4]

Although the two extremes of Japan's political spectrum have no monopoly on insularism or even xenophobia, it is the center-left and center-right that—thanks to their philosophical legacies—have shown the greatest imaginative capacity for liberalism and cosmopolitanism as we understand them. To be sure, Japan's labeling has not always been congruent with American political discourse. The ideological fault lines, too, have blurred considerably since the 1970s. And with specific individuals one finds the usual crisscrossing of ideas—just as many affluent Republicans in the United States, for example, combine the economic conservatism of lean federal budgets with the social permissiveness of pro-choice views.

Nevertheless, the basic assumptions and worldviews are still there as an intellectual and emotional resource that will help to jell the still unsettled political agenda of a nation destined to have a major impact on our own daily lives long into the new century. So let us take a look first to the right, and then, in the following chapter, to the left.

Japanese Conservatism and the New Old Right

The most critical divide in Japanese political values today runs not between the moderate and far left (as it long did) but between Japan's moderate conservatives and the unreconstructed old right. The key divergence lies in their attitudes toward World War II, especially Japan's defeat, and toward the democratic reforms that followed.

The former group, whatever their chagrin, has been able to put defeat behind them, write off the war as a bad job, and get on with the rebuilding of a more liberal, prosperous, and civilian-minded (if still bureaucratically led) Japan. With an inner disposition toward the United States that is relatively unclouded, their roster of prime ministers includes men such as Yoshida, Ikeda, Sato, Ohira, Miki, Kaifu, Miyazawa and

Hosokawa—all from the so-called Yoshida-line or LDP-mainstream factions.

For means to those ends these centrist conservatives have relied on aggressive economic growth and trade expansion coupled with market protectionism to sustain broadly egalitarian and welfarist social goals. On foreign policy they have combined a dovish military posture with a sotto voce deference to American geopolitical goals. And they remain instinctively on guard against any fundamental challenge, from right or left, to Japan's pre- and postwar heritage of political liberalism. They have not made things easy for Americans and others on the market-opening front, but their general worldview has been in rough consonance with that of the Western democracies. It is from the more progressive, imaginative, and younger members of this broader group that the "liberal" ex-LDP rebels of the Nihon Shinto, Sakigake, and Democratic Party of Japan have sprung.

In contrast to all this, the second, more old-fashioned group of conservatives still nurses the shame of defeat, views Japan's postwar democratic dispensation as an American imposition, remains rooted in prewar-style nationalistic psychology, and hankers after some device or development that will settle old scores and wipe the emotional slate clean. Japan's right-wing conservatives—many of them from the so-called antimainstream LDP factions—have shared with the bagatelle postwar ultraright a syndrome of causes and subcauses radiating from that unprocessed stain on the honor of Japanese arms and the imperial line.

Their two great objectives, accordingly, have been to undo the limitations imposed by the postwar constitution of 1947 upon the role of the Japanese military and on the prerogatives of the emperor. Having been blocked by the left and center in their push to revise the constitution toward those two ends, they have sought to prepare the intellectual and psychological ground for them through nationalistic education, revisionist interpretations of the war, hawkish postures on defense, and attempts to reintroduce the old symbols of imperial mystique.

Their well-publicized insensitivity toward Japan's erstwhile victims abroad has been matched by a restless frustration with the finer nuances of democratic process, popular sovereignty, and the individual rights of Japanese citizens at home. They have also been more (or perhaps one should say even more) instrumental in their professed friendship for the United States, although of their four most representative prime ministers—Kishi, Nakasone, Hashimoto, and Mori—the first two were among our most vocal Cold War supporters. More recently, they have tacked the cause of neoconservative economics and deregulation to their standard. It is from members of this more rightish conservative tradition that the nationalistic ex-LDP rebels of the Shinseito (Japan Renewal Party), Shinshinto (New Frontier Party), and Jiyuto (Liberal Party) have largely come, joined on certain issues by the more conservative members of the Democratic Socialist Party or by the Komeito.

Many members of this second strain of Japanese conservatism deserve the moniker of New Old Right, since they increasingly transmute into contemporary guises some of the more problematical features of Japan's prewar statist and chauvinistic ideology. Spanning both a wartime generation of political and ex-military dinosaurs and a younger cohort of nationalistic intellectuals, they are to be found both inside and outside of parliament. And with Japan's newly found clout from the 1980s, the wraps finally started to come off their inherent xenophobia.

The antiforeign animus of this New Old Right cropped up most openly in the public disparagement of American minorities and Asian neighbors by prominent cabinet-level figures and in the anti-American bluster of the provocative 1989 best-seller, *The Japan That Can Say No.* The author, Shintaro Ishihara—then the most outspoken Dietman of the LDP right wing, and since 1999 the governor of Tokyo—has been the politician who most openly typifies this group in intellectual terms and sets it off most clearly from the moderate mainstream. Ishihara was for years a political protégé and factional follower of Okinori Kaya, who had been Tojo's finance minister at the time of Pearl Harbor and for years led the LDP's rightmost faction.

This flamboyant quondam novelist advocates nuclear weapons for Japan while at the same time demanding the removal of all American bases. Having once likened the American military to a "mad dog" rather than a "watchdog," Ishihara was hardly settled in his governor's chair when he publicly demanded the return of the U.S. Air Force's Far Eastern headquarters at Yokota in the Tokyo suburbs—thereby drawing an open retort from the American embassy that it would not deal with Tokyo city hall on a national-level issue. In 1998, in a second book entitled *Sensen Fukoku No to Ieru Nihon Keizai* (The Japanese economy that can utter the declaration of war, "no"), he depicted the Asian financial crisis as an American plot to establish global financial hegemony by undermining East Asian economies through the new "opium" of "money violence"—a "second defeat of Japan" jealously engineered by the "merciless American Jewish trio" of Madeleine Albright, Robert Rubin, and George Soros.[5] As a counterstrategy to America's "market imperialism," Ishihara called for East Asian solidarity in creating a powerful yen sphere and an exclusive Asian Marshall Plan–style recovery program funded by Japan as "elder brother" to the rest of the region.

As if to underline his self-appointed role as Japan's political enfant terrible, Ishihara in April 2000 scandalized the entire foreign community, Asians and Westerners alike, by urging Japan's Ground Self-Defense Forces (i.e., the army) to be ready to rush in at the side of the ineffective civilian police to maintain order during an earthquake disaster, since foreigners were bound to riot and were already "repeatedly" committing "atrocious crimes." Ishihara had long irritated China by habitually referring to it as "Shina"—a term echoing Japan's military past—and by dismissing the Rape of Nanking as a lie. This time he embittered Japan's putatively lawless seven hundred thousand resident Koreans by using a pejorative term, *sankokujin* (third-country nationals), not heard publicly in decades and evoking memories of the wanton killing of thousands of Koreans in the panic following the great Kanto earthquake of 1923, after unfounded rumors that they were committing arson and poisoning wells. Of the 302 telephone calls to city hall in the first two days after his speech, 37 percent supported Ishihara. Considering that many of the 58 percent protesting his racist ranting were probably foreigners, the proportion of Japanese callers supporting him may have been much higher. Given, too, that Tokyo's electorate is the nation's wealthiest and supposedly most internationalized, this is the most ominous proof we have had to date of how far Japanese public sentiment has slid toward the xenophobic right.

Although widely billed abroad as a can-do politician and Western-style statesman, there was much about Prime Minister Yasuhiro Nakasone (1982–87), too, that pointed hindward. His celebration of Japanese racial homogeneity, his insistence on a firmer definition of Japanese "identity" as a prerequisite for any further internationalization, his support for the educational nationalists, and his notorious racial slur on the intelligence of American blacks and Hispanics have only served to undercut the cosmopolitan spirit required for a genuine economic and social opening of Japan.

Unconscionably, just as their country was achieving unprecedented weight in global affairs, the intellectual wing of the New Old Right began to drum into their fellow countrymen the old prewar dogma that they are a people set apart from the rest of mankind and that their cultural and social heritage is racially, that is to say biologically, determined. Those not born Japanese can never fully participate—or even understand. During the prewar years the ideology of Japanese particularism produced both an arrogant superiority toward other Asians based on a sense of being different-and-ahead as well as a nagging self-contempt born of the awareness of being different-and-behind when measured against the West. That notion of cultural uniqueness, still cherished by the New Old Right today, weakened the spiritual and intellectual capacities of the early-twentieth-century Japanese to lead a weaker Asia from a genuine position of noblesse oblige. Conversely, it kept them from relating to the more powerful West with something more constructive than self-pity and the resentment verging on self-destructive rage that was to find its ultimate outlet in war and in the atrocities committed at Nanking and Bataan. Today, if less malignantly, it continues to buttress Japan's closed markets and intellectual institutions.

Political Goals and Visions

The political agenda of the New Old Right has been regressive, and their potential extremism best exemplified by the so-called Spy Bill, introduced but subsequently withdrawn in 1987, which would have mandated the death penalty for the leaking of diplomatic secrets in peacetime—a clear throwback to the mind-set of the thought-control police of the 1930s. Cabinet-level figures among them—including Seisuke Okuno and Seiroku Kajiyama—repeatedly have outraged the Chinese and Koreans with taunting, impenitent statements belittling the historical damage inflicted by Japan on those two countries in the first half of this century.

Most fundamental, and even popular with some Americans, is their demand for the scrapping of the war-renouncing Article Nine of the postwar constitution, both as an assertion of fully restored sovereignty and in order (so the sales pitch goes) to permit a full-scale military "contribution" *(koken)* by Japan to future global peacekeeping operations. Indeed, prior to his summit with President Clinton in September 1998, even the centrist Liberal Democratic prime minister Keizo Obuchi— knowing he would be hearing heavy criticism of Japan's financial mess— coyly remarked to Tokyo's foreign press that Japan would *not* seek a way out of its economic doldrums by building up an arms and arms-export industry. Whether it is to be interpreted as a trial balloon or as merely another instance of psychological blackmail, it was the first time that particular possibility had been aired globally from the highest level.

The vision of some New Old Rightists, however, has included major rearmament and even nuclear weapons, something that would terrify and destabilize Japan's Asian neighborhood and also put the United States in a very awkward position. Some of the proponents, indeed, have argued that possessing a nuclear arsenal would serve to restrain Uncle Sam in his trade demands. Most damaging of all, however, would be the psychological impact on the Japanese mind itself, undermining those civilian, nonmilitaristic values that have gained public acceptance over the postwar decades. As the former socialist Dietman and well-known media commentator Masao Kunihiro once put it to me: The faithful tending of Article Nine has been, in an indirect but very effective way, Japan's apology for World War II.

The contempt and impatience with which one representative writer, Tetsuya Kataoka, dismisses the "pacifist commercial democracy" of postwar Japan sixteen times in a book of sixty-nine pages chillingly suggests the direction in which some of Japan's antipacifist thinking is headed. As with nostalgic reactionaries elsewhere, "dirty" commercialism and world trade were favorite targets of Japan's prewar right. By the same token, they have been the mainstay of Japan's internal democracy and peaceful links with the world today. Kataoka, the author of *Waiting for a Pearl Harbor: Japan Debates Defense* (1980) and a former faculty colleague and drinking companion of mine at Tsukuba University, even took to the *Wall Street Journal* in 1987 the unstartling revelation that "Mr. Hall . . . told me more than once that he adamantly is opposed to a constitutional revision and nuclear armament in Japan."[6] Yes, indeed. Over *yakitori* chicken kebabs, as I recall.

Behind their attack on Article Nine lies the profounder aim of scrapping and rewriting the constitution itself—something that the moderate-conservative, DSP-connected defense intellectual and former Defense Academy head, Masamichi Inoki, warned of in 1991 as the opening of the "lid of hell" that would let out all the other "demons of reactionary conservatism."[7] Should this succeed, attempts would almost surely be made to inch the emperor back toward the aura of his prewar status, refurbishing some of the moral authority that was used as a cloak of immunity for Japan's actual bureaucratic and military power holders and as an ideological weapon to discredit the philosophical foundations of individual liberty and parliamentary democracy in favor of an imperially grounded statism. Although the prewar emperor system was a deliberate political construct of the mid-Meiji government, Japan's cultural right already has come a long way in reviving the general public's acceptance of the imperial institution as the historical touchstone of Japanese culture and in positing Japanese culture in turn—imperially, familistically, and racially defined—as the litmus test of what and who is or isn't "Japanese." In this they have been aided by the vogue since the 1970s of popular books on so-called *Nihonjinron* (theories on [the nature of] the Japanese) that reasserted the old nineteenth-century causal links between race and culture—links that twentieth-century genetics and anthropology have long since demolished.

The debate on constitutional revision finally emerged from the shadows of private discussion to the formal level of parliamentary committees in 1999. And the sleeper issue in it may well turn out to be Article One, on the locus of sovereignty (now residing with the people), rather than the war-renouncing Article Nine. The taboos on too open or critical a discussion of the imperial institution continue in force, as they did with any debate over the late Emperor Hirohito's wartime responsibility, or even the nature of his illness (cancer) as he lay dying in 1988–89. Unlike Britain, any talk of a republic or salacious media coverage of the imperial family is simply unthinkable in Japan today. It is most likely, therefore, that any constitutional move to upgrade Japan's most redoubtable nativist institution will be met by a public psychology not so much supportive as simply too timid and embarrassed to challenge it head-on.

Like constitutional revision, the projects of the New Old Right have all been directed in one way or another at erasing the "shame" of defeat in World War II—without once asking themselves what it was that brought the rest of the world so angrily to Japan's shores in 1945. In practical terms, the moderate conservatives have managed to keep the right wing out of the arenas of economic, defense, and foreign policy, much as one might keep an obstreperous child out of the front parlor when company comes. As a sop, the New Old Rightists have been given their freest rein in the field of educational policy, where they have managed over the years to have references to Japan's aggression and atrocities in World War II diluted in or deleted from school textbooks.

Another of the New Old Right's most vocal demands—and a good litmus test for unreconstructed attitudes toward Asia and World War II—has been their call for the revival of state recognition and support of the Yasukuni shrine to the war dead in central Tokyo. This, the pantheon of pre-1945 militarism and State Shinto, and the spot where the spirits of Hideki Tojo and his fellow class-A war criminals are now enshrined, has been misrepresented to forgetful foreign visitors as being no more than Japan's equivalent of Arlington National Cemetery. What we need to recall here is that the spirits of Japan's war dead have been enshrined not as battlefield heroes in the Western sense but as Shinto gods—and that it is this added weight of deification that makes Yasukuni so widely feared as the reentering wedge of politico-religious absolutism.

Anathema to other East Asians, to whom it still symbolizes the rampages of one of history's most bloodthirsty armies, the Yasukuni shrine remains to Japanese liberals the key sanctifier not only of martial mania but also of the prewar suppression of religious freedom, including Buddhism and Christianity. Inadvertently, almost comically, giving the lie to it all were the architectural plans (sensibly withdrawn) for an adjacent World War II historical museum consisting of two sleek parallel towers of jagged lightning-bolt design—the old Nazi SS emblem! What does strike today's foreign visitor as singularly tasteless in a shrine compound approached through a bombastic, towering bronze *torii* gateway (normally constructed of light wood) is the outdoor display of the steam engine actually used in the festive opening ceremony and first run over the wartime "death railway" linking Thailand and Burma. The prominently posted thank-you plaques to the enthusiastic donors for the engine's repatriation from the junkyards of Southeast Asia belie other signs expressing regret for all the lives lost in the railway's construction.

In organizational terms, today's New Old Right is less a matter of the party affiliations we have noted than a mind-set sprinkled across the entire right half of Japan's political spectrum in a constellation of single-issue councils and committees with overlapping memberships and mutual ideological reinforcement drawing variously on the parties, the bureaucracy, the business community, and on Japanese media and academe.

Typical groupings and leaders since the 1970s have included the following:

- On defense, the Citizens' Association for the Defense of Japan (Nihon o Mamoru Komumin Kaigi), long led by the late composer Toshiro Mayazumi

- On matters of military strategy, the Japan Center for the Study of Security Issues (Nihon Anzen Hosho Kenkyu Sentaa), headed by publicist Hideaki Kase
- On constitutional revision, both privately sponsored and LDP parliamentarians' groups
- On historical revisionism, the Society for the Writing of New School Textbooks in History (Atarashii Rekishi Kyokasho o Tsukuru Kai), featuring the aforementioned Nobukatsu Fujioka of Nanking-debunking note
- And, in the emperor-boosting game, a congeries of groups pushing for the reofficialization of customary practices in symbolic areas such as the national flag and anthem and the reckoning of years by imperial-era names (such as Meiji)

In 1997 the New Old Right achieved a coming-of-age of sorts when Ryutaro Hashimoto—who had climbed the LDP power ladder as the head of the War Bereaved Families Association (Nihon Izokukai), another key subgroup—finally made it to the premier's chair. And in the spring of 2000, with Prime Minister Yoshiro Mori's laudatory public references to Japan as a "land of the gods centered on the emperor" *(tenno o chushin to shite iru kami no kuni),* to *kokutai* (the emperor-centered "national structure," crafted during the Meiji period), and to the Imperial Rescript on Education *(kyoiku chokugo),* the dam on backward-looking nationalism nearly broke.

The implied sense in the phrase *kami no kuni* of Japan as a "divine nation" (as it came across in most English-language dispatches) was redolent of the militarism, aggression, and repressive State Shinto of the wartime period, and Mori's use of it provoked an outraged response from the press throughout Asia, including much of the Japanese. And up until 1945 even implied criticism of *kokutai* was enough to bring the thought police to one's doorstep and land one in jail, if not worse. The term, expunged by the Allied occupation, was a taboo virtually unspoken in public since 1945—to the point where Japanese born since the war know the word only as its homonym, the abbreviated term for the annual high school National Athletic Meet.

Together with "land of the gods" and the Imperial Rescript on Education of 1890—the official prewar moral and ideological guide effectively dictating what it meant to be (and think) Japanese—the very expression *kokutai* was to its erstwhile victims both at home and abroad a deep-stink code word for the oppressive prewar absolutist imperial ideology and the massive and unyielding bureaucratic, military, and educational structures that embodied and sustained it. To Howard French, the Tokyo bureau chief of the *New York Times,* writing on 1 June 2001, Mori's pronouncement on *kami no kuni* was "a perfect summation of State Shinto, the racist official religion that drove Japan's expansionism in Asia and its war with the United States." Accordingly, the emotional voltage of Mori's dragging all three of these skeletons out of the right-wing closet in as many weeks' time was analogous to refloating on the German public discourse of today the old Nazi racial, ethical, and political mantras of *Herrenvolk* (master race), *Kraft durch Freude* (the Strength Through Joy movement), and *ein Reich, ein Volk, ein Führer.*

What was most extraordinary about Mori's bumptiously repeated (and casuistically defended) "gaffes" was the lack of concern shown by the Japanese establishment, including his own LDP. Indeed, it was almost as if he was deliberately being allowed to test and push out the perimeter of admissible ideas and terminology for the upcoming constitutional debate. That the West, for its part, should have reacted so mildly to Japan's prime minister after dumping so heavily on Jörg Haider of Austria for an arguably lesser degree of verbal backsliding—nasty as it was, with its primarily anti-immigrant focus—suggests not only our historical amnesia and reluctance to cope with ideas in Japan but, perhaps more than anything else, a certain patronizing Orientalism—the notion that we simply cannot expect as much of these Japanese, or other Asians.

When Kinhide Mushakoji, former vice rector of the United Nations University in Tokyo and one of Japan's certified internationalist liberals, invoked the UN General Assembly's 1965 resolution against racial discrimination in calling on the foreign media to urge the G-8 powers to move their July 2000 summit out of Japan, his words fell on deaf ears.[8] Had Haider, mutatis mutandis, gone as far (and as tauntingly) as Mori in his politically regressive utterings, the Europeans at least would have pulled out of any confab booked for Vienna forthwith. When Haider in a speech praised Hitler's "full employment" policies—a historical stupidity analogous to the Japanese cabinet ministers who enrage the Koreans by telling them the colonial occupation was good for their economy—he was forced to resign as governor of the rural province of Carinthia. In Japan, Tokyo voters elected right-wing populist Shintaro Ishihara governor of the world's largest city.

Japanese Versus American Right Wings

Unfortunately, the profound antiliberalism of the New Old Rightists was obscured for many American and European democrats during the Cold War by their welcome anti-Communist rhetoric and the presentation of their agenda to the West as a normal and healthy returning pride of country—a new garden-variety nationalism, a mere Gaullism. Although that is indeed part of the picture—and not only on the right—their intellectual baggage is more redolent of the old 1930s chauvinism, warmed over.

There is a special irony in the empathy felt for Japan's New Old Right by some American conservatives. These have included both ex-Democrat neoconservative foreign policy hawks and Republicans of our post-1980 Reaganite New Right who have sworn by a libertarian and patriotic creed and whose central tenet has been the reassertion of individual freedom as against an interventionist state. It is ironic, because these misperceived ideological "allies" of ours in Japan are not only hostile to much of the remaining liberal and democratic legacy of the U.S. occupation, now fitfully tended by conservative and socialist moderates, but are among those (together with Japan's Communists) who would get the greatest emotional kick out of seeing the United States driven out of Japan and Asia and taken down a few notches in the global pecking order as well.

The broader stage for our right-to-right empathy, of course, was set by the Reagan-Thatcher-Nakasone iron triad of economically neoconservative and militarily hawkish Free World leaders throughout the 1980s. Unlike his Anglo-American counterparts, however, Japan's prime minister did little to promote free trade or liberalize his own economy, keeping the West happy with a series of stillborn market-opening "packages" and a drastic upward revaluation of the yen in the Plaza Accord of 1985. More important, the Beltway thought it had at last found a Japanese politician it could understand and do business with. For here was Yasuhiro Nakasone coached to deliver his stateside speeches in English; playing the "Ron-Yasu" game of pseudointimacy with consummate aw-shucks, just-us-folks aplomb; wowing the Pentagon with his tough anti-Soviet talk; and sending his own pacifists reeling with his reference to Japan as an "unsinkable aircraft carrier" *(fuchin kubo)*—at our disposal, of course. So it was no coincidence that when Ronald Reagan, after leaving office, accepted a $2 million speaking engagement in Japan, it was arranged by the *Sankei Shinbun*/Fuji TV group, led by the furthest right of Japan's five great daily newspapers—a frequent tribune of New Old Right causes, including a lot of America bashing on trade.

At the level of institutional collaboration, a classic instance was the joint sponsorship in August 1980 of a binational conference in Tokyo—pragmatic and unexceptional in and of itself—on the next twenty years of the security treaty by the Heritage Foundation and the Japan Center for the Study of Security Issues, whose chairman, Hideaki Kase, would one day head the committee for the production of the Tojo film released in 1998.[9] By any measure other than that of defense philosophy, this was an odd coupling of America's bellwether of the rugged nineteenth-century economic and political liberalism that now goes by the name of conservatism and a Japanese think tank whose members represented a compendium of the New Old Right political and cultural agenda.

Even more improbable was the speaking tour of Japan by our moderate-Republican ex-President George H. Bush and his wife, Barbara, in September 1995 that was sponsored by the Women's Federation for the Peace of Asia (WFPA), a front organization for the Reverend Sun Myung Moon, whose connections with the New Old Rightists (and the ultra-right) in Japan run wide and deep. The United Church of Christ in Japan, a federation of 1,700 Protestant churches, wrote in vain to Bush with the plea: "Please do not be fooled by its name but consider the group behind it and the damage that your association with it could cause to countless numbers of people." The Bushes shared the platform at all six events with Hak Ja Han Moon, the Reverend's wife.[10]

Or perhaps not all that improbable, considering the apparent naïveté or casualness with which another member of the Bush family had allowed himself to be courted and manipulated by murky figures from Japan's gangster underworld a half decade earlier. In July 1991 in an article splashed across the top of its front page, the English-language *Daily Yomiuri* newspaper in Tokyo reported the business deal which the then president's elder brother, Prescott Bush, had struck in March 1989 with Hokusho Sangyo, a real estate firm run by Susumu Ishii, the former head of the Inagawa-kai, one of Japan's largest criminal syndicates. The accompanying photograph—in a pairing that scandalized the Japanese while, as usual, hardly registering with Americans—showed the older Bush seated at a table with Munenobu Shoji (the president of Hokusho Sangyo, and *Yomiuri*'s source for the story), at the time of Bush's 1989 visit. Following that meeting, according to Shoji, Bush advised the *yakuza*-linked corporation on "all of our U.S. investments," including the purchase of two financial firms in New York, Asset Management International Financing and Settlement, and Quantum Access. During subsequent litigation arising from the Asset Management deal, Prescott Bush told a federal court in June 1992 that Shoji and his business colleagues had "deliberately deceived" him into believing that they were "reputable traders and businessmen," and that as soon as he had learned of their reputed mob ties in 1990 he had severed all connections with West Tsusho, the overseas investment arm of Hokusho. But it still begs the question—where on earth were our embassy officials or other Japan experts to steer into safer waters the brother of a president only two months past his own inauguration?[11]

Throughout the 1990s, too, as we shall see, Washington placed its highest hopes on the most powerful and effective of the New Old Rightish conservatives in the Diet today—Ichiro Ozawa. In October 1999 it was Ozawa's personal appointee to the Obuchi subcabinet, parliamentary vice defense minister Shingo Nishimura, who resigned after kicking up a public storm by suggesting in a magazine that the Diet should start debating whether Japan should arm itself with nuclear weapons.

Conversely, it is the issue of base reductions in Okinawa that has highlighted most poignantly the way in which the United States often allowed the imperatives of "defending democracy" in Asia to override the expression of its own liberal values in countries where they were genuinely struggling to the fore, as in the Philippines and South Korea. While granting the need for some type of forward presence in a region still destabilized by an unpredictable North Korea, it was a sorry sight to see the United States in 1996 working with New Old Rightist Japanese prime minister Hashimoto (and he with Japan's bureaucratically oriented courts) against Masahide Ota, then Okinawa's governor, and the much put-upon citizens of Okinawa prefecture to perpetuate the old grievances, including the forced leasing of privately owned real estate. When the regional high court in Kyushu refused to back up Ota's refusal to renew expired leases for base land, he was fobbed off with Tokyo's promise of economic subsidies and a five-to-seven-year Hashimoto-Clinton commitment (its actual implementation still stalled as of 2001) to "close" the Marine Corps Air Station at Futenma by relocating it a few miles up the road on an environmentally destructive and typhoon-exposed offshore platform to be built over coral waters near the smaller town of Nago.

Ironically, thanks to our quarter-century rule of the Ryukyus, Ota, a political scientist trained in the United States, has, like many of his fellow islanders, drunk more deeply of American democratic values than have the mainland Japanese—the very values with which he now confronts us. Indeed, Ota is one of the very few major Japanese political figures today to whom Americans can genuinely relate in terms of our own political mentality. As a final grotesque irony to our betrayal of our own basic principles, we now find the Communists (with whatever ulterior motive) in the forefront of the campaign on Okinawa to assert that quintessential Lockean tenet of American freedom and of the American Revolution itself—the right to private property!

* * *

There are, of course, some historical roots for the soft spot that some business-oriented and dedicatedly anti-Communist American conservatives have held for the Japanese right. After the war there were prominent prewar Japan hands such as former ambassador Joseph Grew (1932–42) and his old Tokyo embassy chief of staff, Eugene Dooman, who, together with Washington's so-called Japan crowd, pushed for a speedy reconciliation with the erstwhile foe in order to contain a China headed for Maoist takeover. Recent years have witnessed an exposé of the role of America's Cold War establishment, particularly the CIA, in passing money through some of Japan's less savory right-wing fixers, such as Yoshio Kodama, to the pro-American ruling Liberal Democratic Party.[12] Since 1993, however, our right-to-right resonance has focused more on the promise of the so-called ex-LDP reformers to work for administrative deregulation and other measures ostensibly consonant with America's own neoconservative economic agenda.

Here, two things have obscured the aforementioned regressive purposes of the New Old Right: first, the fact that their smaller-government line is shared by the more liberal rebels from the LDP, as well as being popular with much of the Japanese public; second, the way they have presented themselves to the English-speaking world as "liberals"—in a truly Orwellian switching of labels that they justify on the basis of their opposition to the LDP establishment. Even an astute Western observer with the impeccable liberal credentials of Dutch journalist Karel van Wolferen, author of the best-selling *The Enigma of Japanese Power*, has come out in praise of New Old Rightists such as Yasuhiro Nakasone,

Ichiro Ozawa, and Nobukatsu Fujioka in the hope that they might move Japan toward its new international responsibilities by restoring "normal" military capabilities, by taming the bureaucracy and establishing a firm chain of political accountability, and by overcoming what van Wolferen sees as a paralyzing negativity toward Japan's own past. In keeping with the recent rightward tilt in Japan, this foreign observer too has adopted an increasingly shrill anti-American tone in depicting American globalization ideology as a U.S.-concocted "political plot" to dominate the world, and in encouraging the Japanese to stand up to American pressures to open their markets and liberalize their economic system.[13]

How many Americans in 2001, however, remember Ichiro Ozawa? He was the Japanese conservative politician who, from about 1994 to 1996, was misperceived by too many foreign journalists in Tokyo and American Japan experts at home as a can-do neoconservative type who would bring his country around to fuller cooperation with U.S. trade and international security objectives. After all, we told ourselves, Ozawa had been pushing for all the right things. He wanted to deregulate Japan's economy and decentralize its society by subordinating the overweening bureaucracy to the enfeebled legislative arm. In order to strengthen that limb, he was calling for the establishment of an effective two-party system along Anglo-American lines that would recast Japanese politics in terms of issues rather than factional loyalties. Finally, by revising the constitution to permit a "normal" defense establishment, Ozawa promised to put not only cash but also Japanese lives on the line for the world community in future crises such as the Gulf War. As a result, American conservatives looking for ideologically congenial elements in Japan began to move beyond the old ties of anti-Communism and defense cooperation to take hope from Japanese politicians and writers with a self-styled neoconservative line on deregulation and small government, in hopes that progress on these goals would help to liberalize Japanese trade practices.

To give Ichiro Ozawa his due, he has been in turn the most influential figure behind the reformist cabinets of Prime Ministers Morihiro Hosokawa and Tsutomu Hata during 1993–94; the driving force behind the more right-leaning umbrella Shinshinto (New Frontier Party), which led the opposition from 1994 to 1997; and, with his own hard-core loyalists of the Jiyuto (Liberal Party) since 1998, the leader of the parliamentary force now furthest to the right. There is also much in Ozawa's *Blueprint for a New Japan: The Rethinking of a Nation* that resonates with current American neoconservative ideals—his prescriptions for deregulating the economy, for calling to account an arrogant bureaucracy, for devolving political power and initiative to regional entities, and for making Japanese troops available for "international contributions" in peacekeeping operations. Indeed, U.S. reviewers on the jacket cover rang out praises for the author as one of the "great reformers" of his country, who was thought to be shepherding a "liberal reformation of Japan" and a "fundamental change in Japanese thinking."[14]

For a time during the mid-1990s American expectations ran high that Ozawa would be the man to recapture power from the bureaucrats, return it to elected politicians, and otherwise remold Japan to our own tastes. These expectations were so high that they threatened to cast the man as Washington's cat's-paw and a turncoat. I recall one American historian of Japan prominent in bilateral cultural exchanges telling me at a Tokyo reception in 1994 that he had just called on Ozawa, and that before long Ozawa would put the bureaucrats in their place and everything would be okay with Japan-U.S. relations.

Unfortunately for us, this was yet another ethnocentrically American misreading of the Japanese political mind. Political rivals and a deep public distrust of the man have kept Ozawa from the levers of power so far. Indeed, for most Japanese, Ozawa—a protégé of the late LDP fixer and kingmaker Shin Kanemaru, who ended his political career disgraced and in jail—has represented too much of the old politics of veiled intentions, byzantine coups, deep-running personal ties to the Ministry of Finance and other centers of bureaucratic clout, and too much rough riding over democratic processes to lead the country toward a genuinely liberalized political and economic system.

In a word, there are too many of the old Meiji statist itches under the veneer of antistatist neoconservatism. Americans, however eager to see Japan's contumacious bureaucrats humbled, should also mind who does the humbling.

CHAPTER FOUR

Limping Liberalism
Civil Courage Derided
as "Leftist Lite"

To the left of Japan's center, the intellectual challenge to the United States at the start of a new century goes well beyond ridding our minds of the old bogey of a strident anti-American opposition hell-bent on depriving us of our bases. The more difficult and important task will be to identify, understand, and encourage those political forces—some of them now on the wane—that are more, not less, inclined to work toward a liberal and outward-looking Japan.

All of the rebels who bolted from the ruling Liberal Democratic Party in 1993 did so in the name of reforming the faction-ridden, bureaucracy-oriented, old-crony style of conservative politics. In their espousal of deregulation, transparency, and bureaucratic accountability, therefore, the more liberal defectors from the old LDP have shared some of the objectives of the Ichiro Ozawa camp. But they do so with an enormous philosophical difference that sees the ultimate purpose of these reforms in the improvement of the people's livelihood and the maturation of a civil society—and not in the strengthening of the Japanese state for the sake of social stability at home and national security and prestige abroad.

The Shaky Liberal Amalgam

The two great questions before Japan's liberal forces in the new decade are whether they will have the accommodating wisdom to forge a new political constellation capable of presenting a viable counterbalance and second-party alternative to a powerful regrouping of the conservative right and, having built such a political base, whether they will succeed in infusing it—despite a smorgasbord of ideological backgrounds—with their shared core ideal of individual liberty governed by reason in a modern, citizen-oriented democracy.

Ozawa's scenario for two conservative parties, tightly disciplined in the British parliamentary style, understandably worries the many liberal-minded Japanese from the moderate center and left who recall their country's prewar party system whereby two entrenched and virtually indistinguishable conservative siblings (for years the Seiyukai versus the Minseito parties, respectively allied with the great Mitsui and Mitsubishi *zaibatsu* industrial conglomerates) swapped governments without serious challenge. Already, the near-rout of the socialists and the increased weight of the conservative right in the parliamentary balance threatens to remove the historical bulwark that the old leftist opposition—with over a third of the seats in the Diet—provided against constitutional revision and a resurgence of the reactionary right.

A more genuine and promising two-party structure could emerge if the Democratic Party of Japan were to realize its goal of uniting an assortment of moderate conservatives, nondoctrinaire socialists, and progressive splinter groups around a broadly liberal standard. This projected amalgam of fractured pieces along the center-left would have to be powerful enough to serve not as the "third force" of which some of its own advocates too modestly speak but as the full coequal of the conservative camp, one that would be capable of governing Japan and holding the country to its postwar democratic heritage.

There are several reasons why this remains a daunting challenge as of 2002. One is the difficulty of making liberal ideals and slogans look hardheaded to an electorate long willing to entrust its interests to more authoritarian leadership as long as it produces results. Learning the hard way, the DPJ raised its initial banner of "comradely friendship" *(yuai)*, rather like the French *fraternité,* only to have former prime minister Yasuhiro Nakasone dismiss it with true New Old Rightish disdain as "soft ice cream."

Another need is for leaders who are not only articulate and committed to liberal principles but also endowed with enough popular appeal and political avoirdupois to inspire public confidence and forge a solid new electoral base. Finally, and most critically, they will have to override the pull not only of conservative versus socialist heritages but even more so their divisive residues of former intra-LDP factional ties and intrasocialist sectarian identities.

All of Japan's liberal leaders today have displayed our previously noted historical linkage of domestic liberalism with cosmopolitanism in foreign affairs. Four of the five most typical figures below have served as prefectural governors while coming relatively late to national politics. That background has left them impatient with Tokyo's central bureaucracy, less beholden to the crony loyalties of the old Diet factions, and possessed of a refreshing sophistication and independence of mind. The fifth (Hatoyama), the heir to an old parliamentary family, comes by the same mental temper by way of personal wealth and an academic career he reluctantly abandoned to carry on the political dynasty. All five, in short, have a certain take-it-or-leave-it aplomb that disdains the frantic, craven attachment to power and factional bosses still driving the old politics of Japan. By refusing to push new ideas by old methods in the Ozawa style, however, they do forfeit some of the practical leverage needed to build a new power base.

Prime Minister Morihiro Hosokawa, the urbane pied piper who led all the rebels out of the LDP in 1993, had been governor of Kumamoto prefecture, where he never tired of telling how he had to get approval from Tokyo's Ministry of Transport just to get a local bus stop moved a hundred yards down the road. A scion of one of Japan's ancient aristocratic families, he had the courage while in office to proclaim publicly that he viewed World War II as a war of aggression on the part of Japan. This was all the more plucky for the elder brother of the grandson by adoption of Fumimaro Konoe, Japan's prime minister until shortly before Pearl Harbor, who was executed as a class-A war criminal. Swept out of politics in 1994 by a minor implication in the LDP's unraveling money scandals, Hosokawa has since become an articulate voice for reducing the U.S. military presence in Japan while maintaining the security alliance.

The small Sakigake Party, founded by the earnestly avuncular Masayoshi Takemura, represented the quintessential liberal force between 1993 and 1998 with its small band of younger reformers who were bound, Western-style, by shared political principles rather than by the traditional mathematics of factional power jockeying. The party served as the fount of reformist ideas on administrative transparency and democratic accountability, and its stress on the control of government from below mocked the special pleading for bureaucratically led reform from above that had characterized conservative thinking from Nakasone in the 1980s to Ozawa and Hashimoto in the early and late 1990s. While serving as the LDP governor of Shiga prefecture, Takemura had personally launched wide-ranging sister-state ties with Michigan, and in his 1994 book, *Chiisakutomo Kirari to Hikaru Kuni Nihon* (Though it be small, a brightly shining nation of Japan), defined a foreign policy based on peace and prosperity at home. Derided by the nationalists, this was Takemura's eloquent warning against the costs of relaunching Japan's great-power hubris.

Naoto Kan, cofounder of the Democratic Party of Japan in 1996, progressed from earlier socialist ties through the Sakigake to the DPJ. Perhaps the most popular politician in Japan during the 1990s, the telegenic Kan became a public hero while minister of public health and welfare by rigorously pursuing his own bureaucrats' cover-up of their failure to stop the supply of untreated AIDS-tainted plasma to hemophiliacs, despite their awareness of the danger and the availability of properly treated stocks (mainly from abroad). Here Kan was acting out—with unprecedented firmness and political courage for a cabinet minister—the very principles of democratic accountability and respect for individual rights that lay at the heart of Sakigake and DPJ liberalism. When his conservative enemies and the media chose to make an issue of the sort of extramarital affair normally permitted to pass in silence for Japanese politicians, Kan handed over the presidency of the DPJ to his cofounder, Yukio Hatoyama, and stepped down to head the party's policy research committee.

Representing the breadth of the DPJ grouping as of 2000 were its president, Hatoyama, a renegade from the LDP, and its vice president, Takahiro Yokomichi, who for years had been a stalwart of the old JSP—the young prince of the socialists, no less—before returning home to become governor of Japan's large northern island of Hokkaido. The still boyish-looking Yukio Hatoyama, who holds a Ph.D. from Stanford University in engineering, has yet to achieve the status of a political heavyweight but carries impressive family credentials as son of the former LDP foreign minister Iichiro Hatoyama and grandson of Prime Minister Ichiro Hatoyama (1954–56), the main conservative rival of Yoshida Shigeru during the 1950s. Yokomichi, who exudes a certain no-nonsense gravitas, is intellectually typical of those former socialists who have broken with the old Marxist obsessions to find fresh outlets for their ideals in progressive citizens' movements and participation in a broader liberal agenda.

As Japan's major opposition party, the DPJ's excellent showing in the June 2000 election for the Lower House, when it surged from 95 to 125 seats (as the LDP dropped from 271 to 229), promised a new lease on life for this pragmatically minded liberal amalgam heading into the new decade. When the rock-star popularity of Prime Minister Koizumi led the LDP to a fresh surge in the July 2001 elections for the Upper House, however, even well-wishers of the Democratic Party had to admit that it might soon become little more than a refugee camp for disgruntled but mutually incompatible defectors from other parties. That was a bit too pessimistic, but in early 2002 there were hints even of a possible tactical rapprochement with Ichiro Ozawa, the old nemesis to the right, in order to drive the LDP from power as Prime Minister Koizumi's ratings started to slip in the polls.

* * *

Since this is a book about American perceptions, it is sad to record here how ignorant Tokyo's foreign press remains of the national burden of authoritarian psychology that Japanese liberals are still trying to break down. Confusing a healthy concern about the past in order to surmount it with a morbid clinging to bygones, too many Western journalists start to fidget when Japan's liberals try to explain historical contexts. Conversely, with gargantuan irony and naïveté, foreign observers inadvertently throw the game to the right-wing crowd—the real stick-in-the-muds—whenever they hail them as the future-oriented forces of Japan who have put the past behind them. In fact, it is exactly the reverse.

Indeed, it was disappointing to see so few of our own correspondents at the Foreign Correspondents Club of Japan on 4 February 2000 when Yukio Hatoyama appeared at a press luncheon to explain the DPJ's boycott of the Diet budget proceedings to protest the majority's railroading of the law to reduce proportional representation. Particularly disturbing to me was the impatience (hostility, even) with which so many of the foreign questioners brushed off his central purpose of illuminating the persistent undemocratic political mentality of so many Japanese conservatives, as evidenced by the Diet steamroller that had provoked the boycott. Some of the foreign journalists heatedly chided him for not having presented his specific recommendations for the Japanese economy. That was not at all the advertised subject of his luncheon address, but it often seems the only thing U.S. editors back home really care about. Pressing on with his message, Hatoyama put his finger on the very nub of the difficulties Japanese liberals face today:

> Democracy does not exist in Japan. The function of the Diet is completely paralyzed. . . . I well understand that those of you who come from the advanced nations have difficulty in understanding the tactics that we in the opposition have adopted. That is because those of you from abroad possess a history of having won democracy for yourselves. Our democracy is at the level of something learned from textbooks; we do not have a history of truly having won it for ourselves. It is precisely because we have mistaken the mere form of democracy for its actual achievement that the morals of our economy and social structure have become so completely corrupted. It is from our sense of crisis about this that we have taken action as the opposition.[1]

Behind the mental restlessness of Hatoyama's questioners lay the triumphalistic, universalistic, economy-obsessed American mind at the end of the century—our assumption that the Japanese political mind works pretty much like ours, and that Japanese history, for all practical calculations, started about ten years ago.

The Japanese Left and the Nub of Civil Courage

Longer historical memories are essential here, and not only because of the regressive sociopolitical mentalities that Japan's centrist liberals have always had to confront. Looking further to the left, we also need to appreciate the critical role that so many of Japan's committed leftists— including their more radical elements—have played in nourishing such civil courage as one finds today in Japan's still nascent civil society. Admittedly, the Japanese left has not always made it easy for Americans to see them as something more than a pesky political "lite."

It seems almost a time warp ago when I stood on the roof of a small office building at the south end of Hibiya Park in October 1971 with Dana Bullen, then foreign editor of the now defunct *Washington Star*. We were there to observe the last mass violent demonstration of Japan's late-1960s student radicals against the Vietnam War. Dana was certain the lunge through the police lines would come at the southwest corner of Tokyo's mini–Central Park, heading for the government ministries.

Suddenly a ball of orange flame went up through the trees in the middle of the park as the rioters—helmeted, masked, and armed with staves and anything loose that would fly—moved from their assembly point at the outdoor concert shell to set fire to a quaint and beloved relic of Meiji-period architecture, the ramshackle old wooden Matsumoto-Ro, a French restaurant. They then attacked in what had seemed the least likely direction—straight out the east exit into the police cordons lined up in front of the Imperial Hotel, torching the well-known flower shop at the gate. The old gent in charge of the store died on the spot, not from the flames but of a heart attack. As the wind shifted clouds of tear gas our way, Dana and I banged in vain on the secured doors of the Imperial, then ran several blocks through the deserted streets of central Tokyo to the Foreign Correspondents Club of Japan, ducking into side alleys as Japan's gendarmes rolled their hissing canisters of tear gas down the pavement at retreating knots of rioters.

To me, after that evening, anything to the right of center in political Japan looked reasonable and good.

Unfortunately for the growth of political liberalism, Japan's postwar ideological pattern has been the unhappy one of mutually repelling opposites. The Japanese nationalistic right would not have become as intellectually respectable as it is today had it not been able to ride the broader conservative mood that set in during the 1970s in reaction to the persistent confrontationalism (and, on the fringe, violence) of the left during the 1960s. Conversely, given the intellectual flabbiness in Japan of the political center—the traditional locus of democratic and liberal ideas in most countries—the most articulate and courageous checks on the unreconstructed right since the war have had to come, too exclusively, from the ideological left.

Here, as with the right, we can draw a line between a larger liberal element that has been genuinely committed to individual rights and democratic institutions and a smaller contingent animated by essentially authoritarian views. The latter were historically represented from the 1920s to the 1970s by the hard-core socioeconomic Marxism plus politico-revolutionary Leninism of the Communists and left-wing socialists, and later by the more radical of the erstwhile New Left sectarians of the late 1960s. Today they hardly count in the arena of political ideas anymore—just as in Europe. Indeed, one almost misses their old function as an intellectual acid on the bland alkalis of the center or the hard cold metal of Japan's right.

What should be stirring the gray cells of American leaders and Asia hands today is, therefore, the imaginative reengagement of Japan's mod-

erate left—a sector traditionally short on jet-setting defense intellectuals. On the party-political side these include people who have joined the
DPJ, such as the former socialist governor Yokomichi, or the recent
SDPJ head, Takako Doi (a nonadvertised Protestant Christian), who led
her Socialists during their recent "cohabitation" with Yutaro Hashimoto's
rump LDP. In terms of their intellectual lineages, they would encompass assorted left-wing progressives and even radicals (as they would
have been labeled in a more ideological decade), together with what I
would call the heirs and survivors of the old philosophical or "modernization" Marxists. Mostly in academe, these were thinkers from the late
1940s to the 1960s who were attracted to Marxism mainly as a vehicle
leading to Western-style rationalism and modernity and as a tool for
rejecting the hoary irrationalism of Japan's prewar emperor-centered,
family-state orthodoxy.

Indeed, in postwar Japan, it has been the left that has most consistently defended the peace constitution; has at least tried to resist the
gradual erosion of some of the democratic reforms of the occupation
(for example, in education or workers' rights); has done the most to
deplore the racist-chauvinist rhetoric of right-wing politicians; has fought
the hardest for justice in what we today would call individual human
rights cases; has put itself out for the rights of minorities and foreigners
in Japan; and has—at the level of its professed ideals, at least—shown
itself the most willing to contemplate a Japan open to the world, eschewing military adventurism, and refocusing its economic energies on
the improvement of the daily life of its own people.

All these the postwar Japanese left has offered—but with a difference that was to limit its electoral growth at home and inhibit its ties
with the Western democracies. That difference was the attraction of so
many left-wingers to Marxist-Leninist dogmatism—an intellectual
framework spun to fine profusion in a Japanese hothouse where they
had no real contact with Communism and nourished by the irresponsi-
bility of being permanently out of power at the national level.

Specifically, the Communist and left-wing socialist forces from the
late 1940s through the 1960s were still talking of an unfinished revolution, had not clearly committed themselves to the continuation of parliamentary democracy should they win at the ballot box, were uniformly
against the U.S.-Japan security treaty, and consistently rooted for the
Soviet Union, China, North Korea, and North Vietnam in the Cold War.
Although never allowed to take power in the Diet by the Japanese elec-

torate, they often ran the larger cities, including Tokyo and Yokohama, where they were popular with a broad stratum of citizens as a protest vote against the smugness—and occasional reactionary flashes—of the ruling conservatives. Paralleling the ideological struggle for Western Europe during the late 1940s and 1950s (and causing similar distress to American policy makers at the time), these hard-left notions achieved a certain fashionable vogue among a much larger number of non-Marxist, essentially liberal members of the Japanese intelligentsia—persons enjoying a wide influence in the universities and elite journals, who continued to find their cachet in being "of the left."

Japan's postwar left argued that their country had done nothing correctly before the Pacific War—a perspective in which they had been enthusiastically encouraged by the occupying Allies. Aggression, atrocities, militarism, imperial autocracy, the greedy *zaibatsu*—a bloody mess, all of it, and it all had to go. Fine by us. But precious little had gone well after the war, either, they intoned, least of all the obnoxious new link to American capitalist imperialism. Not so fine by us.

Typical of the nonauthoritarian intellectual left was Japan's leading postwar political theorist, Professor Masao Maruyama of Tokyo University. Maruyama had drawn variously on Marxist theory, Weberian sociology, and his own personal experience of the militarist boot to plumb the political pathology of Japan's prewar fascism and militarism. He produced a classic body of work that, by confronting the Japanese with the darker roots of their immediate past, has probably been a powerful unseen force in preventing its repetition. The liberal-minded Maruyama, however, was one of those self-styled progressives who were unenthusiastic about the American agenda in Asia and were willing to give the Asian Communists the benefit of the doubt as to being more genuine modernizers than their pro-American nationalist rivals in China, Korea, and Vietnam. In his view, Asian Communists were fast-trackers who could be forgiven for cutting democratic and humanistic corners in order to liberate their traditional societies from the fetters of premodern values.

Maruyama's focus was more on the nurturing of a subjective democratic consciousness among a developing nation's people than on an objective faithfulness to democratic institutions and processes transplanted from the West. That was the key conceptual point on which he found himself either applauded or condemned. Maruyama's ultimate ideal for Japan was a Western-style civil society with a responsible citizens' democracy. His absolute precondition for that, however, lay in a transformation of the old values, and on that count he gave the mainland Communist powers a higher score than he did his own country, which he faulted for its carryover of unreconstructed paternalistic, personalistic, and submissive values from the prewar era.[2] This, precisely, was what Yukio Hatoyama and his colleagues in the DPJ were concerned about when they boycotted the Diet budget deliberations in early 2000— the very same sociopolitical psychology that continues to hold back genuine political and economic reform in Japan at the start of the twenty-first century.

The hard-core left, meanwhile, remained divided over one of those seemingly arcane yet politically portentous theoretical disputes that have dogged the steps of Marxism ever since its inception. This particular one dated all the way back to the early 1930s and concerned the historical interpretation of Japan's modernization process. On one side of the split, the Japan Communist Party (JCP) had argued that Meiji Japan (1868–1912) simply transferred the old feudal repressions of the Tokugawa period (1600–1867) to a devilishly efficient, superficially modernized new autocracy without even passing through the preliminary bourgeois stage of revolution prescribed by Marx. Everything, therefore, was rotten and had to go: the emperor system, the oppressive capitalist economy, the facade of parliamentary democracy, and now— as a postwar addendum to that lingering prewar orthodoxy—the Americans, the archenemy, who were sitting on the lid to keep it from blowing off creatively.

Taking the opposing view was the left wing of the post-1955 Japan Socialist Party (JSP), the heir to the prewar Farmer-Labor ideologues with their more positive interpretation of the Meiji Restoration. According to them, the destruction of the old Tokugawa shogunate in 1867–68 had the markings of a typical European-style bourgeois revolution in which lower-ranked samurai and nascent capitalists had joined hands to overthrow feudalism—a perspective popularized in the English language by the Canadian scholar-diplomat E. H. Norman.[3] It had been a creaky bourgeois revolution at best, however, one that had left much undone in the area of democratic values and institutions. And that agenda had been delayed, so the postwar Marxian socialists insisted, first by Japan's militaristic binge and now by its subservience to American Cold War objectives—although to them it was Japanese capitalism that was the main enemy. Nevertheless, they hoped that a mass movement of left-wing parties, labor unions, students, and intellectuals would suffice to take over the capitalist state peacefully through the ballot box to place Japan on the road to the socialist, neutralist utopia. In the meantime, agitation to hasten that day was essential.

From 1960, however, this great leftist force began its slow retreat as Japan turned away from the turmoil generated in that watershed year by the protracted, violence-prone coal miners strike at Miike in Kyushu and by the tumultuous demonstrations in Tokyo against President Eisenhower's visit and the revision of the security treaty. That year saw the cresting of militant unionism and of popularly validated student power, as the nation picked itself up again and refocused its energies on Prime Minister Hayato Ikeda's (1960–64) bread-and-butter goal of income-doubling economic growth. In 1960, too, the right-wing socialists broke away from the JSP to establish their small but intellectually fertile Democratic Socialist Party (DSP), drawing their ideological lineage more from British Fabianism and Christian Socialism than from the German or Russian variants of Marxism, and allying themselves with the more moderate and pro-American of the two great labor federations.

As the decade progressed, a variety of organized challenges were launched to the left-wing dominance of Japan's intelligentsia. Among the influential opinion monthlies, new journals such as *Jiyu, Shokun,* and *Seiron* were launched to stake out anti-Marxist turf ranging from center to right. Self-styled "realists" such as Shinkichi Eto and Yonosuke Nagai emerged in the academic field of international relations to challenge the JSP's utopianist doctrine of "unarmed neutrality" and to ponder strategic questions in dry, nonidealist, think-tank terms.

Starting with the DSP-connected Japan Cultural Forum (Nihon Bunka Foramu) and the center-to-right Japan Cultural Congress (Nihon Bunka Kaigi), educators, authors, artists, bureaucrats, and Keynesian economists took to the public journals with unaccustomed boldness, so that by the time of the antiwar demonstrations and violent New Leftish campus upheavals of the late 1960s, there was a powerful contingent of moderate proestablishment intellectuals in place to reaffirm the ruling Liberal Democratic Party's emphasis on political stability, rapid economic growth, and support for U.S. foreign policy. Finally, with the automatic extension of the security treaty in 1970, the reversion of Okinawa in 1972, America's resumption of relations with China, the winding down of the Vietnam War, and Japan's march to economic superpowerdom, the left found itself shorn of its most critical issues.

These anti-Marxist intellectual forces from the 1960s onward were characterized in the West as "liberals." Indeed, many of them were, including most of the democratic socialists and moderate conservatives, both of whom were committed to Japan's non-nationalistic postwar democracy. Inevitably, however, they were joined in the antileftist cause by those more reactionary and unreservedly nationalistic ideologues of the New Old Right who would become increasingly outspoken over the following decades. And as the object of their concern shifted from the threat of the radical left to the annoyances of American trade pressures and the challenges of newfound economic power, some of old moderate leftists in the DSP and elsewhere showed themselves more hawkish than the LDP center on security issues and drifting toward the cultural nationalism of the New Old Right.

It was a phenomenon reminiscent of the 1930s and a seemingly intractable dilemma for would-be principled progressives in Japan—the difficulty of avoiding the Scylla of bitter confrontationalism on the left without being sucked into the Charybdis of intellectual co-optation by the right.

* * *

For decades the Japanese left opposed America's Cold War containment policies in Asia, partly out of wishful thinking about Communism but largely because the United States had tied itself so closely to what they saw as the less regenerate and more oppressive forces in their own country. They were a constant headache for the American embassy in Tokyo, but behind what they decried and anguished over as American "adventurism" in the region loomed the specter of Japan's own fateful misadventure on the Asian continent and its painful recoil onto their own soil in 1945. From the standpoint of geopolitical realism, of course, the United States probably had few other practical choices during the heyday of Stalinist and Maoist influence in the region. By ignoring the liberal motivation behind America's commitment to the defense of non-Communist Asia, and by tacking their ideological colors so simplistically to the pole of the Communist bloc, Japan's postwar leftists brought upon themselves the distrust, if not the contempt, of many Americans and Europeans. At worst, we viewed them as the dupes of world Communism; at best, as yet another instance of "airy-fairy socialism"—as Anthony Crosland (the British Labour Party theorist who had recently served as Minister of Education in the first Harold Wilson cabinet) put it to me in Tokyo in 1972.

A decade, however, has passed since the end of the Cold War, and a socialist prime minister (Tomiichi Murayama) has .bestowed his blessing on the security treaty. It is now time for America's public pundits and policy makers to develop a more sympathetic grasp of the intellectual complexities of postwar Japan and to reexplore relations with all Japanese who share our basic liberal ideals. As we do so, we should bear in mind that the very stridency of the postwar left may well have been a precondition, faute de mieux, for the development of a critical and boldly dissenting intelligence—a fragile flower, even today, in Japan's aridly conformist social soil.

Too often, Japan's postwar leftists fell into their own anti-establishmentarian orthodoxy. But at least they helped to hold ground against the old spit-and-polish obedience to the state and against carryovers of bureaucratic high-handedness and secretiveness beyond the imagination of persons raised in the liberal traditions of the West. The outstanding example of what I have in mind here is Professor Saburo Ienaga, who for decades waged largely quixotic battles in the courts against the watering down of wartime aggression and atrocities in Japan's officially authorized school textbooks. Despite all their clichés about monopoly capitalism, American imperialism, and the socialist paradise, we owe these old Marxist Cassandras a debt of gratitude for remaining the most trenchant critics of Japanese militarism, fascism, and expansionism, and—in a country prone to historical amnesia—for refusing to redefine the Nanking Massacre as a Sunday afternoon picnic.

In short, the intellectual challenge to American observers, and to U.S. conservatives in particular, is to see beyond the congenial but limited area of overlap on defense and deregulatory issues to the full panoply of politically and culturally regressive positions represented by Japan's New Old Right—and, by the same token, to perceive and encourage the emergence of more humane, individualistic, and cosmopolitan values and of civil courage, wherever they may turn up on Japan's shifting political spectrum, engaging in particular the remnants of the now disintegrated left.

By "civil courage" I mean, of course, the readiness of the individual or of small-scale citizens' groups to place wealth, status, and even personal safety, if need be, on the line against the authority of the state. It is the perceived weakness of such individual civil courage, more than anything else, that continues to fuel the doubt or distrust of others toward Japan. The fear abides that, in a real crunch, the reasonable and well-intentioned Japanese once again will fail to stand up, even to risk their lives (as the spunkier Koreans and Filipinos recently did), against the excesses of their unreasonable and overweening compatriots. It is a tall order in any society to gird moral conscience and political principle, clearly stated, with physical pluck. Japan has yet to produce its Benigno Aquino or its Kim Dae Jung.

And that brings us to our American misreadings of Japan's political and cultural mentalities outward, toward Asia.

CHAPTER FIVE

Pan-Asianism
Behind the Bromides of East-West Bridging

Is Japan, having drawn its last drop of cultural strength from the West, about to turn its back and abscond with Asia?

Japanese attitudes toward its neighbors will, of course, be heavily affected by the choices covered in our first four chapters. Will Tokyo genuinely open up to globalized free trade, or will it work even harder toward economic hegemony in Asia? Will the strain of close ties to America end with a strategic break? Will an inward-looking nationalism or a more cosmopolitan liberalism win in the contest of political ideas?

On the one hand, American foreign policy assumes that the Japanese will actively promote our agenda of free trade and democracy in Asia, functioning as our junior partner. At the other extreme, some Americans have waxed mystical about the imminent reabsorption of Japan into the welcoming mother womb of Asia. Or there may be something in between—not a judicious cultural compromise, but a messy intellectual muddle. Which is why we need to take a look at Japan's reviving, but poorly understood, pan-Asianism.

Unfortunately we have very few ideological clues from the last five decades to suggest how the Japanese mentality on Asia might develop in the post–Cold War world. Following the collapse and total discrediting of their Asian adventure in World War II, the Japanese after 1945 threw themselves on the West and preferred to stop thinking about Asia altogether—except as an economic opportunity. Since the war, accordingly, very little systematic effort has been made to develop fresh intellectual formulas for a constructive Japanese reengagement with the new Asia. Anti-imperialism, the rallying cry of Japan's postwar left, was too dogmatically Leninist and past-oriented to lay out a positive, forward-looking path. By default, then—and ever so ironically in our high-tech age—that has left the fusty old prewar ideology of pan-Asianism as the richest repository of developed cultural and philosophical ideas for Japan's relationship to its regional neighbors.

Japan's flirtations with pan-Asianist ideology have always gone hand in hand with rising nationalism at home. Indeed, Japanese pan-Asianism has been little more than an extension of domestic chauvinism. Feeding on xenophobia toward the West, and manipulative toward Asia, it has seldom gone beyond being an internal monologue in the Japanese mind and has developed very few tangible human or intellectual ties to the rest of Asia. Yet its historical consequences in the prewar period were catastrophic.

The question today is whether the recent ripples of a reawakened pan-Asianism portend a major wave or just a confused fretting of the waters as Japan sorts out its proper orientation in the post–Cold War international system. The signs of a possible revival are undoubtedly there. The basic premises, language, and frames of reference of Japan's cultural philosophy for the old Co-Prosperity Sphere seem alive and well today among a growing number of government, media, and intellectual voices, although considerably toned down. Japan's Asian neighbors still smart from wartime injuries for which Japanese leaders refuse to make the sort of emotionally convincing amends that their German counterparts have long since undertaken toward Israel and Poland. Nevertheless, there were signs from the early 1990s that Japan intended once again to speak up for Asia, a stance Tokyo made explicit before and at the July 2000 G-8 summit, which it hosted in Kyushu and Okinawa. And with the financial crisis at the end of the 1990s, it is now clear that certain Asian governments are increasingly ready to welcome Japan's leadership vis-à-vis the United States, at least on market-opening issues.

Japan's Autistic Pan-Asianism

One of the central tenets of prewar ultranationalism was Japan's destiny, as the first non-Western nation to modernize, to lead the rest of Asia and—having learned from Europe and America—to serve as a cultural bridge between East and West. For years after the surrender, barely a peep was heard of that old self-appointed mission as postwar Japan repeated the Meiji period's embarrassed flight from poor and fumbling Asian relatives and sought political and cultural alignment with the West, this time with a full seat at the rich nations' club, symbolized early on by the OECD, the G-7 summits, and the Trilateral Commission. Culminating in the successful Sapporo Winter Olympics of 1972, the government had long promoted an image-formation campaign of Japan as "an industrial country with snowfall"—posters, for example, showing high-speed bullet trains streaking against a snow-blanketed panorama of Mt. Fuji. The subliminal intent of this PR was to undermine the frequent Western misconception of Japan as a semitropical, and therefore less developed, country.

Times have changed now, and drastically, with the end of the Cold War, the advancing economic integration of East and Southeast Asia through trade and investment, and Japan's gradual emotional estrangement from the United States. Americans who talk to Japan need to be especially attuned to the nuances and implications of a reviving pan-Asianism, the prewar version of which was virulently hostile toward the West and essentially autistic with respect to Asian neighbors, whom Japan simply sought to incorporate into a vertical trust—a hierarchical downward expansion, so to speak, of its own self.

To what extent is Japan actually adding a new intellectual and ideological dimension to the economic Co-Prosperity Sphere it so dramatically resurrected from the 1970s onward? Geocultural seers in the West have long predicted the "return" of Japan to its Asian roots, and we now find many Japanese announcing the "re-Asianization" of their country. Tokyo's response to the Asian financial crisis of the late 1990s suggests that it may now be less reluctant to proclaim itself the ideological leader of a momentarily discredited bunch of losers. So we may soon find the pan-Asian theme reinvigorated, either positively, in celebration of a quick regional recovery—especially if the American economy starts to slip—or negatively, as a common bond of anti-Western resentment if the crisis continues too painfully for too long.

Any further erosion of the intellectual framework of Western rationalism that dominated Japan's postwar ideological spectrum will give a powerful boost to that trend. Under the old, bifurcated political map of 1955–93 both camps were outwardly hitched to Western lodestars—the conservatives to American democracy, security ties, and anti-Communism, and the socialists to European Marxism and the U.S.-sponsored

peace constitution. That map now lies in tatters. In its place (and especially if things go poorly with America) we may possibly see an implo-
sion of formerly antagonistic ideological forces around a new consensus
nationalism, one that could bring pressures to switch Japan's national
purpose and cultural orientation away from the West toward Asia.

As Japanese enthusiasts for a warmed-over pan-Asianism began tugging at the tillers of national self-definition and cultural diplomacy during the economically heady 1980s, the world noted some high swells of
touchiness and disdain for the now overtaken West together with a froth
of magisterial vade mecums for Asians still bobbing in Japan's wake.
One can only hope that, given the new strength and self-esteem of the
other Asian peoples, Japan's dependence on a transnational postindustrial
civilization, and the humbling experience of its own financial crisis,
Tokyo will not repeat that sort of hubris, and that the Japanese people
will find their way to a cultural dialogue with Asia that is less fixated on
hierarchical power relationships, less dichotomous about East versus
West, and more in keeping with their genuinely global needs and responsibilities.

Regrettably, we recently have been witnessing the latest replay of an
unproductive, six-part cycle that Japan has yet to break out of. In the
opening bars, Tokyo's leaders dissociate themselves from a "backward
Asia," seeking to emulate and join the "advanced West"; next, this exercise in impersonation provokes a nationalistic reaction at home and
Western condescension abroad; in the third movement Japan's intellectuals and statesmen then proudly expound the singularity of their country and its divergence from the West; fourth, their Western counterparts
avidly concur that, indeed, Japan *is* different; fifth, Japan then turns
emotionally and ideologically to a condescending and largely unsolic-
ited "leadership" of Asia and to a resentful anti-Westernism; finally,
that runs into a dead end, so it's da capo, all over again.

One macrocycle ran from the forced-march Westernization of the
1870s to the traditionalist counterthrusts and xenophobia of the 1880s
and 1890s and then through a series of perceived rejections by the West
in the 1920s—Britain dropping its alliance in 1922 and America slamming the door on Japanese immigration in 1924—to the dalliance with
"Greater East Asia" during the 1930s and World War II.

Today we are well into stage five in a microcycle prompted by trade
issues and spanning the past three decades. This cycle began with Tokyo promising Western-style economic behavior but pleading for time.

As the United States and Europe began to lose patience and as domestic resistance built up in Japan in the 1970s, Japanese intellectuals spun their theories of "uniqueness" to justify special treatment for their country. But when European and American revisionist writers in the late 1980s joined this exploration of Japanese dissimilarity, Tokyo cried foul and complained of Western cultural absolutism. The upshot, from the early 1990s, was a Japan tuning in once again to the siren song of "Asian values"—an expansion of the earlier "uniqueness" gambit—as a common regional shield against further U.S. trade and financial pressures.

In a Japanese poll in 1994, 60 percent thought their country should place equal emphasis on Asia and the West (the United States and Europe), with only 6 percent favoring the West as opposed to 28 percent favoring a tilt toward Asia.[1] This nearly two-thirds vote for cutting loose, with Asia-firsters approaching one-third, represented a major shift away from the westward-looking postwar orthodoxy and is a trend that is likely to continue.

By the turn of the century, against a backlog of diplomatic annoyances with Beijing, Japanese polled chose the United States over China 49 percent to 31 percent as the country more important for Japan politically in the future. The exact 43-to-43 percent split as to which country was more important for Japan economically, however, suggested where the more compelling long-term attachments probably lay.[2] Indeed in the mid-1990s, when Japan's media were touting an alleged clash between Asian and Western values and dwelling with some relish on the Clinton administration's failed pressures for human rights in China and numerical targets for Japan trade, cooler heads had to warn that the security, trade, and environmental challenges in the region could hardly be met without a continued U.S. presence—and that a fairer break on economic access would be the chief incentive for that.

In the 1994 survey over two-thirds of the Japanese between the ages of twenty and forty who were queried judged their country to be "disliked" by other Asians—an implicit admission of the long, steep road ahead. By 1996 territorial disputes over offshore islands had pushed China and Korea down again in the polls, and any hint of military adventurism from North Korea or China tends to draw the Japanese back toward their American security blanket. Nevertheless, Japanese who a decade or so ago could not have cared less what other Asians really thought of them now grasp eagerly at any signs of their growing popularity in the region, especially in the nonthreatening field of popular culture, where the appeal of Pokémon, karaoke, and Nintendo seems to be authentic.

"Asia Now Simply Adores *[daisuki]* Japan" read the enormous characters splashed across a third of the hyped-up cover for the Japanese-language edition of *Newsweek* for 17 November 1999. Featuring camera shots of ecstatic young Asian fans of the women's vocal duo Puffy, Japan-chic women's wear selling in Taiwan, and young Chinese males gyrating at a dance-simulation arcade in Hong Kong, the editors asked why one and a half million Asians were now learning the Japanese language. "Because Western ways are out of date. Japan now leads the van, because Japan's [ways] are awfully cute *[kawaii]*," came the reply from a young Chinese woman in Hong Kong, her hair in a ponytail and a "Kitty-chan" bag on her arm. And hip young Japanese were repaying the compliment by taking an interest in contemporary Asian artists, so the boosters gushed on. *Newsweek*'s English-language U.S. and Asian editions carried but a fraction of the text and photos in brief noncover stories.

Pan-Asianism Revisited

Japan's past periods of identification with Asia have typically expressed themselves in grandiose, holistic, pan-Asianist terms—more reminiscent of America's postwar appointment of itself as defender of "Western civilization" against the Stalinist menace than of the quiet, steady flows that defined our earlier view of cultural relations across the Atlantic.

Japan's recurrent pan-Asianist paradigm, simply expressed, is that of two posts and a lintel. On one side is a solidified Asia, much put upon and brimming with resentment; on the other, an equally monistic but predatory West; and 'twixt the twain a cultural gap spanned and spannable only by Japan, which towers above the Orient and serves as its cultural spokesman to the Occident. The Japanese sense of draconian alternatives was first honed by the early Meiji-period slogans of "Escape from Asia" *(datsu-A)* and "Joining Europe [the West]" *(nyu-O)*—terms that are still very much in use along with their increasingly fashionable inversions, *datsu-O* and *nyu-A*—while the visual finality of their Chinese ideograms, like red-or-green traffic lights, further impedes the conceptualization of more nuanced, intermediate choices.

Geographically speaking, although Japan's economic power is now felt throughout the Asian continent, the psychologically intimate Asia of the Japanese mind encompasses mainly China, Korea, and Southeast Asia, closely fitting the area marked in wartime ideology for the Greater East Asia Co-Prosperity Sphere. Leaving out the "white" nations of Australia and New Zealand (despite strong economic links), as well as the Indian and other peoples of South Asia (despite ancient cultural ties), these boundaries betray a natural but powerful fellow-Mongolian racial consciousness. Even in the high-demand labor market of the 1980s, the Japanese government went to arduous extremes to repatriate Malaysian and Pakistani foreign workers and replace them with ethnic Japanese from faraway places such as Brazil and Peru. This suggests—very sadly—that in any extended encounter with actual Asian people, the pervasive underbrush of ethnocentric Japanism may once again strangle the budding shoots of pan-Asian brotherhood.

Historically, Japan's past flings with pan-Asianism have been marred by the failure to assume a more egalitarian posture toward the rest of Asia, by hyperbolic rejections of the West, and by the sterility of a strictly intra-Japanese monologue. Although certain Japanese liberals from the 1880s to the 1990s have been able to envision the nonexploitative nurturing of an Asian comity of nations, Japanese nationalism has always intruded in the end to provoke bitter anti-Japanese nationalism elsewhere, as the Janus face of worship-the-West and eschew-the-East simply switches its Asian mask from one of rejection to that of imperious orchestration. One recent expression of this, of course, has been the "flying geese" development model, for which Tokyo, at least, assumes a permanent Japanese lead. Even the selling of the Pacific War and the old Co-Prosperity Sphere as a struggle for the liberation of Asia did not come into full diplomatic play until the severe military setbacks of 1943, the nation's war aims until then having been couched in terms of Japan's own self-defense and resource needs—the expansion of its own empire.

Too many Japanese intellectuals still find it difficult to reenter Asia enthusiastically without simultaneously denigrating the West, or to celebrate the rise and creativity of their own region without invoking Occidental decline. The frequent inflation of Western cultural threats is suggested by the odd way in which many Japanese cultural nationalists still put the argument in terms of resisting Christianity—a force that has achieved less than 1 percent penetration in Japan and has long been on the defensive in a secularizing West. In his 1976 call for a return to Buddhism, for example, philosopher Takeshi Umehara characterized Christianity as a "bloodstained" religion and its civilization as one of power, assault, and combativeness. Right-wing publicist Hideaki Kase complained to foreign journalists in 1988 of a century's onslaught by Christianity on Japan. And political scientist Yonosuke Nagai in 1994 traced the U.S. containment of Communism to the antiheterodox impulses of Christian theology.[3] What all this hides is probably less concern about Christian religion, in which Japan has very little interest, than vexation with the pressure placed on traditional values by Western rationalism and by industrial society itself. It recalls the yearning of Japan's prewar ideologues for "overcoming modernity" *(kindai no kokufuku)*.

Pan-Asianist ideology in Japan, short on input or feedback from other Asians, has to date served mainly as an expression of cultural nationalism at home. One can only hope that the old reflexes may simply prove to be transitional, as the current surge in student, arts, and sports exchanges, in two-way travel, in new Asian-language electives, and in prime-time TV programming on everything from Tibetan burial customs to train rides in northern Burma gradually transforms Asia from a mere slogan into a compelling human reality. Too often, though, the hype has grated with its excessive prearrangement, as in Fuji Television's pan-Asian singing contests on a recently concluded late-night show called *Ajia Bagus*—"Asia Is Great" in standard Malay/Indonesian. Here, from 1992 to 2000, young Asians in traditional dress singing their native songs were cheered along in English—the only language they all understood—by breathlessly bilingual emcees, who then turned to analyze it all for the television audience in Japanese.

More serious conceptual barriers to the real Asia persist, unfortunately, in Japan's approach to regional cultural diplomacy, in its rather strained advocacy of allegedly shared values, and in its legacy of wartime bitterness.

The old pan-Asianist touch was back again with the cultural policy recommendations for Northeast and Southeast Asia presented at the Second Asia Pacific Conference of the Foundation for Advanced Information and Research (FAIR) in May 1991, following a year's preparation by a panel of scholars under the aegis of the Ministries of Finance and Foreign Affairs. As their sole Western commentator, I was struck by the emphasis on creating a new "organic cultural sphere." This appeal to unity was based on thinly veiled anticolonialist and antiwhite resentment, on the old dichotomy of "Eastern spirit" versus "Western technology," on put-downs of Western rationalism and "modernity," on the same autistic insensitivity to Japan's neighbors (once again, apparently not consulted), and on a presumptuous proposal for an Asian press center in Tokyo to "deliver the ABC's of Asian coverage" to benighted Western journalists. Calls for the construction of imposing pan-Asian cultural centers in capital cities and the staging of flashy events betrayed an expectation that powerful initiatives by Japan could produce the sort of regional cultural blend that in other areas of the world has been the product of centuries of unprogrammed development.[4] A former Western ambassador to Japan who had attended the first conference of this group told me the anti-Western tone (and the Western counter-ripostes) had been downright nasty there. Rushing out of the meeting hall to catch me as I started to enter a subway station, he thanked me for having delivered my cautionary remarks to the conference in a firm yet dignified manner.

Originally seeded by one of the many consultative "brain trusts" launched by Prime Minister Masayoshi Ohira in 1980, Tokyo's cultural stance in the broader transpacific APEC region emerged with its proposal—just before the November 1993 Seattle summit—for an Asia-Pacific exchanges conference that would help remove an alleged "psychological wall" separating the United States from the developing Asian nations.[5] Echoing the government's new theme of American insensitivity was a press cartoon featuring Bill Clinton on a dogsled, whip in hand, stunned as Asia's leaders break out of husky harness to scamper away, muttering, "Can you really expect *him* to understand Asia?"[6]

American negotiators and opinion leaders should rebut Tokyo's concoction of a mid-Pacific cultural divide as a means of enlisting its entire region against U.S. market-opening pressures and posing as the guardian of Asian economic chastity. Compared to Japan's tightly hoisted drawbridges, lowered only to let the economic samurai out, American political, intellectual, and human ties in the postwar period have spanned the region like a freeway cloverleaf—in immigration, intermarriage, refugees, university exchanges, and professional opportunities for Asian artists, scholars, and journalists. Japan should be asked to forge its long-overdue Asian links on its own merits and stop trying to gain points by painting the United States as a common economic and cultural threat.

The immediate business of Japan's "cultural gap" ploy was to latch on to and amplify the emerging postulation by certain Asian thinkers and politicians of a monolithic set of common values under attack by Western cultural absolutism. After the United States fought in Korea and Vietnam to save Japan and Southeast Asia for democracy and capitalism, what an irony it would be to watch the region link arms to reduce American participation under the culturalist rubric that U.S.-style free markets, political liberalism, and individual rights don't really suit their preferences for guided development, Confucian paternalism, and group ethics!

Fortunately, Asian and Western liberals have vigorously pressed the counterarguments on the two most important questions—the universality of human rights and the transcultural appeal of political democracy. More effectively, perhaps, the Asian financial crisis that began in 1997 has put a temporary crimp in the Asian-values gambit. Nevertheless, since the argument is likely to reemerge either with the economic revival of the region or with a more drastic collapse, there are four subthemes that also need to be challenged in the American dialogue with Asian, and especially Japanese, intellectuals.

First, we find an almost heedless proclamation of shared values that overlooks the stark intra-Asian divergence in religious and philosophical systems upon which those values ultimately rest. Since Japan itself has couched the argument in terms of cultural affinity, it is worth recalling the continent's bewildering diversity of traditional civilizations, even leaving out Muslim West Asia. Islam and former colonial influences pull South and Southeast Asia more to the West—toward Mecca and London—than north toward the Confucian orbit, which protrudes southward only into Vietnam and the overseas Chinese communities. Malaysian Muslims and Filipino Catholics have Creator-centered, Western-style religions doctrinally incompatible with this-worldly Confucianism or Japan's group absolutisms. Buddhism, long since extruded from its Indian birthplace by an enduring Hinduism, still supplies in its stricter Theravada form the core of social life and national identity in Thailand, Burma, and Sri Lanka, while its broader Mahayana version yielded primacy to Confucianism in traditional China and in ultra-Confucian Korea and was heavily infiltrated by Shinto in Japan—where eclectic assimilation has diluted the core of every Asian intellectual import.

The second subtheme, within the narrower circle of Northeast Asian values, concerns the celebration of Confucian continuities. Here a distinction needs to be made between the so-called Little Tradition of ancient and extraordinarily stable Confucian popular ethics and the Grand Tradition of mandarin-led, theoretically benevolent, bureaucratic government with its rationalization of political autocracy. The first strain of values, still alive in education, workplace, and family life throughout East Asia, goes back twenty-five centuries to the sage himself. The second is an ideological encrustation gradually imposed on the earlier canon and perfected by the twelfth-century neo-Confucianist philosophers of the Sung dynasty. Its opponents, the late-nineteenth- and early-twentieth-century Chinese and Japanese reformers who viewed the Confucian legacy of agrarianism, anticommercialism, xenophobia, bureaucratism, and imperial authoritarianism as the greatest obstacle to modernization, must be turning in their tombs now—along with Japan's Shintoist scholars of the Tokugawa period, who reviled rigid Confucian squareness as the bane of Japan's native literary and human sensibilities.

The third bromide of the Asian-values debate is that individual rights have no roots in Asian spiritual soil. The Asian-values school conveniently conflates such rights with one particular strand of Western thought—with the lonely, atomistic, culture-bound Anglo-American individualism derived from John Locke and Adam Smith, and its very recent American devolution into a no-holds-barred personal "me-ism" and economic laissez-faire. By the same token, it overlooks the more successful marriages of individual dignity and collective weal in the democratic socialist, Social Gospel, New Deal, Christian Democratic, and Burkean conservative traditions of the West, to name only five. Conversely, throughout Asian history there has been a widespread philosophical awareness of the individual as a morally self-directed and responsible entity transcending the group—in the Brahmin's lonely working out of his individual karma, in the Buddhist's progress toward enlightenment, and in the sort of protoliberalism that the late Sinologist John King Fairbank noted in the personal integrity and humanistic self-cultivation of the traditional Confucian gentleman-scholar. Indeed, only in warrior-dominated Tokugawa Japan (or some of its modern projections) and in the Maoist attempt to mold a New Man have Asians come anywhere close to envisioning the sort of self-denying automaton postulated by the region's latter-day prophets of political obedience.

As a fourth point, others should remind the Japanese that the greatest cultural gap of all—in psychological terms, certainly—remains their country's reluctance to liquidate the emotional residue of its past aggression in Asia and dissolve suspicion among its former victims regarding its true intentions in moving toward greater political leadership in the region, including participation in armed multinational PKO (Peace Keeping Operations) units and the acquisition of a permanent Security

Council seat. Since their universalistic values are weak, and since "justice" ultimately boils down to the well-being of the collectivity—be it clique, company, or country—it is especially painful for the Japanese people and politically awkward for their establishment leaders, publicly and collectively, to admit to any wrongdoing by their nation as a whole.

Asian Responses, American Triangles

No clear, let alone unified, Asian response to Japan's cultural wooing has emerged to date. Professed attitudes toward Japan depend a great deal on whether one has been talking to consumers and economic planners eager for goods and investment, to politicians still playing the old "aggression card," to an elder generation with bitter memories, or to younger intellectuals looking for new and non-Western self-definitions. The nature of Asia's future links with Japan will in any case depend far less on cultural considerations than on economic, political, and military ones—including the nature and extent of America's future commitment to the area. Indeed, it would be fascinating to know precisely what would happen if we actually were to pull out.

Traditional cultures aside, the region is further differentiated by the residual politico-cultural divide between Communist and non-Communist states, by the divergent intellectual residues of colonialism under various metropolitan powers, by emotional gradations in anti-Japanese sentiment, by rival conceptions of Asia, and by dissimilar ties with Japan's primary partner, the United States. Samuel P. Huntington, first introducing his now famous thesis in an article entitled "The Clash of Civilizations?" in *Foreign Affairs* (summer 1993), titillated Japanese readers with his sharp East-West fault lines—and his grand cultural zonings, not in fashion since Toynbee—only to upset them with his clear-cut demarcation of their own country from the rest of Asia. Although some even suspected a politically motivated point here, Japan does have a backlog of bilateral reconciliations blocking any common cultural approach to Asia. And each bilateral tie also partakes of a cultural triangle with the United States—a dynamic in which old synergies may give way to rivalry and strain as Japan moves to replace America as the senior partner.

Korea (for now, the South) will be the litmus test of Japan's willingness to surmount its past. Nowhere have grudges run deeper than in Japan's cultural sibling—closest in race and language, in corporate and educational ethos, and in a joint intellectual inheritance from China and the West.

Unprocessed rage at Japan's colonial attempt to eradicate Korean cultural identity continues to break out, as in the recent demolition of the imposing former Japanese capitol building in Seoul. As of May 2001 the South Korean government continued to ban music tapes and CDs recorded exclusively in the Japanese language, large-scale Japanese concert performances (even of Western classical or pop music), and most Japanese movies and all TV dramas—despite its agreement in June 2000 to let in major international award-winning Japanese films and small pop groups playing to audiences of less than two thousand. For decades now the explanatory signs at museums and historical sites continue to be posted in Korean and English only, although the vast majority of sightseers hail from Japan. Christianity, in part a spiritual riposte to Japan's overlordship, now commands a third of the population, with rickety wooden churches on country hillsides and garish neon crosses on what seems to be nearly every other block in Seoul—a sight totally absent in Japan. And although many Korean youths now study the Japanese language for commercial purposes, the more rancid anti-Americanism among certain younger Korean intellectuals does not necessarily translate into follow-Japan sentiment.

Pragmatists in Seoul, nevertheless, have been calling for a more normal emotional tie, and on the occasion of President Kim Dae-Jung's state visit to Japan in October 1998 a formally negotiated statement expressing Japan's regret and looking to a new, "future-oriented" relationship was signed. Although Kim pronounced himself satisfied, others noted that the document merely committed to paper the roundabout, unconvincing apologies that had been made verbally in the past. Bitterness in Korea runs so deep because the Japanese in very crude and systematic ways attempted to eradicate the Korean language, culture, and national identity—thereby denying to their closest neighbors the very things they themselves had set out to preserve through Japan's own drive to modernization.

Indeed, the commission of Korean and Japanese scholars convened to work out a mutually acceptable version of historical ties already had foundered on the reef of mutual intransigence when the new prime minister visited the Yasukuni shrine in August 2001, leaving many Koreans convinced that Japan would never own up and worried that Koizumi would "lead the nation toward Asian hegemony, based on a sense of superiority, confidence and a closed nationalism."[7] Koizumi, on a one-day trip to Seoul on 14 October 2001 to coordinate global antiterrorism measures, did lay a wreath for the Korean war dead at the National Cemetery in Seoul, the first Japanese premier ever to do so, but his plans to meet with the speaker of the Republic of Korea's National Assembly were canceled when opposition legislators threatened to block his entry into the parliament building. It all keeps coming back to square one—the historical record.

Tokyo in the 1990s seemed to be counting on its economic leverage to bring about a surrender of that lingering bitterness without any gestures toward atonement signifying a genuine change in Japanese attitudes and psychologically credible to the Koreans. Indeed, there were signs that this was working when the Seoul government by the end of the decade had agreed to reimburse Korea's wartime sex slaves of the Japanese army (the so-called comfort women) out of its own funds, and President Kim Dae Jung at least was talking of letting bygones be bygones. Not only that, but as the Seoul-based Canadian journalist Victor Fic has pointed out, one of the more ominous straws now blowing in the East Asian wind is the way in which increasing numbers of the Korean elite are willing to bend over backward to avoid offending their historical oppressor, Japan, while tolerating public abuse of the United States. This first manifested itself in the jeering of American athletes at the 1988 Seoul Olympics even as the Soviet team was cheered, and it continues in the anti-American banners fervently brandished by student demonstrators and in the unabashed personal hostility Americans occasionally encounter on the street.[8]

For probable causes we must adduce more than the ending of the Cold War (which explains so much elsewhere), since the potentially mortal threat from North Korea still remains. Most potent, perhaps, is the power of money—the sheer scale of Japanese lending and investment in recent years as contrasted with America's market-opening pressures and its preachy, tough-cop role in the painful and widely unpopular IMF bailout during 1997–98. Politically speaking, the new devil is always more compelling than the old. Indeed, the recent emergence, by dint of Korean courage and perseverance alone, of a genuine civilian-led democratic government has only mitigated—not erased—the resentment of those who blame the United States for having backed the Republic of Korea's military regimes over three long decades and winked at their army-led slaughter of at least several hundred civilians at Kwangju in 1980.[9] Moreover, among Koreans with long historical memories, there may be some prudent repositioning going on for the inevitable American departure, recalling the casual way in which the United States left their country to the Japanese sphere of influence in 1908, severed it at the waist in 1945, and virtually invited Stalin to try swallowing it all in early 1950.

My own verification of South Korea's new emotional self- restraint toward Japan came in September 1993, after I had spent the summer teaching at Yonsei University in Seoul. Asked to contribute one of my occasional op-ed pieces to the "Seiron" (Sound arguments) column of *Sankei Shinbun* in Tokyo, I decided to put a human face on the depth of the Korean hurt for Japanese readers, who had been told so little about it. One illustration concerned the spacious Independence Hall complex spanning a small verdant valley an hour's drive south of Seoul at Chonan, where five of the seven historical exhibition halls with their dramatic dioramas were devoted to the sundry brutalities of Japanese rule. The other explained how the former Japanese capitol building—slated at last for vengeful dismantling despite the condescending gasps of foreign Art Deco connoisseurs—had been deliberately built not only on a ground plan that copied the Chinese character for the sun (i.e., Japan) but in front of the old royal Kyongbok Palace. Symbolically, that cut off the lines of *chi*—the life force—of the Korean nation, which, according to ancient divination, ran south from the palace to the Han River. That was the politico-geomantic equivalent of castration.

My friendly neorightish editors at *Sankei* had no trouble with the piece, but within days I was invited to an elegant luncheon for two by the economic counselor of the South Korean embassy, and later to a reception by the ambassador himself. They appreciated my sympathetic treatment, but the message between the lines, ever so politely conveyed, was: "Cool it; we need the money." It was clear that the Japanese psychological weapons so long honed against the United States had now been used to bamboozle the Koreans—who in turn had joined with the Japanese to con the Yanks!

In Southeast Asia the historical hurts were shorter in time and shallower in depth than for Korea. Attitudes since World War II have progressed from the severe moral censure of Japan by regional intellectuals—first for its wartime aggression and then for its seemingly mindless unidimensional economic penetration of their countries—to the enthusiastic study of its economic model by today's younger generation of business-oriented students, academics, and entrepreneurs. Where attitudes will come out after the post-1997 financial crisis remains to be seen. Quietly, as we have seen, Japan continues to expand the massive and exclusionary role of its own corporations in Southeast Asia's external, intraregional, and Japan-directed trade. As emotional resentments attenuate with the passage of time, as economic motivations push to the fore as in Korea, and *if* the United States gets itself painted as the villain of the regional financial crisis, this economic integration—already well advanced—just might provide the practical platform for new pan-Asian, anti-Western themes.

At the pro-Japanese end of the regional spectrum, Malaysia has long gratified Japan with its "Look East" economic and educational policies, and Singapore with its resolutely dichotomizing school of "West-versus-Rest" pundits. At the risk of never being allowed to set foot in Kuala Lumpur or the Lion City again, I suspect that the Japanese—avoiding offense to the United States by letting others do the talking—were very much behind Malaysia's promotion of an East Asian Economic Caucus (minus the whites), which they handily would have dominated, and that Singapore's self-generated harping on incompatible values—with a command of English idiom, Oxford Union oratory, and Western guilt buttons far beyond that of the Japanese—has served Tokyo's policy goals well. Prime Minister Mahathir's startling suggestion that the Japanese stop apologizing about the war reflected, of course, the preferred treatment that ethnic Malays received during the occupation in contrast to the Chinese, as well as the wartime education of a number of still active national leaders in Japan. In today's wealthy Singapore, where during wartime the Chinese suffered horribly, the official distaste for human rights probably has had less to do with the glint of Japan-harnessed economic growth than with the desire of Lee Kuan Yew and his successors to remain in power and to strengthen political ties with China.

Whereas America's intellectual presence in Britain's former possessions has always been peripheral and subject to a certain colonially transmitted disdain, Japan's newly funded institutes, chairs, book distributions, and academic exchanges with the Philippines and Thailand have been flowing into the void of receding, or at best static, U.S. cultural and informational activity resulting from the sharp reduction in former strategic ties. Conversely, the Yuchengco Institute of Philippines-Japan Relations in Manila, whose chairman, Alfonso Yuchengco, served as ambassador to Tokyo during the latter half of the 1990s, has been reaching out to key Filipino scholars and artists now increasingly ignored by American cultural officials. To be sure, economic, sentimental, and family links to the United States, shared wartime memories, and sheer temperamental exuberance will keep Filipinos chary of any heavy-handed Japanese cultural embrace. But in Bangkok—as one Thai professor friend put it to me, scrunching his shoulders to make the point—"the American ambassador now looks *sooo* small, compared to the Japanese." Thailand, with its parallel history as the only other noncolonized modernizer in Asia, its fellow monarchical tradition, and its ancient skill in adjusting to new power balances, has moved self-assuredly into close cultural ties with Japan. As for Vietnam, that reunited country—in an ironic reversal—now welcomes an American economic presence to balance Japan's, and the conceivable role of returning U.S.-based refugees as an eventual bridge between the two societies may someday establish the cultural price of Japan's stinginess in turning away so many of the "boat people."

Finally, what of Japan's two giant rivals for the mantle of Asian cultural leadership—China and India? Tokyo's concern with the PRC today focuses far more on economic, political, and military tangibles, while the Chinese have hardly shed their traditional view of the Japanese as culturally peripheral—if technologically adept—barbarians, and retain a historical mistrust of Tokyo-sponsored campaigns on behalf of Sino-Japanese "brotherhood" and "friendship." Chinese inclinations toward Confucian magnanimity and Buddhist forgetting cannot erase the reality of millions of lives lost during the war, while Japan's obtuseness with this historical fact was inadvertently betrayed by a Tokyo journalist now prominent in U.S.-Japan interlocuting who returned from Hong Kong a few years ago amazed by the way the Chinese and British seemed to get along with each other, "in spite of the Opium War of 1842," and puzzling over what was missing in the Japanese approach.

The sleeper in the cultural game may prove to be India, should it shift its political and cultural attention from West to East and vigorously reenter the cultural zone that it once enriched with its religion, philosophy, and art. Several strengths conceivably could override negative reviews pertaining to its slower economy, caste society, and ethnic quarrels. Indian experience in holding together the world's most diverse nation for over a half century—without revolutionary paroxysm or military takeover, and according to Western-derived secular governance—is clearly the *political* miracle of postwar Asia. Indian familiarity with

Western intellectual idiom also positions it as the most effective rhetorical bridge, a sort of super-Singapore mercilessly twitting the Occident if it so chooses—especially America, with which political ties never have been close. More to the point, any *cultural* definition of Asian togetherness will eventually have to go beyond the materialistic appeal of Japanese or Chinese economic performance to something more of the mind and spirit. And as India's preeminent cultural spokesman and pan-Asianist in this century, Rabindranath Tagore, learned during his visits to Japan in 1916 and China in 1924, the Asias of the samurai, mandarin, and Brahmin are different indeed.[10]

India's philosophical bent for tolerance and inclusion, and its preservation of a medley of traditional cultures as the rest of Asia goes looking for its withered roots, could give it the last laugh in a bargain with the modernization devil that was the reverse of Japan's (leave aside the Maoist ruination of China's heritage). Alarmed precisely by India's political subjugation and its cultural bifurcation into an English-speaking, Westernized elite riding a multitude "mired" in tradition, Japan opted for an integrated but hybrid modern civilization with leaders and masses sharing a twice-thinned mix of extracted Western culture and attenuated Japanese tradition, sustained by a permanent political ideology of external imperilment. The dualistic "both-and" of India's looser amalgam— with its deeper accessing of both Western universalism and time-honored roots—may just possibly have more to say to the coming century than the unsettled tension of Japan's "neither-nor," which crops up repeatedly in its sense of cultural loss, its awkwardness in dealing with the outside world, and its outbreaks of xenophobic nationalism.

CHAPTER SIX

Samurai Ethic
Premature Prognoses
of Individualism

In the last five chapters I have framed what I see as America's illusions about a changing Japan largely in terms of our excessive faith in the power of impersonal economic and social forces, set against the intellectual and psychological ability of the Japanese to resist—that is to say, the tenacity of their values.

As a final question for Part I, then, we must ask if there are any core values that subsume all the mercantilist, neonationalist, and ethnocentric isms that we have looked at—and why that core Western value of individualism has had such a hard time sinking roots in Japan.

Arnold Toynbee, writing in 1962, characterized the nature of what he called a small "world state" as follows:

> The smallest human community constitutes the whole world for the people inside it if it is isolated from all other human communities on the face of the planet; and it will be insulated from them if its members feel that outsiders do not count. In this—and it is a very practical sense—even tiny Japan was a world state during her two centuries of insulation under the regime of the Tokugawa shoguns . . . [such] world governments of the past have concentrated their energies on self-preservation; and they have tried to preserve themselves by a policy of freezing. They have tried to freeze not only their frontiers against the outer barbarians and not only the structure of public administration inside those frontiers; they have tried to freeze the private lives of their citizens as well. The most notorious recent instance of this policy is that of the Tokugawa regime in Japan.[1]

Egos on Ice, How Nice

Toynbee's observation captures both the peculiar psychological strength
and historical roots of Japanese insularism and social conformity today.
Private lives still remain frozen by Western and other Asian standards of
self-assertion, and outsiders still don't count. Of course, there are some
in recent years who might like to see American egos put back in the
refrigerator for a while to cool off. Be that as it may, I recall two authoritative Japanese whose off-the-cuff remarks to me bore out Toynbee's
insight from an insider's perspective.

Decades ago, when we were both in our twenties, a close Japanese
friend of mine likened his country to a small, intricate, self-contained
wheel turned on its circumference by the teeth of a much larger wheel.
Preoccupied with the internal whirring of their own closed cosmos, the
Japanese were content to leave the tangential management of that great
world beyond to a small elite of internationally oriented experts. As the
vice minister for international affairs of one of Japan's most powerful
ministries, my friend in later years managed to do a very good job indeed of slowing down the ratchet of that large outer wheel.

Toynbee's remark serves, more importantly, to remind us of the oppressive psychological legacy of the Tokugawa era in its extenuated
shadow today—one that many Japanese are far more conscious of than
the typical foreign academic or journalist. "It's all the fault of Ieyasu!"
leading postwar film director Kon Ichikawa grumbled to me (in equivalent Japanese) one afternoon in 1972 after shooting a rear-view sequence
of me lumbering through a junkyard in suburban Tokyo. We were film-
ing a weekly segment of his TV dramatization for Fuji Television of one
of Catholic writer Shusaku Endo's lesser novels, *Tadaima Ronin*. I had
been dragooned into playing a ne'er-do-well foreign foil to the young
Japanese antihero, who was repeatedly cramming for and failing his
Tokyo University entrance exams—for the nonce *(tadaima)* an academic
ronin, or masterless samurai. Ichikawa, director of major films such as
Fires on the Plain (Japanese title, *Nobi*), was envying my firm American gait, feet planted solidly on the ground, so unlike the tentative, hov-
ering stride of so many Japanese males. By blaming it all on Ieyasu,
founder of the shogunate, Ichikawa was venting a bit of peeve at the
ego-crushing legacies of the quarter-millennium Tokugawa period (1600–
1867).

We saw in Chapter 1 how many Western observers rest their expectations on the perceived emergence of a robust, authority-challenging individualism in Japan. The future political balance between the liberal and reactionary elements we looked at in Chapters 3 and 4 will be also be determined in the long run by the ongoing tussle between a fragile individualism of independently thinking and courageously acting citizens, on one hand, and the enormous pull of Japan's entrenched group mentality, on the other. Similarly, the mentalities toward America and Asia that we explored in Chapters 2 and 5 will be profoundly affected for better or worse by the future strength or weakness of civil society and civil courage in Japan. The problem, of course, is not that this sort of individualism is totally unknown in Japan today, but that the prognoses for its social impact have been vastly overstated.

Pop-psychological theories of the Japanese are a dime a dozen, but two solid professionals on opposite sides of the Pacific have put this weakness of the ego and the tug of the irrational to me in the more abstruse terms of modern psychology. Dr. Ryuko Ishikawa, one of the two Japanese psychiatrists presently licensed to practice in both Japan and the United States and an authority on family systems theory, contrasts the emotional independence fostered by the typical American family with the interdependent, individually undifferentiated "amorphous emotional fusion mass" of the Japanese family (and its fictive extensions in other social groupings such as the corporation or the nation itself). When such an amorphous ego mass breaks down under the buffetings of rapid social change or economic crisis, it does not—*pace* wishful Western prognosticators—give birth to fully formed and emotionally independent individual egos, but simply reconstitutes itself, amoebalike, around a new center. Dr. Ishikawa shared my worry that the new amoeba might well locate itself further to the right on the political spectrum.

Indeed, history reminds us how the 1870s, the first decade following the Meiji Restoration, were originally perceived as a time of extraordinary individual creativity, ideological pluralism, and political pluck, only to be written off by later historians as an era of personal rootlessness, intellectual confusion, and political opportunism—that is to say, no more than a brief if turbulent transition from the social solidarities of the Tokugawa period to the even firmer fetters of late Meiji with its ideology of the emperor-centered *kazoku kokka,* or "family state." These bonds were progressively internalized and destined to hold officially until 1945, and informally for decades thereafter.

Father Gary Hellman, assistant priest at St. John's in the Village Episcopal Church in Manhattan and a practicing psychotherapist, put the emotional dependence and underdevelopment of rationally self-governing individual egos in more starkly Freudian terms: "Japan has made a Faustian compromise with the unconscious."

As a matter of fact, it was only in the mid-1990s that the Japanese began to tout their own protoindividualism, mainly in response (it would seem) to Western expectations. Right up to and through the boastful 1980s, Japan was preaching the superiority of its group-centered values. So let us now look briefly at the broader historical forces that have shaped that orientation and impeded even to this day the development of a more individualistic alternative.

As the United States struggles with frightening cracks in its own social cohesion and public civility, one of the most beguiling messages from Japan has been that of social stability and economic performance rooted in an Asian heritage of communal harmony, cooperation, and consensus. Unfortunately, this ideological gambit, when accepted, has a number of baneful consequences beyond those of placing the United States on the defensive as a penitent learner and lumping Japan together with the rest of Asia against the West. It demeans and sets back those liberal forces calling for the more transparent, even adversarial, conduct of public affairs required by a healthy civil society in Japan. The Asian ploy has been used as a defensive cloak for Japan's market protectionism and for those cartels of the mind that have kept Japan's intellectual shop closed to genuine participation by foreign lawyers, journalists, and academics on the grounds that they would prove too nonconforming and disruptive.[2] Worst of all, this facile harping on a joint Asian heritage obscures a root of Japanese social compliance that is not Asian at all but derives from Japan's unique feudal and military past. The lack of surface nastiness in Japanese society is indeed appealing. But while others would do well to emulate its effects, it is doubtful that many Americans would be willing to pay the price of its chief historical cause.

The garden-variety groupism or xenophobia of like-flocking-to-like is of course pandemic to the human race, and all too evident in our own American record of racial discrimination and ethnic status-definition. What makes Japan fundamentally different is that its racially based national consciousness and exclusivism, far from being the objects of attack, disdain, and public efforts at amelioration, are openly sanctioned by the intellectual establishment, popular consensus, and government policy. Ethnic diversity has been roundly decried as a source of American weakness by Japanese ranging from former prime minister Nakasone to my own university students, who, at the time of the rioting in Los Angeles after the Rodney King trial in 1992, were absolutely convinced of it. The problem, in short, is an ideological one—in the end the product of artificial, politically willed, intellectual constructs running the whole length of Japan's 130 years of post–Meiji Restoration modern history.

Why does Japan's insularism—its group mentality at the international level—retain such an inordinately adamantine edge? We miss both the tenacity and the true root of it when we stop at the two most frequently given historical explanations—those of national security and communal cooperativeness. Having been obsessed with the former ourselves for the past half century, and now mourning the gradual loss of the latter in our own society, Americans tend to nod and say, "Ah, yes," to both of these interpretations, fitting them into the frame of our own values and experience.

Some Japanese attribute their defensive mentality to the strategic sense of insecurity instilled a century and a half ago by China's Opium War of 1840–42, Commodore Perry's black ships of 1853, and the concurrent Russian naval activity in Japanese waters. They seldom stop to ask, however, why their country by the turn of the century had turned determinedly expansionist, the predatory wolf rather than the bristling porcupine. Or why in all of their modern wars, whatever the ultimate allocation of responsibility, they have always been the first to strike—against the Chinese at Seoul and on the sea in 1894, against the Russians at Port Arthur in 1904, in taking over Germany's Far Eastern possessions in 1914, then again in China in 1931 and 1937, and finally at Pearl Harbor in 1941.

The second common explanation of Japanese group-mindedness and insularity stresses the collective consciousness, human intimacy, and cooperative, harmonistic values learned over two millennia of rice-growing agriculture. But we can find other traditional Asian societies that honor family or seniority or tradition or group membership far more than do modern Occidentals yet are not nearly as tightly knit against those outside the group as is Japan—for example, Thailand, another Asian country that managed to avoid colonization by the West. Again, what is it that makes Japanese groups so super-groupy? With hardly any Japanese left knee-deep in the paddies, why do corporate officials trained at the Harvard Business School and jetting first class still go drinking night after night in Manhattan with other Japanese exclusively, lest they be thought "too Americanized"—as one of their New York–based securities analysts, a former student of mine, once confided to me?

The Feudal Plus-Alpha

A more powerful shaper of Japan's group and insular mentalities—and more difficult for us to grasp, since it lies beyond the ken of our own mentality and contravenes some of our most cherished values—is what I would call the survival in various guises of the samurai ethic. This may sound a bit musty and old-fashioned, but Japan explainers should start rummaging through the intellectual attic once again for those concepts that were of serious concern before and after the Pacific War— things such as feudalism; military values; the absolute quality of political, personal, and group loyalties; and the overwrought denial of self (the nub of the matter) to which all of the foregoing have contributed. It is here that we shall find our missing plus-alpha, our clue to the intensity with which the Japanese seal off their groups—or the grand collectivity of their nation—against outsiders.

Until about 1960 Western writers were acutely aware of the strong military thread in Japan's value system from medieval times straight through to 1945. The English philosopher Herbert Spencer, a frequent adviser to Meiji statesmen at the end of the nineteenth century, had taken an intense scholarly interest in modern Japan precisely because it presented a living specimen of the warrior stage in his theory of sociopolitical evolution, a stage that the West had long since left behind. And it was none other than Inazo Nitobe, deputy secretary general of the League of Nations and Japan's most prominent interpreter to the West early in this century, who in his best-known book, *Bushido,* subtitled that ethical code of the "way of the warrior" as the very "Soul of Japan."[3]

As late as the last of the four East-West Philosophers' Conferences held in Honolulu between 1939 and 1964, the Japanese participants were still attuned to the centrality of this ethic. One of them wrote of "that mental tendency of the Japanese which prevents them from exercising their sovereign duties and rights as an autonomous people, a tendency which was fostered in their character during the long period of time when they were subjected to the iron rule of the sword."[4] From the *Hagakure,* often dubbed the "bible of Bushido," he quoted the essence of the samurai ethic as follows:

I serve my master, not from a sense of duty, but out of a blind love of service; I hold my master dear simply because he is dear to my heart above everything else, not because he is kind to me or provides for my living. . . . The *alpha* and *omega* of a samurai's life is service, service, service—nothing but service. . . . A samurai has nothing else in his heart or mind but his master. . . . To a samurai the pledge of loyalty is everything. . . . A samurai gives himself up *in toto* at the free disposal of his master.[5]

In short, we need an imaginative revisiting of the central samurai values of loyalty unto death and total self-abnegation that were spawned not in the warmer solidarities of Asian farming communities close to the soil but in the harsher dispensation of Japan's medieval warrior society and the Tokugawa era with its perfected ideology of unconditional, noncontractual fealties. The Japanese feudal tie (so unlike that of the obstreperous, legalistically haggling English barons at Runnymede) was a deeply internalized existential commitment that tended inwardly toward an absolute identity and submissiveness to one's own lord and group while outwardly creating a posture of aggressiveness and suspicion toward others.

(Indeed, when I viewed one of the originals of the Magna Carta on display in Salisbury Cathedral a decade ago, I could not help conjuring up a lofty Tokugawa Confucian voice tut-tutting the political and moral depravity of those ill-mannered lords, bishops, and London burghers who had the temerity to wrest their rights from a heaven-appointed monarch eight centuries ago. A good head start.)

It is this ethic in its modern mode that has led some astute observers to compare the deepest mind-set of the Japanese nation today to that of a monastic community or to the grand Teutonic Order of the old East Prussian marches. In psychological terms, these similes are far more apt than the mechanical and economically defined stereotype of Japan Inc. or former French prime minister Edith Cresson's hill of busy ants. There is the militaristic aggressiveness and the quasi-religious devotion—although not to any transcendental being or universal principles above the human nexus.

Japan's great religious and philosophical traditions all point away from a Western-style individual consciousness. Confucianism and Shinto stress the social continuities of the family and of the race, while Buddhism prescribes the negation of the ego as a means of escape from suffering and does without a personal, paternal, creator God—that quintessential Westerner who guarantees the infinite, transcendental worth or dignity of the individual personalities He has created (and who, on "walking away" in the deistic eighteenth century, at least had the courtesy to leave behind an immutable universe of natural laws and natural rights). But it is the imposition of the warrior ethic on top of these broadly Asiatic sources of the Japanese mind and spirit that has made Japan so different from all of its neighbors—including China and Korea, with their centuries-long elevation of civilian over military virtues and of family values over those of the state.

The concept of total self-sacrifice and service—not to a religious ideal, as in the Christian, Judaic, or Muslim West, but to political superiors and to one's social group—was nurtured under the Tokugawa shoguns as the ethic of an entire civil and military bureaucracy. It was toughened philosophically and psychologically by nonrationalist injunctions from Zen Buddhism and the Oyomei (Wang Yangming) intuition-and-action school of Confucianism, and blended with the rising tide of Shinto-based nationalism and xenophobia at the end of the Tokugawa period. Then it was foisted on the entire populace by the Meiji educational system after the object of loyalty had been adroitly shifted from feudal superiors to the nation at large and to the emperor as the center and source of all political and moral values. Finally, it was brought to its frothiest pitch in the militarism and ultranationalism of the 1930s, in the quixotic kamikaze missions and in the near-suicidal prolongation of a hopelessly lost war.

Indeed, one could argue that the Meiji leadership, far from having Westernized Japan (save in the externals of material culture and the formal shells of imported institutions), actually managed at the level of values and psychology to samuraize the entire nation. The relatively autonomous mores of the merchants and peasants under the Tokugawa, although not totally swept away, were now overridden and conformed to the loyalty-and-obedience ethos of a single class—that of the old warriors. This was done with all the tools of a modern state: compulsory education, national conscription, and the authoritarian precepts of nineteenth-century German constitutionalism. Much of the actual traditional heritage, most notably Buddhism, was shunted to the side, and only those facets of Confucianism, Shinto, and the imperial tradition that served the purpose of national power—as defined by former samurai— were squeezed into the new ethical matrix. And, in one final irony, the samurai leaders of Meiji Japan, by abolishing their own class and garbing themselves in London-tailored suits, managed to win the plaudits of a duly flattered Western world for their progressive modernism.

To be sure, the feudal ethic they bequeathed was in many ways a debased and distorted one, particularly when one asks what might have become of Japan had that streak of external self-assertion and internal self-possession in some of the old samurai—exemplified by such Meiji liberal or Christian leaders as Yukichi Fukuzawa or Kanzo Uchimura—been nurtured as a stepping-stone to modern individualism.

The Japan-side mentor for my doctoral thesis, the late educational philosopher Takeji Hayashi, once told me what a tragedy it was that the door had been closed to such development by the imposition after 1886 of a mindlessly utilitarian, tightly disciplined, and anti-individualistic educational system on a nation of peasants whose egos had already been beaten to quivering jelly under the Tokugawa class system. Arinori Mori, the education minister from 1885 to 1889 and an indefatigable researcher of serviceable foreign educational models while envoy to London from 1881 to 1884, had totally misread the sociopsychological context of the rigorous regulations, hazing, and military drills that he found at England's great public schools such as Rugby and Eton. Designed to knock the cheeky adolescent stuffing out of Britain's heirs to a ruling aristocracy assured from birth of its financial security, social status, and leadership roles, they proved a singularly inappropriate transplant for Meiji Japan. Prescribing a barrackslike ethos for his new teacher-training colleges, Mori managed to father several generations of inwardly insecure educators, stern and aloof toward students but timid and ingratiating toward their own superiors—what older Japanese still decry as the prewar "normal-school type."

Although discredited in its previous guises by the smashing defeat in 1945, the samurai ethic still survives today as a mind-set—in the devotion to the company; in the single-minded pursuit of market share; in the esteeming of *gaman* (perseverance) and *doryoku* (effort) over imagination and creativity; in university entrance exams set to test sheer memory and stamina, or in other pedagogical equivalents of backpacking rocks to the top of Mt. Fuji; in the instinctive rush to protect Japan against all comers; and in the stoic solemnity of Japan's dark-blue-suited bureaucrats and academics, the true heirs to the samurai style.

This warrior ethic has nurtured many traits Westerners admire—physical valor, self-control, hard work, honesty, and the vigorous if somewhat astringent artistic culture of Noh plays, *sumie* drawings, rock gardens, and tea ceremonies tracing their roots back to late medieval

Zen. Nevertheless, much of its ethical thrust runs counter to the two things that the world increasingly asks of Japan today. One of these is a greater dedication to individual rights; the other, a greater readiness for intergroup (i.e., international) reciprocity and empathy. The dignity of the individual—this root ideal of Western liberalism and democracy and, yes, of consumer comfort—has no place in a code of self-abnegation unable to distinguish between individualism and raw egotism. And the absolute ethical primacy of one's own group (in this case the nation, Japan) militates against the notion of a more relaxed, mutually open, and supportive global community.

I might add that the unqualified temper of samurai loyalty was intellectually and psychologically nourished by (and in its turn fed) the powerful if not dominant streak of irrationalism and intuitionism in Japanese thought and mentality. Drawn variously from animistic Shintoism, Buddhist philosophical idealism, and the experiential immediacy of Zen, this traditional preference for the nonrational over the rational has over the centuries helped to elevate things such as aesthetic taste, ethnonationalism, and unquestioning obedience to the status of moral absolutes. In modern times it helps to account for the attraction of Japanese intellectuals to German idealism from the Meiji period and to French existentialism in the early postwar years. A vast subject in its own right, this hostility to cut-and-dried empirical cogitation (and to Anglo-American thought in general) was best summed up by the American philosopher Charles A. Moore after organizing the four East-West Philosophers' Conferences in Hawaii that over a quarter century set out to explore the Indian, Chinese, and Japanese minds:

> It seems almost as if Japan differs from the rest of the major traditions of the world, all of which would accept the Socratic dictum that "the unexamined life is unfit to live." Japan might even counter by saying that it is the examined life that is unfit to live, because it is not life.[6]

In other words, the ground for individualism is at best shallow in an intellectual culture where rational self-reflection is devalued by so many anti-rational imperatives.

* * *

Historically speaking, the samurai ethic spilled over into a reflexively pugilistic posture toward the intruding and aggressively expansionist West—salutary in the short run but now outdated. This posture was set in the late nineteenth century by two Meiji-era slogans that, absent fresh alternatives, still govern the Japanese mind going into the twenty-first: the overriding national goal to "catch up with and surpass" the West *(oitsuke-oikose)* and to do so by means of a "wealthy country and strong soldiery" *(fukoku-kyohei)*. Motivating these goals were a profound sense of insecurity and a deeply wounded pride, both of which (whether objectively justified or not) have consistently been underestimated by the West. Chastened by the disastrous defeat of Japanese arms half a century later, Japan transmuted the literal armies of its militarist adventurism into the equally energetic and dedicated troops of economic growth and expansionism, achieving by a judicious adjustment of the *fukoku-kyohei* means its original *oitsuke-oikose* end of parity with the West—in all but raw (and now unfashionable) military terms. There has been talk recently of moving beyond the old catch-up goals, but no convincing practical replacement has been put forward so far. The likelihood is all too great that the old wine of a defensive, we-against-them nationalism will simply be poured one way or another into the new bottles of globalization rhetoric.

Others must grasp that Japan's successes have been achieved in a fit of tough-mindedness. There has never been a lack of broad national purpose or public understanding behind the exercise of Japanese power in the world since the end of the Tokugawa seclusion, although the government has made some frightful miscalculations at the level of concrete application. The problem today is that the old overarching and mobilizing goals have become outmoded—dangerously so for Japan—without any fresh conceptual frame of purposes to take their place. The old reflexes remain firmly hooked up, creating new tensions with the outside world and leaving the taste of victory bittersweet.

The Japanese have paid a high personal price for subordinating their individual development and expression to the extraneous goals of the national collectivity—many of them finding it difficult to perceive even their own selves as subsisting independently of "Japan." If American and other Western expatriates, negotiators, and pundits on Japan could just grasp the true depth of this ego weakness and shelve their expectations for the Japanese mentality on this one point of "creeping individualism," it would save them a lot professional frustration, personal heartbreak, diplomatic miscalculation, and fatuous prognostication.

That inability to establish a moral self apart from the nation and state was, according to the distinguished postwar intellectual historian Kiyoko Takeda, the tragedy of Mori Arinori (1847–89). Mori, the subject of my first book, was the radically Westernizing Meiji education minister (1885–89) and first ambassador to Washington (1870–73) who nevertheless had gone on to lay the foundations of prewar Japan's uptight, statist, nationalistically oriented educational system.[7] At the time, Takeda's psychologizing of him struck me as a bit precious. Today, thirty years out of the history books and into Japanese society itself, I know that she was absolutely right—not only on Mori but about most Japanese a century later.

In one of Soichiro Tahara's popular all-night television roundtables in 1997 it took the only non-Japanese panelist present—the young Korean professor Sang Jing Kang from Tokyo University—to suggest that a sufficient solution to the "spiritual malaise" allegedly afflicting Japan in the late 1990s would be a greater emphasis on self-development (*jikko hatten*) for the good life. The Japanese participants pooh-poohed this in a chorus led by the neonationalist political scientist Susumu Nishibe. The Japanese were spiritually adrift because they lacked a firm identity as Japanese, which required a clearer definition of Japan's role in the world. That, in turn, awaited the achievement of full nationhood (by which was understood a new constitution permitting "normal" military forces). Individual happiness, in other words, was still tied to the fortunes of the state. Shades of Meiji![8]

In May 1998 I found myself seated at an Italian restaurant in neocapitalist Shanghai beside an American business couple who had recently spent three years in Japan and another three in China. True, the residual Communist red tape was a hassle, the husband allowed, but the Chinese were more open and straightforward and therefore pleasanter to deal with. "Yes," added the wife, "and above all they are a *happy* people." After all those wars and famines and cultural revolutions, I thought. Then what she had left unsaid, but understood, about the Japanese hit me like a thunderclap.

It all makes one wonder how much the rest of the world may have had to suffer over the past century for the self-inflicted unhappiness of the Japanese.

II
COLLUSION

"With a Twisted Cue"
Binational Cartel for
Sweetness and Light

CHAPTER
SEVEN

Special Pleading
Our Rhetorical Trouncing
on Trade

Needless to say, the transmission of favorable images and psychological pressures from Japan to America that we have looked at in the preceding six chapters does not take place in an immaterial vacuum of pure thought. The enterprise relies on special pleading to make its case, on ostracism to sideline its critics, on money to nurture its activities, on organizations to carry them out, and on people to do the proselytizing. And from Japanese and Americans working together it gets plenty of all five.

At a U.S. embassy press conference in Tokyo that I attended as a reporter for the *Philadelphia Bulletin* in 1971, visiting trade representative William Eberle was asked by a plaintive Japanese journalist why he had come all the way to Japan to upset the Japanese people with his unreasonable demands for market opening. In my recollection of that event, Eberle, probably unprepared for noneconomic argumentation, was not particularly adept at fielding that kind of emotional blackmail. Three decades later it is Americans who have now learned the art of warning their government to go easy on Japan—or else. As former undersecretary of commerce Jeffrey E. Garten admonished in the title to his 27 July 1998 *Time* op-ed piece deploring the Clinton administration's public advice to Japan on the Asian financial crisis: "Stop All the Shouting: America's Japan-Bashing Isn't Doing Either Side Any Good."

This American fastidiousness toward Japanese feelings has been a constant of the Japan-U.S. dialogue ever since trade became a major source of friction after 1970. On the evening of 15 April 1996, for ex-

129

ample, as President Clinton was winding up a brief Korean stopover en route to Japan on a state visit, Cokie Roberts was asking a number of Japan experts on ABC's *Nightline* what they made of a network poll released that evening, according to which the percentage of Americans who viewed Japan as an economic threat had dropped from 60 to 40 percent over the past three years. It was a significant shift in U.S. attitudes toward Japan, Roberts insisted, that had come about despite the "steady diet of negative images" being served up by the press. Was this an accurate reading of the American mind, and if so, what accounted for it?

One triptych of teleconferenced savants—all three of whom had spent much of their professional careers proclaiming the good news about Japan—seemed to agree, in a rather celebratory vein, that the United States had at last returned to its senses. Dr. George Packard, former dean of the Johns Hopkins School of Advanced International Studies in Washington, D.C., argued that Japan was a democracy that shared our values and would "be in our camp" for a long time to come, and that the American people had proved themselves "too smart to be taken in by the baloney that was issued by the so-called revisionists in the 1980s." Professor Ezra Vogel of Harvard found the key to it in the rise of China as the new threat pulling the United States and Japan together once again, as during the Cold War. Professor Yoshihiro Tsurumi of the City University of New York blamed the recent spell of unfavorable images on the effort of the Clinton administration to exploit anti-Japan sentiment politically, and on "elitist phobias" having reached the masses of America. Japan's lengthy recession was cited as one basic reason for the improved U.S. attitude, but not one of the three experts suggested that Japan's trade policies might have had something fundamental to do with the previously bad reviews.

This same glaring omission was even more startling in the case of ABC's main interviewee—Dr. Robert D. Deutsch of EBR Consulting, who had been hired by Tokyo's Ministry of Foreign Affairs in 1993 to examine the American mind on Japan and develop policy recommendations to the Japanese for image enhancement. Neither on TV nor in the eighty-four-page pilot study report he delivered to the Japanese embassy in 1994 did Deutsch even hint that the concrete and specific economic and political behavior of the Japanese state might have been a legitimate, nonillusory cause of the deep strain of negativity that he had found in American attitudes toward Japan.[1]

Deutsch saw Japan's unpopularity not as the product of objective U.S.

experience but as stemming from a largely unconscious, associational image system—a collective American psyche that kept trapping and demonizing current news and positive information about Japan in a set of tenacious subliminal metaphors of economic warfare that linked Tokyo's past military aggression with its recent economic successes, thereby catering to the pervasive American sense of economic defeat at the hands of the Japanese. As Deutsch elaborated in his report, these images—of Japan as unfair, predatory, and threatening—were impervious to factual presentations. What they would require, rather, was a psychological strategy by the Japanese government to publicly expose their primitive emotional roots by presenting on American TV a parade of Japanese officials meticulously coached to a more informal, human, direct, American style of on-screen behavior that would contradict and erode those negative images. "Management of Japan's image," the report emphasized, "must make it possible for Americans to discern the common human heritage and personal human drama they share with the Japanese people. The Government of Japan as well as Matsushita, Toyota, and the Bank of Tokyo could then ride on the coattails of this achievement."[2]

The Deutsch report, the research for which was carried out with the assistance of Japan's consular officials and based on focus groups in Seattle, Detroit, and Washington, D.C., was unexceptionable as a work of image theorizing—although one might question the practical usefulness of its hypothetical model and belabored diagrams to busy Japanese diplomats. What is disturbing in retrospect is the apparent reluctance of the Japanese embassy subsequently to release the full original document, despite the alleged urging of its author to do so. This suggests that Tokyo may have had a more sophisticated awareness than he of the public furor it would have created if Americans had learned how deliberately a foreign government had set out to manipulate Uncle Sam's collective mind—and to carry out the project with the assistance of Americans willing to deep-probe and spin-dry the American mentality on issues of vital national interest as though these were just another object of Madison Avenue consumer research, like household detergents or cat food.

In its wooing of American intellectuals Japan has been greatly aided by the sedulous activities of a binational intellectual cartel that spans the Pacific in the name of mutual understanding. Although Japanese, American, and joint organizations as well as citizens of both countries serve this goodwill industry, the traffic over the bridge is largely one-way. It is a mutual enterprise, but one that functions largely as an arm of Tokyo's cultural diplomacy and political persuasion, since there is very little reciprocal, counterpart activity on behalf of the United States in, or toward, Japan.

Indeed, the United States has been handicapped in its dialogue by a severe imbalance in organized voices, institutional networks, and program activity to get the American view across to the Japanese side. Our Japanese friends may counter with the argument that U.S. culture has had an overwhelming presence in Japan compared to Japanese culture in the United States. Or that Japan has nothing in Washington or elsewhere in America to match our official cultural and informational arm in Japan, the U.S. Information Service (USIS, now merged into the State Department) with its five American Centers in Tokyo, Nagoya, Osaka, Fukuoka, and (until its recent closing) Sapporo.

The problem, however, is not one of general or popular culture—of fashion, cuisine, movies, music, and lifestyle. It is one of ideas, particularly on issues in dispute between the two countries, and of the opportunity to present them effectively to the other side. At stake here are the freedom and quality of America's *intellectual engagement* with Japan— the most essential aspect of our cultural relations with that country. And it should be a cause for national concern how that flow of ideas is being crimped, manipulated, and qualitatively degraded in ways that are the subject of Part II of this book. These have involved structures of argumentation, cash flows, organizational asymmetries, and the personal motivations of individual participants.

In the arena of ideas the Japanese have done better than we have. And that is because they have tried and succeeded (with our permission) in going beyond official governmental channels in the United States to penetrate, fund, and exploit the informal, everyday levels of American society with their public relations push—far more so than has been possible for Americans (that is to say, Americans speaking for America) in Japan.

From the 1970s—after years of entreaty by Americans and others to develop an active cultural diplomacy—the Japanese gradually began to shed their wallflower shyness and inertia, and by the mid-1980s they were at it with a vengeance. Japanese studies, cultural presentations, and issue-oriented symposia mushroomed at American universities, at theaters and museums, and at think tanks and public affairs organizations known for their impact on U.S. policy making and the American public's attitude toward Japan. The unprecedented Japanese governmental and corporate largesse supporting this type of activity today is in some respects routine, benign, and, indeed, long overdue—for example, the language programs, the arts festivals, and the scholarships for study in Japan. Some of it, however, has had a problematical edge that continues to require a watchful eye: the buying into our university and research establishments; the wooing of American opinion by Japan's chosen intellectual propagandists speaking with one voice at lavishly staged international conferences or at exclusive, elite seminars; the proliferation of glossy English-language publications specifically tailored for foreign readers and not always reflecting the fuller spectrum of Japanese views; the promotion of Tokyo's economic policies in the guise of cultural information; and the subtle ostracism of Americans critical of Japanese economic or political behavior.

This Mutual Understanding Industry, as one can only dub it, rests on four pillars, each of them marked by a heavy tilt in Japan's favor. First, there has been the rhetorical assault—both positive, in the unchallenged special pleading on Japan's behalf, and negative, in the sidelining of American voices that disagree. That is the subject of this and the following chapter.

Second, we have had ever since the early 1970s a one-sided flooding of Japanese government, corporate, and foundation money into America's academic and policy-oriented institutions—a flow of cash variously driven by Tokyo's anxieties and cash surpluses and by American need and greed as U.S.-based sources of funding dried up. This has resulted, not surprisingly, in the increasing subordination of our bilateral intellectual engagement to the policy objectives of Japan.

A third pillar is the network of organizations, more extensive and thickly meshed with each passing year, that work on behalf of American "understanding" of Japan—with no reciprocal webbing on the other side of the Pacific. Too much of our intellectual tie continues to be handled by politically motivated intermediaries rather than directly by the principals themselves, thereby aggravating the ongoing denial of reciprocal American intellectual access to Japan's academic, media, and scientific institutions.

Fourth and finally, little of this work would get done without the personal pro-Japan stance of the individual players, Americans and Japanese alike. Japanese hardheadedness has conspired with American naïveté regarding the political exploitability of cultural largesse. Odder still, so many Americans playing Japan's game here seem to think that they are actually serving their own country's national interest by doing so.

The Structure of Japan's Special Pleading

Japan's external propaganda in the postwar period has focused almost exclusively on the defense of its trade policies. Selling Japan's political or military role in the world to others seemed superfluous given Tokyo's commitment to the new pacifist constitution, its American security umbrella, and the geopolitical leadership it had entrusted to the United States.

Even cultural salesmanship remained dormant until it was dragooned into service after 1970 as the handmaiden of economic diplomacy. And what a pity that was, since there was so much in Japanese traditional and modern arts, literature, and lifestyle that would have delighted others—if only Tokyo could have detached it from its economic hard sell. As one Japanese cultural diplomat in Bangkok put it to me in 1971, when Southeast Asia was getting touchy about the extent of Japan's economic penetration: "We can't bring a Kabuki troupe down here, because the Thais would only see 'Toyota' written all over the face of it."

Tokyo's apologia on behalf of its trade policies may be viewed as the sort of nimble advocacy any modern state would employ in defense of national interests it believed to be threatened. And such issues, in recent decades, have been for the Japanese almost exclusively economic. What is unusual in Japan's case is the extent to which its contention on trade issues goes beyond the normal economic stuff of such disputes—my Iowa chickens against your Bordeaux wine—to enlist arguments of a cultural or emotionally manipulative nature. And what is truly astounding is how little Americans and others have done over the past three decades to contest Japan's familiar and repetitive special pleadings in a serious and consistent fashion, or even for that matter to realize that we have been under intellectual attack—thereby yielding the rhetorical high ground to Tokyo by default.

Because of the importance of the U.S. market Americans have been the chief target of Japan's intellectual campaign. To argue back effectively becomes more, not less, urgent as Japan at the dawn of a new century shows itself ready to extend the umbrella of its rhetoric to the protection of other Asian economies against the American push for open markets. To be sure, there have been some serious transpacific debates since the 1980s about divergent forms of capitalism or the relation between economics and national security, as briefly discussed in Chapter 18. What should be struck immediately from the bilateral duet over trade, however, are the polemical ploys Tokyo keeps strumming as an ongoing ground bass.

These gambits have come in three often-overlapping types: the pseudoeconomic, the psychological, and the cultural. The Japanese protagonists have included Tokyo's government officials, distinguished professors of American studies at Japan's leading universities, veteran journalists with the mammoth national dailies, and well-known all-purpose intellectual gurus. Nearly all of them belong to Japan's anointed establishment for the handling of America—a beguiling side job that has induced highly respected professionals to say some silly things. Their American amplifiers hail variously from our academic Japanologists and free-trade economists, from our institutions for Japan-U.S. friendship, and from officials of the Department of State and the Pentagon. Individual themes have come and gone and popped up again, but the overall pattern of Japanese argumentation remains firmly in place. Here are just a few samples of this sophistry—together with some suggested countergrips to Tokyo's intellectual judo.

Japanese special pleading starts—in its logical progression, at least—with trade arguments designed to deflect our attention from the objective import barriers.

1. *Whatever it is, it's different in Japan.* To roast some very old chestnuts: Japanese snow is different, it doesn't like Swiss skis; the Japanese intestinal tract is longer, it has trouble digesting Australian beef; Japanese baseball players don't like the *ping* of U.S-made aluminum bats. Meteorology, dietetics, and otology have all been dragged irrelevantly into the plea for special economic treatment. More pernicious, because automobiles and auto parts still account for the largest and most persistent part of the two-way trade deficit, has been the still-buzzing old saw that Detroit is too lazy to place its steering wheels on the right-hand side to conform to Japan's drive-on-the-left traffic. Thorstein Veblen immediately would have understood the snob value to the Japanese of having a *gaisha,* or foreign car, with the "conspicuous waste" of a driver's seat inconveniently located on the left. Remember from the 1950s, if you are old enough, that aura of one-upmanship—no prosaic American-made Lincolns or Cadillacs, thank you—that clung to those low-slung British MG open-top sports cars with their recondite gearshifts and their steering wheels on the "wrong" side? Roughly half the family vehicles in the designated parking slots at my recent Tokyo apartment residence were

upscale foreign cars, and more than half of these had their steering wheels on the left, including the BMWs and Mercedes-Benzes. Yet we never hear the Germans being twitted for showing the same sloth.

2. *Fighting American protectionism.* Starting with Yasuhiro Nakasone as far back as the early 1980s, Japan's prime ministers have repeatedly vowed to do their utmost to "help the U.S. administration fight protectionism." And Washington continues to buy it. All along, it has been Japan's long-established protectionism that has threatened to incite a merely prospective and reactive American protectionism, but by 1994 the resulting image to the world had become that of a much aggrieved and beleaguered free-trading Japan, hunkering down for the coming onslaught of American protectionism, bravely lending a hand to American free traders in a common front against the ugly monster. The readiness with which America's free trade dogmatists still tumble for this view of Japanese reality continues to underscore their myopic focus on the mote in their own eye.

The final bill for the American failure over many years to challenge this particular Japanese propaganda line was delivered at that disastrous Clinton-Hosokawa summit in February 1994, when Japan succeeded in painting the United States as the spoiler of the free trade system. U.S. officials in Washington and Tokyo could only fume as American intellectuals and journalists bought into a notion that should have been met with a cosmic belly laugh—since Japan has unwaveringly followed a protectionist, mercantilist policy since the war and (as we saw in Chapter 1) has yet to show any credible intention of willingly changing a policy that has proved so successful.

3. *American economic shortcomings.* Most Americans during the 1980s readily admitted that U.S. budget deficits and industrial decline during that decade were in part responsible for our trade deficits with other countries. American economic troubles whenever they do occur, however, should not be used to exonerate the Japanese from opening their own market while they continue to have a free and lucrative run of ours. Yet Japan's explainers on both sides of the Pacific went virtually unchallenged as they perpetuated this non sequitur.

A favorite corollary of Tokyo's line then and now has been that even opening Japan's markets fully would not make much of a dent in the trade balance. During the 1980s the argument was from the noncompetitiveness of American manufactures, and in the 1990s it came from the ravenous appetite of the reviving American economy for imports. Either way this corollary is about as relevant as the strong runner in a race reaching back with a cane to trip up his slower competitors—and, on being asked to desist, retorting, "Well, even if I did, you wouldn't able to catch up unless you lose some weight!" U.S. ambassador Mike Mansfield was particularly prone over the 1980s to tone down Washington's demands for market access with self-abnegating asides about the faults of the American economy—all true enough at the time, but perpetuating the logical fallacy that still serves to buttress Japanese intransigence today.

By 1989 American negotiators had tired of the slowness of institutional change in Japan and the laborious wresting of incremental concessions, sector by sector, under the so-called market-oriented sector-selective (MOSS) talks in 1985. With the new Structural Impediments Initiative (SII) they at last managed to turn the spotlight on Japan's systemic barriers, where it most surely belonged. For a brief moment Tokyo was deprived of its ability to brush off the contribution of those barriers to the U.S. deficit in bilateral trade with Japan by arguing the greater weight of macroscopic economic factors such as comparative productivity, national fiscal policies, or worldwide trade balances. When the SII failed to produce any tangible progress, however, and became tarred with the brush of "cultural imperialism" for presuming to alter Japan's internal behavior, U.S. officials in the early 1990s switched to a third, results-oriented strategy. This sought to establish agreed-on numerical benchmarks for American imports that the Japanese would be left to achieve as they saw fit. Unfortunately, Washington failed to defend this approach against the predictable charge of "managed trade"— for example, by simply showing that Japan does it all the time. Thus, by taking the heat off Japan's structural barriers, the new tactic allowed Tokyo to refocus on American shortcomings.

Freewheeling, loudly public, and at times downright cheeky in their advice for the ailing American economy during the 1980s, the Japanese withdrew into sullen resentment of American analyses and advice for Tokyo's economic woes in the late 1990s. With the economic positions now reversed, they complained that the United States was interfering in Japan's internal affairs. Such advice, they warned, should have been passed on sotto voce through discreet official channels, so as to avoid public embarrassment and a backlash of nationwide anti-American sentiment.

4. *"Good" and "bad" Americans.* When economic sophistry fails to convince, Tokyo often has resorted to the emotional stroking of poten-

tial allies or the psychological intimidation of perceived adversaries to push its case. When directed at the United States, this approach has undermined the rational discussion of objective national interests by personalizing and subjectivizing the entire binational relationship.

Economic disputation too often has been turned into an anti-protectionist morality play featuring vile and virtuous Americans. In Japan's taxonomy of U.S. attitudes on trade, the sheep (sheep indeed, one is tempted to add) have typically included the administration— although Bill Clinton during his first term did briefly try to grow horns— together with influential persons in the private sector thought to be sympathetic to the Japanese point of view. Those Americans who can articulate such opinions effectively have been welcomed into a prestigious circle of cultural bridgers and transpacific interlocutors. Tokyo goes to assiduous lengths to flatter and confirm these "good" American officials, business executives, and intellectuals in their own image of themselves as men and women of conscience, possessed of calm reason, intellectually sophisticated, internationally minded, unswayed by political pressures from America's competing economic sectors or geographical regions, and deeply concerned about the globe rolling off the protectionist deep end.

America's goats have been found variously in the rust-belt boonies, among the revisionist critics of Japan, in our senescent labor movement, and in Congress, which invariably has been depicted as emotional, unreasonable, ignorant, pushy, and immature—and no one more so than the cloven-hoofed Representative Richard Gephardt, arch befouler of the Japan-U.S. pastoral arcadia. This reflects in part the continuing Japanese contempt for their own elected politicians, who, whether as individuals or as parliament itself, have carried far less weight compared to the administrative arm than is the case in the American system of government. The underlying tone taken by Tokyo's spokesmen at economic conferences and cultural seminars with Americans has been that no intelligent, informed American could possibly disagree with the Japanese point of view. That is a fancy dangerously oblivious of the fact that Congress, with all its foibles, still reflects most faithfully among all U.S. federal institutions the voice and mood of the American people.

The implicit charge here has been that of bad manners. It is particularly effective with Americans inclined to deplore their own society's aesthetic crudities and quick to swoon at the refinements of Japanese etiquette. Incredible as it may sound, there are Japanese historians today who will chide Americans for the "rudeness" of Cordell Hull's controlled anger when the secretary of state confronted Ambassador Nomura and Special Envoy Kurusu in his office one hour after the start of Japan's surprise attack on Pearl Harbor. But Hull, of course, was one of those rigid, "puritanical" Americans—so the tut-tutting goes—who lacked the flexibility and sensitivity of mind to deal effectively with the Japanese.

5. *Sanctions are sour grapes.* Yet another way to needle the guilt of the sheep and shame the goats from the late 1980s was to discredit American trade demands toward Japan as the envy of a declining power—a proposition that got a timely boost in 1987 from Paul Kennedy's *The Rise and Fall of Great Powers,* which was immensely popular in its Japanese translation.[3] America's self-confessional openness about its own problems, still admired by the more liberal-minded Japanese, simply went to feed the contempt of cocky bureaucrats and nationalistic politicians—like the prominent conservative party politician at an Australian embassy dinner in 1988 who openly boasted at the table, to the embarrassment of his ambassadorial host, that the American economy was now simply there to service the Japanese. This was alarmingly reminiscent of the prewar self-conceit of Japan as a virile young David confronting a morally and physically flabby American Goliath. This bumptious line, temporarily in remission, draws on a deep-seated obsession to outpace the United States and can be counted on to resurface the moment our respective economic fortunes reverse once again.

6. *Japan bashing.* The reproach of sour grapes is just one variant of a more basic theme that represents Tokyo's most audacious polemical ploy: the grand accusation of Japan bashing. Thanks to Washington's failure to meet it head-on with judicious and timely rebuttals, this hoary old bromide has now sunk tenacious roots into the English language and the American psyche. No matter how factual or problem-specific, American trade complaints or revisionist writings or U.S. advice on the Asian crisis continue to be sensationalized and discounted by deliberately misconstruing them as an indiscriminate emotional attack on everything Japanese. The invention of the term "Japan bashing" and its masterful extension to cover all serious but embarrassing analyses surely was the Great Intellectual Train Robbery of the twentieth century. That was the phrase coined by political historian Clinton Rossiter to describe the way in which big business in the closing decades of the nineteenth century managed to hijack the old American ethic of individualism as an ideological and constitutional cloak for corporate rapaciousness.[4]

In 1992 the conscience-stricken American inventor of the term confessed how he had drawn on the British expression "Paki bashing" in the early 1980s to imply that criticism of Japan's policies was motivated by racism and xenophobia. As his immediate inspiration he noted the successful way in which Washington's pro-Israel lobby had been using the reproach of anti-Semitism to neutralize U.S. critics of Israel's policies. Robert C. Angel, now a professor of political science at the University of South Carolina, was at the time president of the Japan Economic Institute, a Washington-based research and public information center funded and supervised by Tokyo's Foreign Ministry. "I view that modest public relations success with some shame and disappointment," he later admitted. "Those people who use [the term] have the distinction of being my intellectual dupes."[5]

"Japan bashing," nonetheless, has gone on to enjoy a seemingly indestructible life of its own, being first picked up by the American press, then by the Japanese as *Nihon tataki*. It remains a classical example of how a wisp of American self-critical hyperbole can rapidly become a household word with the Japanese, allowing them to indulge their sense of victimization, unite against an allegedly hostile outside world, and slake their own pangs of conscience. Meanwhile, sensitive souls on the Potomac today, ignoring Angel's clarification, continue to wring their hands over accusations of Japan bashing. Indeed, as late as 2001 no less a Beltway economic guru than C. Fred Bergsten brought out a co-authored prescription for "building a new Japan-United States economic relationship" entitled *No More Bashing*.[6] Unable to tune in to Japan's own intellectual hubbub, too many American policy experts remain blissfully unaware of the genuine, frenetic America bashing that has gone on for years—as we saw in Chapter 2—in Japanese mass-circulation magazines, best-selling potboilers, and TV dramas.

7. *Anti-Japanese racism.* This makes overt the true charge encoded in the term "Japan bashing." As a device for emotional intimidation of both individual Americans and the U.S. foreign policy establishment as a whole, it is an artful dodge that simply stops all further discussion. The fear of being tarred with the brush of racism, or of contributing inadvertently to it in the United States, has helped to mute potential criticism of Japan among conscientious Americans. This holds equally for those of us who have not forgotten the history of anti-Oriental prejudice on the West Coast, those who worry about a reactive upsurge of anti-Americanism in Japan, and those who are afraid to provoke a back-

lash against themselves from America's own guardians of politically correct multiculturalism. Such fastidiousness merely permits the Japanese to write off any toughening of American trade tactics as a recrudescence of the old racial and cultural prejudices.

The Japanese, however, should be asked to consider in all sincerity the objective grounds for the unpopularity they encounter as others react to their market protectionism and closed society. During the 1930s the Japanese turned the newly restrictive U.S. immigration law of 1924 into a virtual casus belli, yet half a century later, at the height of their postwar prosperity, they balked at admitting a handful of Vietnamese boat people. And they still give their locally born and raised second- and third-generation Korean residents the cold shoulder. People who keep slamming the door in others' faces—somebody has got to say it, politely—are not going to be popular in anybody's cultural value system.

8. *Growing anti-Americanism in Japan.* The threat of "Yankee go home" was used to good effect throughout the Cold War period by most U.S. allies as an instrument for securing development aid, trade benefits, and political support for established regimes. The specter of a leftist opposition swinging Tokyo toward the Communist camp came in handy during the 1950s and 1960s in negotiations over the security treaty and the reversion of Okinawa. Since 1970 the bogey has been used to deflect market opening pressures, with the putative locus of anti-Americanism gradually shifting to the nationalistic right or to the Japanese public as a whole. The trouble with this device, as we saw in Chapter 2, is that it threatens to become a self-fulfilling prophecy.

9. *Don't derail the broader relationship.* "The broader relationship" (or TBR, as it came to be known among U.S. officials) has been a tune in a more melodious key—one seeking to belittle the importance of U.S. trade grievances relative to the military tie or the cooperative tasks that await the two countries on a global scale. As of the year 2002, these include upholding the world free trade system, ensuring the political stability of Asia, fighting terrorism, addressing threats to the environment, and meeting other grand multilateral challenges of the emerging post–Cold War order. The Center for Global Partnership was the name chosen for Japan's 50-billion-yen fund set up in 1991 by Japan's Ministry of Foreign Affairs for the cultivation of favorable public opinion in the United States. This government endowment was worth at least $500 million until the mid-1990s and was still over $450 million at the exchange rate prevailing in early 2000.

Indeed, Japan's invocation of TBR has been amplified by members of the State Department, Pentagon strategists, and other Americans whose concerns lie in the noneconomic aspects of the binational tie. As a former United States ambassador to Japan asked me, in a gracious private letter in 1998 commenting on my book *Cartels of the Mind,* was it really worth risking Japan's exemplary cooperation on strategic issues by stepping up pressures for economic and intellectual access to that country? That, I submit, is precisely the choice facing the United States at the start of the new century, although the ambassador and I obviously come down on opposite sides of that question. In any case, the focus on TBR got a quick fix—for the short term at least—from the Clinton administration's commitment in 1995 to a twenty-year continued military presence in Japan and East Asia.

Taken a step further, the Japan-U.S. relationship has been consecrated as an indissoluble marriage, as in Ellen L. Frost's *For Richer, for Poorer: The New U.S.-Japan Relationship.*[7] The problem with a gambit deflecting attention from trade issues to nobler tasks is that it is precisely those issues that, if left untended, will drive these economic odd-couple partners off the marriage track. That has been the blind spot of our Japan policy specialists, who loftily warn of the "vitriol" of trade disputes "spilling over" into the defense relationship, while deploring and obstructing any genuine effort to dismantle Japan's trade protectionism. Pushing TBR to its fanciful extreme, some of the Japan-U.S. networking enthusiasts even conjured for a while with the notion of a joint hegemony or "Pax Nipponamericana"—Japanese economic muscle and U.S. military might, judiciously coordinated by a Washington-Tokyo axis of economic, defense, and cultural committees of wise men. It is a seductive whimsy that has fed variously on proclamations of Europe's impending insignificance, conversely on the prediction (as with Professor Lester Thurow) of an emerging European Union behemoth, or more recently on the touting of China as the emerging strategic threat.[8]

10. *Don't abort budding change.* A corollary of the TBR argument is the one we questioned in Chapter 1, namely, that fundamental structural and attitudinal changes are just around the corner, if only the outside world will give Japan the leeway to work them out. This has been perhaps the cleverest rhetorical checkmate of all. Not only does it maximize the time gained for stalling, but it appeals to the American psyche at two of its most vulnerable points—our moralism and our irrepressible grasping after fresh straws of hope. Historically optimistic, believ-

ers in progress and the unlimited capacity of societies and individuals to change themselves for the better, and admirers above all of self-help, Americans are all too eager to stand back—patronizingly—to give the confessed sinner a chance to reform. Because further pressures, negotiations, or deals would be unseemly during the interim, what ensues is a moratorium on American meddling for the period of time prescribed for the changes to take effect.

Despite the failure of a series of short-term market-opening campaigns, the sputtering out of the political reforms promised after the temporary retirement of the Liberal Democratic Party to the opposition in 1993, and the dawdling of the Hashimoto, Obuchi, Mori, and Koizumi cabinets from 1996 to 2002 in addressing the challenge of Japan's longest postwar recession, elements in the American press and government at the turn of the century still seem eager to take the Methuselah's bait of predicted transformations in the Japanese approaches to work, consumer spending, bureaucratic guidance, and individual rights. Such social trends would indeed strike at the root of Japan's insular mentality and mercantilist policies—if and when they come. But, as we have seen in Part I, the evidence of their impending arrival is at best mixed, and even then it would take a number of years for Japanese grassroots pressure alone to force the required regulatory and institutional restructuring, and for those reforms to produce practical results.

11. *Americans don't understand Japanese culture.* When the economic and psychological lines of argument begin to sag, Japanese spokesmen can always retreat to the virtually impregnable redoubt of cultural defenses: Japan is exceptional; it needs to protect its unique heritage (a certified sympathy getter); the outside world fails to appreciate Japanese ways or to grasp Japan's actual intentions. The *Washington Post,* at least, was on to the game in its caustic editorial for 4 November 1995 commenting on the expulsion from the United States of Japan's giant Daiwa Bank for criminal conspiracy to cover up its gargantuan losses. "These revelations," the *Post* wrote, "were followed by a wave of exculpatory hokum from Tokyo about the unique nature of Japanese culture and its admirable inclination toward cooperation and conciliation."

This stratagem is hard for us to focus on because of the conceptual breadth and vagueness of the term *culture* as the Japanese tend to use it. Americans in particular have difficulty grappling with it because of the unpopularity of broad-brush cultural philosophizing in the United States as compared to Japan or continental Europe. The Japanese are the truest

Asian heirs of Hegel and Spengler, of what the Germans grandly call *Kulturkritik.* They have an insatiable appetite for the expansive, nonempirical categorizing of civilizations and historical eras and the differences between them. This takes place not only in scholarly books and op-ed columns but at well-libated student carousings as well, as the analogies and deductions glide giddily over the logical boundaries between fact, theory, and pure speculation. Yet for all that spilling of ink (or sake), the differences between Japanese and American thought patterns, value systems, and social behavior—incessantly rehashed in Japanese scholarly and popular writing—have little if anything to do with Tokyo's deliberately crafted market barriers. Unfortunately these false connections, so easily refuted, have simply washed over the pragmatic American mind, which—most unpragmatically—fails to catch their significance as a political weapon.

12. *Americans can't fathom the Japanese mind.* This is a special adjunct to #11, a form of epistemological protectionism (as we may call it) that is popular when all other forms of ad hominem ruses to discredit a foreign critic have failed. If the writer cannot be shown to be ignorant of Japanese language and culture, or emotional or unbalanced in his or her views, or somehow unhappy or poorly adjusted to living in Japan, then one can still complain that his argument is flawed by a failure to penetrate the Japanese way of thinking. This is particularly true when, as in my own case, that way of thinking is precisely the subject under discussion! Indeed, even in the most favorable Japanese magazine reviews of the translation of *Cartels of the Mind,* the reviewers in their closing paragraphs seemed to take refuge in the disclaimer—"Now, just among us Japanese"—that my book had been written too much from the standpoint of Western values and American interests. As if there were something intrinsically wrong with doing that. As if the Japanese opinion monthlies faithfully eschewed publishing articles written from the Japanese value or policy perspectives. As if these were not the very bread and butter of current-affairs writing in all countries!

13. *Reciprocity is a Western value.* In 1985 no less a figure than future prime minister Kiichi Miyazawa brushed off American demands for equal access, reciprocity, and a level playing field as a form of cultural imperialism. Spinning out his own spurious linkage between Tokyo's mercantilist trading practices and Japanese cultural values, Miyazawa argued that U.S. market-opening demands reflected ideals derived from the reciprocal social relationships that were peculiar to the

West, and from Anglo-Saxon athletic traditions that stressed fair play and abiding by the rules of the game. These were not, he insisted, applicable to Japan.[9]

Quite apart from the fact that Japan's economy has been the greatest beneficiary of the universal rules imputed to Anglo-Saxon sportsmen, one wonders why the Japanese have never been asked where they would be today had the United States and others chosen to apply particularistic Japanese-style standards to Japan. At the very least major American markets would have been closed to Japanese goods, Japan's correspondents barred from key Washington press conferences, and Japanese scholars and researchers denied permanent positions at American universities and laboratories.[10] And any effort by Japan to protest or change all this would have been rebuffed and resented as a culturally imperialist threat to the "American way of life."

14. *America must adjust to its relative power loss.* This final rhetorical ploy, now briefly in abeyance, remains deeply ingrained in Japanese sentiment and is destined to crop up again among Japan's toughly pragmatic leaders as soon as their country gets back on its economic feet, or when the American economy starts to slip—in any case, as the United States gradually loses its place of absolute preeminence in the post–Cold War world. Rules and principles are in Tokyo's eyes strictly situational, reflecting no more than a prevailing power relationship. As American power wanes it will take its noisily proclaimed rules of fairness and reciprocity with it, and the United States will simply have to live with the ancient principle of put up or shut up.

There may be a distant echo here of the old Confucian notion of the mandate of heaven slipping from the hands of incompetent rulers. But that was a distinctively Chinese formula for actual rebellion against an established sovereign, one that never took root in Japan's political cosmos, which was hinged on an inviolable, sacerdotal emperor up to 1945. Basically, the demand that Americans pipe down on preaching universals because they have lost their own particular clout derives from that exaggerated linking of ethics with power that one finds throughout Japanese society. High-ranking Japanese intellectual and political leaders from time to time still proclaim the absence of overriding universal principles as the very genius of Japan's philosophical heritage. Accordingly, more than in any other major nation today, might remains the acknowledged *conceptual* sanction for right, although it is never put quite so crudely at diplomatic receptions.

* * *

The sad fact of the matter is that very little effort has been made by the United States and others to challenge all these sophistries, non sequiturs, and red herrings and to do so directly in Japan, since Tokyo's special pleadings are addressed as much to the Japanese themselves as to others, driving them into a deeper sense of beleaguerment and reinforcing their ancient insular mentality. This absence of foreign rebuttal has been particularly odd in the case of the United States, which during the Cold War managed to develop such impressive psychological warfare capabilities with respect to the old Communist bloc—a time when the United States Information Agency (USIA), the American press, and general-purpose intellectuals were all poised to catch, expose, and refute every subtle twist of the Soviet propaganda machine.

Japan is hardly the old USSR, and it is as entitled as the next country to its own political advocacy, but what has been extraordinary is America's default on effectively reasoned counterargument as opposed to the occasional emotional outburst—or the congressional sledgehammering of Japanese cassette recorders on the Capitol steps. There were plenty of venues where it could have made a difference—at binational conferences, in congressional debates, on the editorial and opinion pages of the U.S. press. Instead, Americans hardly seem aware of the thrashing Japan has been giving us on the intellectual judo mat.

CHAPTER EIGHT

Ostracism
Sidelining the Heterodox

When all argumentation and co-optation fail, the binational Mutual Understanding Industry moves into *mura-hachibu* mode—the traditional Japanese method of containing hard-core dissent not by intellectual counteroffensive but by expulsion from the discourse. *Mura-hachibu*—in premodern times, literally "banishment from the village" and a sentence tantamount to death—still serves as the most feared informal weapon of consensus control in any of Japan's closely knit social groups today.

Admittedly, unlike the West, the ideologically syncretistic Japanese throughout their history have seldom inflicted inquisitions, purges, or martyrdoms on the unorthodox simply because of their deviant religious or philosophical beliefs per se. Buddhist sectarians in the medieval age, Christian converts in the seventeenth century, and Marxists in the early twentieth century were hounded or put to death for more pragmatic reasons—because of their perceived challenge to the established holders or systems of power.

During the Tokugawa era (1600–1867), too, contention among different schools of Confucian thought, or between the Confucianists and the exponents of Shinto studies or the later Western learning, could become nasty whenever they began to impinge on political interests or controversy. The typical strategy, however, was neither to best one's intellectual opponents in argument nor to burn them at the stake. Rather, it was to drive them (either as individuals or as schools gathered around a master figure) into isolation and silence through conspiratorial power plays aimed at cutting them off from their sources of political patronage and public esteem. These intellectual coups were known as *kuzure* (crumblings, ruinations), a term applied as late as the 1930s and 1960s to the collapse of leftist intellectual groups.

What concerns us here is the transfer of these Japanese bully-boy tactics of ostracizing the heterodox to American soil. The exclusion of dissident voices from the public debate on matters of national importance to the United States goes against the entire grain of American political values. The Japanese may be excused on grounds of their own social habits, but the willingness of so many of their American supporters to play along is a deeply disturbing matter, the more specific motivation and psychology of which we will take up in Chapter 12.

Intellectual skeptics about Japan in the United States have been sidelined by targeting their writings, their reputations, or their pocketbooks. Their literary product in some cases has been subjected to coordinated broadsides; in others it is systematically ignored. Quiet campaigns of personal defamation have been conducted against some of the heterodox; others have simply been dropped from the binational conference invitation lists. Where their unflattering analyses are still prospective, they have found themselves passed over for research grants or academic positions. In short, the Mutual Understanding Industry works to render them *salonunfähig*—that marvelous German word meaning "unfit for the front parlor." The velvet glove moves softly and subtly for the most part, but it proves brutally effective in the end, since it cuts all ties to the human web so essential for American scholars, journalists, and businesspeople whose work requires dealing with the Japanese on either side of the Pacific.

Censorship

First, as to the gagging of inconvenient writers: In my earlier study, *Cartels of the Mind*, I described Tokyo's failed attempts to cow the widely read journalist-authors James Fallows and Karel van Wolferen, who were writing at the peak of Japan's economic performance in the late 1980s.[1] A decade later—with Japan in recession and a "third opening" of the country supposedly just around the corner—similar efforts to silence or discredit critical writers, far from abating, were only picking up steam.

The classic example, of course, has been the all-out attack on Chinese-American author Iris Chang and her 1997 best-selling *The Rape of Nanking: The Forgotten Holocaust of World War II* by New Old Right revisionist historians and the entire Japanese diplomatic establishment in the United States.[2] Chang's greatest achievement with her book (and the reason for Tokyo's frantic reaction to it) was that, in addition to outlining the horrors of the Nanking Massacre of 1937–38, it had rekindled American awareness of the reluctance of the Japanese to come to grips generally with their wartime behavior—and it did so just as they were calculating that, with the turn of the century, they could simply sweep the whole thing under the rug once and for all. Japanese investigative journalist Katsuichi Honda had penned a searing Japanese-language indictment with his *Nankin e no Michi* (The road to Nanking) in 1987, but it took an English-language bombshell from an Asian-American woman author to touch the U.S. psyche and provoke sufficient foreign attention—a bit of literary *gaiatsu* (outside pressure)—to get the Japanese to refocus their minds on this issue.[3]

Honda still travels today disguised in a wig and dark glasses and keeps his whereabouts secret—much as did Salman Rushdie—for fear of a right-wing attempt on his life. When heterodoxy is intra-Japanese, the fist of lead or steel can dispense with the velvet glove. But in fact Iris Chang's silencing in Japan has been all the more effective because it has cut her message off from the Japanese reading public altogether. The revisionist historians were not content to organize a peripatetic committee of right-wing scholars to condemn her book with repeated appearances at the Foreign Correspondents Club in Tokyo and throughout Japan. In the end they prevailed on Kashiwa Shobo, the Japanese publisher contracted by Ms. Chang to produce the translation, to insist on incorporating directly into her text "corrections" they wanted made, to delete photographs and alter maps, and to bring out their own rebuttal in a companion volume. That went against the contract, to say nothing of accepted publishing ethics, and led Chang to withdraw her book. As a result, the Japanese have been deprived of her timely reality check and given only the revisionists' 288-page refutation to read, published by Yodensha in 1999 as *"Za Reepu obu Nankin" no Kenkyu* (A study of *The Rape of Nanking*) by Nobukatsu Fujioka and Shudo Higashinakano.

Even more disturbing was the way the Japanese government orchestrated its diplomats to get on the anti-Chang bandwagon. Ambassador Kunihiko Saito in Washington went public to criticize her book as "erroneous" and "one-sided," while Consul General Gotaro Ogawa descended on the editorial office of the *Honolulu Star-Bulletin* the day before Chang's lecture at the University of Hawaii on 24 November

1998 to protest their advance article on the event and deliver a pile of documents topped by historian Ikuhiko Hata's study characterizing Chang's book as a "preposterous fabrication."[4] Seated before a scholarly looking bank of bookshelves for *The News Hour with Jim Lehrer* on 1 December 1998, Ambassador Saito averred that the Japanese felt remorse for the past actions of their military and that he had just that day leafed through a dozen school textbooks mentioning Nanking. Asked by Lehrer if she heard an apology there, Iris Chang, posed against the Golden Gate Bridge, shot back that it was precisely the inadequacy of those references and the lack of apology that continued to infuriate the Chinese today—as the segment faded off the screen with Saito overvoicing his continued remonstrations.

Normally in free societies knowledgeable peers rebut controversial books postpublication in review articles, not by diplomatic interventions or by rushing into print with a countervolume while denying readers access to the original work. Obsessed with the precise number of victims rather than the manner in which unarmed persons were wantonly slaughtered over a period of several weeks, the revisionists were missing the moral forest for the statistical trees in harping on their estimate of 40,000 as against the official Chinese figure accepted by Chang of 300,000 (or Honda's admitted guess of 100,000 to 200,000). Having agreed to revise the handful of minor factual points actually proved wrong, Chang challenged her detractors to explain away the thousands of pages of diaries, intelligence reports, personal testimonials, and other primary-source materials on which she had built her case.[5]

Yet in 1999, when an English translation of Katsuichi Honda's study finally did emerge twelve years late from a U.S. publisher in response to Chang's impassioned breakthrough, certain American tut-tutters from the Mutual Understanding Industry used their praise of Honda to put down Chang gratuitously on the old score of her alleged inaccuracies and polemical style.[6] In fact, it would be hard to find a sharper polemic than Honda's fine book. And it may be thanks to Iris Chang that Honda's book found as many American readers as it did.

Less well known, but directed at a more influential and permanent source of anxiety for Japan's spin masters, was the ongoing attack in the late 1990s on the *New York Times'* reporting out of its Tokyo bureau—a humorless, nit-picking assault that simply did not understand the ethos of independent journalism or its breezy conventions with respect to human-interest stories and investigative reporting. There were a number of observers in Tokyo, myself included, who felt that political coverage by the *Times* was not best served by posting to Japan the prize-winning China-hand husband-and-wife team of Nicholas D. Kristof and Sheryl WuDunn, with their concentration on cultural and economic reporting. We were appalled, however, by the barrage launched against bureau chief Kristof and WuDunn when at New York's behest they produced a series of stories running from 1995 to 1998 on some of the less well known, idiosyncratic, and richly human aspects of Japanese life.

The countercharge began with an ostensibly spontaneous group of offended young Japanese women writers in Manhattan who produced a bilingual book entitled *Japan Made in U.S.A./Warawareru Nihonjin: Nyuyoku taimuzu ga egaku fukashigi na Nihon* (The Japanese ridiculed: Mysterious Japan as depicted by the *New York Times*). Edited and published from New York in 1998 by Zipangu, the name adopted by the group, this volume reached a new high in Japanese victimization mongering. Leading off with "The Ten Worst NYT Stories on Japan," the editors tore into Kristof and WuDunn for their takes on everything from Japanese animism to the marketing of Barbie dolls, Lolita complexes, groping of women on the subway, and wartime memories of the older generation. These were followed by a number of corrective cameo pieces from American Japanologists and journalists saying how much they loved Japan, leaving the reader with the impression that ignorance and prejudice make the *Times'* Tokyo bureau totally unfit to cover that country. In neither the Japanese nor the English half of this book, however, were the *Times'* original stories reproduced—only (as with Iris Chang) their refutations. And there was not a word from the editors about the long-standing parallel world of ethnocentric distortion in the Japanese press' reporting on the United States.

Kristof, who left Japan in 1999, shrugged it off with good grace, but the attack was subsequently picked up and elevated to the national level by the Japanese magazine press and media pundits. Like the Chang book, the presumptuousness here lies in trying to micromanage foreign news coverage toward favorable images of Japan. Unfortunately, we have probably not heard the last of this, for it has been a great favorite of the Mutual Understanding Industry for decades now to fund intrusive conferences and studies promoting "balanced" reporting (in both directions)—thereby sustaining the fancy that good journalism should serve the purposes of sweetness and light.

The Japanese translation of my own *Cartels of the Mind* by Chikara

Suzuki may well have been caught up in this broader backlash against Iris Chang and the *New York Times*. It was brought out by Mainichi Shuppansha in April 1998 under the title *Chi no Sakoku: Gaikokujin o Haijo suru Nihon no Chishikijin Sangyo* (Closed country of the mind: Japan's foreigner-excluding intellectual industries). Selling in Japan for well under half the price of the English original, it was printed in an initial run of thirty thousand copies in hardback, sold very quickly with aggressive advertising up to the twenty thousand mark, then suddenly came to a halt. My editors told me that the great national newspapers—the largest of them with daily circulations of eight million to ten million—had decided not to review my book, a consensus that even Mainichi was not willing to break, but one that probably cost us the sale of a few more tens of thousands of copies. The pressure to blacklist came not from the government but from the media industry itself, since I had been too tough on their exclusive *kisha kurabu* (reporters' club) system. Too tough, I was told, because I had mentioned too many names—not so much those of individuals or even of papers as, repeatedly, that of the Japan Newspaper Publishers and Editors Association (Nihon Shinbun Kyokai). To Japan's media industry, it was as if I had taken the name of God himself in vain.

It was an instance of *mokusatsu,* of "killing by silence"—the literary version of *mura hachibu*. Indeed, a sympathetic Japanese freelancer who interviewed me on my book for the limited-viewer English-study program of NHK-TV's educational channel told me before we began that part of our twenty-minute segment might be edited out before the January 2000 telecast because it was the policy of the quasi-governmental NHK not to carry any criticism of Japanese organizations. And when my Japanese publishers in 1999 were offered the first scholarly book-length study ever of the *kisha* club system, they turned down this work by a young American professor from a major U.S. university press on the grounds (so they told me) that they would only translate books that were *nihonjin-muki,* that is to say, "oriented" toward the taste and interest of Japanese readers. The fix, quite obviously, is in.

Attempts to insulate the Japanese public from unwanted outside views or protest crop up in other modes of communication, too. In a paper entitled "Silencing the Voices of Dissent in Japanese *Newsweek*" (presented to the annual Ph.D. Kenkyukai conference at the International House of Japan, Tokyo, on 2 October 2000), Professor Christopher Barnard of Teikyo University analyzed the consistent differences in authorial stances in articles lifted from the original English-language *Newsweek* for its Japanese-language edition. Barnard concluded that the silencing or muting of protest, inquiry, and criticism in the process of translation had produced "two different archives of public knowledge."

Dr. David McNeill, an Irish research scholar at Tokyo University who also runs a Japanese-language radio program with his Japanese wife on FM Sagamihara, tells of a more direct encounter in the year 2000. In one of their regular on-air replies to faxed responses from listeners, Keiko McNeill, who had lived in China with her husband, deplored the attempt by certain Japanese to deny the truth of the Nanking Massacre and suggested they should go visit the site to see for themselves. Her recommendation was addressed specifically to Tokyo governor Shintaro Ishihara, the steadily growing right-wing groups, the *yakuza* (gangsters), and the hot-rodding *bosozoku*. A young right-wing trucker happened to be tuned in to the broadcast, and within thirty minutes three enraged representatives of a right-wing association presented themselves at the radio station. Two days later, bowing to his Japanese manager's fear that the association would retaliate by harassing corporate sponsors, David McNeill settled the uproar with a "deep apology" for having insulted the right-wingers by mentioning them in the same breath as gangsters.

Subtler is the damper on critical views occasionally exercised by over-zealous moderators of transpacific Internet discussion groups and other electronic or printed outlets for the public exchange of ideas on Japan-related issues. It hardly advances the dialogue when critical observers sense an unspoken imperative to draw in their rhetorical horns, genuflect toward all counterpositions before making their point, and strain to assume the pose of an all-knowing judiciousness normally reserved for the Almighty.

More disturbing still—and flying in the face of its longstanding reputation as the examplar in Japan of the West's traditional freedom of the press—has been the recent blocking by the Foreign Correspondents Club of Japan (FCCJ) of appearances by two foreign authors whose path-breaking books until the mid-1990s would have been dished up for a literary luncheon or dinner not only with enthusiasm but as a matter of course. Recommended to the FCCJ in September 2000 by one of its distinguished former presidents—and then followed through repeatedly over a four-month period by the author herself (and finally by me) without receiving the courtesy of a single reply—was the serious, scholarly study of Japan's controversial and foreigner-excluding *kisha* (reporters') club system by Professor Laurie Anne Freeman of the political science department at the University of California/Santa Barbara. *Closing the Shop: Information Cartels and Japan's Mass Media* (Princeton University Press, 2000) was also the book I mentioned above as having been deemed insufficiently *nihonjin-muki* to merit translation into Japanese.

Five years earlier the veteran Irish economic journalist Eamonn Fingleton ran into a firewall of dodges and excuses at the FCCJ to keep him from reaching an international press audience and overseas readership for his new book, *Blindside: Why Japan Is Still on Track to Overtake the U.S. by the Year 2000* (Houghton Mifflin, 1995). The book controversially argued that the Japanese economic "slump" was a media hoax and that the Japanese establishment was exaggerating the country's economic difficulties and understating its strengths in an effort to stay below Washington's radar on trade. (Japan's "unstoppable juggernaut" image in the 1980s had greatly fanned American anger about U.S.-Japan trade imbalances during that decade.)

Fingleton had just survived an attempt in 1994 by the then FCCJ leadership to have him demoted from the rank of regular members to the nonvoting "professional associate" category on the grounds that, as a full-time author, he was no longer a "journalist!" This, despite the fact that the Club's articles of association explicitly recognized bona fide professional authors as journalists. Finding his requests to speak systematically stymied the length of 1995 by technical quibbles and dilatory tactics on the part of the Western journalist in charge of such Club events, Fingleton wondered what had become of the old celebratory spirit and customary privilege whereby FCCJ authors were given a press luncheon to publicize their new books. A year after the publication of *Blindside,* a new Club president finally overruled the self-appointed book-banner to give Fingleton his say, but by then it was too late to benefit the book's launch promotion.

Both Freeman and Fingleton, with their respective analyses of the Japanese press and economy, were strung out for so long and so elaborately despite their formally submitted interest as to throw the burden of proof, I think, on the FCCJ gatekeepers to show that these exclusions were *not* deliberate—and that they were not more concerned (as some of the Irish writer's friends surmised) about possibly offending the Club's greatly expanded (and budget-underwriting) Japanese media and corporate membership than about helping explain Japan to itself and to the world at large.

Finally, and most sadly of all, I must mention those foreigners who for one reason or another have upon returning home abandoned book-length materials recording various forms of xenophobic treatment they encountered during their stays in Japan—insights forever lost now to our further understanding of that country. I recall here in particular three chroniclers. One was the voraciously note-taking American Ph.D—a grandmother in her late sixties supporting an ailing elderly husband—who returned to the U.S. in sheer exhaustion after losing a protracted court battle to fill out the promised term of her private university post. Another was the young mainland Chinese engineer who took off in disgust (with a hard-won severance package) leaving behind a 100-page account in English of the spiritual "darkness," as he repeatedly put it, of the human relations and anti-foreign discrimination he had encountered in his Japanese company. And, finally, the Western business consultant who fled Japan under perceived threats to his own life as he set out to pen a book-length exposé of his globally feted, "internationalizing," former Japanese corporate boss—as something very different indeed.

Staining Reputations

Second, on the poison of personal defamation: The stain here spreads osmotically through the webbing of the Mutual Understanding Industry and then out into the larger world of American intellectual and public affairs. At its least toxic have been the subjectivized imputations—experienced by many of the revisionist writers—of racism, personal grudges, or psychological maladjustment to life in Japan.

Steven C. Clemons—the Executive Vice President of the New America Foundation, a centrist think tank in Washington, D.C., and a former senior aide to Senator Jeff Bingaman (D-New Mexico)—told me in early 2002 how "sick and tired" he was of the "games being played by Japan's gatekeepers" who were taking it upon themselves to determine which Americans were or were not "politically correct" enough to participate in bilateral Japan-U.S. study groups. Mentioning a number of Japanese gatekeepers like Tadashi Yamamoto of the Japan Center for International Exchange (see Chapter 12), Clemons was particularly incensed at the "Americans and Canadians" who were "badmouthing" him and others as unfit for the binational discourse. On the eve of his January 2002 speechmaking trip to Tokyo, Clemons learned that a long-time Japan-hand journalist turned Asia Foundation (Japan) director had been labeling him as a "real Japan basher" who would have to be "balanced" by others if he were to take part in the Pacific Council on International Policy's Japan Task Force, a project which Clemons and the New America Foundation had strongly supported. Having also helped the Asia Foundation—a "private" American organization almost wholly funded by the U.S. government—from losing its annual $5 million budget from Congress, Clemons wrote in high dudgeon to the Asia Foundation's headquarters in San Francisco and received an apology in writing. It was a rare instance where the victim had sufficient personal courage and political clout to confront his detractors and force them to back down.

In my own case, I had written two articles in the summer 1992 and winter 1994–95 issues of *The National Interest,* the first analyzing Japan's continued reluctance to open up its markets and society, the second emphasizing its ambivalent attitudes toward Asia. Eventually word got back to me that it was being politely whispered at Washington dinner parties and bruited about our own embassy in Tokyo that my views were not to be taken seriously because they had been motivated by my legal confrontation with a Japanese university over the renewal of my teaching contract in 1993. But I had been exposing the closed nature of Japan's academic system in the Japanese and American press ever since 1986, so that was putting the cart before the horse.[7]

Far more destructive and totally inexcusable has been the deliberate rumor-manufacturing directed in desperation at foreign critics who will not give in. These allegations of marital infidelity, sexual misconduct, or other grave transgressions without foundation have been a standard weapon of the *mura-hachibu* game among the Japanese themselves. Since they are libelous in nature, I will go no further with them here except to say that they are the devil's doing. Their victims are damned by their silence if they refuse to respond, and they are damned by their protestation if they do rise to the bait and speak out in their own defense, thereby amplifying the gratuitous gossip and squandering their own time and mental energies—in short, falling smack into the trap that Tokyo has set for them.

Scholarly Funding

Third, as to the crimping of academic grants: As a stunning recent example of this, the Center for Global Partnership (CGP) in the 1999–

2000 rules of competition for its Abe Fellowships for scholarly research ruled out any application "designed or intended to advocate a particular political position or issue area."[8] All too obviously intended to discourage studies of a critical or controversial nature, this is a recipe not for intellectual encounter but for mental disengagement. Indeed, this restriction was seen by some in Washington, D.C., as a panicked reaction by the CGP to an earlier Abe-funded study of the Japanese steel cartel by an intrepid American scholar that managed to slip out of the academic backwaters and find its way up onto Capitol Hill at the very time Congress was debating Japanese steel dumping in the United States. This was a devastating breach of the rhetorical ramparts for the Japanese, who with one voice had been denying the very existence of such a cartel.[9]

In a self-imposed extension of this new "apolitical" constraint to scholars residing in Japan and East Asia, the Tokyo regional committee of the U.S.-based Association for Asian Studies (AAS) turned down a roundtable on human rights in Japanese legal proceedings that had been proposed for the Asian Studies Conference Japan to be held in June 2002 by Professor Michael H. Fox, an American sociologist and specialist in conflict resolution at Hyogo College in the Kobe area. Focusing on the twin issues of forced confessions (including two recent convictions for murder now on appeal) and of media bias toward the criminally accused, Fox's presenters would have included Osamu Watanabe, a criminal law scholar par excellence; Kenichi Asano, author of over ten books mostly on the abuse of media power; and Charles McJilton, the head of a support group for a Filipina accused of murder in Tokyo. In rejecting Fox's proposal the conference organizer, Professor Linda Grove, an American Sinologist at Tokyo's Sophia (Jochi) University, wrote to him that "we believe that our conference is designed for academic study and debate, rather than for advocacy."

Here—with an ivory-towered primness that would have drawn snorts of contempt in a U.S. or European university setting—was the supine surrender of American values both scholarly and political in the pursuit of truth in a free marketplace of ideas. In a subsequent conversation Grove explained to me that her committee had received twice as many proposals as there were time slots, and that Fox's panel would be reconsidered at a future date if he came back with a more "balanced" membership, not only those intent on exposing the wrongs of the Japanese criminal justice system. (Be that as it may, as a longstanding dues-paying member of the AAS, I want my money back!)

Aborting unwanted research before it even gets going is, of course, the most effective means of suppression. I still recall from my years as the associate director of the Japan-U.S. Friendship Commission the American film ethnologist from Alaska who had won a U.S. government-funded grant from the commission and the National Endowment for the Arts with his proposal to study and film the so-called *buraku* community. These are the people, racially indistinguishable from other Japanese, who for centuries were the outcastes of society, although legally equal from the Meiji Period on. In the end our grantee was forced to shift his project to the Caucasoid Ainu communities on the northern island of Hokkaido when his original proposal was blocked by the Cultural Affairs Agency, his mandatory sponsor in Japan. This official guardian of Japan's cultural chastity explained to me at the time (rather disingenuously and irrelevantly) that the target people were not an ethnic entity but a political social pressure group. More honestly, they admitted that they simply did not want to see such a film made. And—in a psychological inversion marking these victims as full participants in Japan's shame culture—they themselves might well have resisted even a sympathetic foreign exposure of their uncompleted quest for integration with the mainstream population.

There is evidence, finally, that the Abe Fund's taboos may be spilling over into American-sponsored academic fellowships as well. In 1999–2000 I met a talented young American anthropologist in Tokyo who was financing his own Japan-based doctoral research on the now virtually extinct protest movement against the expansion of Narita Airport. He had decided to go out on his own, no holds barred, after an American member of the Fulbright screening committee in New York told him informally that he had been rejected for this federally funded grant program because his project was "too controversial." In the *Fulbright* program, that old bellwether of American cultural diplomacy, for goodness' sake!

Whatever the precise forms of ostracism, they have all become possible thanks to the overwhelming Japan tilt in the practical resources— money, organizations, and people—that are available to the Mutual Understanding Industry in dominating the Japan-U.S. dialogue within the United States today. It is to these that we now turn in the following four chapters.

CHAPTER NINE

Yen

The Pavlovian Trot for
Japan's Academic Largesse

Hundreds of millions of dollars over the past two decades have flowed from Japanese business and government into American universities, think tanks, public affairs organizations, and programs for U.S. schools—a phenomenon without historical precedent in any binational relationship. Not in the ongoing Franco-German effort at reconciliation through massive youth and sister city exchanges first launched by Adenauer and de Gaulle, not in the generously manned and superbly professionalized cultural presence of the British Council flung worldwide by retreating British power, and not even in the grand ideological push of the USIA and the Voice of America during the Cold War has the world seen anything quite like this before: the deliberately targeted and one-sided financial penetration by one nation of another's intellectual system.

Highly controversial when first called to the attention of the broader American public around 1990, Japan's academic largesse was stale news by 2000. This is not because the Japanese have stopped giving—although they are doing so less dramatically, thanks to their recession and the reduced trade pressures from an economically triumphant Uncle Sam. Mainly Americans are simply taking it all for granted now and hardly seem to care anymore. If the key story through the early 1990s was the amount of Japanese money being given, the most disturbing tale since the middle of that decade has been the collapse of American scruples about taking it.

The greater portion of Japanese corporate contributions to U.S. institutions of higher learning has been spent on the extraction of cutting-edge science and technology from America's leading research universities. The balance has gone toward the input of approved images of Japan—for the promotion of more (and more-favorable) knowledge, perceptions, and policy thinking toward Japan among American scholars, policy makers, and the general public of all generations. Some of this money covers demonstrable gaps in information—the point American recipients typically invoke in justifying their own receptivity. For the Japanese donors, however, the overall intent has been to build a Great Wall of favorable sentiment in the U.S. intellectual mainstream to secure Tokyo's trade and investment stakes in the United States against any challenges from American workers, politicians, and the more skeptical writers in the media and academe.

These efforts at intellectual manipulation came on top of the $100 million and $300 million respectively that Japan (according to one observer's estimate in 1990) had been pumping annually into the Washington lobby system and into grassroots politicking at the state and local levels.[1] They are also in addition to the activities of America's "revolving door" officials who leave high and often Japan-related U.S. government posts to serve as lobbyists or consultants for Japanese interests—a reversal of advocacy that would be viewed as close to treason were Japanese ex-officials to attempt anything like it in Tokyo. This direct manipulation of the U.S. political system—a theme widely explored by concerned Americans in the press and Congress since the late 1980s—has paralleled, reinforced, and interpenetrated with the more subtle and hence less well understood cultural lobbying that is our narrower subject here.[2]

Who Gets?

To give a rough idea of the donors, recipients, amounts, purposes, and implications of this largesse, the lion's share of cultural cash has come from Japanese corporations and has gone to American universities and think tanks. Here it has been targeted on areas where the stakes for Japanese business in U.S. scientific research—and in what we might call policy protection—are particularly high. With the expiration in 1989 of the 1986 amendment to the Higher Education Act of 1965 requiring U.S. colleges and universities to report foreign funding of over $250,000 to the secretary of education, there is no longer any systematic way to track Japanese contributions to American academe. The study carried out over one year by Stephanie Epstein for the Center for Public Integrity to determine the flow during the half decade 1986–91 (when that federal requirement was still in effect) suggests, nevertheless, some orders of magnitude.

A partial accounting for ninety-three American colleges and universities taken exclusively from public sources lists over $175 million in Japanese money received during that period, all but $3.4 million of it from corporate donors. Even at that, the study found that thirteen of the major university recipients had failed to file disclosure reports for over $46 million in Japanese receipts during 1986–89. The leading beneficiaries of the $175 million were the Massachusetts Institute of Technology ($24.0 million), the University of California at Irvine ($16.5 million), Harvard ($8.3 million), the University of California at Berkeley ($6.1 million), Columbia University ($5.1 million), the University of Michigan ($4.7 million), Stanford University ($4.5 million), and the University of Illinois at Urbana-Champaign ($3.1 million).[3]

The funding came both from Japanese parent companies and from thirteen corporate-sponsored foundations based in the United States, such as the Matsushita Foundation and the Toyota USA Foundation. About two-thirds of the total amount was earmarked for scientific research and teaching. Some of these grants were gargantuan and on the high-tech frontier, as with UC Irvine's $16.5 million from Hitachi Chemical for a biotechnology research facility, or the $85 million to Massachusetts General Hospital for sponsored research by doctors with joint appointments at the Harvard Medical School.[4] Others were more modest but very closely pinpointed both geographically and in purpose—for example, the grants of $100,000 each from Omron Manufacturers of America for scholarships in electronic engineering at five universities in one single state (Northwestern University, Northern Illinois University, Southern Illinois University, the Illinois Institute of Technology, and the University of Illinois at Urbana-Champaign). We may reasonably surmise that these were made with some expectation of eventually tapping into that freshly minted American talent.

The remaining third of Japanese corporate funding during those six years went for chairs and other programs or acquisitions relating to the study of Japan itself, mostly in the professional graduate schools where American interest and demand was highest: $1.25 million apiece from Nippon Life and Nomura Securities for endowed chairs in business at the University of Pennsylvania's Wharton School; $3 million from Mitsui

Life for Asian financial market research at the University of Michigan business school, and another $1.7 million from Sumitomo Bank and Nippon Life for teaching and research on Japanese legal studies at that university's law school; $2 million from Japanese financial institutions for the Center on Japanese Economy and Business at Columbia University, and another $1.5 million for the business school there. By 1996 several American universities were maintaining permanent fund-raising offices in Tokyo to keep the money flowing.

Harvard, even without a Tokyo office, had one of the widest disciplinary spreads, with fifteen teaching positions funded by Japan as of 1996. Donations from 1991 to 1996 alone included $2 million from Toyota for the Edwin O. Reischauer Chair at the Center for International Affairs, a $2 million endowment from the Sumitomo group for a chair at the Kennedy School of Government, $3 million from Nomura Securities to the Harvard Law School for a professorship in international financial systems, $1.25 million from the Todai Corporation for computers at the Graduate School of Design, $3 million from the owner of Kyoei Seiko (a steel manufacturer) for the Takashima Professorship in the Department of East Asian Languages and Civilizations, $3.5 million from the Tsuzuki Integrated Institutes (a conglomerate of some fifty schools running from kindergarten to junior college in Fukuoka) to the Graduate School of Education and the president's discretionary fund, and $3.1 million from the Kinoshiro Taisetsu construction firm in lumber-rich Hokkaido for a chair at the School of Public Health for the study of indoor environments.[5]

Harvard's case illustrates the breadth and ease with which Japan's academic largesse has come to be given and taken nationwide—tracking down endowed chairs gets to be more and more like swatting flies in an unscreened kitchen. Even a cursory glance at the West Coast turns up another Takashima Chair in Japanese Culture at the University of California at Santa Barbara, a $2 million Kiriyama Chair for Pacific Rim Studies at the University of San Francisco (donated by the founder of the Agon Shu Buddhist sect), and a Sen Rikyu Chair at the University of Hawaii endowing, inter alia, a full semester's course entitled "The Way of Tea in Japanese History and Culture."

Most of the money for traditional Japanese studies had been distributed earlier, during the 1970s and early 1980s, when American universities were concerned to strengthen their basic teaching and library resources on Japan in the humanities and social sciences. The Donald

Keene Center of Japanese Culture at Columbia and Harvard's Edwin O. Reischauer Center for Japanese Studies are legacies of that earlier stream of largesse. As the kickoff for its new activist cultural diplomacy toward the United States, the Japanese government in 1973 announced a $10 million package of donations of $1 million each (informally dubbed the Tanaka Fund, after the then prime minister) to ten American universities with established but financially strapped Japanese studies programs: Harvard, Yale, Columbia, Princeton, Michigan, Chicago, Washington (Seattle), UC Berkeley, Stanford, and Hawaii. That same year the Mitsubishi Corporation gave $1 million to the Harvard Law School for a chair in Japanese legal studies, followed by a million-dollar donation from the Sumitomo Group to Yale. Needless to say, it did not take university development officers very long to decide to go for a lot more.

Here, too, Harvard played the role of bellwether when it launched a fund-raising campaign in Tokyo from 1973 to 1976, with the pivotal assistance of the Keidanren (Federation of Economic Organizations). This netted a total of $5.9 million (in addition to the Mitsubishi law and Tanaka Fund politics chairs) from Nissan, Toyota, the electrical power federation, the banking sector, the securities industry, the iron and steel sector, and the Foreign Trade Council (trading firms). As Harvard's Tokyo representative for that fund drive, I watched as other schools rushed over with their own pails to milk the Japanese cash cow, their successes ranging from a few million for MIT to a token squirt of $500,000 for San Francisco State following a visit by its president (and later U.S. senator) S. I. Hayakawa. The Tokyo stampede was on for U.S. "academic beggars—with me in the lead," as Professor Edwin O. Reischauer confessed to me in a pensive moment during one of the three fund-raising journeys to Japan that I arranged for him. I believe the former ambassador to Japan felt deeply uncomfortable in his new money-raising role but was carrying on like a good soldier for the university's sake. Twenty years later, in 1993, undisclosed Japanese business circles leaked to the press a proposed plan to raise the yen equivalent of $271 million for Japan-related activities at the university as a token of gratitude to Harvard for having educated the newly married crown princess, the former Masako Owada (who received a bachelor of arts degree in 1986). In the end nothing came of it ("not one yen," as a Harvard spokesman put it to me), but this time no one raised an eyebrow—nearly anyone who could use a yen had climbed on the gravy train.[6] So much had times changed. (And Harvard never did raise from American sources the matching amount of $5 million for Japanese studies that it had promised its Japanese benefactors during the early 1970s fund drive.)

Some observers thought the flow of Japanese cash might ebb with Tokyo's financial crisis of 1997–98. University administrators were increasingly reluctant to divulge the amount of contributions they were receiving from Japan or (often more to the point) their precise allocation as to programs and purposes. Nevertheless, Harvard by 2000 had successfully completed a vigorous five-year Japan fund-raising campaign for 2.1 billion yen ($21 million at 100 yen to the dollar) toward its projected new Harvard Asia Center in Cambridge. This time the university had a regiment of prominent Japanese business, government, and academic leaders on board as campaign sponsors and fund-raisers to promote the drive in their own country.

Meanwhile, a short paddle down the Charles, the Massachusetts Institute of Technology by 2001 had a total of thirty teaching chairs funded by Japanese corporations, twenty-two of them full professorships at $3 million apiece, but only one of them for the study of Japan per se. Among all industry-sponsored research (omitting multisponsored projects), Japan's share of $4.9 million in fiscal year 1997 paled beside the $40.2 million funded by North American sponsors, but it outdistanced the $4.2 million from all European countries combined, as it has nearly every fiscal year since 1991; Japan's contribution was five to seven times that of Germany, the next largest foreign participant. Japanese funding also helps to support MIT's International Science and Technology Initiatives for educating global managers and engineers, whose MIT-Japan Program is the largest "applied Japanese studies" program in the world and the model for more recent MIT language and cultural enhancement programs on China, India, and Europe for scientists and engineers.[7]

The second major target of Japan's corporate giving has been Washington's quasi-academic think tanks, whose researchers not only cross-fertilize with university-based scholarship but also have a more direct impact on political opinion and national policy formulation through publications, conferences, TV appearances, and testifying before Congress —often on economic issues that are of vital interest to Japan. The study from the Center for Public Integrity listed Japanese contributions of over $5.2 million during 1986–90 to four of the leading policy research centers: $1.8 million to the Center for Strategic and International Studies (CSIS), $1.6 million to the Brookings Institution, $1.0 million to the Institute for International Economics, and $846,000 to the American

Enterprise Institute.[8] To gild its lily, the CSIS also has a Japan chair fully endowed by Toyota. Whether oriented slightly to the right or to the left, these establishmentarian institutions lean toward free-trade advocacy. Even more important for Tokyo, their residue of self-assured, global-oriented internationalism carried over from the Cold War decades makes them uncomfortable with—and therefore a gratifying counterbalance to—the antiglobalist voices in Congress and elsewhere calling for more skepticism with respect to Japanese promises and for tougher, more country-specific measures in dealing with bilateral trade deficits.

Who Gives?

The flagship for Japan's governmental funding of the Mutual Understanding Industry has been the Center for Global Partnership (CGP), established in 1991 with an endowment then equivalent to $350 million for the stated purpose of promoting Japan-U.S. collaboration on global responsibilities and enhancing the dialogue and interchange between individual citizens of the two countries. With a capital fund that by 1998 had grown to the dollar equivalent of nearly $500 million and an annual budget of over $15 million, the CGP is in effect Tokyo's official arm for cultivating goodwill and favorable opinion among America's political, business, civic, and intellectual leaders at both the national and grassroots levels. In its three program areas the CGP operates through short-term project grants, normally in the five-figure or low six-figure (dollars) range, and pegged to binational participation. These go to individuals, collaborative researchers, and public affairs and exchange organizations in both countries rather than underwriting the large permanent endowments that have typified Japanese corporate giving to American universities.

Nearly everything the CGP does has a public affairs (as opposed to strictly scholarly) angle to it that seeks to focus the American mind on the importance of harmonious and collaborative ties (the broader relationship) with Japan—and by indirection, at least, to discredit concern and contention over bilateral trade issues. Indeed, with the tougher line by the first Clinton administration and American trade frustrations heading for a new peak at mid-decade, the new programs of the CGP came on line "just in time." During program year 1994, for example, the Intellectual Exchange Program spent $2.5 million in its subcategory "Policy-Oriented Research" on thirty-four binational studies by universities and think tanks in both countries, ranging from security issues in Northeast Asia to the harmonization of law in the Asia-Pacific region, Central Europe's transition to free markets, bioethics, and the environmental degradation of Tokyo and New York. Another $2.75 million in the "Dialogues" category went to twenty-five organizations such as the American Assembly at Columbia University and the Carnegie Endowment for International Peace for conferences of experts on questions of human rights, nuclear nonproliferation, health care, and the exchange of young American and Japanese political leaders and government administrators. In the category "Access to Current Information," $1.2 million went to six American institutions, including the Library of Congress for its Japan Documentation Center and Public Radio International in Minneapolis for its reporting on Japan.

With its Regional/Grassroots Program the CGP reaches down into local school systems, friendship societies, and service organizations throughout the United States. Preaching to Americans with no hint of Japan's own monolithically homogeneous and ethnically closed society, the annual report for 1994 grandly admonished that "growing diversity and international interaction require us to embrace a new, multicultural model of society."[9] In the subcategory "Educational Outreach," $2.36 million was spent in 1994 on educational resource and development centers at select U.S. universities and foundations to prepare precollege teaching materials on Japan, and on the public outreach forums of Japan-America societies and world affairs councils. Under "Exchange" an additional $1.5 million went to counterpart groups ranging from women leaders, high school students, and NGO professionals to commercial fishing communities in Alaska and northern Japan.

Under its third program, Fellowships, the CGP disbursed $2.25 million through the professional U.S. peer-review processes of the Social Science Research Council and the American Council of Learned Societies to nine American and seven Japanese Abe Fellows in the humanities and social sciences, and another $1.58 million to about eighty American scientists and engineers recruited through the National Science Foundation for short-term stays in Japan. The CGP's fellowships are its closest thing to traditional academic exchange, but once again, the Abe grants have been pegged to public policy research where the mandate for "integrating exceptional individuals into collaborative efforts" serves to expose an increasing number of American Japanologists to Japanese policy views. The really striking feature of the CGP, however, is less its message than the sheer size of its financial commitment and the breadth of its intellectual input into one single foreign country.

The CGP, with its own separate endowment and program, is part of the Japan Foundation, which in turn is a special legal entity under the auspices of the Foreign Ministry, with active-duty diplomats manning its top executive posts. With budget resources of about $200 million in recent years—roughly one-third that of the British Council worldwide— the Japan Foundation similarly has served as Japan's main agency for traditional cultural-exchange work in language, scholarship, arts, and sports throughout the world. Its American programs—outside the purview of the CGP—were worth about $7 million annually as of 1993. They continue to offer dissertation and postdoctoral grants in the humanities and social sciences and support for artistic performances and exhibitions, targeted at Americans who still want to study Japanese poetry, religion, or social institutions in depth or to see a run of experimental films or priceless Buddhist statuary—and to do so without being dragooned into the intellectually thin if frothy rush toward copiously funded and politically baited "issues dialogue" and "policy relevance."[10]

The true accomplice and forerunner of the CGP's public affairs push in the United States is not its parent Japan Foundation but the United States–Japan Foundation (USJF), an entity incorporated in 1980 under U.S. law with a capital grant of $44.8 million from the late right-wing mogul Ryoichi Sasakawa—money derived from legalized speedboat racing, cleared by the Japanese government, and supervised by a binational board. I remember attending the opening gala at the Okura Hotel, Tokyo, in a setting fit for Croesus, with three sitting and former prime ministers and the icons of Japan's political and business establishments in attendance, and Benjamin Hooks hanging a medal around Mr. Sasakawa's neck in recognition of his contributions to the work of the NAACP. Former U.S. presidents Ford and Carter had been wooed onto the board as honorary advisers, but this clearly was not an outfit destined to stray any great distance from Tokyo's policy objectives. Despite its American staff, legal status, and headquarters in New York, I subscribe to the Trojan horse thesis that, being funded exclusively from Japanese sources, this foundation serves the cultural-diplomatic—and political—interests of Japan far better than it does those of the United States or of genuinely disinterested private-sector exchange.[11]

During two decades of operation from 1980 to 2000 the USJF had disbursed nearly $57 million and over 1.5 billion yen in grants. During

1999 and 2000, for example, grants of over $100,000 apiece were made to the Center for Strategic and International Studies in Washington, D.C. (including its affiliated Pacific Forum/CSIS in Honolulu), the East-West Center, the Asia Society in New York, and the following American universities: City College/City University of New York, East Carolina University, the University of Maryland, Ohio State University, the University of Oregon, Stanford University, the University of Tennessee at Chattanooga, and Columbia University (which alone received over $735,000 in two years).

To get an idea of motives and objectives, the USJF by 1993—a typical year about midway through its 20-year history—was supported by a capital base that had grown to $93.4 million and an annual program budget of $5.6 million. Its stated goals were to "build the new stock of intellectual capital from which both countries will have to draw in the management of our relationship during this time of rapid change"—as good a statement as we have had of the Mutual Understanding Industry's self-appointed mission: to help manage the bilateral tie. The USJF concentrates on the public (as opposed to academic) education of Americans on Japan through the support of policy studies, media coverage, leader exchanges, and precollege education. Some of the larger net grants authorized in 1993 included $200,000 for a Brookings Institution study on the integration of the world economy, $158,171 to the Research Institute for Peace and Security (Tokyo) for a U.S.-Japan consultative group on Indochina, $255,257 to National Public Radio toward the establishment of a Tokyo bureau, $260,200 to the Fund for the City of New York for the exchange of urban experts and officials, and $159,829 to the Japan Society of New York for the ninth year of its U.S.-Japan Leadership Program—all of these grants being annual segments of multiyear commitments.[12]

The spread parallels that of the financially more powerful CGP (as do many of the recipients). The largest collective sum of grants from the USJF in 1993, roughly in the $100,000–$150,000 range each, went to seven U.S. universities and five educational organizations to support high school teacher training, curriculum development, and the preparation and dissemination of instructional materials for teaching about Japan at the precollege level. From its earliest years the USJF has worked to establish a network of such programs at key universities such as Columbia University, the University of Maryland, East Carolina University, Wayne State University, Indiana University, the University of Illinois at Urbana-Champaign, the University of Minnesota, the University of Kansas, the University of Arkansas at Little Rock, Texas Tech University, and the University of Alaska, each of which (except Alaska) services a multistate region, with a National Clearinghouse for U.S.-Japan Studies at the University of Indiana. Later on the project was made bilateral, with similar amounts in 1993 going to six Japanese universities to develop model plans and regional networking for precollege teaching about America.

Although a former president of the National Council for Social Studies once warned that "as a profession we leave ourselves open to being bought" by permitting another country to pay for teaching about it in U.S. schools, a great deal of wholesome work is no doubt being done here at a critical level of mutual ignorance or half-knowledge. The slippery part on the U.S. side comes not from input by America's Japan experts but rather from the uncritical introduction of Japan-produced teaching guides and outlines of Japanese history that promote Tokyo's views on trade issues or present a history of mutual ties without even mentioning the Pearl Harbor attack or the conquest of Manchuria—historically fateful turns, to say the least, in the binational relationship.[13] And if the practical challenge for these programs in America's decentralized system will be to get the schools to actually use them, improved teaching on America in Japan will have to buck Tokyo's rigidly uniform, centrally controlled, and nationalistically oriented school system.

Finally, a much larger and Japan-based fund established by the late acknowledged godfather of Japan's postwar ultrarightists is the Sasakawa Peace Foundation (SPF), Japan's largest international foundation, with total assets of nearly $650 million in 1999 for philanthropic projects worldwide. Sasakawa was best known in the United States for his overt grab at high political influence (and, some thought, a Nobel prize) through support of Jimmy Carter's presidential library and Carter Center at Emory University in Atlanta. Far more significantly, his SPF has reinforced the policy-oriented thrust of the CGP and USJF through fellowship and project grants in recent years to some of America's most influential scholarly centers for foreign and economic affairs, including the Council on Foreign Relations, the CSIS, the Fletcher School of Law and Diplomacy, the Johns Hopkins School of Advanced International Studies, the Woodrow Wilson School for International Affairs at Princeton, the Haas School of Business at the University of California at Berkeley, and the American Enterprise Institute.

Who Cares?

For anyone who has worked with Japanese universities, this seemingly endless roster of American blue-chip academic institutions gobbling up Japanese money in multiple millions is simply breathtaking when placed in the context of Japan—where just one campus taking $1 million from a U.S. donor would be news, and hotly debated news at that. But who in America cares any longer? Does academic largesse from a foreign country for our study and research on it matter? Is it really no more than due tribute to the excellence of U.S. higher education, as increasing numbers of Americans have come to think?

As we shall see in the next chapter, it is a more subtle matter than raw cash and Bunraku puppet strings. As with our quasi-academic think tanks, the Japanese subvention of chairs, physical plant, and research projects at American universities does not crudely "buy" scholars at the first flash of free cash. What it does produce when the amounts and conditions are sufficiently intrusive is an altered, Japan-supportive structure and intellectual climate for scholarship on that country. By pouring money (and prestige) into certain lines of study while quietly downgrading others, by commanding the lion's share of grants available for research in Japan, and by co-opting scholars into an ego-stroking transpacific jet set and engaging them as go-betweens on matters of high intergovernmental policy, Tokyo skews the academic playing field for American Japanology. And it is simply perverse to go on insisting that all of this transpires without any political consequences.

Let me close this chapter with two personal vignettes suggesting the enormous political stake that the Japanese, at least, see in their academic spending in the United States.

One evening a number of years ago I was about to enter the International House of Japan (the favored venue for transient foreign scholars in Tokyo) on a private errand when I found the finance minister, Noboru Takeshita, hard on my heels. Popping out of his official black limousine, he was rushing to a small reception hosted by Columbia University, a major recipient of early and continuing Japanese largesse. A distinguished American scholar of Japanese literature whom I recognized through the open door had already started the proceedings.

"The finance minister of America's most problematical economic rival!" I chuckled to myself at the time. How scholarly can we get? I still conjure gleefully with the frenzy that would hit the Japanese press were the likes of Robert Rubin or Larry Summers to turn up in New York to be thanked or entreated at an intimate dinner meeting of dollar-hungry Japanese scholarly experts on America from (say) Waseda University.

Recently, old Harvard friends prodded me to crash a more dramatic scene at Tokyo's most prestigious hotel, the Okura, on the evening of 19 January 2000. Flanked by American ambassador Tom Foley and an aging cohort of Japan-America cultural intermediaries who were still at it after the thirty years I had known them, Prime Minister Keizo Obuchi had come to mark the twentieth anniversary of Harvard's Japan-funded Program in U.S.-Japan Relations together with the retirement of its founding director, Professor Ezra Vogel.

Speaking before a battery of Japanese TV cameras, Obuchi thanked the university for having helped to stem the downward spiral that threatened bilateral ties in the 1980s. Foley then stepped up to the microphone to anoint Vogel as "Number One," a jocular reference to the Harvard sociologist's best-selling *Japan as Number One*. Finally, Vogel (one of those who had beckoned me into the ballroom) recalled how the university, noting the nation's rapid rise to world power by 1980, had wisely sought to bring Japan into a more equal dialogue with the United States by expanding its human and intellectual presence in Cambridge through the resident fellowships, seminars, and colloquia offered by his program. Having myself once been invited as one of the program's speakers—and freeloading off the Okura's exquisite buffet—I kept two wry thoughts to myself. One was to note how far Harvard's Japan money had trailed off into the academic ephemera of public affairs networking as opposed to the scholarly basics of teaching posts and library holdings that had been the purpose of the fund drive I had assisted with in Tokyo in the early 1970s. The other was to recall how the downward draft alluded to by Obuchi had been fanned by Japan's intractable trade surpluses and how my alma mater was in effect being thanked for having kept the American "protectionists" at bay.

The prime minister of Japan, no less . . .

CHAPTER TEN

Dollars
The Long Retreat of American Philanthropy

On the side of American advocacy toward Japan we have today nothing remotely matching these Japanese funding organizations, the grants they disburse, or the network of Japan-related institutions and activities they sustain within the United States for the purpose of cultivating the American mind. Indeed, the flow of what might be called American "cultural cash" to Japan, whether private or governmental, has long since dwindled to a trickle. This has resulted in stark asymmetries in financial and organizational resources for the bilateral dialogue, and it illuminates the sharply contrasting national attitudes toward the taking of foreign "cultural" money. However, the magnitude of the Japanese inflow and its preponderance today is due at least as much to America's abdication of its own former philanthropic commitments and intellectual attention as it is to Japanese initiative and opportunism. We need to set Japan's ballooning largesse within the context of the long retreat of American money.

From Sugar Daddy to Uncle Scrooge

From the entire prewar era into the early postwar period the money flowed the other way. During early Meiji times contributions from American Protestants helped to found and support (among others) Doshisha College in Kyoto, later to become the leading private university in western Japan. After the great Kanto earthquake of 1923 the Rockefeller Foundation helped to rebuild the facilities of the Economics Faculty at Tokyo University, where in 1918 A. Barton Hepburn, board chairman of Chase

172

National Bank, had endowed the professorial chair in American constitution, history, and diplomacy at the Law Faculty that still bears his name and ranks as the most prestigious American studies chair in Japan. From the late 1920s U.S. citizens raised $2.4 million, nearly the total amount needed, for the construction of St. Luke's International Hospital in Tokyo, completed in 1936 with the most modern American medical technology. A similar New York–based fund-raising appeal from 1948 led to the opening of International Christian University in Tokyo in 1953. And the Roman Catholic schools, of course, enjoyed support from both America and Europe.

In short, American philanthropy toward Japan from the Meiji era onward took the form mainly of voluntary, privately organized donations from tens of thousands of individual Americans to Japanese church-related schools and hospitals—an extension of the broader U.S. missionary impulse toward East Asia, including its secularized permutations into medical and educational do-gooding.

The financial involvement of the U.S. government came after the war, most notably with its subvention of the Fulbright academic exchanges that sent 4,300 young Japanese to study in the United States between 1951 and 1980 while bringing approximately 1,000 American scholars to Japan for teaching and research during the same period. For years after 1945 there were dozens of U.S. government cultural centers in cities large and small dotting the Japanese archipelago—first as an educational arm of the occupation's democratization program, and later as regional culture-and-information bastions of the United States Information Service (USIS) during the ideological confrontation of the Cold War. These American Centers, as they are now known, have worked hard to present both the American cultural heritage and the official U.S. foreign policy line to local scholars and public leaders, but their grassroots impact has been limited by their minuscule staffs and budgets and above all by their openly governmental status.

Today all but four of these centers have disappeared in the steady contraction of our officially sponsored American intellectual presence in Japan from the early 1960s onward—a pullback that occurred in Western Europe also as the United States shifted its federally funded cultural diplomacy from politically stable and economically affluent First World allies to new ideological challenges in the Communist bloc and developing countries. The remaining American Centers in Japan are utilized mainly by a narrowly defined clientele of Americanist scholars and others with a professional angle on the United Sates, who are attracted by the lectures, specialized library and data services, small-scale exhibits, and access to American counterparts that they provide. They are not a force, however, among the intellectual and cultural leadership of Japan as a whole today.

It was not until the early 1960s, when the Ford Foundation helped Saburo Okita and other young non-Marxist economists to set up the Japan Economic Research Center at the *Nihon Keizai Shinbun,* that American foundations very briefly got into the business of magnifying sympathetic think-tank voices in Tokyo, as the Japanese today routinely do in Washington. But Ford has not had a representative in Japan since the late 1970s, and the times when our great foundations were acutely attuned to the American cultural stake in Japan have long since passed. These included the immediate postwar era, when John D. Rockefeller III was pouring his own private money into the new International House in Tokyo and the Japan Society in New York; the Cold War years, when the Asia Foundation was active in opening channels to Japan's anti-Communist intellectuals; and the 1950s and 1960s, when the Carnegie Corporation, the Rockefeller Foundation, and the Ford Foundation were the mainstay of the burgeoning new field of Japanese (and other East Asian) studies throughout the United States.

As the American foundations pulled out of Japan they encouraged Japanese corporations to establish their own charitable and exchange institutions—for example, the Toyota Foundation, one of the earliest and most active—in the expectation that the corporations would share with them the burden of philanthropic and other projects to advance free enterprise and democracy in neighboring Asia. There was also the hope that the Japanese would pump up the flagging flow of support to academic and other Japan-related activities in the United States as Ford, Rockefeller, and others shifted their priorities toward domestic urban and minority projects in the wake of the Vietnam War, their stock portfolio losses in 1974, and the wave of populist resentment of "elitist" international projects that hit them after 1970.

By the mid-1990s there were only two U.S. government funding sources (outside the cluster of scientific organizations such as the National Science Foundation) for academic and other cultural exchanges with Japan. In their parsimony and operational philosophy, the Fulbright program and the Japan-U.S. Friendship Commission (which I served as its first associate executive director and Japan representative from 1977 to 1984) have further reflected this long retreat. When Tokyo's Center for Global Partnership was set up with its yen endowment equivalent to $350 million in 1991, it was nine times the size of the Japan-U.S. Friendship Commission—America's one official agency that, like the CGP, is exclusively for cultural and intellectual ties with the other country.

Congress established the Friendship Commission in 1975 as a goodwill gesture toward Tokyo with a $36 million capital fund. This took the residue of Japanese yen repayments to the United States after 1962 for our occupation-era GARIOA (Government Aid and Relief in Occupied Areas) assistance and combined it with a small portion (about 13 percent) of Japan's dollar repayments for American-built facilities we had relinquished on Okinawa upon the island's reversion in 1972.

After fourteen years of operation the commission in 1991 had total assets of approximately $42.1 million, but its grant disbursements were subject to annual appropriation and were crimped by congressional restrictions on both halves of its dual-specie fund. The $14.9 million still remaining in the dollar account was limited to the drawdown of accrued interest plus 5 percent of capital each year, while the yen account (which stood at 3.54 billion yen in 1991) had to be held exclusively in Japanese government bonds and was nonconvertible, which meant it could be spent only on programs for Japanese or Americans in Japan.

By 1994 the appreciation of its yen account had pushed the commission's combined assets up to the $50 million mark, but continuing drops in Japanese interest rates had severely slashed the funds available from the yen side, and the commission's total program budget for fiscal year 1994 was down to about $3 million. By that time the assets of the CGP had climbed to the $500 million range and those of the U.S.-Japan Foundation (USJF) to $93 million. A long-sought legislative amendment was finally passed in 1998 to allow the commission to convert its dollar and yen funds at will for maximum income flow, in effect repatriating the yen account. But with the yen at less than 130 to the dollar, the commission's annual grants budget for fiscal year 1998 still stood at a disappointing total of about $2.5 million. Meanwhile, the expenditure of the CGP for grants alone during the Japanese fiscal year 1998 stood at nearly $8.7 million.

Given that great a disparity, it is ironical that the lion's share of the commission's expenditure—like Japan's own money—has gone for academic, artistic, and public affairs programs to educate Americans on Japan rather than the other way around. In a double irony, the commission's emphasis from the mid-1980s on policy research and public education on Japan for Americans has simply reinforced—indeed, it provided one major model for—the Japanese push in that area. Further aggravating the organizational lopsidedness, the commission closed its Tokyo office in the late 1980s and sharply reduced its original reciprocal commitment to introduce American culture to Japan by whittling its support for American art performances and exhibitions to a token level, and by cutting the American studies portion of its budget from one-fifth during the early years to a mere 4 percent in 1994. By 1995 the two long-standing summer seminars in American studies at Kyoto and Sapporo—funded by Fulbright and the commission, respectively, and providing an annual venue where Japanese scholars and students could mingle with leading U.S. Americanists—had been discontinued for lack of funds.

Indeed, America's greatest declaration of bankruptcy in its cultural exchanges with Japan came in 1979, when it arm-twisted Tokyo into paying half the annual costs of the Fulbright fellowship program, for decades the most effective and respected element in America's cultural diplomacy around the globe. After a lengthy demurral the Japanese finally gave in, but they promptly laid claim to half the seats on the board of the new Japan-U.S. Educational Commission in Tokyo that would run the annual $2 million Fulbright program, with $1 million from each side—no longer a princely sum by competitive standards. Those seats the Japanese deservedly got, and with them an effective lever on grantees and program direction.

This gradual reversal of philanthropic roles over a half century occurred through the confluence of three broad forces: (1) the declining curve of U.S.-based funding for Japanese studies as American scholarly and public interest in Japan continued to climb; (2) Tokyo's political anxieties, which seemed to escalate with each controversial expansion of its economic stake in the United States; and (3) the conviction of certain Americans that it was in the national interest of the United States to put the two together—to keep the bilateral tie unruffled by using anxious Japan's money to fund impecunious American experts to explain Japan and its importance to their discomfited or skeptical fellow citizens.

The number of academic Japan specialists in the United States rose from a mere handful after World War II to over 400 in 1970 and to around 1,500 by the early 1990s. Although as of 1988 only 295 of America's 3,200 accredited institutions of higher education had one or more resident Japanologists, there were by that time 53 schools offering full undergraduate Japanese studies programs, with graduate training concentrated at nearly 20 universities that had the multidisciplinary faculty and Japanese-language library holdings (in the 40,000–200,000 volume range) required to sustain advanced teaching and research on Japan. Enrollments in college-level Japanese-language courses stood at 45,700 in 1992, having overtaken Russian (44,000), but were less than a tenth of those for Spanish (533,600). All in all, though, it was an enormous leap over four decades from virtually nothing to a firm if modest niche in American humanities, social science, and professional education.[1]

None of this would have been possible without the commitment of the Rockefeller and Ford Foundations and the Carnegie Corporation, throughout the 1950s and 1960s, to the development of international studies programs and area studies programs and centers as part of America's new global responsibilities. Japanese studies have never come cheap. Training to functional scholarly fluency in the language normally doubles the time—and fellowship money—spent in gaining the Ph.D.; Japanese-language library materials are both costly and awkward to come by; and as the years passed, research stays in Japan were becoming almost prohibitively expensive. By 1977 the annual cost of running the intensive language-immersion program of the Inter-University Center for Japanese Language Studies in Tokyo had climbed to $600,000, or about $20,000 per head, for the approximately thirty graduate students sent by the ten American universities participating in the consortium. More importantly, there was not an icicle's chance in August that the scattered Japan specialists would get much backing from their own budget-minded administrations or Western-oriented colleagues for the additional faculty positions and cross-disciplinary research centers needed to carry Japanese (or other Asian) studies forward.

When the foundations defected in the 1970s there was a hopeful rush to U.S. and Japanese government money with the establishment of the Japan Foundation in 1972 and the Friendship Commission in 1975. The bulk of the foundation's original academic grants went to American Japanologists, nearly doubling the amount of fellowship money previously coming exclusively from American sources. The limitations on official support, however, were apparent by the new decade as the Japan Foundation went increasingly global and the commission more and more into public education and policy research. The burst of nonacademic interest in Japan throughout the United States created heavy competition for available grant money on the part of American museums, theaters, Japan-America societies, and other nonprofit groups. Yet another new demand came from American college students, with their fresh focus on the Japanese economy and their interest in professional courses that would help them find Japan-related jobs in business, law, and brokerage firms. For American universities, that left the Japanese corporations as the most promising source of support. Unfortunately, in a final twist to a vicious circle, the enormous dependence of the former on the latter since the mid-1980s has effectively undercut any residual sense of obligation by American foundations and corporations to support the Japanese studies field and to help maintain its independence and critical spirit through a predominantly American financial base.

Over the same years, Japanese motives and capacities for cultural funding rose in a precise counterspiral to this American retreat, and in tandem with the much larger surge of Japan-funded lobbying in Washington. The first financial crisis of American Japanology in the early 1970s coincided with the mounting evidence during the Nixon years—the president's sudden opening to China and floating of the dollar in 1971, followed by the 1974 Trade Act—that Tokyo faced powerful new hostile forces in the U.S. business and political communities. The Tanaka Fund for ten American universities in 1973 and the Japanese purses that snapped open for the first stream of academic beggars need to be understood in this context, as do the first approaches to Washington think tanks at that time.

From the mid-1980s the ante of Japanese philanthropy—now fed by the huge cash surpluses generated by Tokyo's bubble economy and the plunge of the dollar after 1985—went up with every creak in the ratchet of America's trade frustrations with Japan. Japanese donors have been known to complain that they're damned if they do and damned if they don't, but they assumed too easily that grants to U.S. nonprofit organizations could somehow compensate for the repeated failures to open Japanese markets or affronts such as the illicit sale by a Toshiba subsidiary of a key submarine propeller-milling technology to the USSR.[2] Faced with the new revisionist voices and repeated brandishing of the Trade Act's "Super 301" big stick, Japan's donors chose to press on—despite the evidence of growing concern among U.S. citizens over the power of Japanese money in American politics and society.

Japan's decision around 1985 to develop its own basic research in science and technology poured a fresh and far more lucrative stream of money into American universities. Keidanren's espousal of "good corporate citizenship" in 1991 provided an authoritative rationale for local or regional giving by Japan's U.S.-based firms. Akio Morita's plan for a grassroots strategy in 1985 had spread like bamboo by the new decade along the regional educational and public affairs pathways so laboriously pioneered since 1980 by the Friendship Commission, the U.S.-Japan Foundation, and the Japan Society of New York.[3] And when the end of the Cold War knocked out the traditional prop for "mutual friendship," Tokyo was ready at the start of the 1990s with its new slogan, "global partnership," and the heftily endowed Center for Global Partnership.

The Philosophical Gap

To put a new twist on an old cliché, he who pays the *shakuhachi* flutist can rewrite the tune. It is abundantly clear now that Tokyo, with its overarching financial presence—and the critical assistance of its American sympathizers—has grabbed the lead in directing and controlling the subject matter, the participants, the timing, and the general direction of the binational intellectual agenda.

The bilateral asymmetry in the flow of academic funding lies not only in the opportunity to get money but also, curiously enough, in the chance to give it away—what might be called eleemosynary non-reciprocity, the refusal to take the other fellow's cash. In *Cartels of the Mind* I called attention to the extraordinary reluctance of Japan's educational establishment to accept U.S. funds—not even a few minuscule grants of $1,000 each from the Friendship Commission to pay for occasional crash courses in American studies at geographically isolated Japanese universities.[4] Surely the time has come to reconsider the way in which American academe now reaches out reflexively for Japanese money whenever new facilities or activities are contemplated with respect to Japan.

Some Americans have defended Japan's largesse in terms of the national need. As a good friend of mine who had once been a high-ranking science adviser to USIA summed up the dominant Beltway view for me: "Ivan, our universities are the best in the world, and they need the money." A more desperate sense of dependence was suggested by the way in which the editors of *Corporate Philanthropy Report* so quickly threw in the towel on a still economically troubled America in their April 1989 issue, arguing that Japan was needed not only for "its capital but also its exasperating efficiency—to bring about changes in U.S. society that we clearly can't realize on our own."

Others, while perceiving the thin ice, have expressed faith in the self-monitoring capacity of the American scholarly community to skate around it. As Professor Richard J. Samuels, director of MIT's Center for International Studies and head of the MIT-Japan Program, puts it: "It seems to me that so long as the research of universities is open and subject to peer review, a blanket proscription on funding from any particular source is unwarranted. That said, all responsible researchers must retain (and occasionally exercise) the right to 'bite the hand that feeds them.'"[5]

It is also true that individual scholars at universities are variously buffered from any direct obligation to original donors. The chairs they occupy have long since been funded, and their research money normally has been passed down through peer committees, study centers, and other layers of campus bureaucracy. The personal indebtedness is heaviest at think tanks or in other situations where a researcher has to raise his or her funds directly. In a gentle admonition, Professor Andrew D. Gordon, director of Harvard's Reischauer Institute for Japanese Studies, laid out the difference to me this way:

> I think you are barking up the wrong tree with this whole matter of endowed chairs. Once they are paid in, they are paid in perpetuity. Especially over time the source or origin in my opinion has no serious impact on the academic or political inclinations of the holders. If one were to seek a link between the funders, their agendas, and sorts of research that was carried out, the much more relevant question is the appropriateness of universities taking soft money, renewable grants, or one-time grants from sources to which a recipient might return in the future, from funders with particular goals. I.e., in the Japan field, CGP or Sasakawa's US-Japan Foundation. Or equally worth examining, the impact of places like Olin Institute, Hudson Institute, AEI, etc. Here is where we find funders with specific political interests and agendas, using their gifts to academics in order to achieve those interests.[6]

Three decades ago, however, there still were prominent American intellectuals who held scruples about institutional as well as individual dependence. When Harvard and other universities started their fund drives in Tokyo in the early 1970s there was acknowledgment by both sides that Japan still had a long way to go to catch up with America's financial contributions to scholarly exchanges after World War II. Something was still owed. Even at that, Harvard's first fund-raising drive in Japan in the early 1970s took three years of repeated visits to Tokyo by Professor Edwin Reischauer to wind up. More significantly, there were absolutely no conditions or deals accepted—no promises of student quotas or trainee slots or joint research positions in exchange for Japanese corporate money. Politely declining one such offer in 1973 cost Harvard a flat million at the time. Fourteen years later, in 1987, the same Japanese corporation on its own initiative offered two chairs, at $1 million apiece, to a school of business at another American university. The dean who clinched the deal told me with a chuckle that he now felt compelled to look for some American money to balance it—a remark one would like to hear more often.

The most fundamental reason for caution, however, is the time-honored injunction against conflict of interest. Brookings Institution president Kermit Gordon cited this in 1972 when he turned down one of the first Japanese grants offered to a Washington think tank, on the grounds that money from foreign countries that were themselves being studied would inhibit the objectivity of the researcher and call into question the impartiality of the research. The intended $1 million donation from the Sumitomo group went instead to the Japan Society of New York, which eventually parceled about half of it out to Brookings for the support of small study groups.[7] Colleagues and competitors, however, soon overcame the sort of scruples early figures such as Gordon and Reischauer had shown about taking Japanese money for policy-oriented studies of Japan or taking it for academic purposes on conditions tying it to the donor's direct benefit.

It is ironic that the conflict-of-interest principle, this bedrock of intellectual honesty and integrity, is self-enjoined far more strictly by journalists than by the scholars who often look down on them. One needs look no further than the 1975 "Statement of Principles" of the American Society of Newspaper Editors or the in-house corporate code of ethics of individual entities such as Gannett Newspapers to realize that some of our university dons seem to have forgotten what the most humble journalist still holds to as an absolute rule: To be trusted and respected as a reporter in search of the objective truth, you don't take money from the subject of your reporting.

What is truly extraordinary today is how few Americans are asking themselves why the Japanese would want to give that much money to

American intellectual institutions. As author and *Business Week* editor William J. Holstein put it in 1992:

> Americans are displaying tremendous naïveté in accepting this money, and that is alarming. Any American nonprofit, for example, would retain a certain amount of suspicion of a major U.S. corporation donating funds to it. What is the expected quid pro quo? . . . The Japanese objectives are simple: to create a climate of positive opinion and political support for continued economic expansion within the United States, which often operates to the detriment of U.S. companies. . . . Nothing is inherently evil about this . . . it is Japan's right to attempt to defend its huge stake in the United States. The burden is on Americans to understand the game.[8]

I would also decry the sheer lack of proportion and balance—the failure to tap American sources, the Pavlovian trot to Tokyo for a hand-out whenever budget shortfalls appear, the naming of new Japanese studies centers after American scholars still active and influential in the dialogue, and the odd lack of what one might call an elementary American pride and self-respect. Even when the conditions on gifts are minimal and straightforward, it is not easy to put a critical bite on the country that fills your coffers. We have studied the French—the premier foreign culture in our book—for two hundred years now without expecting a sou from France. And not even in the heyday of the cultural Cold War—when we were the ones who wanted to be studied, appreciated, and understood—did we offer such huge sums to countries willing to make that effort, nor did others around the world expect it from us. Virtually anywhere, it would have provoked gasps of astonishment, cynical laughter, and an anti-American backlash.

Japan's hypercautious attitude toward foreign funding in Japanese education was encapsulated as early as 1879, when Arinori Mori, then vice foreign minister, although personally sympathetic to Christians and not hostile to private Christian education, advised his close personal friend Jo Niijima, the Amherst-trained Congregationalist founder of Doshisha: "You have a right to exist and also to employ foreign teachers if you use your own fund rather than that of the Board. The Foreign Office objects to your depending on the American Board [of Foreign Missions] altogether." Niijima also recalled that Mori, later to become minister of education and known as one of the most Western-oriented of early Meiji intellectuals, had sent him "word by a friend to be cautious, and advised me to raise a permanent fund at once."[9] Now as then, dependence on money from abroad invites antiforeign sentiment and is seen as interference in Japan's internal institutional order.

Americans and Japanese also hold very different views as to the implications attached to the act of giving itself. We generally like to imagine the best of other people, Japanese the worst—both penchants, needless to say, being off target. Americans can conceive of money without strings tied to it; the Japanese simply cannot. For the Japanese, gifts always imply a counterobligation, which is one reason they are so wary of taking them. So, to the extent that their current largesse exceeds the perceived repayment of earlier American favors, most Japanese would assume the American takers to be, somehow, in their debt. We believe it possible to take money from the devil and then kick him safely out the door. That was how the great American foundations, capitalized by the tainted gains of robber barons, eventually achieved public respectability. (It was also, I might add, the absolving thought my own clerically ordained father leaned on, as president of a staid little Presbyterian sagebrush college, to dun contributions from Idaho's legalized slot-machine operators during the lean wartime years.)

This was also the axiom by which certain Americans in the early 1980s, after considerable soul-searching, decided to establish the U.S.-Japan Foundation. At the outset quite a few Japanese friends of the United States were in doubt as to the wisdom of the American side in taking this money—Sasakawa, with his open support of right-wing causes and groups, and his well-researched and substantiated ties to Japanese gangsters, still remained beyond the pale for most Japanese intellectuals and political liberals. Ever since the foundation's establishment, the International House of Japan, sensitive to its own Japanese constituency, has refused to take any money from the USJF for its own projects and has been reluctant to extend its full collaboration and liaison services. I myself have seen books and photographs featuring Sasakawa prominently displayed at both the Tokyo and New York offices of the foundation, and although he was not openly involved in the foundation's activities, his son Yohei has been a member of the board from the start.

What is germane here, of course, is not the late Sasakawa's speckled reputation but the highly divergent views that Japanese and Americans hold with respect to the seductive potency of money. Inevitably, the nonchalance shown by the foundation's U.S. organizers set a new attitudinal standard for Americans willing to take megadonations from Japan.

Organization
The Mutual
Understanding Industry

This new promiscuity in taking foreign academic money, originally pioneered along the U.S.-Japan axis, soon bred a litter of copycats whereby other East Asian countries such as South Korea and Taiwan were induced to help underwrite the study of themselves at American universities. Success in the United States also encouraged Japan to take its intellectual funding to other strategically important countries, particularly to Thatcherite Britain, where Tokyo managed to isolate the same Anglo-Saxon gene for nonchalant, cash-hungry serviceability.

The purpose of these chapters is to stitch the imbalance of academic money into the broader weave of Japan-U.S. intellectual relations rather than to fully address the broader question of foreign academic funding per se. Nevertheless—to barely skim the comparative surface of that extended story—it was not long before other countries followed Japan's suit. The Korean Traders Association endowed Harvard's new chair in modern Korean history in the mid-1970s; by the late 1980s the University of California at Berkeley had received two Taiwan-funded chairs for the study of China; and the University of California at Los Angeles now has a Korean-funded chair in Korean studies. To mention only two cases in the Islamic field, the University of Maryland has its Anwar Sadat Chair in Egyptian Studies, and on 12 September 2001 CBS reported that the brother of Osama bin Laden had given about $1 million to Harvard for Islamic legal studies.

In the United Kingdom (where Japanese business was anxious to establish a manufacturing platform before the doors of the European Union shut too tightly) Oxford from the mid-1980s has had its Nissan Institute of Japanese Studies, housed in a functionalist cube adjacent to St. Anthony's College. Equipped with library, offices, and an auditorium, the institute also supports a professor, a reader, and the subvention of books and other publications on Japan. At Cambridge, in addition to a chair on Japan donated by the head of the Tokyo Electric Power Company, the airy new multistory East Asian wing of its central library was given in the early 1990s by a single Japanese private citizen to house not only the university's Japanese collection but its Chinese collection as well. And as Japanese investment poured into the economically depressed Cardiff region, Tokyo residents were suddenly treated to a succession of tweedy male choral groups booming out musical goodwill from Wales. Examples such as the last aside, it is striking how lavishly Japanese donors have targeted what arguably are the top five research universities in the world, from Oxbridge to MIT, Harvard, and UC Berkeley.

What, then, is so problematical (or at the very least unique) about Japan's academic and other cultural largesse in the United States? Basically, three things, beyond the concern for scholarly independence noted in the previous chapter: (1) the sheer size and number of donations (for example, chairs) to individual institutions; (2) the remarkable geographical spread and sectoral depth of Japanese support for organizations addressing scholarly, economic, and political interests across the entire fifty states; and (3) the way this funding has helped to create and sustain the informal but powerful network that pulls together so many American individuals and institutions in work related to Japan.

Indeed, politically speaking, the most significant function of all this money has been to drive yet another critical imbalance: the organizational tilt. For there are now in the United States tier after tier of cultural, business, civic, and grant-making organizations helping to promote bilateral friendship and a greater understanding of Japan. Whether under American, Japanese, or joint sponsorship, they tend to reinforce each other's voices and—more importantly—have no real counterparts doing the same thing for the United States in Japan. This asymmetry in networking has received very little attention, since most Americans at home know or care little about Japan's internal intellectual arrangements, while those resident in Japan have long since come to take the difficulty of access and the lack of reciprocal organizations as part of the established order of things.

An approximate paradigm of the Mutual Understanding Industry's work in the United States would highlight the following. At the university level, American Japanologists who have become dependent on Japanese money for their chairs, centers, and research visits to Japan feed their expertise into the policy studies of our think tanks, the lecture circuit of the Japan-America societies, and the proliferating curriculum projects on Japan in American schools. In public affairs, former U.S. officials of a Japan-protective stripe help boost the message to the practical level of policy and politics through their positions in the funding organizations, friendship societies and think tanks, or legal and PR firms retained by the Japanese. In exchanges, key American and Japanese players such as the Japan Society of New York and the Japan Center for International Exchange work together closely to organize Japanese from Japan who can convey Tokyo's views to America. Finally, for the purpose of building community support for Japanese manufacturing plants at the grassroots level—and checkmating those members of Congress who would put pressure on Japan to open its own markets—Japanese corporate and government money has also been channeled into American charities, nonprofit organizations, universities, and colleges at the local and regional levels, thereby completing the circle.

Among those regional strategies, one frequently cited model for Japan-saturation at the state level has been Tennessee. At best a medium-sized state, far removed from the nation's metropolitan corridors, Tennessee nevertheless has its Japan-Tennessee Society and its Tennessee-Japan Friends in Commerce; its Japan for Teachers Pilot Program at the University of Tennessee at Chattanooga, with special school programs on Japan in Memphis, Nashville, and Knoxville as well; its Center for United States–Japan Studies and Cooperation at Vanderbilt University; the Nissan auto plant, of course, at Smyrna, and Komatsu's tractor assembly at Chattanooga; and in Lamar Alexander—who later became secretary of education and even made a bid for the presidency in 1996—a grateful ex-governor. Indeed, while still in office in 1986, Alexander prefaced his 190-page photo study *Friends: Japanese and Tennesseans* with the admonishment: " 'Don't discuss the War.' That's the Supreme Command, the one thing an American Governor seeking Japanese investment does *not* do. . . . By early 1985 ten percent or $1.2 billion of all Japanese investment in the fifty United States was in one state: Tennessee. We had learned our Japanese manners."[1] Ah, yes, the Japanese are sensitive to criticism and chafe at dissent, so let's not be crude.

Scraping Along in Japan

Unfortunately, the Mutual Understanding Industry is not mutual, and there is no remotely comparable nexus in Japan working for the American interest.

It must be acknowledged that all Japanese college students have had to study English; that American literature is widely taught; that the United States gets its due mention in general survey courses (for example, world politics) that are not specifically about America; that Japan's media report widely, if superficially, on U.S. affairs; and that the tiny band of pioneer Americanists in the 1930s bravely weathered a great deal of opprobrium from Japan's ultranationalists. It is likewise true that their postwar successors in American studies have on the whole (hard-core Marxist ideologues excepted) explained the United States sympathetically while being, like Americans themselves, critical of racism and divided on certain policy issues such as the security treaty or the Vietnam War.

However, Japanese universities both national and private have been virtually impermeable to U.S. financial participation in the development of American studies. Moreover, Japan's America specialists tend to remain primly in their ivory tower, rarely commuting in and out of public life, as have so many of our Japanologists. Indeed, Japan's Americanists typically close ranks on trade issues, and relatively few of them have ventured into the bilateral dialogue. Those who do so tend to function more as apologists for their own country toward Americans rather than reciprocating the role of those American Japanologists who defend Japan on trade to their fellow U.S. citizens. It is accepted that the deans of the profession will preside for years on end (creating marvelous institutional memory) as Japan's appointed go-betweens with the United States on matters concerning American studies in Japan. One thinks here of the former Hepburn Chair occupant Makoto Saito, who served on CULCON (the bi-governmental advisory Conference on Cultural and Educational Interchange), or the retired Tokyo University historian Nagayo Homma, who until recently ran the Center for Global Partnership as its executive director.

Given Japan's academic factionalism, its allergy to foreign philanthropy, and the Ministry of Education's rigid controls on curriculum, it is inconceivable that American studies could ever experience the sort of brushfire spread that took place in Japanese studies in the United States after 1960, followed by its timely, flexible extension to professional education in law, business, and journalism starting in the 1980s. There are only two universities, Tokyo and Doshisha, that have a center for American studies with library holdings, interdisciplinary research, and a spectrum of undergraduate course offerings on campus comparable to the ten major university-based Japan research centers in the United States. Chair systems established decades ago in reflection of a world long since vanished have left American history at many schools squatting on stools while German history reclines on couches.

For years, as American educators and fund-raisers were falling over each other to help Japanese promoters shoehorn the study of Japan into U.S. academe, the American embassy (USIS) and the Friendship Commission pleaded in vain with Japanese scholars and bureaucrats to address the serious lack of faculty positions in American politics, economics, and society, where the key to a genuine understanding of the contemporary United States presumably lies. Here the Americanist go-betweens often seemed more concerned to protect than to prod and pry open the vested teaching and research structures. More conferences and fellowships for advanced study in the United States were always welcome, but no push for additional teaching positions, please. Those were Japan's (and the established scholars') own sacred preserve.

Turning for a moment to Japanese think tanks, the overweening role of the Tokyo government in all aspects of policy formulation makes it difficult for an American to introduce his or her individual views through private research channels. Japan's fledgling private-sector think tanks for policy affairs are for the most part jealously guarded one-man side-shows, with a stable of ideologically congenial experts as in America but grouped around a more limited topical agenda than we would find, say, at Brookings, Hoover, or the American Enterprise Institute. With some but not nearly enough parliamentary input, most Japanese policy decisions emerge from the administrative ministries themselves, their affiliated research institutes, and their bureaucratically orchestrated advisory councils (the *shingikai*). These councils, like the think tanks, occasionally solicit the opinion or even the participation of foreign persons, often resident in Tokyo, under the nominal rubric of garnering fresh intelligence or testing overseas reactions—something they hardly need, given their own far-flung resources for information gathering. Most foreign invitees, however, are loath to admit that the real reason they are there is not to engage the Japanese in an open-ended dialogue but to ratify with the stamp of foreign approval policy thrusts or decisions that already have been agreed on. Any American regularly employed by a think tank would of course function strictly as the *gaisho,* or foreigner-handling factotum safely committed to the institution's agenda.

It is in the public affairs sector, however, that the profoundest asymmetry lies. The bilateral friendship societies in Tokyo and a few other major cities, known as Nichibei Kyokai (America-Japan societies), are the nominal equivalent of the Japan-America societies throughout the United States, but they serve little function beyond that of monthly luncheon clubs providing a podium for the occasional visiting American celebrity. They have not developed the dynamic multiprogram operations of the Japan-America societies in the United States, which they would need in order to get American views widely presented to Japan's political, business, media, and cultural leaders at the national, regional, and local levels.

In the subarea of business sector ties, this imbalance has long been epitomized by the Japan-U.S. Businessmen's Conference, which regularly issues pronunciamentos on the state of bilateral economic relations together with recommendations to both governments. For the national-level meetings there have been secretariats for each side, in Washington and Tokyo. The Japanese secretariat, however, has also run exclusive exchanges with six regional organizations in the United States, such as the Japan–Western U.S. Association, based in California. There have been no such regional counterparts for the United States in Japan, nor has the secretariat in Washington made any effort to reach back across the Pacific to court Japanese businessmen and public opinion at the regional level in Japan. For years Sony Corporation's Akio Morita, through the California association of local Japanese businesses, was instrumental in massaging West Coast corporate and political opinion toward Japan. It was as if the highest U.S. business and political leadership had decided over cigars and brandy that Lee Iacocca of Chrysler was the one to cultivate Japanese corporate leaders and galvanize local American firms into exchange activities in the seven prefectures of Western Honshu, stretching from Osaka to Yamaguchi.

Meanwhile, as U.S. business executives—with reduced numbers of American staff and in concert with the American Chamber of Commerce in Japan—continued butting their heads against "informal" trade barriers in Tokyo, Japan's visiting corporate leaders spilled over into the Japanese-owned Essex House and the opulently appointed twenty-one-story Nippon Club Tower to talk up "free trade" with America's financial and business magnates in Manhattan.

Riding High in America

The lack of official cultural centers abroad is not necessarily a handicap to a given nation's cultural diplomacy, and the Japanese have in fact had a very modest diplomatic base for their cultural and intellectual work in the United States. What Americans have failed to match in Japan, rather, is the extensive unofficial web that the Japanese have managed to stretch out in the United States. The American assumption that our free flow of scholarly, media, and business contacts across the Atlantic can be duplicated across the Pacific without special attention or effort on our part has been proved wrong.

In taking its message beyond American universities and sympathetic U.S. government officials to reach the broader U.S. public at the regional and grassroots levels, Japan has relied heavily on the public-spirited enthusiasm of its American friends. Indeed, one of the cardinal rules of official cultural diplomacy is to allow your host country to do your work for you as much as possible—to have your nation's history taught by its own colleges and schools, your government's viewpoints carried in the local press as news, your national arts promoted by the host country's own mainstream concert halls and museums. In other words, get a free ride rather than trying to make your case directly through PR bulletins and costly cultural centers managed and paid for by your own embassy. Japan has *no* official cultural centers in the United States, and only six of them under Japan Foundation auspices elsewhere in the world. These are the two venerable academically oriented Japan Cultural Institutes in Rome and Cologne, lineal carryovers from the old Axis alliance, and the four recently established multipurpose cultural centers in Bangkok, Kuala Lumpur, Jakarta, and Sydney as part of the new cultural push toward Southeast Asia.

Apart from the small, trade-oriented reading rooms known as Japan Information Centers in several American cities, Tokyo's real cultural and informational diplomacy in the United States is carried out by Americans—most promisingly through a rapidly maturing chain of Japan-America societies (or Japan societies, as the larger ones are often called) now reaching into a majority of the fifty states. As of 2000 there were thirty-three of these organizations, stretching from Hawaii to New

Hampshire, that were receiving program services through their umbrella National Association of Japan-America Societies (NAJAS), with financial contributions from the governmental and private sectors of both countries to help educate the U.S. public on Japan and the importance of the bilateral tie.

The preeminent friendship institution, the Japan Society of New York, has long been an aggressive presenter not only of Japan's culture but of the Japanese viewpoint generally to the East Coast elite and the U.S. foreign policy establishment. A private American organization established in 1906 but greatly expanded under the aegis of John D. Rockefeller III after the Second World War, it has a chic four-story building on East Forty-seventh Street distinguished by its sleek, black-painted facade. Japan House offers on the cultural side a stage adaptable for Japanese theater performances and featuring a run-on *hanamichi* ramp for Kabuki; an art gallery, library, and film collection; and an ongoing menu of artistic performances, exhibitions, and scholarly lectures. In the public affairs arena, Japan House hosts intimate seminars or luncheon meetings with Japanese VIPs that focus on the current political and economic scene in Japan, Japanese business methods, trade issues, and U.S.-Japan relations in general. Finally, it serves as the practical orchestrator and expediter of a number of nationally based fellowship, speaker, and traveling artist programs for which other institutions (such as foundations) provide the money.

Of these three functions it is the first, or cultural, one that gives the Japan Society of New York its cachet, the second that endows it with political clout, and the third that makes it such a key player in the nationwide network for mutual understanding.

The society has a seasoned staff of Japan experts to supervise these activities, and it has become the organizer and starting point for many of the Japanese groups that go on to tour the United States—everything from puppet theater to "caravans" of Japanese intellectuals analyzing the causes of economic "friction." Financial support comes from a lengthy roster of U.S. and Japanese private corporations, but the Japanese government has long viewed the Japan Society as its key partner in winning over the American public. On the American side, too, the U.S. Information Agency for a number of years contracted out to the Japan Society its responsibility for organizing the American subcommittees and biennial planning for CULCON.

Since the late 1970s a large number of other American nonprofit organizations have joined the effort to make Japan better known among Americans, including the world affairs councils, United Nations associations, and foreign relations groups in major cities of the United States other than New York. For years a small number of regional Japan-America friendship societies worked out of cubbyhole offices with volunteer staff, renting hotel space for their public functions and catering to a narrow, nostalgic, culturally oriented clientele of local Japanese-Americans and former American residents of Japan. Today, having graduated from flower arranging to hard-nosed economic and political issues, they are professionally run and reach out to influential businessmen, lawyers, journalists, and politicians in their respective cities, states, or multistate regions. Since the establishment of NAJAS in 1979 the Japan-America societies in major cities such as Atlanta, Boston, Chicago, Los Angeles, and San Francisco have dramatically expanded their activities with assistance from the Japan-U.S. Friendship Commission, which matched a 1981 Japanese government donation of $2 million that the commission had requested from Tokyo for what it called its "regional public programs on Japan."[2] In 1986 a second, unrestricted $2 million was contributed by the government of Japan to the commission's Japan Gift Fund for distribution at the discretion of the U.S. government's Japan-U.S. Friendship Commission to these regional societies, and in 1988 it gave another $1 million. In effect, Washington itself was "laundering" this money on behalf of Tokyo, but with Americans only at the controls.

Most regrettably, this lopsidedness at the organizational level is further aggravated by the asymmetry in roles permitted to Japanese and American intellectuals resident in each other's country. In contrast to Japan's cartelized intellectual scene, America is a veritable international freeway of the mind. It is the Japanese who always make the greater fuss over the briefly visiting American VIP, but I am thinking here of those respected Japanese professional voices that have become "embedded" in the American system, or even of a Japanese corporate leader such as Mitsui's Hisao Kondo in New York, who has sat on the boards of Lincoln Center, the Kennedy Center in Washington, D.C., and the New York Chamber of Commerce.

The English-language *Japan Times* of 3 May 1994 carried—for Western consumption and feedback to the American mainstream—an op-ed piece by the previously mentioned Professor Yoshihiro Tsurumi of the City University of New York roasting President Clinton, who had "de-

monized Japan" and forced it into "slavish concession." There is nothing unusual about this sort of hyped-up public criticism of American
policies in the United States—we do it ourselves all the time. What the
United States lacks, however, is a reciprocal fulcrum in Tokyo—that is
to say, Americans employed at major Japanese universities or other institutions who utilize their position and the Japanese-language media to
reach the Japanese people directly with open (let alone sharp or biting)
criticism of Japanese leaders or Japanese government policy. It is literally impossible to conceive, for example, of an American (or other foreign) equivalent in Japan of the Indian economist Jagdish Bhagwati at
Columbia University, who led the intellectual attack on Clinton's get-
tough trade policy toward Japan during the president's first term. Any
such foreign critic in Japan would have been yanked, figuratively speaking, out of his chair—that is to say, ostracized. Rather, the anticipated
opprobrium would be so great that he or she would have learned long
since not to even contemplate anything so rash.

By coincidence (perhaps) Japanese television the very next day
brought on a resident American to join the attack on the U.S. trade stance
toward Japan—hardly the reciprocal of Tsurumi that I had in mind here.
On 4 May 1994 the NHK nightly op-ed lecture featured a Japanese-
speaking American businessman, graphic charts and all, running through
the standard Japanese government rebuttal to U.S. trade complaints.[3]
As I watched, my immediate reaction was that I wanted equal time—
my next thought being, of course, that I would never get it. There are no
Americans who take the American viewpoint into serious Japanese television programming in the limited English-language telecasts, much less
who could do so in Japanese, thereby reaching millions of viewers. Again,
the featuring of a hard-hitting American defense of American views in
fluent Japanese on an NHK program would be virtually inconceivable—
not because the U.S. talent isn't there, but because official Japan cannot
tolerate an unvarnished foreign challenge to its policies directly before the Japanese public. All that Japan's viewers got at the height
of the trade tensions in the mid-1990s was at best a few snippets in
English—with Japanese voice-over and tightly edited in Tokyo—
from high-ranking U.S. officials in Washington: a few raspy sec-
onds from the likes of an angry-looking, gabby Mickey Kantor or
Laura Tyson, set against a clichéd studio montage of the White House
or Capitol Hill and promptly rebutted by some meticulously prepared Japanese commentator.

* * *

One would have expected the sheer size and diversity of the United States—as opposed to the compactness and centralization of Japan—to give the Japanese a certain disadvantage in the intellectual persuasion game. For if both sides were equally accessible, this geographical difference would of course make the United States the more difficult country to get a purchase on. The Japanese, however, riding smoothly on America's magnificent social openness, have gradually learned to engage the multicentered poles of power and influence throughout the United States—once they realized that the country was not hinged on a Washington–New York–Cambridge axis similar to their own national hegemon, Tokyo.

For Americans, however, Japan's massive central structures—political, economic, and cultural—remain tightly protected, while its regional cities and prefectures pull pathetically little weight. Accordingly, the more that Americans—out of a well-intentioned but misplaced populism—stress regional penetration in exchange work, the greater the advantage to Japan. The so-called grassroots in the United States are of enormous political consequence—rather like tall pampas grass—whereas in Japan's unitary state their relative political clout is more on the order of a closely cropped putting green. People-to-people exchanges are a worthy objective, as is the encouragement of Japan's political and cultural decentralization away from Tokyo. But Americans must see to it that they do not get shunted off into the Japanese boondocks before they have established meaningful access at Japan's center—while the Japanese continue to roam the heights of American life, which are by their very nature decentralized.

CHAPTER TWELVE

People
Of Buffers, Barnacles, and Gatekeepers

There are, as we have just seen, very obvious practical financial and institutional reasons for America's ineptness in its current dialogue and psychological tug-of-war with Japan. Ultimately, however, it all depends on people—on the Japanese and Americans active in the transpacific dialogue. And the basic problem here lies in what we might roughly call the psychology and sociology of the Mutual Understanding Industry, a moniker I first used in an op-ed piece for the *Wall Street Journal* in 1987.[1]

The patriotic drive and quasi-official stamp of approval for Japan's standard-bearers in this game are clear enough, but how do Americans driven by softheaded sentiment or hardheaded geostrategic conviction find places of greater or lesser prominence in the structure of American-side advocacy for Japan?

The heart of the matter here is, once again, intellectual—namely, our lack of sophisticated thinking and "street smarts" in dealing with the peoples of East Asia, of whom we remain considerably more ignorant than we do of the peoples of Europe, Russia, the Near East, or Latin America. The root failing (as we shall pursue further in Part III) is that too many Americans personally or professionally involved with Japan have been prone to extract the positives from an ambivalent reality too complex or burdensome to behold in its totality, tucking the negatives away in remote corners of the mind. (The obverse holds true, of course, for those of us who zero in on the negatives.)

Basically, in East Asia we are up against attractive "high" cultures on a par with and in some respects surpassing our own, but organized in

195

poorly understood non-Western ways. In the rush to supplement our own cultural shortfalls in art and human relations and religion, to establish strategic partnerships in the region, or simply to push trade, it has been all too tempting to minimize the depth and downsides for us of political, social, and psychological dissimilarities. From Voltaire on China to our own patronizing idealizers of Japan today, there have always been Westerners who seem bent on denying East Asians their own fair share of mankind's innate orneriness.

As Japan, China, and Southeast Asia draw ever closer to us without a parallel upgrading of our intellectual understanding, this tendency can only get worse. Indeed, the habit has a venerable historical pedigree.

Forerunners

At times when U.S. nerves were fraying to the quick over strategic or economic confrontations with Japan in the 1930s or 1980s, it has taken a special type of American to assist and sympathize with Tokyo's stance and still believe in one's heart that such actions were in our greater national interest. The leading tribunes of mutual understanding in U.S. academic and public affairs circles today have been educators and former diplomats whose archetypes—the mind-set toward Japan—may be found in two Americans who worked in Tokyo during the height of the militarist era, were interned after Pearl Harbor, and came home together on the enemy-aliens exchange steamer *Gripsholm* in 1942.

Eugene V. Dooman, Ambassador Joseph C. Grew's second in command in Tokyo and his special assistant when Grew took over as undersecretary of state in 1944, threw his weight behind the group of fellow Japan experts—linguistically trained and with direct experience of the country—who were developing less punitive positions for Washington's presurrender planning process. Stressing the differences between Japan and Nazi Germany, they argued the feasibility of working through the established bureaucracy, the importance of retaining the emperor, the existence of a prior liberal political tradition, and the goal of allowing Japan to rebuild its economy quickly and return to its erstwhile role as a great trading nation alongside the United States and Great Britain. Afraid that any social revolution would lead quickly to Communism, they locked horns with the non-Japan-expert economists, New Deal social reformers, and China hands who wanted drastic democratization not only on behalf of Japan's broader masses (with whom Grew and Dooman had hardly rubbed shoulders) but to secure a sufficient institutional base for Japan's transformation into a peaceful, democratic nation.

When the outbreak of the Cold War clinched the argument for bringing Japan into the Western camp quickly, Dooman in the late 1940s helped to found the American Council on Japan—the first bud of a Japan lobby in Washington—to press for tempering of the occupation's more draconian social and economic directives. After revisiting Japan in 1952, he lamented that "the divesting of the Imperial institution of all political and social significance has eliminated any spiritual values from national life"—a page torn right out of Japan's Old Right bible.[2]

Dooman's was a business-oriented, avuncular vision of Japan that played down past confrontations (and their possible structural roots within Japan itself) in favor of globally focused American objectives such as trade opportunities and the strategic containment of Communism—Japan, in other words, as a serviceable pawn in a much larger game, whatever the Japanese might eventually make of themselves internally. Here Dooman was in many ways the ideological grandfather of those later American diplomats who retired into the headship, actual or honorary, of so many of our Japan-boosting foundations and friendship societies. Theirs, like his, is a personally committed policy position, the wisdom of which we can question, but one with plenty of precursors.

Academic boosters of mutual understanding often share that geostrategic view while adding a more personally protective, missionizing touch to their advocacy of Japan. Indeed, some of the earlier Japanologists, such as Edwin O. Reischauer and John W. Hall, were the offspring of missionary parents in Japan. The readiness of a very decent man to defend a very troublesome Japan, however, was best typified by Paul Rusch, the fondly remembered Episcopal layman who brought Jersey cows, model dairy farming, and rural youth training to the alpine meadows of postwar Japan at his Kiyosato Educational Experimental Project (KEEP).

Rusch, who had led the fund drive for St. Luke's Hospital and introduced American football to Japan while teaching at Rikkyo University (St. Paul's, Anglican) before the war, was a close friend of Vice Foreign Minister Renzo Sawada, a former ambassador to Britain, and his Japanese Anglican wife, Miki, who was to found the Elizabeth Saunders Home for orphans of Afro-Japanese parentage after the war—both patrician liberals of the type admired by Dooman and Grew. In early 1939 Sawada suggested to Rusch that he undertake an observation tour of

China, Korea, and Manchukuo under Foreign Ministry auspices so that he could explain Japan's foreign policy goals to Americans during a fund-raising trip he was planning to the United States later that year.

Eagerly agreeing to that, Rusch, upon returning to Tokyo from the Asian continent, defended Japan's invasion of China in an NHK short-wave broadcast to the United States and in the *Japan Times and Mail* of 8 March, which reported his words as follows: "The Japanese people are too modest in speaking out for their nation. With confidence and sincerity, they ought to assert their rights for the construction of a New Asia to the rest of the world. . . . The American people misunderstand the current incident [the invasion of China] and the true motives of Japan." Rusch later recalled that the commander of the Kwantung Army, which had taken over Manchuria, had the "demeanor and philosophy of Abraham Lincoln." And the trains in Korea ran on time. Here was the voice of mutual understanding, full throttle.

Rusch's Asian tour brought anguished protests from American missionaries in Shanghai, a lecture from Grew at the embassy, a reprimand from his American missionary bishop (who was chancellor at Rikkyo), and the demand from the U.S. Episcopal Church that he cancel his stateside fund-raiser.[3] Fiercely loyal to the students, Christians, and Westernized elite who made up his immediate circle of Japanese friends, Rusch obviously had difficulty seeing through his personal attachments to the oppressiveness of the Japanese state over its own subjects and its patent cruelties abroad. Like many missionaries, he wanted to believe that his protégé, in this case Japan, was going to turn out all right.

There is less altruism (misplaced or otherwise) among America's young Japan specialists today, and that is probably a good thing. It is sad to think, however, that those among them whose youthful idealism might have led them to work in Japan on behalf of American goals have instead been drawn to lucrative jobs as legal or public relations advisers to Japanese firms in the United States—or into the new projects and positions being funded by Japan's philanthropy throughout America—because American corporate, governmental, and media organizations have neither interest in their expertise nor the aggressive presence in Japan that would require it.

Buffers

America's top-drawer intellectual, political, and business leaders (unlike Japan's) have relatively little in-depth knowledge of or well-thought-out opinions about the other country. This makes them vulnerable both to Japanese PR and to simplistic Japanophobia. By way of contrast, Japan's international interlocutors have gone beyond the school-level English required of all their countrymen to a fluent command of the language, often combined with graduate training in the West, which enables them to exploit our entire intellectual GNP and to tune in on everything we say to each other—an imbalance for which we can fault only ourselves.

Meanwhile, America's academic and governmental Japan experts— those who do know the language and the country—are often distinguished in their own callings but have relatively low stature on the elite level. They typically speak more to other narrowly based specialists than to the broader public, and are sometimes blinkered in their analytical assessments by a sentimental Japanophilia that comes naturally enough with years of personal friendships and professional investments in that country. And it is into this gap between the eminent and the expert that the Japanese have now come crashing with their extraordinary financial resources and organizational skill, enlisting our experts in their wooing of our eminent.

The imbalance here also partakes of the contrasting national temperaments—the freewheeling, antigovernment, individualistic ethos of American society as against the Japanese ethic of fitting in with the group and rallying to the official national position on any given issue whenever one finds oneself in formally structured international or media-covered meetings. It reflects, too, the organizational difficulty in establishing a nonmanipulative binational dialogue between a tightly held intellectual arena ridden with cartel-like academic and media barriers and one that is wide open, at times even anarchic. Unlike the free transatlantic flow of ideas between the United States and Europe, therefore, the Japan-U.S. discourse is largely determined by a small group of Japanese and American experts on each other's country who have bridged the great linguistic and cultural gap.

Ostensibly dedicated to mutual understanding, this narrow channel of diplomats, scholars, businessmen, and journalists tends, on the whole, to tilt the binational dialogue in Japan's favor. Participants from both sides help to amplify Japan's culturalist special pleading, to fend off revisionist analyses of Japan as being harmful to "mutual friendship," to skirt issues that are domestically sensitive in Japan, and to promote the cardinal tenet that while the Japanese have adequate knowledge of the United States, Americans are basically responsible for the trade disputes because of their ignorance of Japan.

One risk in having so much Japanese financial control of collaborative policy research and public affairs dialogue is that it gets too much of a free ride on American naïveté. American participants typically enter upon a bilateral policy study or join in a conference with the Japanese on trade or other issues as though it were a search of disinterested individual minds for hitherto elusive truths. The conclusions then get reported as "objective" recommendations to both governments—the scientific model, in other words, rather like AIDS research or the exploration of dark matter. Unfortunately, the Japanese participants typically allowed into the network already share a general consensus and are well primed for argumentation and results that will serve the national interest. Americans who might interject a genuine challenge are kept out and discredited—not so much in the larger public forums, where some opposition is welcome as a foil, but in the more intimate seminars and tête-à-têtes where reputations get buzzed around, academic egos stroked, and new projects funded.

The upshot, then, is that today's bilateral web of individuals and organizations for mutual understanding rests on yet another asymmetry. On one side we have America's interlocutors, still typically focused on enlightening their fellow Americans about Japan rather than presenting U.S. views to the Japanese. From a lofty sense of noblesse oblige they persist in seeing themselves as objective, disinterested, strictly individual operators, dispensing their own wisdom-of-Solomon judgments and playing a strictly cultural, apolitical game. On the other side we have Japan's internationalist crowd, who, although capable in private of voicing doubts about their country's way of doing things, will in public settings almost always speak out in support of discreetly agreed-upon national goals.

To be specific, the Mutual Understanding Industry today is populated by three major types: Japanese appointed to handle American opinion, American "America handlers" enlisted to reinforce that effort, and Japanese who in the name of facilitation also guard the sluice gates of reverse American persuasion, thereby preempting a more direct sort of "Japan handling" by Americans in Japan. Facetiously—for they are honorable people, many of whom are my longtime personal friends—I have come to think of them as the Buffers, the Barnacles, and the Gatekeepers.

Japan's insular awkwardness in dealing easily and candidly with other peoples may be likened to the elaborate ritual docking of a ship. As the pilot inches his vessel ever so cautiously toward the pier, there are deckhands and dockhands who throw over a variety of rubber tires, padding, and other protective gear from both sides of the narrowing water to soften the crunch of direct contact. The most visible of the lot have been Japan's Buffers, internationally prominent Japanese who have been able to present Tokyo's views at a direct and high personal level to their counterparts overseas—well-known unofficial spokesmen on the order of the late former foreign minister and distinguished economist Saburo Okita, the late Sony chairman Akio Morita, and more recently Fuji Xerox chairman Yotaro Kobayashi or the former vice minister of finance Eisuke Sakakibara.[4] Eminent American diplomats and scholars in the game have included former ambassador Mike Mansfield, Harvard professor Ezra Vogel, and the late Edwin Reischauer, who qualified as both.

Barnacles

At the working level on the U.S. side, we find a lower order of American Buffer that needs a bit more explanation. Also to be found among Europeans and Asians mediating on the intellectual interface between Japan and their own countries, this breed is more personally dependent on the good ship Japan and more symbiotically attached to the boat. Some of them are nonspecialists who somehow found their way into the dialoguing business, but the essential core are genuine experts on Japan. Fluent in the language, versed in Japanese culture, and fortified with the experience of having lived in Japan, their livelihood and professional status rests on continued social and intellectual access to that country.

Foreign Japanologists in apolitical specialties (such as art or literature) find it easier to make their peace with Japan on its own terms and happily cultivate their own aesthetic gardens. The choice is starker for those university scholars who study, write, or care about contentious political, economic, and social issues. The price of engaging in public criticism or dissent can be an effective debarment from the net of access. Contrariwise, the rewards of becoming a sympathetic, protective guru on Japan can be enormous—in subsidiary income, in media appearances, in the enveloping glow of appreciation. But one risks the desiccation of one's own independence of spirit through too much accommodation. The Barnacles.

For intellectuals at think tanks—with their Japan-funded research, conferences, and even chairs—the problem usually faced is less one of in-depth access to Japan itself than of functioning effectively in the American groove, where a resident scholar often has to raise his or her own salary and where professional reputation depends on participation in projects with a substantial impact on government policy. As Stephanie Epstein has remarked, "There's no evidence that scholars involved have *revised* any positions to please Japanese benefactors" (italics mine).[5] Her study, nevertheless, uncovered a wide congruity of "pro-Japanese" positions among the four Washington-based think tanks with substantial Japanese funding—as evidenced in their published studies on points of contention between the two countries with respect to Japanese trade practices, direct investment, and sharing of the defense burden.

Although precise correlations between the thrust of particular research projects and the Japanese grants to their sponsoring think tanks were not established in her study, Epstein aptly reversed the old adage to note that "Washington is not overflowing with people who feed the mouths that bite them." At the very least, she concluded, the voices of American policy researchers congenial to the Japanese embassy had been amplified on positions where national opinion polls by the *New York Times/* CBS and the *Washington Post/*ABC News in 1990 and 1991 showed the think tanks to be out of kilter with the mainstream of American opinion on Japan.[6] Washington's think tanks today have become less accommodating in disclosing to independent researchers the amounts (or disentangling the precise allocations) of foreign grants for specific study projects, such as those with a focus on Japan.[7] Indeed, it may well be enough for Japanese donors nowadays simply to get certain issues on a think tank's agenda, knowing full well that with Japan's multiform presence in the nation's capital, Tokyo's voice will at least be heard, and very likely it will serve to leaven the study reports.

In the funding organizations and friendship societies promoting American understanding of Japan, retired American diplomats and other former U.S. officials with East Asian experience have long maintained a key if not dominating presence. They have gravitated to such positions not only to supplement their pensions but also to stay in the swim of Japanese affairs—to remain active, relevant, and appreciated.

William Clark Jr., a former deputy chief of mission at the Tokyo embassy, was appointed president of the Japan Society of New York in 1995, succeeding William H. Gleysteen Jr., former ambassador to Korea. In the early 1980s the first president of the U.S.-Japan Foundation, Richard W. Petree, and the second executive director of the Japan-U.S.

Friendship Commission, Richard A. Ericson, had both served as heads of our Tokyo embassy's political section. Petree's wife, Virginia, was active in organizing the early activities of the National Association of Japan-America Societies out of an office in the Japan Society of New York, whose then president, the late David MacEachron, had come to his post from the Council on Foreign Relations. The USJF in 1993 had as its chairman William Eberle, who had served as the U.S. trade representative in the Nixon administration and later as a lobbyist for Nissan, and as its president Stephen W. Bosworth, a former envoy to the Philippines. Richard Finn, yet another former political chief in Tokyo, later served as executive director of Harvard's U.S.-Japan Program, while James Auer, a former Japan expert with the Pentagon and U.S. naval forces in Yokosuka, now runs the influential Center for United States–Japan Studies and Cooperation at Vanderbilt University in Japan-conscious Tennessee. The list could go on and on.

This is not a conspiracy, just an all-too-predictable old-boy web. The problem with it lies in the way these ex-officials bring to their new private sector work the intellectual verities of the State and Defense Departments, including the axiomatic imperative to place military and political ties ahead of the nation's economic difficulties with Japan. By taking that line, they help not only to amplify Tokyo's cultural and public affairs push among their fellow Americans but also to orchestrate it. Even more than the Japanophile scholars, they tend to bristle at the revisionist critics of Japan—as if some ill-bred guest had belched loudly at an ambassadorial dinner. And they do so totally convinced that they are working in *our* national interest.

Becoming something of a Barnacle is an understandable occupational hazard, if not a prerequisite, for those who work in American nonacademic private organizations that are dedicated exclusively to the Japan-U.S. tie and lack the broader intellectual horizons of a university or the national-interest imperatives of U.S. government cultural-exchange agencies. Like mutual friendship societies the world over (Franco-German, Anglo-Argentine, or what have you), they cannot function without an active and sympathetic involvement by the other partner, in this case Japan. Here, too, guaranteed access to Japan—with all its stated and unstated conditions—is essential.

The smaller regional Japan-America societies still rely for many of their operations on American volunteers—on local Asia scholars, retired Japan-hand diplomats, housewives beguiling their time with flower arranging and other Japanese domestic arts, all of them in it mainly for the fun. This represents an extraordinary—and, as we have seen, largely unreciprocated—self-mobilization of Americans to spread the good word about Japan. These grassroots activists have pitched in out of their own curiosity, public-spiritedness, or a concern for the foreign relations of their country. While they view their own role as broadly educational, apolitical, and for the long term, their Japanese cosponsors for various programs usually have a more immediate and hardheaded agenda in mind— the expectation that with ever more information, statistics, and explanations in the hands of the U.S. public, altercations over the trade deficit and market access will evaporate like mist under the morning sun.

One final subspecies of the Barnacle makes its habitat in Japan. A minority are long-termers, well known locally and often fluent in Japanese, who have learned to butter their bread by promoting Tokyo's side of bilateral issues among the resident foreign community and toward the Japanese public itself as authoritative evidence of foreign support. Far more numerous are the transient Americans—ranging from latter-day hippies to luxuriously ghettoized corporate and diplomatic officials— whose detached or privileged circumstances permit them to string out their initial love affair with the country indefinitely, brooking no complaints from fellow foreigners who have gone deeper or stayed longer.

Gatekeepers

Finally, we come to those Japanese who not only mediate the foreign intellectual and cultural access to Japan but also see to it that it does not get out of hand.

There is a very special crimp in Japan on the sort of free foreign penetration of local society that is available to the Japanese in America. Once they have found their initial point of entry into the United States and know where else they want to go, they are usually free to proceed on their own. The Japanese, however, are uncomfortable with an unfettered, loosely structured multilateralism in dealing with foreign organizations in their own country. Following a custom that applies equally among fellow Japanese, they prefer to have the business in a particular line of exchange activity with a foreign country channeled through a single intermediary Japanese individual or group—sort of a central broker or brokerage known as *madoguchi*. This means service or ticket window—in effect, the Gatekeeper.

Foreign individuals or organizations that rely on a particular Japanese entity for their initial debut but then try to dance around with rival partners may quickly find themselves spurned by their original sponsor and effectively shunned by all the others. This gives the Gatekeepers, of course, a stranglehold on the volume and nature of foreign people, programs, and ideas they allow through their respective gates. And since Japanese organizations dedicated, if not assigned, to work with the outside world are informally meshed into other Japanese entities reaching up to the very top of the national policy establishment, few of the Japanese Gatekeepers for U.S. cultural ties are likely to buck the broader consensus. That is not to imply, of course, that many of them do not work extremely hard and enthusiastically on behalf of their American clients (who would be lost without them) within the limits permitted by Japan's heavily compartmentalized and personalized social order.

Naturally enough, there is a wide personal and institutional overlap between Japan's own propagandists, their American apologists, and the Japanese orchestrators for America's would-be Japan handlers visiting or stationed in Japan. Indeed, during my eight years with the Friendship Commission I sometimes caught myself wondering at hotel receptions whether I was in Tokyo, New York, or Washington, D.C.—it was almost always the same crowd. Where the gatekeeping function becomes deeply problematical is when Japan's exchange managers export the *madoguchi* principle into their U.S.-based cultural and informational activities, as we touched on briefly in Chapter 8. That is the way they prefer to deal with foreigners in their home countries, too, and at its worst it has led to Americans ostracizing fellow Americans where U.S. organizations of a "chrysanthemum"—that is, Japanophile—stripe have sought to exclude American critics of Japan from their programs.

One classic instance of this was when a Japanese consul general in Los Angeles sought to have the "revisionist" scholar Chalmers Johnson removed from the board of directors of the Japan Society of Southern California. Johnson—one of the few American intellectuals who can say things the Japanese do not want to hear and still maintain status in both Tokyo and Washington—blew the whistle on him, loudly, and before long the hapless diplomat found himself transferred to the post of ambassador to a minor Central American country.

When the National Association of Japan-America Societies was putting together my own book tour of several U.S. cities in February 1998 to promote *Cartels of the Mind,* they warned me sympathetically that some of their member societies might find my volume "too controversial."[8] Recalling with irony how I had helped to lobby for the initial Japanese and U.S. governments' funding for NAJAS when I was with the Friendship Commission, I realized how far the network had strayed from the chief purpose originally envisioned for it—precisely the discussion and working through of controversial issues! When the Japan Society of Northern California (San Francisco) passed, a journalist who came to my presentation at the University of California at Berkeley told me he thought my rejection had indeed been politically motivated. With the Japanese consul general and CEOs of major Japanese corporations in the Bay Area on the society's masthead, it was not too hard to guess why.

With the Japanese now controlling so much of the input on both sides of the Pacific, the bilateral dialogue begins to resemble nothing quite so much as a large liver sausage neatly crimped and sealed at both ends. Gatekeeping, however, is simply not the way we do things in the United States, and the need in Japan-U.S. relations today is for a dynamically expanding, nonorchestrated crisscross between all sorts of groups and individuals in all fields and at every level. No single American group should ever attempt to become the central broker for Japan-related cultural and public-affairs activities.

Unfortunately, to descend to specifics, that has been the general tendency of the oldest and most distinguished American group dedicated to the furtherance of U.S.-Japan ties: the Japan Society of New York. With its close ties to the Council on Foreign Relations and other pillars of the East Coast foreign policy establishment, the Japan Society (i.e., the Japan Society) shed its narrower Gothamite identity in the late 1970s for the broader ambition of serving as a nationwide clearinghouse for cultural and public-affairs activities relating to Japan. It has already become a force in the field equaled only by the American universities with Japanese studies programs and by the collective Japan-related activities of the U.S. government. Indeed, until 1991 the society served under contract to the USIA as the American secretariat of CULCON, while at the same time turning itself into Japan's chief de facto cultural and informational center in the United States—an extraordinary feat of politico-cultural symbiosis. However, not all of America's Japan crowd has been happy with this arrangement, and from my vantage point with the Friendship Commission in the early 1980s I watched the struggle of the newly created NAJAS grouping of regional Japan-America societies to free themselves from the would-be hegemony of their great-aunt in New York.

To give one eyewitness example from my own experience, the lengths to which Americans infected with *madoguchi*-itis will go was illustrated by a backstairs attempt by the executive head of the Japan Society of New York in 1978 to abort the previously mentioned request of the U.S. government's Friendship Commission to the Japanese government for a matching $2 million donation to rejuvenate those smaller, regional Japan-America societies. At that time I was the commission's associate executive director and Japan representative. Unknown to us, this gentleman while in Tokyo had gone over the head of the Foreign Ministry's cultural section (our point of contact) to advise the ministry's political arm against this donation. I caught the stratagem by sheer chance on November 8 in the course of a routine courtesy visit to the ministry's cultural chief, who informed me that the North American Bureau, acting on the Japan Society's advice, was on the point of sending the prime minister's office a recommendation to turn down our request. Only days before I had been sitting with my own executive director in a Washington cocktail lounge, clinking glasses with this Japan Society executive. I phoned at once from Tokyo to my chairman and executive director in the United States, and shortly thereafter a cable was on its way to the foreign minister from the society's sympathetic chairman, putting his organization's full weight behind the commission's grant request. We were back in business, but it had been a close call—and an unconscionable power play by a private organization against a U.S. government agency seeking a benefit for Americans nationwide.

There are, to be sure, a growing number of Japanese universities, corporations, media organizations, and small foundations that run their own exchanges with the United States. But many of the flows that constitute the heart of the binational discourse—namely, between intellectuals with an impact on public life and people of affairs who influence the realm of ideas—are still tended by two Japanese private organizations that between them replicate the sort of predominance enjoyed on the American side by the Japan Society of New York and, indeed, work very closely with it.

The International House of Japan in Tokyo's leafy Roppongi district, a residential and program facility also generously funded by John D. Rockefeller III in the postwar years, provides attractive lodging, impeccable service, and indispensable liaison for many American scholars and artists trying to find their way around Japan, in addition to being the sanctioned meeting ground in Tokyo for Japanese and American intellectual and cultural leaders. The Japan Center for International Exchange (JCIE), more politically oriented and run by its founder, Tadashi Yamamoto, specializes in Japan-U.S. exchanges of parliamentarians and business leaders and for many years served as the Tokyo anchor for the private Trilateral Commission grouping of American, Japanese, and European bigwigs. "I House" and the Japan Society of New York operate as virtual sister institutions, while the JCIE maintains a permanent U.S. office that was housed well into the 1980s on the society's Manhattan premises. For many years now this Tokyo–New York triad has often functioned, faute de mieux, as a virtual binational superbroker, a self-appointed mutual-admiration nexus that has been hard to budge for those without an inside track.

The system has opened up a bit as more Japanese organizations begin to establish their own bilateral links with U.S. counterparts—as with the artists' exchanges of the Seibu Group in conjunction with the Asian Cultural Council of New York. But at the political level and what we might call the high intellectual level there is still plenty of leeway for more friendly competition, more parallel tracking, and more alternative points of entry to Japan. The "pipes"—the *paipu-yaku* (pipe operatives), as the intellectual-exchange facilitators are sometimes called in Japanese—should never let themselves become plugs or stoppers. Indeed, they should be working in both countries toward the day when—on the transatlantic model—their own services will no longer be needed.

Japan's unfettered entry into the American intellectual scene, to say nothing of the U.S. economy and political system, stands in stark contrast to the Japanese barriers to foreign participation (for which the reader is referred, once again, to *Cartels of the Mind*). To get a broader historical sense of *why* America's leading thinkers and intellectual organizations have allowed Tokyo to steal the lead on the transpacific dialogue, we must now turn, in Part III, to a consideration of the American mind itself in its wavering and all too frequently gullible fix on things Japanese.

III
Self-Delusion

"And Elliptical Billiard Balls"
American Roots of Wishful Thinking

CHAPTER THIRTEEN

Gullible's Travels
Our Four Faulty
Vision Things

Why have Americans, as Japan's chief postwar partner, been so slow to see (and see through) the intellectual and psychological game Japan plays with us, so tardy in reckoning its cost to our practical national interests, and so hesitant to do or say anything much about it? The answer lies deeper than the effectiveness of the Mutual Understanding Industry, which simply piggybacks on certain habits and vulnerabilities of the American mind when it turns its ill-focused and unsteady gaze toward Japan. The intellectual muddles of our own making have long, and exasperatingly repetitive, historical roots stretching the fifteen decades from Commodore Perry's time to our own. We never seem to learn from our past mistakes. That is the burden of Part III.

* * *

For years after World War II, Japan's "soft-core" persuasion was of little concern to Americans because its "hard-core" trade barriers were acceptable to a United States that had little need to export and was willing to wink at Japanese trade practices in order to build up a staunch anti-Communist ally in Asia. The intellectual upshot of the narrowly military and political focus of U.S. Asian strategy in the 1950s and 1960s was that it permitted a great deal of wishful thinking and sentimentalism about internal economic and social arrangements in Japan.

In the 1970s and 1980s, when American attention finally shifted to economics and the trade imbalance became a major foreign policy con-

211

cern, one might have expected a realistic analysis of the barriers preventing our exports from penetrating the Japanese market. That process
of rethinking, however, was hampered not only by our own lingering
credulity but also by those rhetorical defenses (recounted in Chapter 7)
that the Japanese quickly put into high gear. Most importantly, in mobilizing their intellectual arguments to justify their economic barriers, the
Japanese were abetted by an American foreign policy establishment
unwilling to abandon its old priority of defense over trade.

It was not until the end of the 1980s that the first—and much too long
delayed—breakthroughs finally came toward a more hardheaded U.S.
trade policy and an intellectual reformulation of Japan. The two respective mileposts were the congressionally mandated trade sanctions on
Japanese consumer electronics in 1987 and the stream of revisionist
books and articles by American and European writers at the end of the
decade. But it had been a lengthy and emotionally draining process, one
that left the long-indulged Japanese resentful of their new exposure to
critical scrutiny and Americans bitterly divided between affirmers and
challengers of our earlier 1950s–1960s conceptualization of Japan. Not
until the reversed economic performances of the late 1990s did the emotional tension between Japanese and Americans, and among Americans
themselves, see a temporary respite.

Going into the new century, we must learn to hold our positives and
negatives on Japan in a single line of sight—as we do for most countries, including our own—without flip-flopping between dismissive euphoria and obsessive anxiety. Specifically, we need to get an intellectual
handle on the harsher side of Japan, but do so without flying into "yellow peril" or Pearl Harbor rhetoric. Every national culture has been an
interweaving of softer and harder surfaces—of Beethovens and
Bismarcks, of flamencos and Falangists, of church suppers and corporate greed. You never get it all one way. The Japanese long complained
of our outdated romantic images of a Mount-Fuji-and-geisha Japan—
we were not taking them seriously enough, the lament went—but they
then took umbrage when American observers laid bare the internal work-
ings of the *keiretsu* industrial groupings or market conquest through
dumping.

We need to reassure the Japanese, and those Americans who are solicitous of Japanese sensitivities, that there is no reason why we cannot
continue to be mutually respectful partners and friends in the decades
ahead—once we have gotten Japan's ways of doing things and its inten-

tions more clearly in focus and made the required adjustments in our own tactics and expectations. But what are the cobwebs in our own mind that may have helped to keep such insights into the less comforting aspects of Japan so slow in coming?

Sheer ignorance and distance—like a blindfold or nearsightedness—largely explain the failure of Americans to see much of what goes on in Japan. The inability or reluctance to properly comprehend what we do see, however, is more like a bad case of astigmatism or a succession of heavily tinted lenses. It is the product of a constantly shifting interplay of at least four major factors: (1) American strategic needs of the moment; (2) a spectrum of contrasting images of Japan, selectively drawn on, that serve the immediate need; (3) a reservoir of deep-seated American philosophical proclivities that help to shape those images; and (4) the generational tilt—namely, a historical procession of American "Japan hands" both inside and outside of government, each generation trained to a specific set of foreign policy requirements, interpretations of Japan, and American thought patterns, and then stuck in their own era's particular mental fix on Japan.

This unstable kaleidoscope of lenses is the main reason for the blurring of American vision. It has a century-long pedigree and needs close tracing through several postwar permutations to understand the complex and often contradictory accumulation of ideas, emotions, and perceptions with which Americans confront their Japan relationship today. But before turning to that, a quick word about the two simpler optical refractions of ignorance and distance.

In today's interlocking high-tech world the United States is the most intimately involved of all nations with Japan, and Japan the most intertwined with America of all non-Western countries. Trade and finance, the postwar occupation and subsequent security ties, cultural exchanges, and a converging high-tech and media-drenched lifestyle have all conspired to make it so. This de facto togetherness is one that the self-protective Japanese find hard to accept emotionally, and one that Americans, with their orientation toward Europe and other regions of the world more broadly represented in the U.S. population (like the Near East, Africa, and Latin America), have yet to digest intellectually.

For our sheer ignorance of Japan and East Asia—proportionate to their importance to the U.S. national interest, as opposed to their weight in the national census—we have only ourselves to blame. The continuing superficiality of knowledge and focus on Japan in American schools and media and in the institutional memories of assorted U.S. government agencies means that we are continually discovering (or, more often, rediscovering) new layers or fragments of the Japanese totality. Lacking a broad, nationally shared, base of information and understanding on Japan (as contrasted with, say, Germany or Mexico), we tend to embrace each new layer or fragment as the long-missing key, the open sesame, to the entire Japanese puzzle. Not only that, but to the extent that our Japan watchers, who produce these new discoveries and interpretations, have a strategically driven axe to grind, each new take comes with a certain polemical sharpness to it. By assuring or warning Americans, as the case may be, of something splendid or something awful about to come, they merely accelerate our wild swings between positive and negative images of Japan.

As for the distance factor in our viewing of Japan: This myopia has been not only horizontal—across the great geographical and cultural spaces that lie between the two countries and peoples—but also vertical, in the positioning of so many foreign commentators on Japan high above the surface of Japanese life rather than in the thick of it. The horizontal telescoping expresses itself in our familiar temptation to squeeze Japanese variants on things such as capitalism, democracy, education, law, or consumer behavior into an American mold. Given the fuzzy resemblances at such a remote distance, we comfort ourselves that the Japanese are "just like us," or are about to become so, or that we would do well to become more like them. Then, as we zoom in closer and discover deviations, we tend to panic or to feel betrayed.

The vertical remoteness is something Americans are far less aware of, yet it affects nearly all of the U.S. attitudes toward Japan discussed in the six brief chapters below. For many of the harsher aspects of Japan —particularly intangibles such as the depth of xenophobia or the residues of the samurai ethic—are things a foreigner is not likely to see, or appreciate the full force of, until he or she has struck against them through direct personal or professional experience.

The smooth surface of everyday life is something the Japanese would strive to maintain among themselves in any event. When foreigners do appear, extra veils and curtains are drawn over any protruding blemishes. Foreign VIPs, particularly those likely to comment publicly on Japan, are lifted extra high above the surface on a palanquin of exquisitely polite and celebrative attention. It is consummate PR, the world's most breathtaking construction of a virtual reality. And if the visiting

VIPs may be likened to magisterial birds eyeing the pretty hues and ripples on a lake from their lofty line of flight, much of Japan's expatriate community—comfortably ghettoized and working entirely through interpreters and Japanese go-betweens—resembles those water bugs that skitter and skim over the water without ever really touching down. To realize that the lake is wet, cold, and sticky-bottomed, one has to be pushed off the dock.

Unfortunately, two of the major generators of American perceptions of Japan—our scholars and our diplomats—tend to operate in a place that the Japanese call *kumo no ue,* "above the clouds," rather than in the *doromizu* or "muddy waters" of Japanese life known from the inside. State Department personnel posted to Tokyo not only help to shape our official Japan strategy but upon retirement often have an impact on U.S. public opinion through their writings or their leadership of civic organizations devoted to the discussion and influencing of foreign policy. Like foreign service professionals from all countries at all times, their job is to tap their host nation's policies at the highest level, not to mingle with its masses. As a result, however, they circulate almost exclusively in a government-to-government nexus, and their "diplomatic immunities" have inoculated them all too well against a direct experience of the foreign country's society.

Less appreciated is the fact that many of the West's academic Japanologists, despite their mastery of the language and extended periods of research in Japan, share in this remoteness of the diplomats. Residing and working in their own countries—as is quite natural and proper—their contacts are usually limited to the interacademic nexus, and relatively few of them have stepped outside the soft cocoon of reciprocal scholarly courtesy to bump against the rougher realities of Japan.

To say all this is not to imply that the diplomats and academics are not technically competent in their respective professional tasks—in reporting the immediate political and economic trends, or in solid scholarship on specialized aspects of Japan. The *kumo no ue* aloofness that is built into their work situations becomes problematical only when they graduate to a more general punditry on things Japanese—when they attempt overall assessments, especially patronizingly positive or absolving ones, without factoring in the psychological and experiential grasp of negativities that can come only from having waded, however briefly, alongside the long-suffering Japanese themselves through the *doromizu* of everyday Japan. Most of them do know about Japan's assorted downsides intellectually, but it is the difference between reading about tooth-aches in a dental journal and actually having one. It is not until the foreign diplomat has tried sending his children to a Japanese school or the visiting scholar stays on to actually join a Japanese faculty that plush—so to speak—comes to shove.

Not surprisingly, then, most of the critical analyses of Japan have come from that more energetic fraction among foreign businessmen, lawyers, journalists, and resident scholars who have actually encountered and challenged the gamut of economic and intellectual barriers—from the pens of entrepreneurs, Department of Commerce staffers, and Office of the U.S. Trade Representative officials who have fought for market access; from veteran Tokyo correspondents trained to skepticism; and from foreign educators who are long-term residents yet continue to find themselves excluded by the system.

Having myself served not only on the Olympus of American Japanology and U.S. government cultural diplomacy but also in the Styx of journalism and university teaching in Japan, I may say that the scales do not fall quickly or easily from one's eyes. To inject a personal aside, my affection for the Japanese people as individuals, my delight in the softer textures of their way of life, my enjoyment of Japan's vibrant cultural scene—none of these have been diminished or disturbed. But they can no longer serve me as a tinted glass, screening out the less attractive social and political realities.

Let the example of a more eminent personage suffice to encapsulate the shock of this descent from lofty patronization to Japan Encounters of the Direct Kind. When the new head of a major U.S. organization for cultural relations with Japan first visited Tokyo in that capacity a few years ago, he was heard grandly dismissing the revisionist writers as soreheads who, after spending some time in Japan, had discovered that they "didn't like the Japanese." A year later he was back to head an ostensibly cultural get-together that was boycotted by its original Japanese cosponsor, the Foreign Ministry no less, because of the conference topic he had insisted on—mutual education about defense. In the post-mortems, those of us who had given papers were treated to his railings against the contumacy of Japanese bureaucrats and his avowals to raise an American posse to set things straight. He was like a little boy suddenly deprived of his favorite toy. Welcome to the real Japan, my friend!

CHAPTER FOURTEEN

Roller Coaster
The Prewar Matrix of Plus-Minus Images

From Commodore Matthew Perry's knocks on the door in 1853–54 to the collapse of the Meiji system in 1945, U.S. views of Japan rolled uphill and down again at least twice, sowing the seeds of many of the contradictory postwar images that are our inheritance today.[1]

At the strategic level, what counted was whether Japan was seen as a threatening rival, an innocuous sideshow, or something in between. Reflecting that power relationship, there were two pairs of conflicting images that dominated American perceptions during these seven pre–World War II decades. One pair was that of a softer, geishalike, "feminine" Japan as opposed to a tougher, samurailike, "masculine" Japan. The other pair featured a country leaping ahead of the rest of Asia to become Westernized, as against one destined to remain indelibly and inscrutably Oriental.

Reinforcing these conflicting images were strands from our own conflicted intellectual history—including the competing arguments for the universalism of America's message as against the particularism of the American experience. Our cheerleaders for Japanese Westernization drew on the Enlightenment-bred notion that peoples everywhere were fundamentally similar and progressing toward a more rational, modern model of society best represented at the time by the United States. Our skeptics about Japan were more likely to take the late-nineteenth-century Anglo-Saxonist position that only the northern European races had it in their genes to practice modern democracy.

Americans in the mold of Henry James, who deplored the barrenness

of their own culture compared to that of Europe, often looked to feminine Japan for similar high-artistic enrichment. Meanwhile, those in the
lineage of Emerson and Whitman, who celebrated American democracy and individualism as against European autocracy, tended to view
the conformist efficiency of masculine Japan with disdain if not alarm.
The first group had their Buddha-head statuary in socialite salons to
gush over, the second their battlefield dispatches from the bloody siege
of Port Arthur in 1905 to spoil their breakfasts for them.

Among the American groups willing to think the best of Japan were
missionaries, educators, and businessmen with Japan experience or connections of one kind or another. Those more on their guard included
certain scholars and journalists haunted by the cultural differences, as
well as diplomatic and military officers who had to worry about geopolitical contingencies, especially the U.S. Navy.

1870s: Up

Distance and noninvolvement *can* make good neighbors. During the
last three decades of the nineteenth century both countries were turned
inward—the United States preoccupied with post–Civil War reconstruction, economic growth, and continental expansion, the Japanese busy
with their own sweeping internal reforms. Until Japan's annexation of
Taiwan after the Sino-Japanese War in 1895 and the U.S. takeover of the
Philippines from Spain in 1898, the two countries had stood aside from
the great European scramble for colonial real estate, and neither was
viewed by the other as a strategic rival or threat. Americans took pride
in their lack of European-style territorial ambitions in Asia and were
early supporters of the revision of the unequal treaties that had given the
Great Powers extraterritorial privileges and control of Japanese tariffs.
The Japanese, for their part, welcomed the Americans as relatively disinterested bearers of the new Western civilization.

The Japanese often refer to these years as the honeymoon period of
their relations with the United States, an era that was the seedbed of the
romantic, feminine, Westernizing images of Japan in the American mind.
During the 1870s Japan was awash with American educators and high-
level advisors, such as the Rutgers University mathematician David
Murray, who virtually ran the new Ministry of Education in its earliest
years, or General Horace Capron, who was brought over to mastermind
the development of the large northern island of Hokkaido. Then as now,

Americans tended to do better as teachers to other cultures than as learners from them, the Japanese better as learners than as teachers—and in these years each side was playing its elemental role to mutual perfection.

Younger Japanese men and women, particularly from the uprooted ex-samurai class, found a new sense of liberation and direction in New England–style Protestantism, in the egalitarian thrust of American-inspired schools and educational methods, and in the libertarian messages of America's nineteenth-century poets, philosophers, and political heroes. In return, American missionaries and schoolteachers and technical advisers (as we would call them today) basked in the adulation of their earnest pupils and took home with them an upbeat message about a New Japan that was energetically shedding the corrupt old Asian ways— in which China seemed hopelessly mired—and was rushing to join the West with its new railway lines, civil codes, ballroom dancing, and budding parliamentary institutions.

At a time when the sprouts of Japanese democracy were extremely fragile and in need of sympathetic encouragement, well-meaning Western bigwigs such as ex-president Ulysses S. Grant (in his visit to Tokyo in 1879) and Herbert Spencer (the dean of English liberalism, no less, in his advice from London throughout the Meiji period) urged the Japanese to go slowly, for there was plenty of time. The prototype of today's "magisterial birds" flying by on high, these stalwarts of Western democracy delivered themselves of patronizing injunctions not to push freedom too fast—what we might call an overcompensating conservatism. This played directly, if unwittingly, into the hands of Japan's more autocratic political forces, which were only too delighted have the cachet of foreign approval in constructing—as they went on to do—the authoritarian Meiji state with its politically regressive imperial ideology.

Japan's coming industrial and military prowess, however, still lay well over the horizon. It was easy enough during those early years to enjoy not only the ultimate flattery of another people busily imitating us but also the sentimentalizing romance of a quaint, artistic, and essentially harmless Old Japan. Americans conjured up a land of geishas and teahouses and painted screens, of Mt. Fuji rising majestically in the woodblock prints of Hiroshige or Hokusai. They sighed with Lafcadio Hearn for the passing of the old social ways with their limpid purity of heart, and shed tears for much-abused Madame Butterfly or for Gilbert and Sullivan's lovelorn prince Nanki-Poo. They stood in awe of the great treasures of Buddhist art that were salvaged in the nick of time from the wrecker's ball by the American philosopher Ernest Fenellosa, a visiting professor at Tokyo University. They lapped up the "wisdom of the East" that lay behind those temples, statues, paintings, Zen gardens, and tea ceremonies, all eloquently expounded by Fenellosa's Japanese collaborator, Tenshin Okakura. And with great enthusiasm they transported many of those treasures (along with Okakura himself) to the Museum of Fine Arts, Boston, where the Brahmins of Anglo-Saxonism could get a good look at them.

America's optimistic images of early Meiji Japan also drew on the dominant intellectual trends of the Western democracies as a whole during the mid- and late nineteenth century. These were the years that saw the high tide of liberal economies, free trade, and open borders under a Pax Britannica; the flowering of cultural cosmopolitanism, peace conferences, and embryonic multinational peacekeeping organizations; and the peaking of an unseasoned scientific rationalism, which assumed that men of goodwill everywhere, by simply reasoning with each other, would hit on the right institutional devices to secure continuing peace and prosperity. That entire intellectual cosmos came crashing down with the First World War, and the likes of it was not to be seen again—nor, with it, such positive American takes of Japan—until the emergence of a Pax Americana from the 1950s, with its rededication to free trade, to international political structuring, and to the badly shaken rational, universalistic, and cosmopolitan parts of the Western philosophical heritage.

Turn of the Century: Down

The U.S.-Japan honeymoon was bound to fade as the power gap between the two countries began to narrow, as strategic rivalry came into focus, as the Japanese turned increasingly to Europe for their modernization models, and as Americans—after sustaining the greatest immigration surge in U.S. history—began to close their doors along racial and cultural lines. During the first two decades of the new century, the old images started to peel away on both sides, leading to mutual distrust and occasional hostility. During Japan's wars with both China (1894–95) and Russia (1904–5) Americans had cheered the Japanese on as a young, doughty, modernizing nation taking on the decrepit dragon and the reactionary bear. Their pro-Japanese president, knowing Japan's weakness in a protracted struggle with Russia, mediated peace terms at Portsmouth, New Hampshire, in 1905, but the Japanese public—riding a wave of unprecedented chauvinism, and convinced that Theodore Roosevelt had cheated them of their just spoils—repaid the favor by staging history's first massive anti-American demonstrations in the streets of Tokyo.

Washington began to have second thoughts about its erstwhile protégé, too, seeing Japan for the first time as a potential military foe in the Pacific and a powerful competitor for the commerce of the world. In 1907 Roosevelt sent the sixteen battleships of the Great White Fleet (nicknamed for their hull paint, not their paleface crews) on a courtesy call around the world, pointedly stopping in Japanese waters. American alarmists who had warned of treacherously planted mines were proved wrong—the U.S. sailors were serenaded in English by thousands of Japanese schoolchildren. But the two new East Asian colonial empires were now separated by a bare two hundred miles of open sea between Luzon and Taiwan, and it took two agreements between the increasingly touchy neighbors (Taft-Katsura in 1905, and Root-Takahira in 1908) to guarantee their respective free hands in the Philippines and Korea and to reaffirm an open door to China's lucrative markets. And while Japanese resentment grew over the exclusionary treatment of their immigrants in California, American popular sympathy shifted to the nascent nationalism of the Chinese as they began to stand up to the new bully on the block—Japan.

With the strategic equation deteriorating, the American mind began to conjure up negative images for both the Old and New Japans—of a ruthless and inscrutable samurai heritage of flashing swords, hara-kiri, and feudal oppression, and of an ominously well oiled military and heavy industrial machine. By combining these two masculine images, traditional and modern, it was possible to imagine a colossus of Asia incarnating Kaiser Wilhelm's paranoia about a "yellow peril." What nagged at American intellectuals and policy makers—and made this new power on the global chessboard seem a bit Frankensteinian—was the growing conviction that Japan, far from becoming Westernized except at the material surface of its national life, had taken artifacts and institutions of Western origin and simply grafted them onto a value system and ways of thinking that remained profoundly alien—and had done so for purposes that remained distressingly obscure.

The vision of a threatening, inscrutably Asiatic Japan drew on several strains of American thought that came to the fore as the old century gave way to the new. The anti-imperialist movement in the United States

after 1898—an idealistic protest against our own colonialist debut—
sharpened the distaste most Americans had always felt for Prussian militarism, which had embarked on a fresh spree of saber-rattling under
Wilhelm II. It was easy enough to superimpose our images of samurai
Japan on the new military and industrial might of the kaiser's Germany,
since the Japanese had largely modeled their army, parliament, legal
codes, and imperial system on those of Berlin.

Also influential in our gradual alienation from the Japanese was the
racially conceived politico-cultural doctrine known as Anglo-Saxonism,
which taught that the American capacity for self-government traced its
roots back through the New England town meeting and the old English
shires to the tribal councils of the ancient German forest through ge-
netic inheritance. Modern democracy was not something one could learn
through education, imitation, or osmosis—one had to have it in the blood.

Subsequent American history was to prove that tenet totally wrong,
but early-twentieth-century Anglo-Saxonists argued that America's
free institutions themselves would be endangered by widening that
bloodstream beyond the British Isles and Teutonic northern Europe—
conveniently overlooking the fact that contemporary Germany had somehow lost the democratic thread. Anglo-Saxonist ideologues fed on the
turn-of-century wave of Anglophilia and on Kipling's talk of the white
man's burden. Demagogues among them envisioned a literal overseas expansion of rapidly breeding flaxen-haired Yankees bringing
American-style elections and Protestant hymns to benighted races around
the globe, but the serious thinkers were more defensive, concerned mainly
to preserve what they saw as a fragile democratic political culture at
home. And if Italians and Slavs could not be expected to mark a ballot
intelligently, so much the worse for the East Asians, who did not even
partake of European civilization.

The fact that conscientious American scholars and statesmen could
reason from such premises to the restrictive Immigration Act of 1924
derived from the assumption that they were only being scientific in equating culture with race—more specifically, political behavior with bio-
logical forebears. Eventually advances in modern genetics and
anthropology would explode the race-culture link and its derivative myth
of inherited political characteristics. But at the turn of the century the
entire West was under the spell of powerful racial ideologies—Aryanism,
Teutonism, and pan-Slavism, among others—all proclaiming some kind
of cultural superiority based on genes, and tragically eroding the earlier

cosmopolitanism. It was the distinguished Harvard astronomer Percival Lowell who in 1888 had described the Japanese mentality, with its lack of "individualization," as the polar opposite of the American, and no less than the great tribune of free enterprise and anti-imperialism, William Graham Sumner, who in 1906 warned that not even in a thousand years could the Japanese masses learn the mores of the West. That, added to the growing strategic uncertainties, began to suggest the inevitability of a military clash someday in the Pacific.

Finally, stashed away in the attic of American historical memory were remnants of the seventeenth-century Puritan attitude toward the American Indian—savages beyond the pale of God's grace, devils sent to torment and test the elect of New Zion, ferocious fighters who picked at the fragile frontier of the early settlements and sought to impede the manifestly destined spread of American civilization across the Great Plains to the Pacific and beyond to the Asiatic shores whence the red man himself originally had come.

Calvinist diabolism about the black race, too, has of course survived to this day among Afrikaaner fundamentalists and has been richly repaid with the white demonology of the early Malcolm X and other Black Muslims. Afro-Americans, however, had been Christianized and "domesticated" from the earliest times; they had been brought into the country by design, had no powers of resistance, and in the South had been forced to become, literally, "part of the family." The racial images subliminally transferred from black to yellow in the white American mind were, therefore, probably minimal. The shift from red to yellow (as the colors themselves incidentally suggest) was more powerful, if never quite explicit—cropping up in that curious mixture of wariness, alarm, grudging respect, and nostalgia Americans directed at the more militant peoples, Amerindian and Asiatic, who loomed across our successive western horizons.

It is only fair to add that Japan's own emotional distancing from America had begun even earlier. Any teacher-pupil relationship, especially between nations, harbors the danger of a nasty break when the pupil grows up—if the senior partner fails to adjust to the new equality, or if the junior one chooses to resent his earlier dependence. The rise of anti-Western cultural nationalism from the late 1880s into the 1890s was an inevitable reaction to the Meiji government's forced march toward modernization, but there were three additional trends that served to dilute the American intellectual and cultural presence in Japan.

First, Europe with its monarchies and class society was in the end chosen as a more appropriate model for the New Japan than the republican, egalitarian United States. Meiji leaders looked to Germany for their army, constitution, and universities, to Britain for their navy and menswear, and to France for their artistic sensibilities. Hegel and Descartes displaced the earlier Anglo-American empiricism in the lecture halls, and the only American author taken seriously by Japan's literary mainstream was Poe—the most French of our writers.

Second, America increasingly came to be viewed by Tokyo's political and literary elites as the inspirer or exile haven of Japan's ideological malcontents, visionaries, and revolutionaries—a source of dangerous radical, socialist, or anarchist notions, and of the subversively individualistic and humanistic ideals of Emerson and Whitman. America's libertarian, antiestablishment influences would continue to feed an undercurrent of admiration and empathy for the United States throughout the new century, but during the highs of Japanese nationalism they simply strengthened the image of an alien, if not irrelevant, United States.[2]

Third, the Japanese were quick to develop their own Yamatoist[3] version of racial-cultural uniqueness—and of superiority, at least within Asia—stressing the homogeneity of their population and its unbroken allegiance over two millennia to the same imperial line.

1920s–1930s: Up and Down

The brighter images of the 1870s and 1880s were to have a strong revival in the 1950s. Similarly, the darker ones of the 1900s and 1910s presaged the steep decline during the 1930s and World War II. It was the ambivalent set of images in the 1920s, however, that most resembles the era we have been in since the mid-1980s. This is probably all to the good, if not much fun. Ambiguity is always harder to live with than one-sided positivity or negativity, but it is usually closer to reality. Americans have generally been one step behind in their images of Japan, or rather, they have often missed the continuity at all times of both softer and harsher weaves in the Japanese tapestry by overcrediting the one that has a momentary edge over its opposite. The goal of a powerful military and industrial state should have been clear from the early Meiji in the government's assiduous promotion of modern factories and armaments in line with its repeatedly stated national policy of *fukoku kyohei* (rich country, strong army). Conversely, post-1900 Japan registered a continuing growth of Western-oriented intellectuals, progressive social movements, and experience with parliamentary institutions that ran parallel to the dominant and more dramatic rise of nationalism, xenophobia, militarism, and imperial autocracy prior to the First World War.

To begin again with the strategic equation: The 1920s represented an acceptable, if somewhat uncertain, equilibrium for both countries. Japan had fought alongside the Allied powers during the war, abandoned its alliance with Britain in 1922 to the great relief of the U.S. Navy, and joined the new quest for international cooperation, undergirded by a series of disarmament and naval-limitation treaties. These in turn had reduced U.S. military presence in the Western Pacific, and the United States was retreating into one of its most pronounced isolationist eras. Both countries had pulled back somewhat to less rivalrous or threatening postures.

Within Japan, the military triumph of the Western democracies gave the democratic ideology a pragmatic boost among Japanese intellectuals and voters as the nation entered its brief years of "Taisho democracy," with its introduction of universal male suffrage in 1925 and its fleeting ascendancy of the parliamentary leadership and their civilian ethos over the bureaucratic and military elites. Riding the new liberal mood and the advent of radio broadcasting, phonograph records, and the movies, American popular culture reached one of its historical highs in 1920s urban Japan—with baseball, jazz, Hollywood films, and flappers in cloches with their beaus in boaters strolling the Ginza together and experimenting with cigarettes and gin.

Once again the Japanese were becoming more like us. Indeed, after visiting Tokyo University as a guest lecturer in 1919, John Dewey—America's leading philosopher, whose progressive educational theories were to be in vogue in Japan during the new decade—opined that Japanese liberalism had taken a giant leap forward and deserved the warmest U.S. support. Charles Beard, Ida M. Tarbell, and other Progressive academics and journalists in the early 1920s even went so far as to pronounce American imperialism and militarism worse than—if not, indeed, responsible for—their Japanese counterparts. With the Japanoiserie of Fenellosa and Okakura now penetrating to a wide American public, the feminine images also had their revival and were sufficient in many minds to override the nagging awareness of Japan's divergence from U.S. political and social norms. Meanwhile, among the aesthetes, those rare American travelers who had been lucky enough to know a more intimate and ramshackle turn-of-the-century Tokyo now decried the modern office buildings and trolley lines that were turning it into another coldly efficient Western metropolis.

All was not well, though, with mutual perceptions. Like no other country similarly affected, Japan chose to take America's exclusionary immigration law of 1924 as a supreme national humiliation and to nurture the hurt over the following years as a virtual casus belli—something Japanese intellectuals can still wax indignant over even as they plead the necessity of their own hermetically tight immigration policies today. Both tradition-minded Japanese and those with a European or "high-culture" Western orientation tended to view the America of the Roaring Twenties with contempt as a materialistic, mechanistic, barbarian society, thus preparing the ground for the more virulent anti-American sentiment of the 1930s, with its loud ultranationalistic trumpeting of Japanese spiritual superiority. Many Americans, in turn, continued to question the depth of Japan's new spurt of Westernization and the strength of its commitment to democratic values and peace in Asia. As Japanese labor movements and parties came under ever stricter surveillance, as the thought police began to infiltrate university campuses, and as the new decade was ushered in with a series of political assassinations and the takeover of Manchuria in 1931, the pessimists could argue that they had been right all along.

What was new about American opinion on Japan in the 1920s (continuing into the 1930s) was its split into two sharply opposed camps, much as we are seeing in the United States today.[4] The defense of Japan rested on three main groups. America's liberal intellectuals had had their fill of realpolitik in the First World War. Among them were carryovers from the old Progressive movement destined to reappear as ardently isolationist America-firsters in 1939–41. As the latest outcropping of America's bedrock of Enlightenment universalism and optimism, they were hopeful for a new world responsive to scientific planning and human reasonableness, willing (many of them) to give the new Soviet experiment the benefit of the doubt, dismissive of warnings about fascist mischief brewing abroad, and intent above all on debunking the devils at home.

American missionary-educators in Japan were the group closest to everyday Japanese society and culture, although still on their elevated pedestal (which some of them were rather taken with). Their contact, moreover, was more with the humanly admirable common folk of that country than with its ruling elites, and it was understandable that some of their own missionary idealism and love of the Japanese people (as in the case of Paul Rusch) might transmute into a certain idealization of Japanese realities and a need to believe that relations with the United States were somehow going to turn out all right. Edwin O. Reischauer (the U.S. ambassador to Tokyo from 1961 to 1966) recounts in his autobiography how proud he and other missionary children "born in Japan" were of their "B-I-J" status, and how eager to refute what seemed to them ignorant U.S. criticisms of Japan. [5]

Most influential, perhaps, was the internationally oriented element among U.S. business and financial leaders who then—as now—saw vigorous transpacific trade as the glue that would hold the two nations together against divisive political and cultural pressures. In a gesture that was to be built on by John D. Rockefeller III after World War II, a group of Japanophile New York businessmen and professionals established the Japan Society there in 1907 to promote U.S. public understanding of Japan and its people. After making its customary disclaimer about taking "no part in political controversy," the society in its 1933 report (two years after the global uproar over Tokyo's takeover of Manchuria) averred that its "dissemination of a broader knowledge of cultural relationships" with Japan had "helped to develop a sympathetic attitude on the part of the United States towards that country."[6]

The trouble with placing too much faith in the creative interaction of the two nations' business elites in the 1920s—a prescription to be reissued from the mid-1990s as the fast track to opening Japan's markets—was that the pillars of the American haute bourgeoisie tended to read their own strengths and convictions into that tiny, atypically Westernized sliver of Japan's upper-crust *zaibatsu* whom they had gotten to know personally. U.S. businessmen were not only the archetype of American individualism and antistatism, but in the 1920s they were running the country. The Japanese gentlemen in top hats and patent leather pumps, in chauffeured Rolls-Royces and with their reassuring Princeton or Oxford accents, were wealthy indeed, and charming into the bargain. But as a beleaguered element in an unstable power structure increasingly dominated by their bureaucratic and military rivals, politically dependent on two quasi-corrupt conservative parties, and personally exposed to right-wing assassins and growing popular opprobrium, Japan's prewar economic leaders were in no position to significantly influence the geopolitical course of their country.

Then as now, Americans tended to lean too heavily for their interpretations and expectations of Japan on those few members of the Japanese elite who appeared to be Westernized or internationalized, and who—whether by individual inclination or broader design—were the first to reach out to foreign people. Like the peripatetic cultural spokesman and League of Nations deputy secretary-general Inazo Nitobe, they too often were viewed as a genuine avant-garde, as the wave of the future, rather than as an anomalous if not precarious part of the larger Japanese scene. The mistake here, of course, lay with the Americans, who—possessed neither of the language nor of sufficient knowledge of the country—had little other access to developments in Japan.

This probably holds true for the courtly Joseph C. Grew, ambassador from 1932 to 1941 and the first American envoy to Japan to leave any mark in the history books since Townsend Harris opened the first American consulate in Shimoda in 1856. Sensitive, sophisticated, and arguably the most distinguished diplomat of his era, Grew was obviously moved by his urbane and liberal-minded Japanese friends, who deplored their country's lurch toward war but asked for enough American patience to permit them to work things out internally. To his dying day the aristocratic Grew believed that war might have been avoided had his fellow Grotonian, Franklin Delano Roosevelt, and Secretary of State Hull gone along with his promotion of an eleventh-hour summit—to take place behind the backs of Japan's seething military—between the U.S. president and the nobly born but vacillating prime minister, Prince Fumimaro Konoe. Historians continue to debate the might-have-beens, but to many it would suggest the limited usefulness for Japan-U.S. ties, in that era, of interpatrician or interplutocratic mutual admiration.

Most of the U.S. government, indeed, including the State Department and especially the navy, had remained wary and pessimistic about a Japan that was increasingly regimented at home and clearly embarked on military conquest in Asia, and as the 1930s drew on they came to view the Japanophile groups as the dupes and unwitting instruments of Tokyo's propaganda. In 1925 the Washington-based British naval commentator Hector C. Bywater published his fictitious *The Great Pacific War: A History of the American-Japanese Campaign of 1931–33,* which predicted with uncanny accuracy the actual course of the conflict to come, including a Japanese surprise attack on Pearl Harbor. The Hearst papers and the "yellow peril" crowd lapped it up, but the *Wall Street Journal* and other tribunes of the U.S. business elite throughout the 1920s derided talk of an inevitable war with Japan as kooky—and as counterproductive for the trust and the trade that should undergird the relationship.

Exactly one decade off schedule, history obliged Bywater and his U.S. Navy sources.

* * *

In short, the ambivalent American perceptions of Japan in the 1920s—and their reciprocals in Japan—were essentially extensions of the positive and negative images of the two earlier periods, revved up by the new mass communications technology and an expanded flow of goods and people. Likewise, the steeply plunging mutual images of the late 1930s and wartime years simply took the negative set to hyperbolic extremes.

The conundrum of Japan watching in the opening decade of the twenty-first century, as in the similarly ambivalent 1920s, presents us with the same three basic options:

1. Do we view Japan with hope and trust, as an entity gradually approximating us and deserving our patient understanding and encouragement, its temporary political and social shortfalls sweetened by the softer, feminine aspects of its culture?

2. Or do we perceive it with foreboding and distrust, as something radically and permanently different, defining its harsher, masculine aspects as the real Japan, with the cultural attractions no more than window dressing?

3. Or can we—in something that has never yet been tried—sort it all out into a single integrated and pragmatically serviceable formula? This would require shedding the false expectations and indulgent sentimentalizing of option #1 without losing our ability to identify and applaud genuine (not imagined) Japanese trends that are in the U.S. national interest, and making an honest effort to live with real cultural differences. By the same token, it would mean rejecting the unqualified pessimism and goading cynicism of option #2 while standing on our own values wherever the U.S. national interest is directly affected and maintaining a skeptical and constantly probing mind toward things Japanese to protect ourselves against the return, on cat's feet, of our own gullibility and wishful thinking.

The American mind on Japan during the successive postwar decades, as we shall now see, was to swing exclusively between the first two alternatives—although in a drastically altered strategic context of U.S. Cold War dominance and Japan's rise to economic parity, and against a social background of steadily firming Japanese internal cohesion as opposed to the accelerating decline of American togetherness.

CHAPTER FIFTEEN

MacArthur Maxim
Democratic Missionizing
Through the 1950s

After seven years of Allied (read: U.S.) occupation, postwar Japan regained its independence in 1952. American images of the erstwhile enemy were to be overwhelmingly positive over the following three decades, but they were largely of a Japan seen through the prism of American hopes and values, as a country that was (once again) becoming more like us. In the 1950s it was Japan as an emerging model Asian democracy; in the 1960s, Japan as a loyal Cold War ally; in the 1970s, Japan as a miracle of economic development and a paean to the free enterprise system in dramatic refutation of Communism's planned economies. Again, a sense of certain American shortcomings helped to strengthen those positive interpretations. In the 1960s we started to decry our own ignorance of Japanese culture and values, while in the 1970s we began to measure our own economic flaws against Japan's superior performance.

The old negative images had not disappeared entirely, but they intruded mainly as bogeys from the past, projected onto the future. Often they were skillfully used by the Japanese as leverage against undue American pressures—the specters of a militantly leftist, or resurgently nationalistic, Japan if the Americans pushed too hard on rearmament (in the 1950s) or market access (from the 1970s). In the 1980s trade frictions revived the harsher images directly in the new guise of a threatening economic titan, and by the mid-1990s, with the end of the Cold War and the international order once again in flux, the ambivalent juxtaposition of positive and negative images returned to center stage.

Our chapter division from here on by decades is a bit procrustean, yet not far off the major watersheds. The year 1950 marked the start of the Korean War, which drastically changed the United States' strategic orientation toward Japan, with 1951 ushering in the peace and security treaties. Nineteen sixty saw the peaking of Japan's political leftism, the inauguration of a new Japan-U.S. security pact, and the start of Japan's single-minded commitment to capitalist growth, while 1961 marked the start of the Reischauer era at the Tokyo embassy with its clarion call for mutual understanding. The new bilateral focus on trade relations started in 1970 with the untroubled extension of the security pact together with the highly symbolic publication of Herman Kahn's best-selling *The Emerging Japanese Superstate,* and in 1971 Richard Nixon floated the dollar largely in response to Japan's new economic muscle and its intransigence in opening its markets further to American goods. Nineteen eighty-one brought the Reagan years to America, with their heavy dependence on Japanese finance and the ideological commitment to free trade (one-way, if need be), which was to come under heavy attack later in the decade from the U.S. Congress. And from 1990 came the reunification of Germany, the unraveling of the USSR, and the loosening of the Cold War glue in the U.S.-Japan alliance.

Democratic Tutoring

The decade of the 1950s saw a dramatic reversion to the positive, "feminine" images of the early Meiji period. Once again Japan was Westernizing, learning from us, a delicate flower to be protected, a source of spiritual balm for some of our own ailments.

During the 1950s—in many respects an extension of the occupation years—Japan remained to all intents and purposes a protectorate of the United States, serving as the backyard arsenal, staging point, and R-and-R retreat for our military during the Korean War. The American strategic interest in 1945 was to pull out the roots of militarism, ultranationalism, and Japanese-style fascism; in the late 1940s was added the goal of preventing Japan from veering leftward into the Communist camp. In both instances, making Japan more like America seemed the obvious solution. During the occupation, there was no question as to who was in command, and in many ways both peoples rose to their best in a repeat of that old teacher-pupil relationship of the 1870s honeymoon.

Unlike the dramatic self-modernization of the Meiji period, the sweeping reforms of the occupation era had been carried out under the dictate of a foreign conqueror.[1] The Japanese people, however, fundamentally welcomed most of them. These included the introduction of constitutionally legitimated parliamentary supremacy, whatever the informal bureaucratic powers; the launching of a democratic constitution spelling out more citizens' rights than were ever mentioned in America's own national charter; the promotion of land reform and women's rights and the less successful attempts at the democratization and decentralization of education, local government, and the police. All of these could be viewed as the fulfillment of trends, potentialities, or at least hopes among the Japanese themselves that had been thwarted during the militaristic 1930s.

Many Japanese, remembering the previous subservience to their own jackbooted masters and the misery of the wartime years, were experiencing a genuine sense of liberation—as did their forebears in the 1870s after the collapse of the Tokugawa feudal autocracy. They took enthusiastically to the American slogans of liberty, individualism, and personal fulfillment, actively seeking to realize them in the new institutional framework the Americans had provided. And in the background—power always counting heavily with the situation-oriented Japanese—their new model, the United States, was clearly on top of the world.

The crown prince had an American Quaker lady as his personal tutor; there were Parent-Teacher Associations in every school; young Japanese were into Coca-Cola and boogie-woogie; and some girls were even going so far as to have their eyelids surgically altered to look more Caucasian. It is hardly surprising, then, that Americans in the early postwar years tended to view Japan's new liberal dispensation as a direct transplant or unadulterated graft from our own institutions and culture—and as a gift, rather like the Hershey bars tossed out by good-natured GIs to appreciative Japanese children. The hopeful image of an Americanizing Japan overlooked, however, not only the native roots of the eagerness of many Japanese themselves for the occupation's democratizing agenda but also three critical carryovers from the authoritarian past that would seriously retard the emergence of a genuinely liberal-minded Japan.

First, the deep-set human values and social relationships and worldview of any given people—forged over centuries of living together—do not respond all that quickly to freshly imposed institutional and ideological dispensations. We are being reminded of this today as Moscow struggles fitfully with the introduction of Western capitalism and democracy and as some of the religious and chauvinistic features of the old imperial Russia resurface after seven decades of Marxist experiment. Likewise with Japan, it should not have surprised anyone (although it did many Americans) that the old deference to authority and reliance on personalistic ties continued to pervade the political and social system. Too many Americans during their tutelage of Japan mistook Japanese cooperation and emulation for a conversion to American ways of thinking. Too few Americans were aware of the extent to which they themselves had simply taken over the old Japanese authority roles. Their proconsul in Tokyo, General Douglas MacArthur, had grasped that traditional psychology to perfection and exploited it to the hilt.

Second and third, the occupation, with its down-to-earth American pragmatism—effective in the short term but problematical in the long run—leaned on two institutional carryovers from prewar Japan: the emperor and the bureaucrats.

.Fearing a massive nationalistic uprising—or, alternatively, a social breakdown leading to Communism—if the imperial institution were to be abolished, MacArthur (with a strong assist from Grew behind the scenes in Washington) insisted on the retention of Emperor Hirohito and quietly dropped the question of his responsibility for the war.[2] To be sure, he would now serve as a model democratic monarch tipping his fedora to coal miners. Japan's renunciation of war-making capability in Article Nine of the new constitution was also pushed through as a political and psychological trade-off for retaining the Chrysanthemum Throne. While the final judgment is not yet in, that trade-off—while undoubtedly securing the internal stability and civilian-oriented values of postwar Japan—left the emperor as a lodestar for right-wing nationalist sentiment as it revived, while turning the war-renouncing clause into a rallying point for leftist opposition to U.S. bases and military commitments in East Asia.

The most costly and least perceived shortfall of the occupation was its failure to come to grips with the enormous powers of the Japanese central bureaucracy. These, despite the dismemberment of the most reactionary units such as the old Home Ministry (Naimusho), were carried over into the postwar era in the command of the economy, in the cowing of the nominally superior legislative arm, in the enmeshing of daily life in a web of regulations, and in the fine-tuning by fiat of all levels of education. Least fathomable to the American mind—precisely because it was so un-American—was the psychological inheritance by postwar officialdom of that inchoate yet intimidating authority of established power that keeps the Japanese, as individuals and as citizens, docile and undemanding. This is a legacy that runs in a direct line back from the militarists and deified emperor of the prewar era to the warrior rulers of the Tokugawa period, and is one that has yet to be definitely severed—*pace* the new "individualism" of Puffy and Pokémon.

At the time of the occupation the United States had no other means for running the country, and Japanese officials were—or seemed to be—doing our bidding. But this shortfall would come back years later to haunt the United States in its market-opening efforts. And it would take decades, right up to the political changeover of 1993–94, before the Japanese electorate itself would get up enough gumption—briefly and so far ineffectively—to demand a relaxation of bureaucratic power.

The occupation of Japan began over half a century ago—even further removed from Americans today than the Spanish-American War of 1898 was from MacArthur's men. (Who, after all, cared anything about *that* war in 1948?) We easily forget, then, the extraordinary boldness and reach of the American experiment represented by that occupation, and our need then and later to believe in its success. Having thoroughly digested that faith during the 1950s, we are seldom aware of the ways in which it continues to nourish our proclivity to think and hope the best (for our own interests) of Japan decades later. This remaking of Japan in our own image has provided Americans with a succession of reassurances down through recent decades. It redeemed the sacrifices of the Pacific War; it insured us against resurgent Japanese militarism; it fit Japan smoothly into our internationalist vision of the new postwar order; it guaranteed Japan's loyalty and cooperation in the ensuing global struggle against Communism; and, beginning in the 1970s, it led us to believe that the Japanese were genuinely working to shed a few residual habits that still kept them from becoming full-fledged, American-style free traders and free entrepreneurs.

Since the Grew years the more prominent American envoys, such as Reischauer, and the foreign service staffs they gathered in Tokyo were to help shape not only American policy but also the broader public view of Japan to an extent unique for U.S. diplomats, with the possible exception of those posted to the Soviet Union. None of them, however, came close to matching what we might characterize as the MacArthur maxim—the attitudinal legacy of the supreme commander with the hundreds of high-level American military, legal, economic, and educational experts who had a hand in his reshaping of Japan and then returned home to speak enthusiastically of the country (often, too, their wives had become enamored of the Japanese arts or recalled a pleasant social contact with the people). The U.S. military, in what may be a professional trait, were among the most ready to forgive whatever had to be forgiven. They were quick to proclaim the full compatibility of the two nations' interests and to view the resurgence of the Japanese economy, nationalism, and even some modest rearmament as things that could only serve to strengthen this reliable new bulwark of democracy in Asia. Tens of thousands of American GIs and lesser civilian officials of the occupation, many of them with Japanese brides, rounded out this new honeymoon era in transpacific relations.

Three additional historical conditioners were to help keep U.S. perceptions of Japan positive for the rest of the 1950s. Behind the American diffidence in looking too clinically at Japan stood, most obviously, our guilt (or remorse) over the bomb. Beyond the natural revulsion it evoked—and the mea culpas quickly pronounced by a number of prominent scientists who had helped to create it—the possession and possible use of nuclear weapons became a bitterly contested moral and military issue that agitated U.S. theologians, strategists, and general-purpose intellectuals throughout the decade until the first test ban treaty in 1961 took off some of the edge. And as a constant reality check for this debate stood the actual immolation of two Japanese cities. Most Americans—and not only ban-the-bombers—were focused on the putative horrors of a future World War III and were quite willing to let the cowed and seemingly penitent Japanese grasp at their one straw of moral superiority in the past conflict, as the first and only victims of a nuclear attack.

What few Americans at the time realized—save those few who were capable of spotting the telltale signs in Japanese journals, popular films, and academic controversy—was the alacrity and thoroughness with which the Japanese by 1960 had turned their atomic suffering into an exculpation for their own aggression and atrocities in World War II and relieved themselves of any sense of culpability toward the United States. Except for certain pockets of leftists and liberals, the Japanese, after a brief period of national regret—mainly for having lost the war, and with little of the soul-searching or self-cleansing of the Germans—were ready to cast themselves entirely as the victims of America and quick to exploit every sign of Yankee guilt.

The postwar Germans were lucky in having had an earlier, humanistic "good German" culture to fall back on. For the Japanese, their civilization and national identity had been so closely bound to a deeply inculcated faith in military invincibility that defeat on the battlefield knocked out virtually every ego prop the country had. To climb out of this state of near-total psychic and cultural collapse (attributable in part, I would once again argue, to that too-rigid and brittle samurai ethic), it was comforting and perhaps even essential for the Japanese to believe that, despite the acknowledged excesses of their own military, their country really had been dragged against its will into the conflict with America. Whether by diplomatic encirclement, by economic sanctions, or by racial and cultural prejudices, it really didn't matter. In any case there was that enormous magnet FDR had somehow managed to install on Oahu, pulling the Japanese fleet willy-nilly like so many bathtub toys across the North Pacific toward Pearl Harbor.

Although few Americans at the time were willing to accept Japan's historical revisionism, many were too hamstrung by their nuclear guilt and traditional sympathy for the underdog to undertake a forthright rebuttal as postwar Japan regained its strength. Too often Americans rushed to scold their own dog for having mauled the Japanese cat, overlooking the blood and bones of the Asian field mice that barely had been wiped from its whiskers. Having been kept under wraps too long, this issue of Japan's failure to acknowledge the wartime pain it inflicted on others came back in the 1990s with a vengeance. Along with Asians still waiting for apologies, American veterans and congressmen in 1994–95 castigated the Smithsonian Institution for planning to portray Japan too much as the victim in its Hiroshima exhibit, and by 2000 former GI prisoners of war were suing Japanese firms in American courts for the time they did slave labor.

Aesthetic Romanticizing

When Oliver Statler wrote his best-selling *Japanese Inn*, American readers were treated not only to the architectural and culinary delights of an ancient Japanese hostel perched among windswept pines above a crashing sea but to the spectacle of a visiting Emperor Hirohito fumbling out of his shoes, like an absentminded old professor, at the entrance porch— hardly the Darth Vader of our wartime imagination. It was a classical instance of the way in which the aesthetic touch from the 1950s on into the 1960s spilled over into our political judgment of things Japanese.

A second historical atmospheric, therefore, was the sheer pleasantness of life for Americans stationed in Japan as economic recovery gradually took over. Japanese were still deferential to a degree inconceivable to foreign residents of Japan today. Teachers, junior diplomats, and young American businessmen in Tokyo lived in spacious, cheaply rented houses with gardens where their wives and children got to know the Japanese family next door. On weekends they could pile into the Buick and wander over uncluttered roads to explore remote mountain hot springs or quaint seaside inns. Even for the humblest of Americans it was a life high above the surface of the real Japan.

Indeed, most of our senior generation of Japan experts and many others still active in transpacific dialogue today first encountered Japan in the 1950s. It was a decade when Japan was well out of the rubble but not yet into high growth and nasty trade disputes, an era when American attitudes—at 360 yen to the dollar—were typified by the sentimental exotica of James Michener's novel *Sayonara.* Japan was not only a haven for soldiers on leave from the Korean battlefields and an appreciative cocoon for the gestating Japanologist but a pastoral arcadia for American aesthetes in flight from the Levittowns, gasoline guzzlers, and presidential soporifics of the Eisenhower years. Steaming themselves in hot baths or rattling open their old Japanese farmhouse shutters to watch the moon rise behind the twisted pine branches, these would-be denizens of Eden were totally oblivious to the sweating masses of workaday Japan, packed into their streetcars and commuter trains and hell-bent on rebuilding their country. So they helped to conjure up a Japan that never was nor ever would be—sweetly feminine, vulnerable, and mystic, a Japan grossly unappreciated (so they complained) yet basically inaccessible to the average American mind (so they patronized). This fancy of a gentle Japan was presciently challenged by Paul Goodman in *Growing Up Absurd,* where he chided the Kyoto-nurtured West Coast Beats for seeking respite in a Zen shorn of its tough feudal samurai backbone.[3]

The third intellectual conditioner of Japan perceptions was America's growing restlessness with its own smug affluence and complacent sociopolitical "consensus" of the 1950s. During the last half of the decade social critics as varied as William Whyte, Vance Packard, C. Wright Mills, and John Kenneth Galbraith were bemoaning the organization men, the hidden persuaders, the power elites, and the worship of material quantity over cultural quality that were robbing the American lifestyle of its old individualism and spontaneity.

Most of that debate remained within the familiar grid of Western psychology, religion, and political thought, but just as some Americans disaffected from the Gilded Age had turned to Theosophy from India or to fresh artistic sensibility from Japan, the Beat writers and gurus of mid-1950s San Francisco were now starting a new search for light from the East. Indian yoga and Chinese Tao were part of the quest, but the object with the widest intellectual impact and the greatest focusing of interest on its country of origin was Zen Buddhism from Japan. The mania for Zen ran the whole gamut from trivial to ponderous. America was treated to the faddish koans of Jack Kerouac's hot-rodding dharma bums; the search for *satori* enlightenment by Allen Ginsberg (who at least had visited Japan and India); the serious Zen poetry of Gary Snyder, who had meditated at Kyoto's Daitokuji temple; the analyses of East-West pop psychologist Alan Watts; the prolific English-language promotion of Zen by Japanese philosopher Daisetz T. Suzuki; and the prodigious effort by Suzuki and Eric Fromm in 1960 to put Freud and Zen together in their *Zen Buddhism and Psychoanalysis.*

Unlike the social critics, these pilgrims to the Orient were seeking an internal, spiritual liberation from what they decried as the overly rational, technocratic, and puritanical psychic binds of the mid-twentieth-century American mind. Their full impact was to come in the early 1960s with that great outburst of alienation among U.S. youth known as the counterculture, with its often drastic rejection of Western religious and philosophical values—a time to cancel one's admission to Yale and hop the first Pan Am flight for Katmandu. In fact, however, the extraordinary self-discipline of the Zen Buddhist tradition, like the square-toed and uptight Confucian ethics that have held Japanese and other East Asian societies together, were the very antithesis of the self-indulgent side of the American counterculture.

Two decades later Allan Bloom was to characterize the New Left in 1960s America as "a Nietzscheanized-Heideggerianized Left," and one probable effect of the counterculture's selective and badly digested celebration of antirationalism in the name of the Eastern mind may have been to make American youth more vulnerable to the irrationalist gurus of the Western mind.[4] Some of the roots of today's multiculturalism and New Age religion can also be traced to that midcentury turning to Eastern thought. But its broadest public impact at the time probably was to make ordinary Americans more aware—however superficially—of the existence of higher systems of thought and belief outside the Western tradition that were worthy of study, respect, and understanding.

* * *

This "greening" of the American cultural horizon—and with it a new willingness to learn about Japan and take its culture seriously—came just in time, as the political relationship took some hard knocks at the end of the 1950s.

Pursuing the defense of free Asia, the United States had come to rely too exclusively on Japan's conservative crowd—some of them thinly disguised reactionaries—to bring the rest of Japan along. Students and intellectuals on the left had long deplored the occupation's eventual retreat, in the name of anti-Communism, from some of its own reforms. Accordingly, the late 1950s witnessed fresh strength in the socialist and labor movements together with a growing neutralist-nationalist swell that resented the subservience of the ruling conservative LDP to U.S. foreign policy goals.

True, Prime Minister Shigeru Yoshida had shrewdly turned down economically burdensome and politically unpopular American demands for a Japanese military buildup on the model of our NATO allies. But when his successor Nobusuke Kishi rammed a new security treaty through the Diet in early 1960, the leftist opposition and large numbers of intellectuals and moderate citizens—outraged by the prime minister's parliamentary high-handedness—took to the streets. The massive and occasionally violent demonstrations were enough to force the cancellation of a planned visit by President Eisenhower and the resignation of Kishi himself.

By late 1960 the Japanese were reflecting how close they had come to wrecking their own democracy, while Americans pondered the near snap in their Japan tie. It was with this shaken but sobered-up mood on both sides that President Kennedy sent to the Tokyo embassy Harvard's adroit Good Humor man—Professor Edwin O. Reischauer, America's foremost Japan historian—to establish a dialogue with the neglected sectors of Japanese opinion and to proclaim a new era of mutual respect and understanding as between equals.

CHAPTER SIXTEEN

Reischauer Rubric
Cultural Sensitizing
from the 1960s

The task facing America's "Japan handlers" at the start of the new decade was to get the relationship with Japan back on the honeymoon track, but under an updated marriage contract. The implicit compact that gradually emerged was that the Japanese would entrust their geopolitical and military initiatives to the United States in return for unrestricted access to the huge American market. It was a formula that would hold for the rest of the century, but one destined to renew conjugal strife as the partners moved toward economic parity beginning in the 1970s. During the 1960s, however, it was assumed that any rough edges in the deal would be softened by the assiduous massaging of cultural appreciation and understanding—particularly on the part of the loutish American husband. The key, in short, was to keep the mutual images upbeat.

The strategic situation of both countries during the 1960s was such as to make this, in an imperfect world, the best medium-term arrangement for both sides. Japan still required U.S. military protection and political sponsorship in the global arena, and its startling rise to economic gianthood still lay a decade ahead. The United States, for its part, was still in need of the Japanese bastion during the decade that saw the Vietnam War and continuing tensions with China, North Korea, and the USSR in Northeast Asia. Accordingly, Americans were downright eager to applaud the economic advances and to certify the democratic achievements of Japan's exemplary Asian alternative to Communism.

For their part, the Japanese under Kishi's immediate successor, Hayato Ikeda, pulled back from distracting internecine political confrontations to focus single-mindedly on Ikeda's plan to double income within the decade—the stunning success of which totally undermined the Marxists' prediction of inevitable capitalist emiseration.

This exclusive emphasis on economic growth, however, meant continuing Prime Minister Yoshida's old formula of leaving security matters to the United States while abiding by the peace constitution. Since the first part of that formula was as unpopular with the left as the second half was annoying to the right, Japan's establishment had to steer an ideologically bland, pragmatic middle course between two types of anti-American nationalism. On the left lurked the passions provoked by the U.S.-imposed security treaty with its abominable American bases; on the right, the xenophobia stirred by the U.S.-imposed constitution with its detested Article Nine.

As we saw in Chapter 2, Tokyo was not above using the threat of anti-Americanism as a bargaining tool, but the mainstream Yoshida line of conservatives who dominated the ruling LDP from 1960 to the end of the century were genuinely concerned to keep the more overt forms of Japanese nationalism under wraps. Unfortunately, that feat of economic sublimation and psychopolitical repression seeded two intellectual trends that came to maturity in the 1970s and continue to affect the psychological climate of Japan-U.S. relations today.

First—on the internal side—economic performance itself became the new lodestar of Japanese identity. The long-standing drive to overtake the West, to erase the humiliation of the lost war, and to establish Japan's rightful place in the sun was transmuted into the economic nationalism of conquering world markets, establishing technological superiority, and besting the capitalist West at its own game. This mobilization toward raw economic goals produced an imperative for political stability, which in turn required a new—or, more properly speaking, resurrected—ideology of social harmony that reached back into the prewar era and traditional Japanese values for its stock of ideas. Typifying the gradual erosion of the American occupation's ideological legacy during this decade was the steady weakening of Japan's organized labor movement as against management, and the dramatic subsidence of labor unrest. With the great antiwar demonstrations and university upheavals at the end of the 1960s, Japan was to live through its own brief version of Daniel Cohn-Bendit and his New Left student cohorts on the Paris barricades. The accompanying violence, however, was offensive to the public at large and in the end served merely to accelerate Japan's parabolic plunge into 1970s conformism.

The new ideological emphasis on harmony, consensus, stability, and hard work—not just as ideals but as innate Japanese traits—fed into that growing school of "uniqueness" and other *Nihonjinron,* or theories about the Japanese. This intense contemplation of the collective navel was to set the Japanese apart from the rest of the world, erode the earlier post-war attraction of Western democratic or socialist ideas, and create a far more powerful and unifying nationalism of the center than either the leftist or rightist poles of Japan's political spectrum had to offer. Cheered on by the Americans, the Japanese went into the 1970s convinced of the historical inevitability and moral rightness of their economic and trade expansion, and united in their determination to continue it at all costs.

Second and externally—in its relations with the United States—Japan's pro-American establishment soon found in the two types of re-pressed nationalism, left and right, those convenient means of political leverage on the United States with respect to trade, security, and other issues on which the two partners disagreed. It was, in fact, a stunning application in reverse of the *gaiatsu,* or foreign pressure, allegedly used by Washington to get results from Tokyo.

Japan's spectacular economic growth depended above all on the American market, and such leverage became especially important for managing the Americans as Japanese imports started to hurt U.S. manu-facturers and workers and to arouse the ire of their congressional repre-sentatives. Japan in the 1960s, by faithfully following the U.S. foreign policy line worldwide, could honestly argue that it was taking a firm stand on behalf of free enterprise and democracy in Asia.

Having spoken thus as a loyal ally, the Japanese could then go on to admonish gently that if the United States pressed too hard on market opening, tried to involve Japan in the Vietnam War, or delayed too long in returning Okinawa, then the Marxist, anti-security-treaty left might take to the streets again. Alternatively, if Americans pushed too hard for Japan to arm itself further, to contribute more directly to the war in Vietnam, or to embrace a wider collective security structure in East Asia, that could raise the specter of reviving militarism and right-wing Japanese nationalism in the prewar mold. It was the beginning of the emotional in-timidation and special pleading we looked at in Chapters 2 and 7.

Modernization Theory

In support of the American side of the renewed strategic compact, the Edwin O. Reischauer years at the Tokyo embassy, 1961–66, saw the emergence for the first time of a distinct school of American thought about Japan, both among the diplomats who had served at his embassy and among like-minded colleagues and protégés in Japanese studies back home. The tenets of what we might in retrospect call the Reischauer rubric upheld the following: in politics, a view of Japan as an emerging democracy, to be judiciously researched and positively explained to the American people; in diplomacy, the acceptance of the basic trade-off of Japanese geopolitical loyalty for U.S. economic indulgence; and in scholarship and cultural exchange, an unflagging effort to educate Americans to a sympathetic understanding of Japan and to an awareness of the vital importance to them of this particular transpacific tie.

From 1960 onward the images themselves came to be treated like independent actors in the binational relationship. A younger, middle-level group of State and Defense Department officials—with their counterparts on the Japanese side, and a coterie of temperature-taking American and Japanese opinion pollsters—became concerned about the cultivation of positive images and the preservation of a constructive outlook on both sides. Increasingly they came to exercise what we today would call spin control, keeping passions and resentments from getting out of hand. These officials were still convinced of the congruence of their nations' interests but feared the two countries might be driven apart—against those true mutual interests—either through the partisanship of politicians or by the hyperbole of the media on either side of the Pacific.[1]

This intergovernmental concern for solicitous tending of the relationship, and for official promotion of goodwill, received support from four trends in American academe during the decade of the 1960s: the new interest in Eastern culture, the application of so-called modernization theory to Japan, the proliferation of Japanese studies throughout the United States, and the cultivation of American Japanologists as future cultural and political bridges to Japan in the Reischauer mold.

Modernization theory (best known through its hopeful hypothesis of "economic takeoff") was a scholarly effort to demonstrate that the economic, social, and political modernization of "underdeveloped" societies was possible without passing through a violent revolutionary upheaval, particularly a Marxist one, as had befallen China. Given the proper material assistance and military protection from the developed world, it was argued, Asian and other countries still bound by the heavy weight of tradition and economic backwardness would be enabled to walk the classical Western road from entrepreneurship through social mobility to democracy. The argument had important political implications (and motivations) and was particularly tempting when applied to Japan—for several reasons. If Japan could be shown off as a non-Communist success story, that would reduce the attraction of the Soviet and Maoist alternatives. Second, within Japan the most bitter opposition to the conservative government and its American security tie came from Marxist or other "progressive" thinkers such as Masao Maruyama, who viewed their own country's social and political modernization as half-baked and in need of more drastic, even revolutionary, reforms, which the American connection held back. Finally, those few American intellectuals who had any interest in Japan at all seemed to be inordinately influenced by Japan's own overly pessimistic postwar schoolmen.

From the standpoint of the modernization theorists, too many Americans had adopted the perspective of those Japanese "progressives" who continued to view their own country in the 1950s as an unregenerate extension of the prewar era, or at least in danger of a sudden backslide into the past. To Washington's policy makers, the failure of both Japanese and American intellectuals to appreciate Japan's capacity for change and the depth of its postwar democratizing reforms was an ideological impediment to the maintenance of American strategic interests in the Far East. As Nathan Glazer was to surmise in 1974, Maruyama—by osmosis through the few Japan specialists the United States then possessed—had been the most important single influence in forming the broader American intellectual view of postwar Japan.[2] Like Maruyama himself, most of America's and Europe's nascent Japanologists were still obsessed with the backward-looking question of what went wrong.

Japan's old left, as we saw in Chapters 3 and 4, has gone steadily downhill from the 1960s to the point of virtual irrelevance today. But any Western diplomat or scholar who was in Japan even as late as that decade can recall the stridency, intolerance, and virtual domination of the intellectual discourse by the left wing socialist perspective. The new American ambassador had his work cut out for him when he arrived in 1961.

It was against all this negativity that Reischauer and the younger Japan historians such as Marius Jansen at Princeton, John Hall at Yale, and Albert Craig at Harvard had started to ask a different question, wondering what had gone right—since postwar Japan was beginning to surprise so many practical observers quite pleasantly. These second-generation Japanologists helped to reinvent yet another Japan—one that stressed the values of social harmony as well as the strength and authenticity of indigenously grown democratic roots. This reconceptualization, in turn, would come under attack during and after the Vietnam War by John Dower and other members of the Committee of Concerned Asian Scholars (CCAS). This subgroup of third-generation Japanologists returned to the emphases of E. H. Norman on class conflict and stunted democratic growth, particularly in his evaluation of Meiji Japan. They faulted the modernization school for understating the backwardness of Japanese politics and society today and denounced Reischauer and company as cold-warrior lackeys of U.S. foreign policy who had set out to prettify the Japanese status quo.[3]

The assumptions of modernization theory, long since disproved in so many parts of the world, were basically three: (1) that sufficient inputs of capital, technology, and education would catalyze, in W. W. Rostow's term, an "economic takeoff"; (2) that a growing economy would, in turn, promote social mobility and the emergence of a middle class that would demand increasing commitments to democracy; and (3) that democratic countries would then of their own volition stay out of the Communist camp. This was the rationale for the U.S. government's worldwide economic aid programs, for our technical and cultural exchanges, and for America's support of free trade and the generous opening of its own market to foreign imports during the first quarter century after World War II.

In applying that general framework to Japan, the Reischauer school (as we may call them) argued that the steady growth of the Japanese economy from the Meiji period on had inevitably brought in its train a long-term undercurrent of social changes, including urbanization, an educated middle class, and the gradual permeation of modern Western ideas and values into Japan. It was not all that different from the path out of medieval feudalism and early-modern despotism that had been traveled by the Western European nations. Just as inevitably for Japan, those changes would lead to the emergence of a Western-style political democracy, to a more liberal and individual-centered society, and to more open and cosmopolitan attitudes toward the outside world.

Postwar Japan's seeming movement in these directions, they argued, was for real—not illusory—precisely because the changes were *not* American transplants. Rather, they were deeply rooted in Japan's own historical soil. Those roots stretched back all the way from the socialist and labor movements of the 1930s through the "Taisho democracy" of the 1920s to the slow but persistent push toward genuine parliamentarism stemming from the more rational and enlightened aspects of the Meiji era's constitutional, legal, and social reforms. In one word, moderniza- tion theory became a paean—with all the bells and whistles—to Meiji Japan.

Cultural Sensitivity

Finally, the increasing number of academic Japanologists, and their grow- ing extracurricular service as cultural bridges and internuncios, were to reinforce the trend toward wishful thinking about Japan in the 1960s.

After a brief sojourn at Harvard in 1959, author Makoto Oda likened the study of Japan there to his own major in ancient Greek at Tokyo University—esoteric, impractical, and very sparsely populated.[4] When I joined Harvard's M.A. course in East Asian studies in 1961, new en- rollments in the Japan track had jumped to two or three dozen in the wake of Edwin Reischauer's ambassadorial appointment. The early 1960s marked the takeoff of Japanese studies in the United States. Boosting this academic launch were the Sputnik scare of the late 1950s, the Cu- ban missile crisis of 1962, and the increasingly aggressive Soviet and Chinese cultural and economic offensives toward the Third World, which combined to create a new sense of strategic vulnerability.

President Kennedy's Peace Corps was only the most symbolic ges- ture of a briefly internationalizing America, ready to meet every foreign challenge—including quite consciously, for the first (and last?) time, the cultural one. Washington came to see that shortfalls in U.S. higher education were not only threatening America's technological lead but also hindering its ability to deal effectively with unfamiliar cultures in the global rivalry with Communism. In response, the federal govern- ment began to pump money for graduate scholarships and other pro- gram support into basic science, and, with a parallel commitment by the Ford Foundation, into the study of "difficult" non-Western languages and their related cultures, such as Japanese, Chinese, Arabic, Hindi, and Swahili.

Having trained under prewar Japan experts such as Reischauer, the small group of second-generation specialists who emerged from the wartime interpreter pool or from service with the occupation went on to become the academic empire builders of Japanology throughout the United States. Like their colleagues in Sinology, they pried loose the required financing by proclaiming the strategic Cold War significance of their hitherto neglected and presumably exotic field. Many in the much larger successor generation they in turn trained—and who now occupy the major Japan chairs—were similarly imbued with the spirit of cultural bridging, and were still rare enough to feel themselves rather special and to be treated as such by their American sponsors and Japanese hosts.

These were no mere professors of Spanish or Shakespeare researchers, mind you—scholars who would hardly elicit a yawn in Mexico City or London—but a thin, precious line of interlocutors to one of America's most vital but touchy allies. Heady stuff. From the early 1970s, federal budget trimming and the defection of the big foundations to the inner cities and other domestic problems started to dry up the graduate school grant tree. In spite of that, many in the financially strapped third generation, now at the top, managed to stake out their own niches of strategic relevance by cornering the avidly sought expertise on Japan's superior economic performance and business strategies.

In short, historical timing and funding dynamics conspired to imbue America's Japan specialists from 1960 onward with a sense of mission, of participation in international events, and of serving the national interest *precisely* by being sensitive and nice to the Japanese. And that, above all, meant explaining to fellow Americans what was commendable and hopeful about Japan. Indeed, the academic effort to educate the nation on Japan in the 1960s took on some of the proselytizing fervor with which earlier Americans—sometimes the same people—had sought to Christianize prewar China or democratize occupied Japan. It was the same missionary spirit, now turned inward upon the United States itself.

To dip once again into personal testimony, I can remember from my own graduate student days the glow of excitement Reischauer's ambassadorial appointment in 1961 cast over East Asian studies at Harvard. Long before exploration of Japan's managerial wizardry was to become the academic fashion, it was possible to feel that even studies of Japanese medieval landholding, seventeenth-century playwrights, or minor Meiji-period thinkers were somehow contributing to the grander task of transpacific togetherness. And, for those of the first and second generations who enjoyed a bit of public affairs moonlighting, there were foundation consultancies, appointments to cultural exchange committees, and top-drawer access to the two nations' intellectual and political establishments—opportunities that were beyond the reach of the average American scholar in a Western-oriented field.

The archetype—although hardly the lone representative—of this fusion of scholarly and public activity was, of course, the man who as Harvard professor and Tokyo envoy had reached the top rung in both careers.[5] Having helped to institutionalize Japanology at Harvard and elsewhere, Reischauer now brought to his embassy young officers with language fluency and promoted the professional advancement of American diplomats with a serious career commitment to Japan.

Reischauer was a soft-spoken gentleman of the old school, a man of human breadth and warm humor, and a scholar well versed in the classical traditions of China and Korea (an oft-forgotten fact) as well as in the whole sweep of Japanese history. His appointment had raised eyebrows among Japanese leaders (mightn't he, as a Democrat, be too leftish?) and American foreign service professionals (would he be sufficiently tough-minded?). Some Japanese, of course, set out to con him and exploit his personal love of their country. For many, however, it was a flattering and long-sought gesture of equality—to send the first U.S. envoy who knew the language, one who loved the country and even had a well-connected Japanese wife. Reischauer's genial personality, and his forgiving nonchalance when he nearly died of a would-be assassin's stab wounds, made it difficult for all but the most cynical not to go along with his new gospel of cultural understanding. Nothing better testified to his effectiveness in damping anti-American sentiment through the broad reaches of Japanese society than the resentful hostility with which both extremes—the chauvinist right and the Marxist left— regarded him.

The lures of modernization theory and cultural bridging lingered for a long time, perhaps more as an ambience than a conscious set of imperatives. But there were also purely scholarly trends at work during the 1960s to make the growing profession upbeat and to avert mistier eyes from the downsides of Japan. Reischauer's widening of the hitherto narrow door leading from Japanese studies to public service was matched by three other developments in the field during the course of that decade. One was the interdisciplinary enrichment of the new area studies approach; another, the infusion of a certain humanistic sensibility as a preliminary to all disciplinary specialization; and finally, a natural cyclical swing of the research pendulum toward more affirmative takes on Japan.

The 1960s were in many ways a charmed decade for the budding Japanologist. The laborious, groundbreaking, surveylike studies had been done during the 1950s or earlier, while the specialization that crowds thesis writers into increasingly fragmented topics lay a good decade ahead. It was still possible to write books that were of large-scale interest—more entertaining for the author as well as the reader. The "great books" and "great ideas" approaches of Western civ courses in the 1950s were now applied to the 1960s curriculum on East Asia. Japan historians were encouraged to draw on Japanese literature and vice versa, and all beginners were expected to strive not only for functional mastery of the Japanese language but for a passing familiarity with the cultures of neighboring Asia, particularly that of China, as well.

The attempt to attach a certain side-angled Japan expertise to mainline disciplines such as economics, management, or political science *without* these deeper linguistic and cultural underpinnings was to come later. It was the economic performance of Japan in the 1970s that would first attract the theoretical interest of scholars outside the Asian field. And it would be a couple of decades before the economic approach itself—through mathematical, econometric modeling—was transposed to produce those abstracted rational-choice analyses of Japanese politics that were to blight the 1990s.

The 1960s were also the golden age of the now old-fashioned cultural and humanistic approach to Japanese studies, something that flavored the work in anthropology, sociology, and psychology as well as the humanities proper. Insights were still to be drawn from Japanese novels, art, and philosophy as well as the hard facts of the nation's political and social history. Reflecting a continuing concern for "what went wrong" before the war, ideas, intellectual history, and a grasp of the Zeitgeist or spirit of the times were still in fashion. But there was also a new eagerness to consider the brighter side, not only in the booming, pacifist Japan of the 1960s but also by tracing the more promising threads of the future back as far as possible into the past.

With the old research horse of Japanese militarism and fascism seemingly flogged to a pulp, it seemed wiser and more fun to stake out new turf and original interpretations (the key to academic advancement) along the optimistic line. At the very least, in the culturally disputatious America of the 1960s, one could enrich one's own Western heritage by drawing on the ancient stores of Japan and its sister East Asian civilizations. The emerging scholarly type, in short, was rather Renaissance. But when later confronted with the rise of Japanese power and the countertrend to scrutinize it critically, the old Japanese studies camp was more prone to the demure idealism of Erasmus than to the cynical realism of Machiavelli.

All of this had its seductive side for the individual scholar who had taken the better part of a decade to master a recondite language and subject matter of little interest to American colleagues with a mainstream Western orientation. It was a bit like having had advanced neurosurgical training on top of medical school, only to be asked about Band-Aids. Young American Japanologists were beginning to understand that they would remain dependent throughout their professional lives on Japanese individuals and organizations for access to informants and materials—and, as Japan became an increasingly expensive place for research, for financial sponsorship and logistical support. It was still an era in which American business, journalism, and academe were relatively uninterested in Japan expertise. Accordingly, it often seemed as though the only sources of appreciation and encouragement were the Japanese themselves, or those Americans in the nascent Mutual Understanding Industry who were politically concerned to keep the state of transpacific ties positive.

Reflecting on my own experience, one went to Japan with one's dissertation project in the 1960s—or later in the 1970s as a correspondent who could actually interview in Japanese, or as a foundation official who knew the local terrain—and was lionized. The Japanese, having waited for it ever since Perry, understandably were delighted to be taken seriously. And for the older generation of Japan hands who found themselves elevated to the stratosphere of cultural go-betweening, there was even headier stuff—rubbing shoulders with cabinet ministers, corporation presidents, and members of the cultural elite whom most Americans met only in books. The eminent Japan historian John W. Hall, my first chairman at the Japan-U.S. Friendship Commission, remarked to me in 1981—with self-deprecating New England wit—what a letdown it always was after a Tokyo trip to go back to being "just another Yale professor."

All this was harmless enough, except that the American players in the cultural bridging game were for the most part scholars with a higher level of name recognition in Japan than in their own country, innocents of the old school who consistently saw themselves as operating in a genuinely reciprocal goodwill undertaking devoid of any power-political implications. Continuing to bask in the approbation of their Japanese counterparts, the American team—its intellectual and emotional roots in the 1950s and 1960s—failed to revise this perception as tougher economic and political issues began to infiltrate the cultural-understanding channels from the 1970s onward. Meanwhile, Japan's own suavely Westernized and personally charming interlocutors swung ever more firmly into the orbit of Tokyo's hard-core trade and foreign policy apologia. Add Japan's national-interest-minded cultural spokesmen, consensually attuned to the highest policy goals, to a well-intentioned, transnationally minded specialist coterie of Japanophile Americans, and you are bound to get a distorted dialogue.

To its credit, the cultural bridging of the 1960s—as opposed to its abusive manipulation for Tokyo's propaganda purposes later on—was in its day an accomplishment of historic proportions that wove human and institutional ties between the intellectual, cultural, and policy-making communities of the two countries so that they could at last talk to, not simply past, each other. What happened thereafter, simply stated, was that Japanese power grew much faster than the awareness of it on either side, leaving Americans stuck in a posture of patronizing indulgence, which the Japanese—also out of long habit—were, and still are, only too happy to exploit.

CHAPTER
SEVENTEEN

Number-Oneism
Economic Giantizing
in the 1970s

The more recent and better-known story of the 1970s, 1980s, and 1990s is that of the failure of America's policy makers and intellectual interlocutors for Japan to keep up with the ongoing shifts in strategic interests, mutual images, and intellectual climates in both countries. The 1960s Reischauer formula of steering between the Scylla and Charybdis of left- and right-wing anti-Americanism by eschewing any possible offense to Japan's "national sentiment" *(kokumin kanjo)* gradually hardened into dogma, leaving the American mind consistently vulnerable to emotional blackmail.

At first the 1970s looked like yet another reconstruction of the honeymoon era, but at a level of greater equality to accommodate Japan's growing economic power. The security pact still served the basic foreign policy goals of both countries and was quietly extended in 1970. The reversion of Okinawa in 1972 and the gradual winding down of the war in Vietnam reduced organized anti-American sentiment, while the new American fascination and praise for their country's economic performance gratified the Japanese and heralded the approach of economic parity.

The growing divergence in economic interests, however, was starting to nibble away at the political relationship. The first wake-up bite came when Prime Minister Eisaku Sato failed to deliver on his 1969 promise, as Americans had taken it, of export restraints on Japanese textiles. President Nixon had viewed this as a partial quid pro quo for the return of Okinawa and had counted on it as the key to his southern-state election strategy for 1972. The United States retaliated with the double "Nixon shocks" of 1971, floating the dollar and going over Japan's head to reopen contacts with China without informing Tokyo in advance.

Trade relations continued to sour as delegation after U.S. trade delegation visited Japan during the 1970s to plead for market opening. It was that previously mentioned Japanese reporter who best encapsulated Tokyo's attitude when, in a peevish and highly personalized tone, he asked William Eberle (Nixon's top negotiator) why he had come to irritate the Japanese people with such persistent and unreasonable demands.[1] This theme of American arrogance and pushiness on trade issues soon became a buzzword with the Mutual Understanding Industry throughout the decade and beyond—the Japanese warning against the provocation of anti-American sentiment, and the U.S. side chiming in, "Yes, yes, what we Americans need is a better understanding of Japan."

The incipient political erosion was suggested by Japan's overnight pro-Arab tilt during the 1973 oil crisis, indicating its willingness to defy Washington's strategic orchestration in a global confrontation that affected its vital economic interests, and by Tokyo's icy reaction to President Carter's plan in 1977 to withdraw U.S. troops from Korea. This initiative, although wisely retracted, was the most disquieting of a series of U.S. strategic wobbles in Asia—from the help-to-those-who-help-themselves Guam Doctrine of 1971 and the fall of Saigon in 1975 to the spectacle of a hapless American Gulliver immobilized by the revolutionaries in Teheran and Kabul at the end of the decade. These were to jolt the credibility of U.S. security guarantees at the very time that Americans were beginning to complain of Japan's free ride on defense.

Nixon's unilateral moves and brusque style toward their countrymen alienated the Japanese—in fact, they were deliberately calculated to break Japan's expectation of continued favored treatment by the United States. Henry Kissinger was known to dislike the Japanese personally and to have mimicked them mercilessly in the privacy of his office. And there was a growing element in the U.S. government and business communities —those annoyed by the budgetary costs of the free ride and the burdens of unfair competition—who were reverting to the old negative images. Japan, once again, was being seen as different, threatening, and headed for increasing conflict with the United States. Reining in their personal distaste, however, the president and his secretary of state continued to play the old 1960s script—that of keeping Japan quiet by going easy on trade disputes, thereby freeing America's political energies for more critical tasks (as they thought) around the globe.

One result was the successive appointment to Tokyo in the early 1970s of three ambassadors with little political weight in the United States and little to no previous experience of Japan: one miscast Near East diplomatic hand (Armin Meyer) and two ex-corporate chiefs (Robert I. Ingersoll and James D. Hodgson). Carrying on the old Reischauer line, they managed to keep impatient U.S. journalists and businessmen at bay while assuring Tokyo that the old terms of the relationship would hold. Determined not to rock the strategic boat on behalf of mere trade grievances, the Department of State and the political section of the American embassy were not keen to sustain the sporadic outbursts of official American distress. Indeed, American public diplomacy through USIS during this decade was largely squandered on quixotic justifications of the Vietnam War and of President Carter's human rights agenda, rather than developing an effective voice on economic and trade issues.

It was from the early 1970s (as we noted in Chapter 9) that the Japanese government and corporate sectors, importuned by American Japanologists and cultural exchange officials, embarked on their active cultural diplomacy toward the United States by funding American organizations with programs on Japan. This largesse helped to nourish the central intellectual preoccupation of the decade—America's growing fascination with Japan's economic "miracle"—and, with that, to sustain a fresh set of positive images of Japan for another ten to fifteen years. These drew on the notion that Japan's success was due to innate cultural characteristics, resonating the views of Japan's new school of cultural uniqueness and superiority. Among Americans, too, Japan's darker past and its arguable political backwardness were suddenly forgotten in the exploration of lifetime employment, quality control, government-business cooperation, and worker-management harmony as possible talismans for the ailing American economy.

Conveniently overlooked by writers in both countries was the price being paid by the Japanese themselves in marathon working hours, cramped living quarters, a subhuman "commuters' hell," and the immersion of the individual in a suffocating corporate ethos. Also ignored—perversely so, since they were the sine qua non of the equation—were the two great macroscopic factors behind Japan's economic success. First, what had secured Japan's lucrative and one-sided access to world markets were America's free trade policy and its global military commitments, for which the U.S. economy was paying an increasingly high price. Second, the American defense umbrella over Japan itself had relieved Tokyo of the enormous financial, domestic political, and foreign policy costs of maintaining a major military establishment of its own.

Americans in the 1970s, however, were smarting from their defeat in Vietnam, obsessed with the Watergate scandal, and baffled by a recalcitrant stagflation. Given the national mood, they were less interested in political disaster news from Asia than in the new, upbeat messages about economic growth and social stability that were pouring in from Japan.

Riding the "Japan boom" that rose in a crescendo from the early 1970s to the mid-1980s were four types of authors: (1) foreign writers with global name recognition but with no previous expertise on Japan, such as Herman Kahn; (2) home-based Western Japanologists, such as Ezra F. Vogel of Harvard, who wrote initially for domestic consumption but were in short order translated, lionized, and brought into Japan's inner circle of transpacific bridgers; (3) a few foreign expatriates in Japan who wrote mainly for, and were similarly feted by, an appreciative Japanese audience, which had waited so long to be told something nice; and (4) the Japanese intellectuals themselves, who were spinning the *Nihonjinron* ideology of Japanese uniqueness.[2]

It was Kahn, with his think-tank cachet and his controversial theorizing on thermonuclear war, who brought an aura of geostrategic excitement to the enterprise early on with the publication of his *Emerging Japanese Superstate* in 1970.[3] Predicting Japan's imminent surpassing of the West and its claim to the twenty-first century, his best-seller was a mixture of derivative social description, economic projections now long since come true, and patented Herman Kahn futurological scenarios. The latter managed to tickle not one but two of the old Western nerves with speculations about Japan's coming greatness: fear and admiration.

In hopeful preparation (one may surmise) for the role he would soon be playing on the Carter foreign policy team, Zbigniew Brzezinski followed on Kahn's heels with a cautionary corrective, *The Fragile Blossom,* in 1972.[4] This book was more in line with the long postwar emphasis by official America on Japan's inherent weaknesses and the continuing need for U.S. sensitivity and restraint—a volume to warm the hearts of Japan's trade expansionists as yet another foil to any coordinated American pressure. Finally, striking a semantic balance between Kahn and Brzezinski, the former Tokyo-based journalist and author Frank Gibney in his *Japan: The Fragile Superpower* in 1975 took advantage of the new curiosity about Japan to delve into details of Japanese business, media, and intellectual life that until very recently would have been beyond the range of U.S. popular attention.[5] And in 1976 came the massive study from the Brookings Institution in Washington that provided the chief scholarly underpinning for the Japan boom: *Asia's New Giant: How the Japanese Economy Works,* edited by Hugh Patrick of Yale and Henry Rosovsky of Harvard.[6]

At the far end of the decade stood Ezra Vogel's *Japan as Number One: Lessons for America*.[7] Vogel, publishing in 1979, was one of a new generation of linguistically trained American social science experts on Japan—another was the young Columbia political scientist Gerald Curtis—who, unlike the older generation of ivory-tower, stay-at-home humanists in Japanese studies, were spending more and more time now in Japan, not only on research and fund raising but in the rough-and-tumble of getting to know and mingle with the business, political, and bureaucratic elites of Japan on their own Tokyo turf. Few at Harvard were as close to the dynamic pulse of 1970s Japan as was Vogel. It was no longer possible for any single person to fill the seven-league boots of Edwin Reischauer as *the* grand cultural interlocutor, but if the shoes now were smaller, there were many more pairs of them to go around, and plenty of new feet jostling to fill them.

Vogel went well beyond the usual 1970s paeans to Japanese miracles in management and productivity to portray an entire society functioning with enviable smoothness. His book was an encomium to Japan's successful mastery of problems in education, crime control, pollution reduction, and effective political governance with which Americans were still struggling. In his emphasis on conscious, rational institutional structuring as opposed to hoary inborn Japanese instincts, Vogel stood against the culturalist crowd and the *Nihonjinron* writers. He caught the attention of his American readers with his hopeful message of institutional renovation and transferability, placing himself among the apostles of cultural convergence—with the new retro twist of America now converging toward Japan—while still standing in the continuing line of 1960s modernization theory.

What caught the eye of the status-conscious Japanese who read Vogel's megaseller translation, however, was, very simply, its title: *Japan as Number One*. There it was, at long last, and from a Harvard don, no less. What more could one possibly want than the recognition, after a century's bitter struggle, that Japan was now on top?

Japanese able to laugh at their fellow countrymen's susceptibility to flattery soon coined the term *Vogelization,* while in the West there was widespread criticism of the book's failure to spell out the deficit side of Japan's social ledger. The one thing certain was that this study, and the notion of number-oneism that it spawned, probably had a greater impact on the psychological interface between the two countries than any single volume previously published—and it was working overwhelmingly to the benefit of the Japanese. A few years before writing his best-seller, Vogel—an old Harvard mentor and fellow fund-raiser—had told me how he felt something had to be written to disabuse Americans of their ignorance, nonchalance, and poor preparation in dealing with the leaders of Japan. A decade later, not long after publication, he mentioned his regret that the book, by catalyzing a cheeky new self-confidence among the Japanese, had probably weakened the hand of the United States at the trade negotiation table.

Representative of foreign writing directed at the Japanese was a book in 1977 by the Sophia University scholar Gregory Clark entitled *Nihonjin: Yuniikusa no Gensen* (The Japanese: Sources of their uniqueness).[8] Clark, restirring the pot of *Nihonjinron* bromides, called on the Japanese to reaffirm their collectivistic, emotionally binding "tribal" values, nurtured over centuries of relative seclusion, as a positive strength in a world tiring of divisive Western ideologies. The author went on to numerous (and by his own admission very lucrative) appearances on Japanese television and the public lecture circuit, but his study never went into an English edition and seems to have been written exclusively for a Japanese readership.

All of these authors, and their Japanese counterparts in the *Nihonjinron* school, were writing not only at a time of seemingly unstoppable economic conquests but during an era when Japan's university students and intellectual elite were rapidly becoming more conservative, prone at times to a new smugness or even arrogance. These were the years for self-congratulation and for the proliferation of academic courses, textbooks, and public lectures on topics such as cross-cultural communication, mutual images, or the interminably puffed-up similarities and differences between Japan and Countries X, Y, and Z. When the gatherings were international they featured wherever possible the participation of foreign heavyweights such as Daniel Bell or Claude Lévi-Strauss—conferences where the Japanese could indulge their age-old pastime of regarding themselves in the great global mirror, but with far less of the old, anxious self-deprecation than before.

* * *

When analyses of Japan's extraordinary economic performance became the new academic rage, Americans too often failed to challenge the assumption that allegedly superior social or managerial arrangements somehow absolved the Japanese of the obligations of market reciprocity. Taking Japan's economic success as yet another confirmation of modernization theory—and confident of the social and economic liberalization that theoretically should follow—it was during this decade that the U.S. interlocutors in the transpacific dialogue gradually allowed the moral initiative and psychological edge to slip into the hands of the Japanese.

The basic problem was that too many Japanese and Americans—from the early 1970s right up to today—have remained captive to that 1960s formula for mutual discourse that prescribed ever greater knowledge, sensitivity, and understanding on the part of America in return for bolder self-explanations by Japan. This formula was specific to the peculiar needs of the early 1960s, when the great menace to the relationship was the occupation-bred Yankee arrogance and Nipponese self-contempt that had come to a boil by the late 1950s. In its time, this Reischauer rubric was a political masterstroke, rescuing both countries from an earlier prescription that had gone sour. By 1960 the old MacArthur maxim—that of American democratic tutelage to a people weary of militarism and yearning for a new ideal—had degenerated into an inflammable mixture of Japanese servility and American nonchalance. By 1970, however, it was the Reischauer rubric itself that had outlived its day. Unfortunately, it was to cast its long shadow into the 1980s as the Mansfield mandate—encouraging Japan's spokesmen to ever greater insouciance while America's Japan experts stood by, all but tongue-tied for fear of appearing crude.

Behind that diffidence lay one of our most elementary difficulties in dealing effectively with Japan, namely, our halfway mastery of Japanese etiquette—our failure to factor in Japan's deeply felt distinctions between virtual and actual reality. Japanese etiquette, as every tourist guidebook explains, requires the covering of true but problematical intentions (*honne,* the "true root") with a mask of face-saving pleasantries or excuses (*tatemae,* the "false front"). Within Japanese society both sides of this elaborate equation are fully understood. One party either accepts the nominal excuses of the other and backs down or finds additional leverage to change the other party's true intent. Too many Americans too often (Japan hands included) have mistaken that facade for reality. Or, having been told that the Japanese eschew direct confrontation, and not wanting to be disliked or thought gauche, have pulled back and remained silent without playing the other half of the game—that of a decently veiled but convincing power positioning. This has allowed the Japanese to gain precious time at no ethical cost to themselves, since this game is not only accepted but also indeed mandatory in their way of doing things. Whenever Japan pulls the wool over Uncle Sam's eyes, it is Americans who provide the fleece.

To engage in that game effectively, it has to be understood by the top American player in Japan—the U.S. ambassador. Before too long diplomatic historians will start to appraise the unusually protracted (1977 to 1989) Tokyo stewardship of Mike Mansfield.

Any ambassador ultimately works within the constraints of administration policy, and the esteem in which Washington's makers of Japan policy held the former senator from Montana was underlined by the decision of both Presidents Carter and Reagan to keep him in Tokyo. Through personal style and by lines of advice, however, an ambassador can affect the tone and direction of American policy toward the country in which he or she is stationed. Unfortunately, Mansfield was prone to bask in the fawning appreciation of official Tokyo, taking the hook of *tatemae* deep into his throat and repeatedly faulting his own country on trade issues while patronizingly exonerating his Japanese hosts. Although the embassy's rhetorical stances were to become more realistic under succeeding ambassadors Armacost and Mondale, the resilience of the old Mansfield manner was displayed under their successor, Tom Foley. And as young Ph.D. candidates begin to sift the public record and tape their interviews there will be three points to ponder.

First, even a cursory check of the press files will reveal a surprising number of times when Ambassador Mansfield in public statements toned down or otherwise distanced himself from a tougher Washington stance on trade disputes, echoing Japanese criticism of U.S. economic behavior and calling, with lofty impartiality, for greater American patience. Second, if they can get the right people to talk, they will learn of numerous instances when more pessimistic evaluations of Japanese intentions by embassy officers were "spiked" by higher-ups and denied transmission to Washington. Finally, they will have to calculate the political cost—spread over more than a decade—of an ambience best encapsulated by the celebration in honor of Mr. Mansfield's birthday in 1986, at which Prime Minister Nakasone compared his own relationship with the American envoy to that of a son to his father, and likened Mansfield himself to a Japanese ambassador to the United States.[9]

But that was precisely the trouble. This retro ambassadorial role was doing more to erode than to preserve the binational relationship, which Mansfield himself never tired of calling "the most important one in the world, bar none." Since trade relations were by that time in a full tailspin, this charade left some observers asking if Alice had been posted to Wonderland.

CHAPTER EIGHTEEN

Brief Awakening
Revisionist Turnaround
in the 1980s

If Americans in the 1970s were learning from the Japanese economy, by
the next decade they were leaning on it. During the 1980s there were
two portentous shifts in the American intellectual climate toward Japan,
laying down lines of confrontation that have continued to this day. First,
many Americans were beginning to view Japan's economic prowess as
a threat; second, there was an increasingly nasty split between those
who saw it that way and those who didn't.

   With poetic justice, the United States was now experiencing some of
the emotional turmoil and intramural enmity that broke out among the
Japanese after the war between those who chose to work closely with
the Americans—the acknowledged masters—and those who resented
such collaboration. At a deeper level still in the national psyche, Americans were getting a tiny whiff of the anxiety that had overtaken East
Asians 150 years ago with the appearance on their shores of the materi-
ally more powerful and culturally alien Western civilization. Not since
the days of King George III or the London financiers of the nineteenth
century had Americans in great numbers sensed that their lives were
somehow beholden to forces outside their borders and beyond their control. And imperial Britain, after all, was still something of a great-aunt,
not an Asian unknown. Once again, sweet and sour formulations of Japan were competing for primacy in the American mind.

   As Tokyo continued to expand its exports and investments together
with its financial and political clout in the United States while adamantly
keeping its own markets closed, the group of Western scholars and jour-

nalists who were dubbed revisionists began to scrutinize the roots of Japan's economic and political behavior in dry-eyed, skeptical terms and to question the further (or even the original) usefulness of the old Reischauer rubric. On the counterattack against them, echoing and abetted by the powerful propaganda machine Tokyo now had in place throughout the United States, America's own defenders of Japanese economic behavior raised the old appeal to an overriding strategic partnership. Throwing the blame for the trade imbalance on American economic shortcomings, they joined Japanese spokesmen in writing off the bearers of revisionist tidings as sloppily researched, emotionally driven Japan bashers—that thinly clad circumlocution for "racist." Revisionists returned the compliment by tagging as members of the "Chrysanthemum Club" the opposing ranks of American public pleaders for Japan. Broadly identified with that flower were the free trade ideologues in academe and journalism, the scholarly Japan apologists behind ivied walls, the hard-core Japan trade lobbyists in Washington, sentimental Japanophiles in all walks of life, and American cultural exchange professionals with an institutional stake in the Mutual Understanding Industry—the trench fighters for the club.

Through the early 1980s Americans persisted in their economic adulation of Japan, even while slipping into unprecedented financial dependence on it. Strapped by its double budgetary burden of tax cuts plus higher defense spending, the new Republican administration turned to Tokyo as the leading buyer of U.S. Treasury securities to finance the growing federal deficit. The Japanese were quick to make full, if discreet, use of the political indebtedness thereby incurred to thwart any development of effective trade strategies by Washington, coating the pill of financial blackmail with outspoken fidelity to American Cold War objectives and repeated accolades for Ambassador Mansfield's diplomacy of good feelings.

Yasuhiro Nakasone—arguably the most right-wing and nationalistic of Japan's postwar prime ministers—was quick to establish a close personal and ideological "Ron-Yasu" rapport with the new American president and to claim, alongside Reagan and Margaret Thatcher, the third corner of that newly regnant conservatism espousing free economies and a strong anti-Soviet military stance. Presenting himself as an anti-Communist stalwart and defense hawk, and skillfully playing on Reagan's preoccupation with the Free World's final checkmating of the USSR, Nakasone (in office 1982–87) managed to wring from the Americans yet another respite on trade issues with his magician's bag of highly touted but largely unfulfilled trade liberalization measures and special-commission reports. Speaking to American audiences in English and coming across as the sort of outspoken leader the United States had been longing to deal with, Nakasone got away with mere lip service to the free trade part of his neoconservatism. Once again, ethnocentrically blinkered Americans and Europeans had set down their own Cartesian cookie cutter in the amorphous dough of Japanese political life and come up with a confection they were quick to pronounce as a great Western-style statesman.

Within the United States itself, Tokyo's establishment—long hooked, rather snobbishly, on the academic totems of Democratic liberalism such as Harvard and the Brookings Institution—was now discovering and learning to work with the Heritage Foundation and other conservative research centers and foundations representative of America's New Right. In a minor but richly symbolic appointment, the Japan-U.S. Friendship Commission in 1983 welcomed as its new chairman the economist Glenn Campbell, director of Stanford University's Hoover Institution, who with Milton Friedman had been one of the two gurus of laissez-faire economics advising Barry Goldwater in his campaign for the presidency in 1964. The Japanese, naturally enough, did all they could to encourage the dogmatic Reaganomic commitment to free trade, which was almost too good to be true. Incredibly, the United States now seemed determined to keep its own markets open, whatever the protectionist behavior of its trading partners, lest the American economy succumb to the alleged blights of managed trade and industrial policy—the very cornerstones, in fact, of Japan's unremitting trade surpluses.

Not surprisingly, Japanese public sentiment—which for years had been wary of Nakasone's hawkishness at home and inclined to empathize with the suitably liberal and dovish Democrats on the American side—swung to an unprecedented enthusiasm for Yasu and for Ron's Republican camp. By the 1988 election, with the Democrats demonized as the party of protectionism, ordinary Japanese were now rooting for a GOP win—in a marked shift from the Eisenhower-through-Carter years. In the months leading up to the 1988 election, Japanese money was quietly pumped into U.S. capital markets, and, confirmed by Uncle Sam's own self-deception, the Japanese were now solidly united in the defense and rationalization of their protectionist, mercantilist system.

By the latter half of the 1980s, however, economic reality was beginning to tear rents in the Reischauer rubric—still being tended as the Mansfield mandate as America's longest-serving ambassador to Tokyo became the most distinguished spokesman for the new chrysanthemum corollaries to the old argument. America's deficit, so ran the refrain, stemmed from lower productivity traceable to low savings, high consumer spending, flagging worker morale, and excessive management perks. American businessmen in Japan simply weren't trying hard enough, and the hostility to Japanese investments in the United States, in contrast to those of the front-running British and Dutch, smacked of racial prejudice.

Events, however, were running against the apologists. The Plaza Accord of September 1985 launched the dollar on its long decline against the yen—from 235 yen at the time to as low as 85 by mid-1995—but with little impact on Japan's trade surplus despite good results with Europe. Instead, the United States was suddenly faced with a wave of Japanese investment in real estate and industry, much of which managed to worry or offend American local or national sentiment. There were those trophy purchases—Rockefeller Center, Universal Studios, Columbia Pictures, the Pebble Beach Golf Course, and nearly all of Waikiki—that seemed to some like the selling of America's own soul. There were the ranches and sawmills that were bought out by Japanese in lieu of importing American beef or finished lumber directly into Japan. And there were those wholly owned Japanese plants in several states that, while contributing to local employment, were too often held hostage politically for the good behavior of their local congressional representatives on U.S.-Japan trade issues. The Anglo-Dutch financial presence was less controversial, of course, because it was concentrated in traditional blue chips for the long term. Above all, those two countries were reciprocally open to American investment.

Japan's economic leverage on the United States was dramatized not only by its discreet financial manipulations on behalf of the Bush campaign in 1988 and by the contributing role played by Japanese insurance companies in Wall Street's Bloody Monday crash of October 1987 but most shockingly by the linkage of economic to military dependence made explicit in 1989 by the taunting challenge to America by rightwing Dietman Shintaro Ishihara and Sony chairman Akio Morita in *The*

Japan That Can Say No. As a result of the extended controversy over codevelopment of the new Japanese FSX fighter during 1987, the Pentagon was already on edge about the unreciprocated flow of dual-use military/industrial technology to Japan when Ishihara asserted that the world power balance would shift overnight if Japan were to deny the United States the semiconductor chips essential for ballistic missiles and offer them to the USSR instead. It was a point of critical technological dependence that the coming Persian Gulf War would serve to confirm. But then, Ishihara gratuitously added, the Russians and Americans, as fellow Caucasians, were more likely to gang up on Japan. This was the first public unveiling of the bumptious, racially toned technonationalism that was to increasingly characterize Japan up to the start of its severe recession in the late 1990s.[1]

* * *

All these hard-reality knocks were bound to produce intellectual reevaluations of Japan, which came in rapid-fire succession from the revisionist camp in the latter half of the 1980s. The seminal text was already at hand with Chalmers Johnson's 1982 landmark study of the bureaucracy, *MITI and the Japanese Miracle: The Growth of Industrial Policy, 1925–1975.*[2]

Johnson, anointed by *Business Week* (7 August 1989) as the "intellectual godfather" of revisionism, was a political scientist at the University of California at Berkeley with a distinguished record of publication on both Japan and China. In *MITI and the Japanese Miracle* he had traced the historical rise of Tokyo's powerful economic bureaucracy and the continuities of collaboration between the state and the private sector under the direction of the Ministry of International Trade and Industry and its predecessors from the premilitarist 1920s straight through to the late postwar era.

In so doing Johnson clarified the model for national-security-oriented economic growth that he found implicit in Japan's successful bureaucratic-business cooperation. This he called the "developmental state," or, as the public debate extended to similar Asian economies, the "capitalist development state" (CDS), which he contrasted with the "regulatory state" of American capitalism with its emphasis on rules and reciprocal concessions to maintain economic competition and consumer protection. Johnson's take-home message was that any nation attempting to match the economic achievements of Japan would have to adopt the same priorities, and beginning in the middle of the decade he began to call publicly for an American industrial policy, particularly with respect to Japan.

This was inconvenient not only for the Japanese, who were having the true thrust of their economic behavior exposed, but for those Americans who had thought that they could have their own miracle *à la Japonaise* simply by working a little harder, but without surrendering the basic values and institutions of their individual-oriented political economy. As one U.S. industry after another succumbed to Japanese competition, however, the matter was no longer academic, and in 1988 veteran Commerce Department negotiator Clyde V. Prestowitz Jr. detailed a depressing series of American industrial surrenders in his *Trading Places: How We Allowed Japan to Take the Lead*.[3] Prestowitz showed how difficult it was in practice for official representatives of a regulatory state—with its strict antitrust laws, its adversarial government-business postures, and the primacy it gave to political over economic diplomacy—to match the single-minded dedication, thorough coordination, and long institutional memories of Japan's negotiating teams and policy makers.

The following year Dutch journalist Karel van Wolferen, after fifteen years' reporting from Tokyo, brought out *The Enigma of Japanese Power: People and Politics in a Stateless Nation,* which limned the unstructured, arbitrary, and oppressive nature of power in Japan and traced that country's unresponsiveness to the needs and demands of the outside world to the lack of the center of accountability that is essential to any modern state.[4] While also zeroing in on Japan's bureaucrats, van Wolferen stressed the element of anarchic, internecine power struggle and the lack of ultimate goals in contrast to Johnson's and Prestowitz' sense of national objectives deftly pursued. Further exposing the fiction of Japan as a free market economy and challenging its claim to be a normally functioning parliamentary democracy, he depicted a bureaucracy unbeholden to the people's representatives, locked in unceasing battles for turf, and wed to an echelon of cognate administrators in the private sector. Working in tandem, they constituted an imperious, Tokyo University–trained ruling class that kept the Japanese public from the levers of power yet was incapable of taking ultimate responsibility for the nation in its dealings with the outside world.

Popularizing these and other revisionist insights for the broader U.S.

public while adding some of his own was the *Atlantic Monthly*'s James Fallows, who had lived for nearly two years with his family in Tokyo. Combining the iconoclastic eye of an H.L. Mencken with the gracious wit of Ogden Nash, Fallows managed to spell out—in terms of everyday living to which average Americans could relate—the human cost to ordinary Japanese of the system being described by his revisionist colleagues. Although calling provocatively in 1989 for the "containment" of Japan's one-sided trade practices, he was particularly concerned that Americans understand the difference in the values that kept each of the two societies humming each in its own way. Questioning the myth of impending convergence, Fallows challenged the propensity of his fellow Americans to place any given Japanese achievement in their own value context. At a time when praise of Japanese youngsters' math scores was the fad of the day, Fallows caught the entire subjective ambience of Japan's school education in the two-word title of one of his pieces: "Gradgrind's Heirs."[5]

Meanwhile, from the hand of a scholar at Oxford in 1986 had come an erudite, hard-hitting strike at the roots of the intellectual nationalism supporting the economic, political, and social arrangements now under revisionist scrutiny. In *The Myth of Japanese Uniqueness* Peter N. Dale dissected the *Nihonjinron* ideology of Japanese singularity.[6] Why were the Japanese constantly harping on their racial homogeneity and radical difference from other peoples, and how was one to account for the procedural hostility among nationalist intellectuals to non-Japanese modes of analysis? In a fresh answer to these old questions, Dale construed them as an ongoing effort to construct a fictive national mentality—a defensive intellectual project that went back in time to the political and social crises of the first decade of this century. Indeed, Carol Gluck at Columbia had just shown in *Japan's Modern Myths: Ideology in the Late Meiji Period,* a major study of modern Japanese intellectual history, how a variety of patriotic, imperial, familistic, and other ideologies that had been floating through the Meiji educational and political systems began to congeal during that same decade as conscious instruments of social control.[7]

In 1982 Roy Andrew Miller, in *Japan's Modern Myth: The Language and Beyond,* had driven a scalpel deep into one of the central axioms of cultural nationalism—the concept of a mystic, ineffable spirit of the Japanese language (*kotodama*) totally inaccessible to non-Japanese.[8] In so doing, Miller struck the nerve center of Japan's mentality toward the outside world—the assertion that, because of a fundamental cognitive and ratiocinative uniqueness (on top of all the rest), others could never really comprehend Japan. Since Japan's propaganda was ascribing trade pressures, foreign criticism, and now revisionism itself to an alleged lack of cultural understanding, the exposure by Western cultural scholars of this mythical dimension in Japan's special pleading was an important adjunct to the revisionist argument—and deserving of a much wider nonacademic readership.

When American journalist Marvin J. Wolf wrote his provocatively titled *The Japanese Conspiracy: Their Plot to Dominate Industry World-Wide and How to Deal with It* in 1983, it created little more than a brief sensationalist stir, although much of what he had to say was to get a better hearing later.[9] What had accumulated by the end of the 1980s was a critical mass of writing by respected Japan scholars and top-drawer journalists in the West sufficient, at long last, to budge the old verities of 1960s modernization theory and 1970s number-oneism and to make plausible a Japan that was more different and more problematical than the world had wanted to imagine. Americans were also becoming more aware of the presence and impact in their own country of Japanese investment and of the political arm-twisting by Tokyo's lobbyists to be chronicled by economist Pat Choate in 1990 in *Agents of Influence: How Japan's Lobbyists in the United States Manipulate America's Political and Economic System*.[10] In short order, the predictable flow of more apocalyptic writing by those less familiar with Japan but eager to climb on the bandwagon followed: in 1991 the nonfictional, systematically argued *The Coming War with Japan* by George Friedman and Meredith Lebard; in 1992 Michael Crichton's best-selling *Rising Sun,* followed by the movie; and in 1994 Tom Clancy's *Debt of Honor,* with its fantasy of an all-out U.S.-Japan war narrowly averted. The awesome, negative samurai images of Japan were once again in vogue.

The Japanese didn't like any of it. But it was the serious revisionists that they were most concerned to discredit. Japanese potboilers featuring betrayal by or war with the United States had been churned out for years, but they, too, took a new lease on life as the Cold War retreated into history. By the early 1990s a new layer of confrontational ideas and images had been laid down on top of the earlier postwar positives, giving us the basic stock that Japanese and Americans will have to draw on as they grow closer together, or further apart, going into the new century.

CHAPTER NINETEEN

Dumbing Down
PC and Other Intellectual Follies of the 1990s

After 1990 many began to wonder how long the U.S.-Japan alliance would hold together without the old strategic and ideological glue of the Cold War. For the moment, slippage was confined to the level of emotions, rhetoric, and geopolitical punditry, as the military tie remained firmly in place. Both sides had it too good to tinker, as yet, with the old security arrangements.

It was a sign of the times, however, that America's next two envoys to Tokyo were at long last speaking more frankly to the Japanese about their closed markets, albeit with no more visible results, and that their hosts were less than enthusiastic about it. At his maiden press luncheon at the Japan National Press Club in September 1989 Michael Armacost delivered a cool and reasoned explanation of the U.S. position on trade, the sort of straight talk one had been waiting over a decade to hear from his predecessor, Mike Mansfield. The response of the crowd was chilly, and the few questions that followed were adversarial in tone. "The man has none of Mansfield's charisma, he's just a bureaucrat," one of Japan's cultural bridgers remarked to me as we were leaving the auditorium. It was the old ad hominem put-down the Japanese fall back on when the argument hits too close to the *honne*.

When Walter Mondale arrived in 1993 he was even more outspoken, but so were many Japanese in their disdain. One national daily gratuitously crowed over the fact that workers in an office building overlooking the route to the imperial palace couldn't be bothered to step to the window to watch the new American ambassador ride by in the traditional horse-drawn carriage of state to present his credentials to the emperor.[1] The Mansfield manner would be in abeyance until the arrival in 1998 of Tom Foley, whose appointment had been held up for months in the Senate by members who felt he was already too close to the Japanese.

With the mutual stock of contentious ideas largely in place by the early 1990s, the bilateral intellectual relationship during the decade was remarkable less for any fresh input than for those barometric drops in American attention span we noted in Chapter 1. Protestations and special pleadings continued on trade, as did the mutual punditry on Japan's emerging role in Asia. As also noted in the opening chapter, economic takes on Japan were the one new cottage industry, many of them arguably off target. The one major intellectual trend in Japan that should have provoked American interest and concern, but didn't, was the rapid rejuvenation of New Old Right ideology and the parallel decline of Japanese liberalism. These were spelled out in Chapters 3 and 4, which also limned the basic political story of the 1990s.

The more lively and problematical arena of ideas during the 1990s was to be found within the United States as the full range and nature of American intellectual blinders on Japan was becoming more apparent every year. The subject of the two following sections in this chapter, these include four older intellectual habits specific to Japan as well as more recent controversies with a narrow intra-American reference that are nevertheless exercising a powerful yet virtually unnoticed influence on the way we think about Japan. Indeed, the intellectual terrain among Americans themselves has been shifting so rapidly in an unhelpful direction that it becomes increasingly difficult to see how, or whether, the United States will ever come to a nonbamboozled grasp of Japan in the opening decade of the new century.

The Intellectual Looking Glass

American universalism has been the most persistent philosophical factor in the intellectual interaction between the two countries, as frequently noted in the foregoing chapters. It has also been, understandably, the one most divisive to the Japanese.

Less overarching—yet particularly influential during the three decades since the emergence of major tensions and rivalry around 1970—have been American attitudes and assumptions with respect to bureaucracy, nationalism, historical progress, and cultural relativism. These four deserve special mention here because they reach well beyond the realm of formal ideas and ideology to something like a national consensus at the level of gut instinct. The problem with all of them, too, is that they mainly reflect an American face in the mirror.

Americans, liberal and conservative alike, have at heart been disciples of Adam Smith, differing only in what they consider to be the appropriate response to their common guru. During the 1980s and 1990s it was repeatedly pointed out—with little effect on U.S. policy—that the assumptions of classical economics simply do not apply to Japan, where competitive economic energies and commercial activity are channeled within broad parameters by a powerful bureaucracy in the overall service of predetermined national security and development goals.

It has been the quality, or "feel," of Japan's overweening bureaucracy and of the nation's almost pathologically defensive economic mentality that has been hardest for Americans at home to appreciate. Both lie outside the American historical experience and have presented two of the greatest intellectual stumbling blocks to dealing effectively with Japanese trading behavior. Tokyo's bureaucrats are not our bumbling Washington civil servants, nor does our extroverted, flag-waving, 300-percent-American sort of patriotism really give us much of an empathetic clue to the taut, anxious, inwardly drawn coil of Japanese chauvinism. Part of the problem still lies with that effort by post-1960 scholarship and journalism to rectify the earlier overemphasis on Japan's exoticism by searching out reassuring points of similarity or gradual convergence.

From my own graduate work at Harvard in the early 1960s, for example, I recall the admiring functionalist slant many of us then had on Japanese bureaucracy. It was rational, efficient, and disinterested—unlike so many Asian countries with their structural corruption—and it was still playing a crucial role in Japan's rapid development. All of this was true. The undemocratic aspects of the one major system of prewar Japan left virtually untouched by the Allied occupation were sloughed over.

We knew this was not our freewheeling American way of running a country, but then one should consider—so we told ourselves—that there were other major Western societies, such as France, that had accommodated themselves to the administrative state without selling their liberal souls. Japan, in other words, was a sort of Code Napoleon democracy with Oriental trimmings. The centralized mandarinate in Paris and the elite higher schools that produced it had indeed provided the main models for their Japanese counterparts from the Meiji period on. But the Napoleonic analogy perniciously ignores the manner in which the administrative incubus on the Seine rests on the national commitment of France to political liberty and to the institutions for its expression, and ultimately on the irrepressibly individualistic temperament of the French people.

To truly appreciate the intimidating powers of the Tokyo mandarinate, one has to have dealt with it directly—as American trade negotiators and other foreign supplicants can well attest. From my own work in Japan as a U.S. cultural representative dealing directly with Japanese officials in the 1970s and as a national university professor in the 1980s I gradually came to understand why serious Japanese could fly into emotional rages—fits that I had mistaken for childish anger—about their bureaucracy. No longer an isolated researcher in Japanese studies or a foreign correspondent comfortably cocooned in the international press corps, I could now see why independently minded Japanese thinkers could pepper their discourse with imprecations about the "power establishment" *(kenryoku taisei)*—something that I had too easily written off as the ritual incantation of the intellectual left.

The hopes that the outside world pins on a more open Japan depend almost entirely on bureaucratic plans and promises in the areas of economic and educational policy. The prognosis is not very good, since bureaucracy-led solutions harbor the oxymoronic goal of planning for and managing spontaneity. The Japanese bureaucracy simply does not know how to let go, nor does it ever intend to—barring as yet unforeseeable internal political or external economic pressures.

Japanese nationalism, too, is something most Americans still tend to behold through the prism of the 1950s and 1960s. During those decades we liked to think that the serpent of prewar-style nationalism, although not entirely scotched, lay wriggling rather irrelevantly way over in right field. By far the greater threat was from Japan's left—febrile, quasi-revolutionary, and avowedly anti-American. Japan's ruling troika of business, bureaucracy, and the Liberal Democratic Party seemed basically centrist albeit temperamentally conservative, and in their essential commitments freedom-loving and comfortingly pro-American. Occasional outcroppings of chauvinism were written off as mere Gaullist cravings for greater autonomy in foreign policy, all quite modern and forward-looking. Japanese cultural nationalists touting Japan's unique forms of consensus and harmony were seen largely in the context of

American neoconservatism—that is to say, as springing from similar libertarian and democratic roots. What these American perspectives failed to factor in was not only the subcutaneous strength of the New Old Right that we looked at in Chapter 3, but also the carryover into the postwar decades by the bureaucrats of their resilient techno-nationalism.

Another very basic American intellectual blinder has been our eighteenth-century faith in historical progress, together with the nineteenth-century corollary that the United States has come to embody it and the late-twentieth-century assumption that with globalization we are almost there—QED.

This overweening self-assurance has prevented us from taking an unsentimental look at a society that has proved economically successful by our own yardstick but that works (rather disturbingly well) without our cultural values of individualism and universalistic rules. More distressing yet, it seems to have shifted to an adversarial relationship between itself and the world at large the sort of energizing tensions we have created in our own society between business and government.

Our need to feel that Japan really is falling into step after all was pathetically evidenced by the euphoria with which much of the American press and public greeted the Tokyo stock market plunge of 1990–92, the recession that set in during 1992, and the financial crisis of 1997. Wiser watchers, more attuned to Japan's long-term strategies and worldview, tend to believe that the present difficulties may eventually be shown to have been merely another adversity-induced opportunity for *reculer pour mieux sauter,* that is to say, for retrenchment and restructuring in order to become the center of a rapidly integrating East Asian bloc or, some distant day, what Leon Hollerman once predicted: the "headquarters nation" for the entire world economy.[2]

Being great admirers of progress not only in ourselves but in others, American observers are, furthermore, prone to assume that commendable achievements in other societies must somehow spring from familiar philosophical roots—even when they derive in fact from very alien values, methods, and goals. The most familiar historical example, of course, was the long romance of many American liberals (e.g., John Dewey) throughout the 1920s and into the 1930s with the excitement and promise of the new Soviet experiment.

The building of mammoth hydroelectric projects and of whole new cities east of the Urals struck nostalgic chords with Americans recalling their own nineteenth-century taming of the West; five-year plans seemed a more rational way of running a national economy than our own failed Coolidge-era capitalism; and the USSR, it was hoped, might yet create a socially cooperative New Man reminiscent of the lost communitarian spirit of an earlier, rural America. For a while, until the Moscow trials of 1935, the political price of the Stalinist system could be discounted by its apologists either under the pragmatic rubric of breaking eggs to make an omelet or from the cultural relativist thought that the Russians had never known democracy anyway.

Although its object is very different today, America's shift toward a less illusioned view of Japan—if and when it ever comes—may resemble in its inner dynamics the sobering up about the Soviet Union that finally took place among the majority of American intellectuals in the late 1940s. Arthur Schlesinger Jr., in *The Vital Center,* pinned the pejorative label "doughface" on those progressives of the 1930s and 1940s who had been unprepared for Hitler and who refused to face up to the ugly facts of Stalinism. The term came from a Civil War epithet for Northern men with Southern principles, that is to say, for softheaded Yankee sympathizers with the Confederacy.[3]

For the post-1970 decades we could probably speak of "doughface Japanophiles" to characterize those who, when conceptualizing Japan, stand in the tradition of Dewey's economic and social optimism as opposed to Reinhold Niebuhr's political and moral pessimism—the two great philosophical poles between which America's ethical view of international affairs oscillated during the twentieth century. Perhaps some of the intellectual wellsprings cited by Schlesinger in 1949 are relevant to our perplexity about Japan today—too dogmatic a faith in the goodness and perfectibility of man; too sentimental an approach to politics and culture; too great a trust in the efficacy of purely economic arrangements; and too much debilitating naïveté about power and its manifold corruptions.

Perhaps the hang-up most blocking America's effective intellectual engagement of Japan is the sort of facile cultural relativism skewered by Allan Bloom in *The Closing of the American Mind* in 1987.[4] More specifically with respect to Japan, an oversimplified conception of cultural tolerance can lead Americans to lose sight of the fact that our tolerance of cultural intolerance and our relativism toward nationalist-racialist absolutism are both inconsistent and self-defeating. Although dovetailing with our more recent obsession with multiculturalism, this also has a long history closely tied to the notions of universalism and progress.

The fact of the matter is that Japan still practices against foreigners and many of its own citizens various types of discrimination that cultural relativists in the United States would be the first to decry were they to be perpetrated by Americans.[5] Perhaps as Japan increasingly imports its insularism into the United States itself—with more litigation in our own courts over discriminatory employment and promotion practices affecting American women, minorities, and white male executives in U.S.-based Japanese corporations—my point here will become clearer.

Indeed, it is ironic how some high-minded Americans who once denounced discriminatory barriers in the United States or South Africa have executed a 180-degree turn to join Japanese spokesmen in characterizing American requests for access and reciprocity as another instance of Western cultural absolutism. Such exercises in righteous indignation are easy enough for Americans who have not been personally affected by any of the barriers erected by Japan's insular-mindedness. Japan, however, is being asked to change and bring under mutual rules only those practices that palpably impinge on others in a globally interdependent age—what John Stuart Mill would have called "other-regarding" behavior—and not to overturn its entire heritage. To insist that the first is tantamount to the second stops all discussion, and it is one of the most effective ploys in Japan's public relations quiver.

Americans should of course be willing to step back in the interest of cultural tolerance (or relativism) when a solid case can be made for it. But very often, as a cognitive process, we need initially to react to any given aspect of an alien culture in terms of our own value system—to allow our natural responses full play—simply to see that particular feature for what it actually is. Having first grasped the objective fact of the matter, we can then safely step back and put that initial evaluation through our cultural relativist calculator and arrive, perhaps, at a posture of toleration or acceptance.

If that sounds a bit ponderous and belabored, two simple illustrations may help. Before rendering a value judgment on seppuku or suttee, both highly honored in their traditional samurai and Hindu settings, persons grounded in Western values must first perceive that they involve, respectively, a man slashing his abdomen in ritual suicide and a widow joining her deceased husband on his funeral pyre. Both acts would be thoroughly reprehensible in Western (or any multicultural definition of contemporary American) culture. But they have to be seen for what they are and *not* sloughed off as something else—for example, as the moral and physical equivalent of an act more familiar but less offensive in our own culture like wife-beating, or as something encountered harmlessly in the movies like a self-dispatching bullet to the brain. (The same, of course, would hold for any Japanese making a value judgment on America's gun culture, or for a Roman Catholic bishop from the Congo trying to figure out same-sex marriage and gay rights.)

Less obviously, but more to the point, U.S. trade representatives would be more effective if they could overcome their cultural relativist resistance to concluding that the Japanese may not at all times be negotiating in good faith—according to *our* notions of good faith, not theirs—and then simply proceed, as diplomatically as possible, on that more cynical assumption.

American failures to fathom Japanese intentions and develop realistic strategies to deal with them often rest on that sort of muddle in our own mind. From our basic values of universalism and inclusivism we feel compelled—in our initial and natural reactions—to fault Japan for its group-based exclusion and discrimination. But then, in a premature application of cultural relativism, we lash our consciences for having violated another American ideal—that of tolerance—in arriving at such a negative judgment. And in the end we swallow Japan's own assertion that it is *not* practicing exclusion or discrimination, but rather is doing something else—something that our Western mind is not capable of fathoming. This mental mix-up makes it very difficult for us even to see what it is we are trying to grapple with, particularly where the Japanese *honne* of true intention and the *tatemae* of formal facade are so hard for us to distinguish.

The Intellectual Shackles of PC, MC, RC, and DC

This older sentimentalist bent, so inhibiting for our ability to cope with Japan, received further impetus during the 1990s from academic fads of a more recent provenance. Four of them have proved to be particularly debilitating for a clear focus on Japan today: (1) the strictures of political correctness, or PC; (2) the PC corollary of multiculturalism, or MC, and the ethnic confrontations that feed it; (3) the culturally blinding blight of rational-choice theory, or RC, which applies the assumptions of classical economics to political analysis; and (4) the destructive impact of deconstructionism, or DC, on that grand old literary road for learning something about Japan by reading its best novels, poems, and plays.

As applied to Japan, political correctness in the United States functions mainly to reinforce the multiculturalist verities. It makes it increasingly difficult—for example, at certain academic conferences of Asianists—to speak critically of Japan, or even to be known as a critic, without being written off as a Japan basher and shunned as a pariah. The wet blanket of assorted PC taboos not only dampens the scholarly Japanese studies debate—as when the Dutch author-journalist Karel van Wolferen broke off a one-on-one recording session in a Boston radio studio after Harvard's Edwin Reischauer suggested his views might be "racist"[6]—but also helps to account for that odd reluctance of some of the Japan-America friendship societies to place "controversial" issues before the American public.

Most perversely of all, by ruling out negative critiques of Japan, the unwitting result of America's PC orthodoxy has been to throw the weight of its liberal, leftist, and countercultural adherents to the side of the New Old Right chauvinists while leaving their natural allies among Japan's liberal and leftist moderates in the lurch. Added to the contempt of American conservatives for Japan's "leftist lite"—for Japan's own internal critics, that is—that means a double dose of American intellectual support for the Japanese right.

Multiculturalism per se presents additional obstacles to the serious study and discussion of Japan. Indeed, the multiculturalist animus works far less for the genuine presentation of Japanese culture—the serious understanding of non-Western peoples never having been the main purpose of MC—than as a force dragging the debate on Japan down into the vortex of domestic racial sensitivities, ethnic resentments, and the psychology of victimization with its sundry academic and political agendas. What gets damaged in this process is the capacity of Americans to sort out legitimate political analysis and criticism of Japan from genuine racial prejudice, with the result that far too much of the former now gets attributed simplistically to the latter.

In an odd way, multiculturalism in the United States has come to resemble nothing quite so much as Japan's autistic pan-Asianism. Its gaze, too, is almost exclusively inward, a mere subtheme of national navel gazing, engaging very few of its alleged partners directly. And although in the American case its expression has been antichauvinistic rather than nationalistic like Japan's, multiculturalism as an academic or educational cause has shown little respect—or stomach—for the radically different "other" of non-Western civilizations. By trashing the

European heritage while presenting a superficial kaleidoscope of foreign cultures (through thick, crude American lenses), the multiculturalists have eroded American cultural understanding from two directions at once—both of ourselves and of others. Above all, they have made it harder than ever for average Americans on a rapidly shrinking globe to surmount their deeply ingrained universalism, develop an awareness of the depth and pain and poignancy of genuine cultural divides, and stop thinking of them as minor irritants amenable to the instant ministrations of orchestrated diversity.

The Japanese, for all their incessant muttering about a national identity crisis, are arguably the most identity-certified nation in the world today—beating even the Koreans and the Chinese at it thanks to their century of ideological stroking from the Meiji state orthodoxy through to the *Nihonjinron* fancies of today. In its intellectual ties with Japan, the United States is now paying a price for not having moved more quickly beyond its old Anglo-Saxonist melting-pot certainties to a more effective manner of accommodating both national and ethnic imperatives within its own society, such as the formulations of dual identity proposed by sociologist Nathan Glazer in his *Affirmative Discrimination* or by the pacifist Randolph Bourne during World War I.

Since the Japanese-American community is relatively small and has taken some pains not to be seen as pro-Japanese in bilateral disputes, the reflexive rejection of Japan criticism has come as much from the younger generation of other Asian minorities that are canvassing for some sort of pan-Asian identity, and most of all from well-to-do mainstream whites with no blood ties to Asia at all. Indeed, it was downright bizarre to see the street protests against the movie version of Crichton's *Rising Sun* being led by Chinese-, Korean-, and Filipino-American youths whose older cousins in the mother country, with sharper memories of Japan, probably would have been out in droves demonstrating in favor of the film. The fact that multiculturalism is most popular among those young Asian-Americans whose families have been longest in this country serves to strengthen one's impression of it as a project fired primarily by the countercultural heritage of the Old New Left professoriate now securely tenured at America's elite universities, and abetted by the misplaced idealism of comfortably situated Caucasian students.

Rational-choice theory and deconstructionism, the two more purely academic fads, function not so much to inhibit critical expression as to divert the minds of Japan scholars—and, most injuriously, the minds of their graduate students, the future teachers of America—from the substantive mastery of things Japanese to an epiphenomenal stratum of theoretical, methodological, and exegetical concerns.

On top of the taboos placed by PC and MC on the unfettered discussion of Japanese values, systems, or social behavior, rational-choice theory in effect proclaims it a waste of time to even bother. Since Japan's political decisions and social choices are said to proceed from the same desiccated Benthamite hedonistic calculus as our own—that is to say, from the same dry computations of the greatest happiness of the greatest number used to determine maximum benefit under the classical economic model—there is little need to account for political or cultural factors particular to Japan. Given that, Americans can also dispense with the traditional area studies approach to Japan and do without scholars (or diplomats or journalists) fluent in the language, versed in the culture, and adept with such disciplinary tools as history, anthropology, or political science.

Concerning the application of RC to Japan by one of its leading exponents, two of the scholar's Harvard colleagues commented on the lack of ideological, historical, and international perspectives in his interpretation of the politics of the Meiji oligarchy.[7] Based on a narrow calculation of the oligarchs' individual self-interests (to bowdlerize an abstruse argument), the study was totally dismissive of the role of ideas in the events leading up to the great political turnaround of 1881, which locked Japan on course for an imperial autocracy, closing the door to more liberal alternatives. Extended to the broader sweep of modern Japan, this approach would reduce to idle curiosities the intense scholarly and ideological debate over the true nature of the Meiji Restoration, the practical impact of right-wing versus liberal ideals in Japan today, and the entire subject matter of this book! Needless to say, this hotly contested school of thinking will continue to draw strength—for a while at least—from the dominance of classical economic theory in American universities and the current economic ascendancy of the United States.

Like rational choice, deconstructionism was also pulling intellectual energies away from the *Ding an Sich*—from the imaginative teaching about Japan itself. Ask any American graduate student of Japanese literature, eager to get on with the plays of Chikamatsu or the novels of Mishima, who has had to slog through Jacques Derrida first. To some extent it was the sheer growth of the Japanese studies field that had permitted younger scholars of Japanese literature to shift their research and writing from general works to specialized monographs and then to these less substantive theoretical capers. As with the economists and political scientists, increasing numbers of them no longer saw themselves as broadly grounded Japan experts so much as members of a traditional subdiscipline, such as literary criticism, to which they had added a special Japan angle.

Harboring the insight that things are almost never what they seem, DC was hospitable to the antiestablishmentarian campus ethos of PC and MC. For those students stuck with the wrong teachers, it was no longer possible to tap the rich and immediate lode of Japanese feelings and outlook on life by an ingenuous plunge into the texts. Worst of all, it was no longer fun.

* * *

The cumulative blows of PC, MC, RC, and DC have left the American mind more supine, apologetic, and vulnerable than ever before to special pleading, emotional blackmail, and professional co-optation on behalf of Japan. So, too, has the much broader retreat on all intellectual fronts bemoaned during the 1990s as the "dumbing down" of America.[8] It is enough to make one ask, why does the sole remaining superpower on earth today regress so nonchalantly into its intellectual adolescence? Are we driven by America's fleeting triumphalism of the moment? Or is it that historical lack of a sense of limitations for which the Japanese— in one of their sounder critiques of America—have so often chided us? Can we go on forever being the cocker spaniels of international society, fancying every guest in the room an easily made friend, loath to be thought the least bit cold or cynical, squeamish even of the biblical injunction to be wise as serpents?

In any case, now that the twentieth century has drawn to a close, it is time for Americans to take some intellectual stock of the past few decades—to flatten out the wild swings in their perspective on Japan based on the grievance or enthusiasm of the moment; to understand the long historical pedigree of each of these competing views; to strive for a steady, objective focus independent of the immediate U.S. strategic need in Asia or the passing intellectual fads and fashions at home; and, above all, to be aware of the strategic use that the Japanese so skillfully make of our perceptions of their country.

Conclusion
The Punishment
Fits the Crime

To conclude this book, there are very few recommendations one could make that have not already been indicated or implied in the foregoing chapters. I can only hope that our failure in the relatively easier game of wits with Japan may alert us to our national penchants for overidealized images, lackadaisical counter-argument, and America-centric assumptions that will hobble our progress toward an effective comprehension and intellectual engagement of the long-neglected world of Islam.

Broadly speaking, the intellectual challenges to the United States from Japan (and the rest of Asia) have presented Americans with two types of processes: those we cannot control (as in Part I) and those we can (as in Parts II and III). There is not much we can do to change the ways in which Japanese and others are going to act and think, but that is precisely why we need to grasp the nature and resilience of perspectives that are different from our own. What Americans *can* change, however, are the ways *we* think and act on our side of the intellectual game—meaning by "we" in these closing pages America's government and private sectors taken together.

Japan as a "Reverse Teacher"

Values, policy thrusts, and social trends in Japan are not likely to follow American prescriptions for free trade, liberal democracy, individualism, and a collegial engagement of Asia—not nearly as much as we like to imagine. In any case, these will be matters for the Japanese to decide in their own interest. But it can only help the national interest of the United States if we develop some suitable skepticism on these points and convey those reservations to the Japanese side—two moves we have never seriously tried to make. It can hardly hurt us to deprive Tokyo of its comfortable assumption that we see Japan the way they want us to see it. More importantly, it would sweep the mental cobwebs out of our own heads as we set out to reconceptualize U.S. policies toward Japan in a world that changed forever on 11 September 2001.

A clear and steady focus on U.S. interests is particularly crucial when we come to those beguiling debates about "whither Japan?" and "is Japan changing?"—as if there were some magical or portentous turn just down the road that we can simply wait for while the lucrative business of instant Japan punditry unlocks the riddle for us. In fact, none of the three major hypothetical scenarios promises an easy trek on the intellectual track.

If Tokyo decides to rev up and push outward with a new constitution, an expanded military establishment, and a serious big-power bid for Asian economic hegemony and ideological leadership, Washington will be scrambling to pick up its intellectual shards. If, on the other hand, Japan opts to rev down and turn inward—settling for the low-posture status of a neutral middle power willing to pay the price of an occasional WTO slap on the wrist in order to keep its markets closed—the United States may well face even more virulent forms of mercantilist apologia and cultural nationalism, with Japan's academic and media institutions as closed as ever to foreign participation. The third alternative would be for the Japanese simply to stay put—the horse on which the U.S. defense and diplomatic establishments have long been betting. But that would simply perpetuate the old intellectual racket of special pleading, emotional blackmail, and the funding and manipulation of our binational dialogue by the Mutual Understanding Industry. So, whatever the scenario (or any mix of the three), we are left with problems.

Postmortem reflection on how we Americans managed to get ourselves bamboozled in the intellectual game with Japan will be particularly important as the United States draws into closer and more equal relationships with the rest of East and South Asia. This is especially true in the case of China but applies also to the two Koreas, to the Southeast Asian nations, and, as they gradually put on real economic and military muscle, to India and its immediate neighbors as well. Indeed, there is the ironic probability—almost totally overlooked—that as Asians move

toward the very goals of greater material prosperity and political participation that we have deigned to set for them, the more challenging
our intellectual ties with them will become. Singapore with its eloquence
in the "Asian values" campaign has demonstrated this on the score of
greater affluence, just as South Korea with its rising anti-Americanism
has done so on the point of greater democracy.

Intellectually speaking, we—meaning, once again, America's official and private sectors in informal partnership—had it a lot easier with
the old Communist and Third World states of the early postwar decades.
Circumstances then dictated a less sophisticated game. In the Stalinist
dictatorships the United States faced walls it could not scale to reach
people on the other side, while in the underdeveloped countries (as they
were then called) our dialogue was at best with a tiny Westernized intelligentsia. Most importantly of all—and the greatest difference from
today's emerging Asia—there was very little the governments, people,
or business interests in non-Communist Asian countries could do to
mount sustained campaigns of persuasion toward the United States. It
was enough for Americans in those days to counter heavy-handed Soviet propaganda with simple and loudly broadcast countermessages of
our own and to trust that the dazzle of Broadway and the friendly ambience of a state college or Ivy League campus would suffice to nudge the
emerging intellectual elites of South Korea or Indonesia toward a political and cultural rapport with the United States.

Looking at Asia today, we are foolish to assume that a more open and
well-heeled China (among others) will fall into a shared intellectual orbit with us, like our erstwhile enemy in West Germany, rather than repeat the pattern of postwar Japan—the far more likely model. Indeed, it
is precisely an affluent, high-tech, communications-drenched Japan—a
Japan that with all its warts is far more democratic and open to us now
than during the militaristic 1930s—that has mustered the financial resources, the self-confidence, and the mental energies to play the intellectual game so successfully vis-à-vis the United States.

China's nationalism, its economic ambitions, its cultural sensitivities, and its historical resentments are likely to become more, not less,
of a problem for us as the Chinese continue to integrate themselves into
global society. To engage them effectively, Americans would do well to
develop the fine-tuned, hands-on mental dexterity that we neglected to
cultivate in our ties with Japan. For, as with Japan, it is precisely a more
open China, empowered by democratic pressures and popular expres-

sion, that will be able to talk back and be free to establish an active public relations presence in the United States. Indeed, it is all too likely that the Chinese will drag their own variety of culturalist special pleading into purely economic disputes and set out to fund their own Mutual Understanding Industry in America—which, come to think of it, might be rather fun to watch as Beijing starts to give Tokyo's chrysanthemums a run for their money.

Beyond Asia, the Japanese case described in this book provides a point of reference for the gathering intellectual donnybrook over the pros and cons of globalism—the most recent form of American universalism. This hyperbolic term got the debate off to a bad start by provoking too much unthinking hucksterism in favor and not enough seasoned rebuttal against. The Mutual Understanding Industry today has served in effect as the Japan-specific wing of the globalist forces in America. Boosters of globalism and apologists for Japan join in discouraging tougher trade policies toward Tokyo and in heralding the imminent free-trade opening of Japan—a tenet essential to the new globalist faith.

There is much irony here, since Japan, a successful capitalist economy and nontotalitarian state, provides the most persuasive evidence we have that globalism as envisioned by its American enthusiasts simply may not work in the long run. Already functioning on a veritable compendium of contraglobalist premises, the world's second-largest economic power presents itself as what is known in Japanese as a *hanmen kyoshi*— literally, "reverse teacher," meaning a person or situation from which one learns what *not* to do. Unfortunately for the United States, too many countries that are uncomfortable with an American-sponsored globalism, particularly those in East Asia, may learn from Japan's economic mercantilism, ethnocentric nationalism, and social insularism *exactly* what to do—and how to get away with it as long as they can bamboozle Uncle Sam into beholding a silk purse in a sow's ear.

This is a great pity, since there are compelling reasons to refute a simplistically conceived globalism on behalf of the cultural integrity, political freedom, and economic justice that will always be served better by nation-states and other entities closer to home than by any globalized corporate management. The problem with the Japanese example, however, is that it has taken the particularist alternative to an exclusivist extreme—one that rests, however subtly, on a strong ideologically and institutionally sanctioned xenophobia. Accordingly, Americans and others arguing against the globalist persuasion should take care lest they inadvertently provide Japan with a philosophical cover for abandoning any further movement toward a politically liberal, economically open, and culturally cosmopolitan society.

What Americans Can Do

There are, as I suggested, limits to what the United States can or should attempt in seeking changes of heart among the Japanese. We can, however, be in full charge of our own side of the binational discourse, try to establish the most advantageous context for it, and work toward the ultimate goal of a transpacific dialogue as free and straightforward as the one has long spanned the Atlantic. This will require a sophisticated two-track approach—sophisticated, because the tracks at first glance seem mutually contradictory.

The first track, broadly stated, is the political. We need to beef up the American voice where the economic and other national interests of two sovereign states are at variance, as they will often continue to be. In other words, we need a stronger intellectual advocacy toward Japan. This means not only more effective counterpleading by the U.S. government but an end to the ostracism in America and exclusion in Japan of American private citizens who have critical views on certain aspects of Japan or who could join the argument on the American side.

The second track is what we might call the purely cultural. We also need to relocate the broader intellectual and cultural bonds between Japan and America on a path apart from narrow-gauged national-interest advocacy by either side. To be sure, this can only be a matter of degree, since one can never separate the political and cultural entirely in any sphere of life. But there are arrangements that can minimize the intrusion of politics and maximize the sphere of cultural autonomy—which redounds to the long-term benefit of the political interest itself, as historically demonstrated by the Rhodes and Fulbright scholarship programs. Where government cultural money is involved, professional screening committees and other nonpolitical mediating entities have long shown that they can do the job if given genuine independence. The greater threat usually comes from private funders with a hidden national-advocacy agenda. Above all, we need to return the academic study and public discussion of Japan throughout the United States to an American-style "free marketplace of ideas."

As to the first track, this book has been a virtual manual on how to revitalize American advocacy by changing our ways of thinking about Japan. Summed up in one sentence, we need to cut through illusory perceptions, PR blandishments, and old intellectual habits to develop the two things we need most—more intellectual savvy and mental toughness. But what practical actions might we also undertake to empower the American voice?

The three aces now in Tokyo's hand are a steady national focus on its American relationship, a strong establishment consensus on how to handle it, and an army of players trained to the game. What the United States obviously needs is a more deliberate enlisting of its own educational, academic, business, governmental, and media resources to develop the informational, analytical, linguistic, negotiating, and communication skills to truly fathom the Japanese and other East Asian peoples and get our message across to them. In giving the American public a rationale for this effort we should dispense with patronizing bromides about "sensitizing" ourselves to "exotic" cultures in a "multicultural world," and do it as a straightforward matter of urgent national interest.

In speaking to or about the Japanese, American politicians should trade in their blustery, lectern-thumping style for more dialectical smarts, and wherever there has been honest educational spin-off from the Mutual Understanding Industry it should not be rejected. We need more, not fewer, American diplomats who can read the Japanese-language press and distinguish between the fine flavors of sushi.

Our Tokyo embassy, however, demands the type of ambassador we routinely sent to the old Soviet Union—career professionals with a sound and unsentimental knowledge of the country and a sharp nose for power politics, men on the order of George Kennan, Llewellyn Thompson, and Malcolm Toon. Since most of the State Department's Japan hands are products of the old policy and viewpoint, we may have to wait awhile for a new generation of less dewy-eyed diplomats to emerge. Indeed, at a time of continuing trade disputes in the late 1990s it raised more than a few eyebrows to see posted as our deputy ambassador (deputy chief of mission) at the Tokyo embassy William LaFleur, a man married to the daughter of Japan's finance minister, Kiichi Miyazawa. In any case, the American ambassador to Tokyo should no longer be expected to function as a symbol of Japan-U.S. friendship, nor be judged by his popularity with the Japanese.

With America still in a populist mood, it would be quixotic to try to match the hundreds of millions of dollars Japan now spends on its intellectual propaganda in the United States. Eventually, however, we may be able to lean on the self-protective vision of American industry, or even encourage the partial return of our big foundations to critical sectors in the Japanese and Asian studies field. To make the Friendship Commission (the only Japan-specific agency in the U.S. government) the rough equivalent in size and function to Tokyo's Center for Global Partnership would require several legislatively difficult quantum leaps: a tenfold infusion of new capital, a shift of target from Americans to Japanese, and a level of governmental supervision that would override the commission's traditional autonomy. These are noted here not as recommendations but simply to suggest the magnitude of the gap.

What would be helpful in Japan right now is a major sustained cooperative effort by the U.S. public and private sectors to open up Japan's universities, reporters' clubs, and research laboratories to the same degree of American participation that is permitted to the Japanese in the United States. And, if the Japanese side of our taxpayer-funded CULCON continues to obstruct such liberalization, the federal government should simply let this ossified relic of 1960s cultural sensitizing go.

We need a stronger forensic presence altogether inside Japan. Of course, the informational work of the American embassy can be no better than the policies out of Washington that it is called upon to elucidate and defend. But there must be more that our official spokesmen can do to meet Tokyo's special pleadings head-on, if politely phrased—in news releases, in press briefings, or at seminars and conferences at which they have been invited to speak. Intellectual engagement of the Japanese *within* Japan has rested far too heavily on the shoulders of a small group of journalists, businessmen, and scholars, some of whom are not even American and all of whom run some risk in being so outspoken. Whether private or official, we need more Japan-based Americans who are fluent in Japanese, familiar with the country, and well versed in the issues—people who can get a hearing on Japanese television, handle public speaking, hold their own in the give-and-take of intimate seminars, and establish a beachhead in Japan's monthly opinion journals. Some grand American retro-Buffers, if you will.

For the part of the intellectual game that takes place in the United States, we need to get more non-Barnacle Americans into the institutionalized networks—a tall order bound to collide with the interests of entrenched Japan apologists. Many of the regional Japan-America societies that work for mutual understanding, however, are still American to the core, so it might be possible to hijack some of the network in the reverse direction—that is to say, have them also carry America's message back to those Japanese who fund or take part in their activities. The large Japanese funding organizations should be told that they are welcome to underwrite intellectual labor in the United States, but only under genuinely scholarly goals and criteria set by and for Americans of all views including those critical of Japan. The Japan Society of New York presents a somewhat special case, where the missions of cultural education and political advocacy have become so inextricably entwined. If Americans were less generously minded and were to go by the ancient Confucian injunction to "rectify names"—that is, to make the term for something conform with its actual function—we might be tempted to ask the Japanese to take over officially on Forty-seventh Street and do their own work among us.

Some of the Americans who work in cultural relations with Japan need an emergency transfusion of red-blooded political sense as well as a sharper intellectual skepticism. The spurious linkages that the Japanese are constantly making between politics and culture need to be severed, once and for all. The German cultural envoy who exhibits sketches of Dürer at Goethe House on Manhattan's Fifth Avenue does not expect this to enhance the American viewer's agreement with Germany's fiscal policy or its official position on foreign affairs. And certainly no German in his right mind would expect the glories of Bach to obscure the horrors of Hitler.

Most urgently of all, some standard of exposure and opprobrium must be set for American organizations that practice a Japanese-style ostracism of fellow Americans who choose to go public with critical analyses of Japan. By the same token, we need to multiply the number of organized American platforms now giving voice to such heterodoxy and dissent—along the lines already set out, for example, by the Japan Policy Research Institute in Cardiff, California, or the Japan Information Access Project in Washington, D.C.

Deficiencies along the second, or nonpolitical, track are best suggested in terms of atmosphere and ambience. It is time to move Japan and America off the manipulative, strategically fixated thrust of their intellectual and cultural relations and onto a more natural and humanly enriching plane. And this does not mean being nice by withholding sharp analyses of each other—quite to the contrary.

Let ideas, scholarship, and simple conversations revert to their own natural delights without being dragooned into the stultifying service of policy goals—in both countries. Let the ties among individuals and organizations on opposite sides of the Pacific unfold along more substantive and ingenuous lines of cultural and intellectual stimulation than the grim-faced advancement of national interest or the maudlin mandate of "mutual friendship and understanding." The manipulative aspect has been more apparent on the Japanese side in this book, and as long as it continues Americans will have to parry the thrusts. But we should not forget the whole gamut of intellectual superficiality, psychological ineptness, and wild image swings on the American side of the ledger, or the way these have had their roots in U.S. strategic purposes and ethnocentric mind-sets of the moment.

* * *

In conclusion, the United States can afford to be a bit philosophical—tough-minded but not frantic—about the intellectual challenge from an economically advancing East Asia. With poetic justice (again), Americans from 1970 onward have been treated to a faint inkling of the mental anguish thrust upon those countries by the pressures from our more dynamic civilization a century ago. Some of our quandary stems, ironically, from our very success in winning the three world wars of this century—First, Second, and Cold. These put us so far ahead that, with the peace and prosperity we all want, catch-up by others has led inevitably to our own relative decline.

America's old religious and political missionizing impulses toward the region should take satisfaction, however, from the fact that hundreds of millions of East Asians are no longer starving and from the tenacity of the modern democratic idea in societies as different as Korea, Taiwan, Burma, and the Philippines. Going into the new century, what will continue to challenge us most is the economic vitality of Northeast Asia. But even here this traces back to the economic impact of our successful twentieth-century agenda on nations with a significantly greater social cohesion than ours and with a political leadership more clearly focused on the comprehensive national interest, including the programmatic linking of economic activity to strategic security.

Americans should take advantage of what still remains of our turn-of-the-century economic high—to say nothing of our recent jolt from radical Islamic terrorists—to deliberate what it is in our own values and way of life that we most wish to preserve. And we should do so before resurgent economic competition from East Asia—given a reasonable containment of the terrorist threat—starts to aggravate the pressures already unleashed on American society by our own commitment to globalism. For example, some of the goals we have not typically shared with East Asia—things such as workdays that really end at 5:00 P.M., secondary education that still takes pains for personal development, the modicum of nonmobilized and nonpurposive psychological space required for the survival of our type of individualism, and the basic Western proposition that human beings work to live out their own intrinsic and transcendental ends rather than live to work in the service of some collective entity, be it corporation, race, or state. And then, having set our sights, we should engage the economic and intellectual challenges from Japan and its neighbors with the same political and mental concentration with which we met the less benign competition from the Soviet Union from the late 1940s—or which the Japanese, for that matter, have always mustered to field the challenges we toss their way.

Finally, while honing our Japan focus, there are good reasons now for extending our intellectual attention to all of East Asia without zeroing in obsessively on Tokyo—an emotionally cool and judicious "Japan passing," if you will, in our own frame of mind. One occasionally hears talk from the more sanguine Japan-America bridgers of a "Pax Nippon-americana" (as if the rest of the globe were beneath consulting) or of the interpenetration of the two economies and even the two political systems. As a U.S. citizen, I have always found the latter a rather frightening prospect as long as Japan remains socially and intellectually a closed country. A Japan that was both powerful and insular-minded would be less worrisome if we could at least feel that democracy, individual rights, and freedom of expression were firmly rooted within the nation itself. But I find little comfort in contemplating a substantial penetration of my own country's economy, politics, and internal discourse by a Japan that still refuses to come to terms with its own darker past; that avoids a meaningful dialogue over serious criticisms directed at it from outside; that responds to its own newly felt power with the reassertion of an outmoded, regressive, race-centered, particularistic national consciousness; and that shows less gumption and civil courage in support of controversial ideas and individual self-expression than it did two or three decades ago.

Alas, as a prominently situated American politico-cultural bridger put it to me in early 2002, the intermeshing of the two nations' political, economic, and intellectual elites already has been permitted to proceed so far as to make critical positions and proposals on Japan increasingly difficult to air and discuss intramurally within the higher levels of United States leadership.

An energetic intellectual engagement of *all* of East and South Asia commends itself to us not only because of the rapid rise of China and the smaller economic "tigers" in the region relative to Japan, but also on account of a greater overlap of compatible intellectual traits. The other regional peoples—even the Chinese and Koreans, with their own cohesive and hard-edged cultural nationalism, and the pluralistic Indians, of course—are more attuned by their various cultural heritages to a sense of universals than are the Japanese. They are more at home with open, rational disputation and entreaty (even when in heated altercation), and they share with us distaste for the veilings and circumlocutions that they have encountered in their own intellectual contacts with the Japanese. That means—whatever our military ties with Tokyo, or Japan's high level of Western material lifestyle—enlisting the rest of Asia's intellectual classes, *ahead* of Japan's, in a serious search for values and understandings that can honestly span the Pacific.

Indeed, the time has come for Americans to ask themselves whether there is really any good reason left for not treating Japan as we would any other country—especially a fellow advanced nation—in the exchange of ideas.

Gilbert and Sullivan would poke fun at us if they were still around to compose an operetta on Japan-U.S. intellectual encounters a century after *The Mikado*. Their wry advice would be:

- Stop stumbling around on the Cloth Untrue of Japan's rhetorical and emotional manipulation.
- Learn to parry the Twisted Cue of the Mutual Understanding Industry.
- Turn in your Elliptical Billiard Balls of the old American thinking on Japan for a new set.

If you don't, the punishment, most surely, will fit the crime.

Notes

Notes to Introduction

1. Betty Friedan, *The Feminine Mystique* (New York: W.W. Norton, 1963).
2. Ivan P. Hall, *Mori Arinori* (Cambridge, Mass.: Harvard University Press, 1973).
3. Ivan P. Hall, *Cartels of the Mind: Japan's Intellectual Closed Shop* (New York: W.W. Norton, 1998).

Notes to Chapter 1

1. For two of the most recent and robust examples of this sanguine scenario, see Milton Ezrati, *Kawari: How Japan's Economic and Cultural Transformation Will Alter the Balance of Power Among Nations* (Reading, Mass.: Perseus Books, 1999), and M. Diana Helweg, "Japan: A Rising Sun?" *Foreign Affairs*, July–August 2000.
2. James Fallows, *More Like Us: Making America Great Again* (Boston: Houghton Mifflin, 1989). Fallows' call, of course, was for Americans to return to their own strengths, challenging both the applicability of the Japanese model to the United States as well as the broader possibilities of convergence.
3. Thomas L. Friedman, "Japan Fatigue," *New York Times*, 11 January 1995.
4. For this emphasis, see Chapter 18 and especially three books published in the same year from varying political standpoints: Patrick Smith, *Japan: A Reinterpretation* (New York: Pantheon, 1997); Walter LaFeber, *The Clash: A History of U.S.-Japan Relations* (New York: W.W. Norton, 1997); and Michael Schaller, *Altered States: The United States and Japan Since the Occupation* (New York: Oxford University Press, 1997).
5. Quoted in Louis Uchitelle, "Puffed Up by Prosperity, U.S. Struts its Stuff," *New York Times*, reproduced in the 2 May 1997 edition of the *Asahi Evening News* (Tokyo).
6. "Japan Prefers Private Criticism," *Asahi Evening News*, 30 April 1998.
7. See note 1.

8. Francis Fukuyama, *The End of History and the Last Man* (New York: Free Press, 1992).

9. For exposition of the triumphalist line in extenso see Ezrati, *Kawari*; more particularly on convergence, see Jagdish Bhagwati, "Samurais No More," *Foreign Affairs* 73, 3 (1994): 7–12.

10. Nicholas D. Kristof, "In Eclipse: A Special Report," *New York Times*, 1 August 1999.

11. Thomas L. Friedman, "Japan's Nutcracker Suite," *New York Times*, 30 April 1999.

12. "Keizaishakai no arubeki Sugata to Keizaishinsei no Seisakuhoshin" (The appropriate form of socioeconomy and policy directions for economic rebirth), Economic Planning Agency, Tokyo, July 1999.

13. Hans van der Lugt, Tokyo correspondent for *NRC-Handelsblad*, recalling the briefing with Sakaiya in his Internet posting to the Dead Fukuzawa Society, fukuzawa@ucsd.edu, 15 August 1999. Later, in a follow-up call to the Economic Planning Agency, the Dutch reporter was told that Sakaiya had not meant to imply that the entire Japanese establishment was already of one mind about these changes.

14. Masakazu Yamazaki, *Yawarakai Kojinshugi no Tanjo* (The birth of gentle individualism) (Tokyo: Chuo Koronsha, 1984).

15. For a classic statement of this view, see Roger Goodman, *Japan's "International Youth": The Emergence of a New Class of Schoolchildren* (Oxford: Clarendon Press, 1990).

16. This phrasing is intended descriptively, not to give offense. The parasitic military trade-off, one could argue, has been the lazy and clinging dependence of the United States on its forward bases in Japan.

17. Murray Sayle, "The Social Contradictions of Japanese Capitalism," *Atlantic Monthly*, June 1998.

18. Peter F. Drucker, "In Defense of Japanese Bureaucracy," *Foreign Affairs* 77, 5 (1998): 80. See also 68–80, *passim*.

19. Ibid., 79.

20. For the most trenchant exposition of this viewpoint, see Karel van Wolferen, *The Enigma of Japanese Power: People and Politics in a Stateless Nation* (New York: Alfred A. Knopf, 1989).

21. Glen S. Fukushima, "Perception Gap Hurts U.S. and Japan," *Los Angeles Times*, 13 November 1998.

22. Eamonn Fingleton, *Blindside: Why Japan Is Still on Track to Overtake the U.S. by the Year 2000* (New York: Houghton Mifflin, 1995).

23. Eamonn Fingleton, *In Praise of Hard Industries* (New York: Houghton Mifflin, 1999).

24. Personal communications from Eamonn Fingleton to the author, 12 May 1999 and 15 January 2002, and his article, "Quibble All You Like, Japan Still Looks Like a Strong Winner," *International Herald Tribune*, 2 January 2001.

25. Fingleton's contretemps with Peter Tasker of Dresdner Kleinwort Benson and Alexander Kinmont of Morgan Stanley took place in March–April 1999 postings to the now defunct Dead Fukuzawa Society. The entire exchange is available on www.fingleton.net.

26. For a representative study, see Tatsuo Arima, *The Failure of Freedom: A*

Portrait of Modern Japanese Intellectuals (Cambridge, Mass.: Harvard University Press, 1969).

27. For example, see: Frederic Lilge, *The Abuse of Learning: The Failure of the German University* (New York: Macmillan, 1948).

28. See my remarks on the *kikokushijo* in Ivan P. Hall, *Cartels of the Mind: Japan's Intellectual Closed Shop* (New York: W.W. Norton, 1998), 143–44.

29. Masao Miyamoto, *Straightjacket Society: An Insider's Irreverent View of Bureaucratic Japan*, trans. Juliet Winters Carpenter (New York: Kodansha International, 1994) (published in Japanese by Kodansha as *Oyakusho no Okite*).

30. President of Mikuni & Co., Tokyo, and from 1963 to 1975 an executive of Nomura Securities. My discussion here draws on his three articles for the Japan Policy Research Institute (JPRI), Cardiff, Calif.: "Japan's Big Bang: Illusions and Reality," JPRI working paper no. 39, October 1997; "Why Japan Can't Reform Its Economy," JPRI working paper no. 44, April 1998; and "The Mirage of Japanese Financial Reform," JPRI critique, August 1998.

31. Mikuni, "The Mirage of Japanese Financial Reform," 1. Fingleton in his earlier *Blindside*, 192–94, exposed the politically dictated nature of suppressed consumption.

32. Mikuni, "Why Japan Can't Reform Its Economy," 3.

33. Mikuni, "The Mirage of Japanese Financial Reform," 1.

34. R. Taggart Murphy, *The Weight of the Yen* (New York: W.W. Norton, 1996).

35. R. Taggart Murphy, "Don't Be Fooled by Japan's Big Bang," *Fortune*, 29 December 1997.

36. Associated Press story, "Government Enshrines Set of New Goals," *Honolulu Advertiser*, 9 July 1999.

37. Lonny E. Carlile and Mark C. Tilton, "Preface," in Lonny E. Carlile and Mark C. Tilton, eds., *Is Japan Really Changing Its Ways? Regulatory Reform and the Japanese Economy* (Washington, D.C.: Brookings Institution Press, 1998), v.

38. Mark C. Tilton, "Regulatory Reform and Market Opening in Japan," in Carlile and Tilton, eds., *Is Japan Really Changing Its Ways?* 188, referring to a survey in the 19 October 1996 *Nihon Keizai Shinbun*.

39. Lonny E. Carlile and Mark C. Tilton, "Is Japan Really Changing?" in Carlile and Tilton, eds., *Is Japan Really Changing Its Ways?* 206.

40. The following paragraphs on Japan's regulatory and administrative reform have drawn variously on all six of the scholars contributing to Carlile and Tilton, eds., *Is Japan Really Changing Its Ways?:* Carlile, Tilton, and Elizabeth Norville (American); Hideaki Miyajima and Kosuke Oyama (Japanese); and Yul Sohn (Korean).

41. Naoto Ide, "Suggested Remedies for the Japanese Economy No. 4," April 1999, Resolution Inc., Honolulu. Private paper received courtesy of Ide.

42. Tilton, "Regulatory Reform," 185.

43. Edith Buchanan Terry has made the argument here in *How Asia Got Rich: Japan and the Asian Miracle* (Armonk, N.Y.: M.E. Sharpe, to be published in 2002). My comments here were drawn from Terry's adaptation in her paper "Crisis? What Crisis?" JPRI working paper no. 50, October 1998, from the Japan Policy Research Institute, Cardiff, Calif..

44. Walter Hatch and Kozo Yamamura, *Asia in Japan's Embrace* (Cambridge: Cambridge University Press, 1996).

45. "Promoting Comprehensive Economic Cooperation in an International Economic Environment Undergoing Upheaval: Toward the Construction of an Asian Network," Economic Planning Agency, Tokyo, 1988. See Terry, "Crisis?" 4.

46. Terry, "Crisis?" 5.

47. Chalmers Johnson, "Economic Crisis in East Asia: The Clash of Capitalisms," *Cambridge Journal of Economics* 22 (1998).

48. Joseph Stieglitz, "How to Fix the Asian Economies," *New York Times*, 31 October 1997.

49. Chalmers Johnson, "Let's Revisit Asia's Crony Capitalism," *Los Angeles Times*, 25 June 1999.

50. Ibid.

51. Terry, "Crisis," 3.

Notes to Chapter 2

1. My translation from the original German carried on Deutsche Welle TV on 13 September 2001, from remarks made directly for domestic consumption, not to impress an American audience.

2. Tetsuya Chikushi, Yoshimi Ishikawa, and Masao Kunihiro, "Goman na Amerika, Jujun na Nihon" (Arrogant America, submissive Japan), *Shukan Kinyobi*, 10 April 1998.

3. For concrete examples of such a threat, see Eamonn Fingleton, *Blindside: Why Japan Is Still on Track to Overtake the U.S. by the Year 2000* (New York: Houghton Mifflin, 1995), 47.

4. Kurt Singer, *Mirror, Sword and Jewel: The Geometry of Japanese Life* (Tokyo: Kodansha International, 1981), 39–40.

5. Taichi Sakaiya, *Hibiwareta Niji* (The rainbow cracked) (Tokyo: Nihon Keizai Shinbunsha, 1978).

6. Naoki Komuro, *Amerika no Gyakushu* (America's counterattack) (Tokyo: Kobunsha, 1980); and *Amerika no Hyoteki* (America's target) (Tokyo: Kodansha, 1981).

7. *Japan Times*, 16 August 1991.

8. Takeo Doi, "A Psychiatrist's View on Zeitgeist," *Solidarity* (Manila), August 1971, 19.

9. For a detailed account of Japan's actual war aims as they developed before and during World War II, see Peter Duus, Ramon H. Myers, and Mark R. Peattie, eds., *The Japanese Wartime Empire, 1931–1945* (Princeton: Princeton University Press, 1996), especially the introduction by Duus, Chapter 7 by Peattie, and Chapter 12 by L. H. Gann.

10. Gavan McCormack, "Holocaust Denial à la Japonaise," Japan Policy Research Institute working paper no. 38, Cardiff, Calif., October 1997, 2.

Notes to Chapter 3

1. Particularly helpful in tracing the intellectual dimension behind the shifting party kaleidoscope of 1993–2000 have been the following articles, from which I have drawn for parts of both Chapters 3 and 4: Lonny E. Carlile, "The Left in Japa-

nese Politics: Is There a Movement Toward a Third Pole?" JPRI working paper no. 17, Japan Policy Research Institute, Cardiff, Calif., March 1996; Ronald Dore, "Japan's Reform Debate: Patriotic Concern or Class Interest? Or Both?" *Journal of Japanese Studies* 25, 1 (1999); Mayumi Itoh, "Hatoyama Yukio and Political Leadership in Japan," *Asian Survey* 39, 3 (1999); Koichi Nakano, "The Politics of Administrative Reform in Japan, 1993–1998: Toward a More Accountable Government?" *Asian Survey* 38, 3 (1998); Hideo Otake, "Forces for Political Reform: The Liberal Democratic Party's Young Reformers and Ozawa Ichiro," *Journal of Japanese Studies* 22, 2 (1996); several articles on Japan's liberal left in *Ronza*, October 1995, especially Ikuro Takagi, "'Kyodai Hoshu' Tanjo o Yurusu Na" (Don't permit the birth of a giant conservative [force]), and "Shamin-Riberaru ni Chansu Ari" (There *is* an opportunity for the social-democratic/liberal [forces]), a dialogue between Keiichi Kamoshida and Uwe Schmidt. Two longer works are referenced in notes 2 and 14 below, for *Sekai* magazine and the book by Ozawa, respectively.

2. See the special issue of *Sekai*, November 1999, "Sutoppu! Jijiko Boso: Nihon no Minshushugi no Saisei no tame ni" (Stop the reckless run of the LDP/Liberal Party/Komeito: For the sake of the rebirth of Japan's democracy), in particular the lead article by Shuichi Kato, "Watakushitachi no Kibo wa doko ni aru ka" (Wherein lies our hope?).

3. Ivan P. Hall, "Samurai Legacies, American Illusions," *The National Interest* 28 (1992); Rawdon Dalrymple, "An Exchange on Japan," *The National Interest* 30 (1992–93).

4. For an example, see Peter Duus and Daniel I. Okimoto, "Fascism and the History of Pre-War Japan: The Failure of a Concept," *Journal of Asian Studies* 39, 1 (1979). For a fine study of Japanese liberalism from Meiji up to World War II, one that makes the requisite distinctions yet does not hesitate to use the term, see Germaine Hoston, "The State, Modernity, and the Fate of Liberalism in Prewar Japan," *Journal of Asian Studies* 51, 2 (1992).

5. Shintaro Ishihara and Akio Morita, *No to Ieru Nihon* (The Japan that can say no) (Tokyo: Kobunsha, 1989); Shintaro Ishihara, *Sensen Fukoku No to Ieru Nihon Keizai: Amerika Kinyu Dorei kara no Kaiho* (The Japanese economy that can utter the declaration of war, "no"—Liberation from financial slavery to America) (Tokyo: Kobunsha, 1998).

6. Tetsuya Kataoka, *Waiting for a Pearl Harbor: Japan Debates Defense* (Stanford, Calif.: Hoover Institution Press, 1980); and in his letter to the editor of the *Wall Street Journal*, 28 July 1987, commenting on my op-ed piece, "Stop Making Excuses for Japan's Insularity," 6 July 1987.

7. *Asahi Shinbun*, 7 August 1991.

8. In an appeal by the Japan Committee of the International Movement Against All Forms of Discrimination and Racism (IMADR-JC) issued on 2 June 2000. Mushakoji, the author, saw the xenophobic outbursts of Tokyo governor Ishihara and the religious exclusivism of Prime Minister Mori's "divine nation" claims as expressions of racial discrimination. The text portrayed Mori as "at least as serious a threat to the international community as Jörg Haider. . . . If the G-8 will not meet in Austria, why should they in Japan?" The son of Japan's ambassador to Berlin who signed the Axis Pact, Mushakoji recalls looking down from the balcony as a child on Hitler's head during the ceremony, and quips that he has been doing "penance"

for that ever since (personal discussion with Mushakoji at the Foreign Correspondents Club of Japan, 2 June 2000).

9. The proceedings were published by the Heritage Foundation, Washington, D.C., in 1981 under the title *U.S.-Japan Mutual Security: The Next Twenty Years*, edited by Edwin J. Feulner Jr., president of the Heritage Foundation, and Hideaki Kase, chairman of the Japan Center for the Study of Security Issues.

10. "Bush Trip Harshly Criticized," *Japan Times*, 9 September 1995.

11. "Bush's Brother Linked to Ex-Crime Syndicate Boss," *Daily Yomiuri*, 27 July 1991; "Prescott Bush Files $8 Million Countersuit," *Daily Yomiuri*, 27 June 1992; "Tokyo Company Sues Bush's Brother for Millions," *New York Times*, 16 June 1992.

12. See the pathbreaking *New York Times* article of 9 October 1994, "C.I.A. Spent Millions to Support Japanese Right in 50's and 60's," by Tim Weiner, Stephen Engelberg, and James Sterngold; and Michael Schaller, *Altered States: The United States and Japan Since the Occupation* (New York: Oxford University Press, 1997).

13. Karel van Wolferen, *The Enigma of Japanese Power* (New York: Alfred A. Knopf, 1989). For van Wolferen's views on Japan's historical revisionism, see "Rekishi Shikan o Motenai Kuni Nihon" (Japan: A country without a view of [its own] history), *Ronza*, May 1997, and *Naze Nihonjin wa Nihon o Aisenai no ka* (Why can't the Japanese love Japan?), published only in Japanese translation (Tokyo: Mainichi Shinbunsha, 1998), Section II. For his views on America's "political plot," see *Amerika o Kofuku ni shi Sekai o Fuko ni suru Fujori na Shikumi* (The absurd contrivance that makes America happy while making the world unhappy) published only in Japanese (Tokyo: Daimondsha, 2000). Evaluations of Nakasone and Ozawa are from numerous passionate contentions with van Wolferen, a personal friend.

14. Ichiro Ozawa, *Blueprint for a New Japan: The Rethinking of a Nation* (Tokyo: Kodansha International, 1994), translated from the Japanese original, *Nihon Kaizo Keikaku* (Plan for the restructuring of Japan) (Tokyo: Kodansha, 1993).

Notes to Chapter 4

1. My own translation of Yukio Hatoyama's reply to a question following his Japanese-language luncheon address on 4 February 2000. From the tape recording of the address, with questions and answers, on file at the library of the Foreign Correspondents Club of Japan, Tokyo.

2. See, for example, Masao Maruyama, "Aru Jiyushugisha e no Tegami" (Letter to a certain liberal), *Sekai*, September 1950. Maruyama's political thought is available to readers of English in Masao Maruyama, *Thought and Behavior in Modern Japanese Politics*, ed. Ivan Morris (London: Oxford University Press, 1969).

3. E. Herbert Norman, *Japan's Emergence as a Modern State* (New York: Institute of Pacific Relations, 1940).

Notes to Chapter 5

1. *Asahi Shinbun*, 23 August 1994.

2. *Daily Yomiuri*, 29 December 2000.

3. Takeshi Umehara, *Nihon Bunkaron* (On Japanese culture) (Tokyo: Kodansha, 1976), 53–54; Hideaki Kase in a speech to the Foreign Correspondents Club of

Japan, 26 September 1988; Yonosuke Nagai as reported in *Asahi Shinbun* evening edition, 14 September 1994.

4. See "Bunka Shakaimen Kenkyu Guruuppu Hokoku" (Report of the cultural and social study group), Second Asia-Pacific Conference, FAIR (Foundation for Advanced Information and Research), Tokyo, 1991.

5. *Japan Times*, 11 November 1993, quoting the Foreign Ministry.

6. *Asahi Shinbun*, 23 November 1993. My translation.

7. Professor Hang Sang-Il of Seoul's Kookmin University in the *Dong-a Ilbo*, translated in the *Asahi Evening News*, 2 May 2001.

8. In personal discussions with Victor Fic in Tokyo, July 1998.

9. The South Korean government admitted to at least 240 killed; sources in Kwangju claimed more than 3,000 killed or maimed. See Chalmers Johnson, *Blowback: The Costs and Consequences of American Empire* (New York: Henry Holt, 2000), 116.

10. See the superb study by Stephen N. Hay, *Asian Ideas of East and West: Tagore and His Critics in Japan, China and India* (Cambridge, Mass.: Harvard University Press, 1970).

Notes to Chapter 6

1. Arnold Toynbee, "How to Change the World Without War," *Saturday Review*, 12 May 1962, 17. Quoted in Mikiso Hane, *Premodern Japan: A Historical Survey* (Boulder, Co.: Westview Press, 1991), 130.

2. See my recent book on this subject: Ivan P. Hall, *Cartels of the Mind: Japan's Intellectual Closed Shop* (New York: W.W. Norton, 1998).

3. Inazo Nitobe, *Bushido: The Soul of Japan* (Rutland, Vt., and Tokyo: Charles E. Tuttle, 1969) (first published in 1905).

4. Furukawa Tesshi, "The Individual in Japanese Ethics," in Charles A. Moore, ed., *The Japanese Mind: Essentials of Japanese Philosophy and Culture* (Honolulu: University Press of Hawaii, 1975), 239.

5. Ibid., 232–33.

6. Charles A. Moore, "Editor's Supplement: The Enigmatic Japanese Mind," in Moore, ed., *The Japanese Mind*, 289.

7. Ivan P. Hall, *Mori Arinori* (Cambridge, Mass.: Harvard University Press, 1973).

8. *Asa Made Nama Terebi*, program on Asahi Television, 26 April 1997.

Notes to Chapter 7

1. *Understanding and Enhancing the Japanese Image in the United States*, Pilot Project Final Report, prepared for Counselor Seiichi Kondo, Embassy of Japan, by Robert D. Deutsch with Richard E. Hayes, Arthur Alexander, Robert Hitlin, and Jill Lavigne, EBR Consulting, Vienna, Va., 1994. The author's copy was received from a confidential congressional source. A brief summary was issued by the Japan Economic Institute, Washington, D.C., in May 1996.

2. Ibid., 71.

3. Paul Kennedy, *The Rise and Fall of Great Powers: Economic Change and Military Conflict* (New York: Random House, 1987).

4. Clinton Rossiter, *Conservatism in America: The Thankless Persuasion* (New York: Vintage, 1962), 130–31.

5. Quoted by John B. Judis, "Campaign Issues: Trade," *Columbia Journalism Review*, November–December 1992.

6. C. Fred Bergsten, Takatoshi Ito, Marcus Noland, *No More Bashing: Building a New Japan-U.S. Economic Relationship* (Washington D.C.: Institute for International Economics, 2001).

7. Ellen L. Frost, *For Richer, for Poorer: The New U.S.-Japan Relationship* (Rutland, Vt., and Tokyo: Charles E. Tuttle, 1988).

8. Lester Thurow, *Head to Head: The Coming Economic Battle Among Japan, Europe, and America* (New York: William Morrow, 1992).

9. Kiichi Miyazawa, then chairman of the LDP Policy Affairs Research Council, in a seminar at the Japan National Press Club that I attended on 27 November 1985.

10. See Ivan P. Hall, *Cartels of the Mind: Japan's Intellectual Closed Shop* (New York: W.W. Norton, 1998), Chapters 2, 3, and 4.

Notes to Chapter 8

1. Ivan P. Hall, *Cartels of the Mind* (New York: W.W. Norton, 1998), 164–67. For earlier illustrations and further analysis of Japan's treatment of foreign probers and skeptics, see Chapter 5, "Manipulated Dialogue: Crushing the Critics," especially the sections "Cultural Exchange as Cultural Buffering" and "Discrediting Dissent."

2. Iris Chang, *The Rape of Nanking: The Forgotten Holocaust of World War II* (New York: Basic Books, 1997).

3. Katsuichi Honda, *Nankin e no michi* (The road to Nanking) (Tokyo: Asahi Shinbunsha, 1987).

4. *Honolulu Star-Bulletin*, 25 November 1998.

5. Iris Chang, "It's History, Not a 'Lie,'" *Newsweek*, 20 July 1998.

6. Katsuichi Honda, *The Nanjing Massacre: A Japanese Journalist Confronts Japan's National Shame*, trans. Karen Sandness, ed. Frank Gibney (Armonk, N.Y.: M.E. Sharpe, 1999). The main text is taken from *Nankin e no Michi*, with excerpts in the appendix from some of Honda's more recent writings on the subject.

7. Hall, *Cartels of the Mind*, 170, 197.

8. From the Web site for the Social Science Research Council, http://www.ssrc.org, 23 June 1999.

9. Mark Tilton, *Restrained Trade: Cartels in Japan's Basic Materials Industries* (Ithaca, N.Y.: Cornell University Press, 1996).

Notes to Chapter 9

1. Pat Choate, *Agents of Influence: How Japan's Lobbyists in the United States Manipulate America's Political and Economic System* (New York: Alfred A. Knopf, 1990), xi, 133.

2. Choate has given us the most thorough account to date of Japan's political lobbying, and in his two final chapters introduced problems and personalities in what I have chosen to distinguish here as the cultural lobby. Three other writers who helped to blow the whistle were: James Fallows, "The Japan Handlers," *Atlantic*

Monthly, August 1989; John B. Judis, "The Japanese Megaphone," *The New Republic*, 22 January 1990; and, in especially useful detail, Stephanie Epstein, *Buying the American Mind: Japan's Quest for U.S. Ideas in Science, Economic Policy and the Schools* (Washington, D.C.: Center for Public Integrity, 1991), to which I am indebted for many of my academic-grant statistics for the late 1980s.

3. Epstein, *Buying the American Mind*, 46–66.

4. Epstein (ibid., 50) listed Harvard as the leading beneficiary, with a total of $93.3 million, including $85 million (covering ten years from 1989) from the Japanese cosmetics giant Shiseido, "to build, in partnership with the Massachusetts General Hospital, the Cutaneous Biology Research Center." There has been some criticism of the Epstein report for its occasional misinterpretations of the internal allocation of Japanese grants. For example, in a telephone interview on 14 May 1996 a Harvard fund-raising official explained to me that none of this money had been passed to or through the university but had gone directly to the hospital for a new laboratory building and "sponsored research" there by doctors who held joint appointments at the Harvard Medical School. Whether that overturns the basic argument here is another question.

5. Telephone interview with the Harvard fund-raising official, confirming a total of fifteen teaching positions, the first four grants from the Epstein study, and adding the last three items.

6. See note 5. The story was carried in the *Japan Times*, 24 April 1993. According to Harvard, the original suggestion came from Japanese diplomats as part of a more ambitious concept for raising anywhere from $300 million to $500 million for a package of donations in the greater Boston area, but it fizzled out along with the brief euphoria over the royal wedding.

7. From data and public documents courtesy of the MIT Industrial Liaison Program.

8. Epstein, *Buying the American Mind*, 39–41.

9. The 1994 annual report of the Center for Global Partnership, Japan Foundation, Tokyo, was the first to state the philosophy behind each program area and subcategory in full detail.

10. Japan Foundation, *Overview of Programs for Fiscal 1993/Annual Report for Fiscal 1992* (Tokyo: Japan Foundation, 1993).

11. For this reason, the study by the Center for Public Integrity chose to list grants from the U.S.-Japan Foundation as Japanese-source money. See Stephanie Epstein, *Buying the American Mind*, 40–41.

12. For the quotation and grants made in 1993 see United States-Japan Foundation, *Report from January 1993 through December 1993*, New York, 1993.

13. Frederick Risinger, as quoted in Stephanie Epstein, *Buying the American Mind*, 31. For Manchuria and Pearl Harbor, see p. 36; for further examples of Japan-biased materials, see pp. 26–38 and passim; and for grants to American universities for the development of precollege education programs during 1986–91, see pp. 47–62.

Notes to Chapter 10

1. For the statistics and some historical reflection by the Japanese studies profession on itself, see Marius B. Jansen, "History: General Survey" and "Stages of

Growth," *Japanese Studies in the United States: Part I—History and Present Condition*, Japan Studies Series XVII (Tokyo: Japan Foundation, 1988), and Patricia Steinhoff, "Japanese Studies in the United States: The Loss of Irrelevance," *The Postwar Development of Japanese Studies in the United States: A Historical Review and Prospects for the Future* (Tokyo: International House of Japan, 1993). The language statistics are from the annual *Statistical Abstract of the United States*, as reported in the *Japan Times*, 4 November 1992.

2. See, for example, Jennet Conant, "Secrets of the Nippon Club," *Manhattan, Inc.*, April 1990, 62.

3. Pat Choate, *Agents of Influence: How Japan's Lobbyists in the United States Manipulate America's Political and Economic System* (New York: Alfred A. Knopf, 1990), 137.

4. Ivan P. Hall, *Cartels of the Mind: Japan's Intellectual Closed Shop* (New York: W.W. Norton, 1998), 161–62.

5. Letter from Richard J. Samuels to the author, 31 July 2001.

6. Letter from Andrew D. Gordon to the author, 22 September 2001.

7. Interview on 21 February 1996 with Mindy L. Kotler, director, Japan Information Access Project, Washington, D.C. One of the most active trackers of Japan's payments for access to influence in the nation's capital, Kotler's JIAP is a rarity on the U.S-Japan scene in that it neither receives nor solicits funding from Japanese organizations.

8. William J. Holstein, "We're Naive About Japanese Philanthropy," *The Chronicle of Philanthropy*, 14 January 1992.

9. Quotations from Arthur S. Hardy, *Life and Letters of Joseph Hardy Neesima* (Boston, 1891). See also Ivan P. Hall, *Mori Arinori* (Cambridge, Mass.: Harvard University Press, 1973), 293–94.

Notes to Chapter 11

1. Lamar Alexander, *Friends: Japanese and Tennesseans: A Model of U.S.-Japan Cooperation* (Tokyo: Kodansha International, 1986), 15. For Japan's grassroots campaign in Tennessee, see also Stephanie Epstein, *Buying the American Mind: Japan's Quest for U.S. Ideas in Science, Economic Policy and the Schools* (Washington, D.C.: Center for Public Integrity, 1991), 26–29, and Pat Choate, *Agents of Influence: How Japan's Lobbyists in the United States Manipulate America's Political and Economic System* (New York: Alfred A. Knopf, 1990), 138–40. Choate's bombshell devoted considerable space to some of the concerns of this chapter as they had developed over the 1980s. Accordingly, I have confined myself in this thumbnail sketch to delineating the general pattern and adding some description of the reverse situation in Japan.

2. As the associate executive director of the Friendship Commission at the time, I was heavily involved in the proposing, pursuit, and implementation of this donation. For my discussion of goodwill societies and Japanese and American studies in these pages I have drawn extensively on my own professional experience.

3. William Totten, of Assist Software, Tokyo. See also several books (appearing in Japanese only), including Bill Totten, *Amerika wa Nihon o Sekai no Koji ni suru* (America is turning Japan into the world's orphan) (Tokyo: Goma Shobo, 1998), and *Nihonjin wa Amerika ni Damasarete iru* (The Japanese are being fooled by

America) (Tokyo: Goma Shobo, 1998). My point here is not that there is anything wrong with such advocacy, merely that an American private citizen making his or her living in Japan would never make it to market with a Japanese-language polemic arguing the U.S. side of trade issues.

Notes to Chapter 12

1. Ivan P. Hall, "Stop Making Excuses for Japan's Insularity," *Wall Street Journal*, 6 July 1987.

2. Quoted by Marlene J. Mayo in "American Postwar Planning for Japan: The Role of the Experts, 1942–45," paper given at the Washington and Southeast Regional Seminar on Japan, University of Maryland, 18 February 1978, 30. For the American Council on Japan see also Mindy L. Kotler, "Making Friends: A History of Japan's Lobby in Washington, D.C.," *Venture Japan* 2, 2 (1990).

3. Toshiyuki Ijiri, *Paul Rusch: The Story of KEEP: And What a Man with Vision Can Do* (Cincinnati: Forward Movement Publications, 1991), 117–23.

4. The role and sobriquet of Japan's Buffers was first set out by Karel van Wolferen in his *The Enigma of Japanese Power: People and Politics in a Stateless Nation* (New York: Alfred A. Knopf, 1989), 11.

5. Stephanie Epstein, *Buying the American Mind: Japan's Quest for U.S. Ideas in Science, Economic Policy, and the Schools* (Washington, D.C.: Center for Public Integrity, 1991), 39.

6. Ibid., 40–45.

7. In my own case, and also in the experience of Professor Robert Angel of the University of South Carolina as personally related to me.

8. Ivan P. Hall, *Cartels of the Mind: Japan's Intellectual Closed Shop* (New York: W.W. Norton, 1998).

Notes to Chapter 14

1. For the decade-by-decade sketches of the intellectual history of Japan-U.S. relations that follows in these final chapters, I have drawn on the books mentioned in the text; on personal observation and experience; on general sources in American and Japanese intellectual history, generally not referenced below; and on the cornucopia of studies of mutual images that is now available, especially for the earlier decades in the transpacific tie discussed in this chapter. The last include Sadao Asada, "1920 Nendai ni okeru Amerika no Nihonzo" (American images of Japan in the 1920s), *Doshisha Amerika Kenkyu* (Doshisha American studies) 2 (1965); Akira Iriye, *Across the Pacific: An Inner History of American-East Asian Relations* (New York: Harcourt, Brace and World, 1967); Akira Iriye, ed., *Mutual Images: Essays in American-Japanese Relations* (Cambridge, Mass.: Harvard University Press, 1975); Harold R. Isaacs, *Images of Asia: American Views of China and India* (New York: Harper Torchbooks, 1958); Sheila K. Johnson, *The Japanese Through American Eyes* (Stanford: Stanford University Press, 1988), also in an earlier Japanese version as *Amerikajin no Nihonkan* (English title rendered as *American Attitudes Towards Japan, 1941–1985*) (Tokyo: Simul Shuppankai, 1986); Shunsuke Kamei, *Meriken kara Amerika e* (From "Meriken" [Meiji-period term for America] to "America") (Tokyo: Tokyo Daigaku Shuppankai, 1979); and Hiroshi Kitamura, "Psychological

Dimensions of U.S.-Japan Relations," Harvard University Center for International Affairs, Occasional Papers in International Affairs no. 28, August 1971.

2. Readers of Japanese will find a fine literary-intellectual history of Japanese attitudes in Kamei, *Meriken kara Amerika e.*

3. The informal term designating the Japanese cultural theory and form of cultural nationalism which emphasizes the roots of Japanese identity in the political and social system and the imperial myths of the Early Yamato Period (ca. A.D. 300–550) before the advent of Chinese civilization.

4. For my references to American perceptions in the 1920s I am largely indebted to the brief but pathbreaking study by Asada, "1920 Nendai ni okeru Amerika no Nihonzo."

5. Edwin O. Reischauer, *My Life Between Japan and America* (New York: Harper and Row, 1986), 3–7.

6. Edwin O. Reischauer, *Japan Society 1907–1982: 75 Years of Partnership Across the Pacific* (New York: Japan Society, 1982), 36.

Notes to Chapter 15

1. For the most authoritative and very recent account of the occupation era, see John W. Dower, *Embracing Defeat: Japan in the Wake of World War II* (New York: W.W. Norton, 1999).

2. As to American motives for, and the consequences of, retaining Emperor Hirohito on the throne, see the equally recent and masterful study by Herbert P. Bix, *Hirohito and the Making of Modern Japan* (New York: Harper Collins, 2000).

3. Paul Goodman, *Growing up Absurd* (New York: Vintage, 1960), 172, 181.

4. Allan Bloom, *The Closing of the American Mind* (New York: Simon and Schuster, 1987), 314.

Notes to Chapter 16

1. For the interplay and shift of dominant attitudes toward Japan among postwar American elites—from an upbeat military (typical of the 1950s) to anxious bureaucratic experts in the 1960s and exasperated business leaders from the 1970s—see Priscilla A. Clapp and Morton H. Halperin, "U.S. Elite Images of Japan: The Postwar Period," in Akira Iriye, ed., *Mutual Images: Essays in American-Japanese Relations* (Cambridge, Mass.: Harvard University Press, 1975).

2. Nathan Glazer, "From Ruth Benedict to Herman Kahn: The Postwar Japanese Image in the American Mind," in Iriye, ed., *Mutual Images*, 166.

3. The modernization theory controversy between the two academic generations of Japanologists has been set within the broader political context of Japanese studies by Richard J. Samuels, "Japanese Political Studies and the Myth of the Independent Intellectual," in Richard J. Samuels and Myron Weiner, eds., *The Political Culture of Foreign Area and International Studies: Essays in Honor of Lucian W. Pye* (New York: Brassey's, 1992).

4. Makoto Oda, *Nandemo Mite Yaro* (Let's go look at anything we darn please) (Tokyo: Kawade Shobo Shinsha, 1961).

5. On a personal note I should mention that it was precisely this dual-function aspect of Reischauer's career that had attracted me to Harvard's program in the first

place, only to have him defect to the Tokyo embassy for five years. He returned to the Harvard faculty in time to vet my doctoral dissertation, and it was my privilege later to work closely with him as Harvard's Tokyo representative for its Japan fundraising drive during 1973–77.

Notes to Chapter 17

1. As mentioned in Chapter 7, this is my own recollection of a press conference I attended in 1971 as Tokyo correspondent for the *Philadelphia Bulletin*.

2. For a thumbnail sketch of what *Nihonjinron* was all about, see Ivan P. Hall, *Cartels of the Mind: Japan's Intellectual Closed Shop* (New York: W.W. Norton, 1998), 175–76.

3. Herman Kahn, *The Emerging Japanese Superstate: Challenge and Response* (Englewood, N.J.: Prentice-Hall, 1970).

4. Zbigniew Brzezinski, *The Fragile Blossom: Crisis and Change in Japan* (New York: Harper Torchbooks, 1972).

5. Frank Gibney, *Japan: The Fragile Superpower* (Tokyo and Rutland, Vt.: Charles E. Tuttle, 1975).

6. Hugh T. Patrick and Henry Rosovsky, eds., *Asia's New Giant: How the Japanese Economy Works* (Washington, D.C.: Brookings Institution, 1976).

7. Ezra Vogel, *Japan as Number One: Lessons for America* (Cambridge, Mass.: Harvard University Press, 1979).

8. Gregory Clark, *Nihonjin: Yuniikusa no Gensen* (The Japanese: Sources of their uniqueness), translated from an unpublished English draft into Japanese by Masumi Muramatsu, Tokyo, Simul Shuppankai, 1977.

9. *Yomiuri Shinbun*, 15 March 1986.

Notes to Chapter 18

1. Coauthored in the original Japanese version by Shintaro Ishihara and Akio Morita, *No to Ieru Nihon* (The Japan that can say no) (Tokyo: Kobunsha, 1989).

2. Chalmers Johnson, *MITI and the Japanese Miracle: The Growth of Industrial Policy, 1925–1975* (Stanford: Stanford University Press, 1982).

3. Clyde V. Prestowitz Jr., *Trading Places: How We Allowed Japan to Take the Lead* (New York: Basic Books, 1988).

4. Karel van Wolferen, *The Enigma of Japanese Power: People and Politics in a Stateless Nation* (New York: Knopf, 1989).

5. James Fallows, "Containing Japan," *Atlantic Monthly*, May 1989, and "Gradgrind's Heirs," *Atlantic Monthly*, March 1987. In *Looking at the Sun: The Rise of the New East Asian Economic and Political System* (New York: Pantheon Books, 1994), Fallows consolidated his analysis of Japan and placed it in its broader East Asian context.

6. Peter N. Dale, *The Myth of Japanese Uniqueness* (London: Croom Helm, 1986; reprinted, London: Routledge, 1988).

7. Carol Gluck, *Japan's Modern Myths: Ideology in the Late Meiji Period* (Princeton: Princeton University Press, 1985).

8. Roy Andrew Miller, *Japan's Modern Myth: The Language and Beyond* (New York and Tokyo: Weatherhill, 1982).

9. Marvin J. Wolf, *The Japanese Conspiracy: Their Plot to Dominate Industry World-Wide and How to Deal with It* (New York: Empire Books, 1983).

10. Pat Choate, *Agents of Influence: How Japan's Lobbyists in the United States Manipulate America's Political and Economic System* (New York: Alfred A. Knopf, 1990).

Notes to Chapter 19

1. *Asahi Shinbun*, 25 October 1994.

2. Leon Hollerman, "The Headquarters Nation," *The National Interest* 25 (1991).

3. Arthur M. Schlesinger Jr., *The Vital Center* (Cambridge, Mass.: Riverside Press, 1949); from the 1962 paperback edition, 36–41.

4. Allan Bloom, *The Closing of the American Mind* (New York: Simon and Schuster, 1987).

5. See, for example, Ivan P. Hall, *Cartels of the Mind: Japan's Intellectual Closed Shop* (W.W. Norton, 1998), in all five chapters.

6. At WGBH, Boston, some time in 1989–90 in Karel van Wolferen's recollection to this author in December 2001.

7. J. Mark Ramseyer and Frances M. Rosenbluth, *The Politics of Oligarchy: Institutional Choice in Imperial Japan* (Cambridge: Cambridge University Press, 1995). The review essay was by Joseph P. Gownder and Robert Pekkanen, "The End of Political Science? Rational Choice Analyses in Studies of Japanese Politics," *Journal of Japanese Studies* 22, 2 (1996): 363–84. For a scathing indictment of rational-choice theory from inside Japanese studies itself, see Chalmers Johnson and E.B. Keehn, "A Disaster in the Making: Rational Choice and Asian Studies," *The National Interest* 36 (1994). Johnson and Keehn (referring to a different pair of rational-choice theorists) complained of "worthless research" showing "an arrogant disregard of Japanese scholarship about Japan that borders on academic malpractice" (p. 18).

8. For the classic text, of course, see Katherine Washburn and John Thornton, eds., *Dumbing Down: Essays on the Strip-mining of American Culture* (New York: W.W. Norton, 1996).

Index